VIOLIN AND KEYBOARD:
THE DUO REPERTOIRE

Abram Loft

Violin and Keyboard: The Duo Repertoire

VOLUME II

*From Beethoven
to the Present*

AMADEUS PRESS
Reinhard G. Pauly, General Editor
Portland, Oregon

Reprinted 1991 by Amadeus Press (an imprint of Timber Press, Inc.)

ISBN 0-931340-36-5 (Volume I)
ISBN 0-931340-37-3 (Volume II)
ISBN 0-931340-38-1 (Two-volume set)

Printed in the United States of America

AMADEUS PRESS
9999 S.W. Wilshire
Portland, Oregon 97225

Library of Congress Cataloging-in-Publication Data

Loft, Abram, 1922-
    Violin and keyboard : the duo repertoire / [by Abram Loft].
       p.   cm.
    Reprint. Originally published: New York : Grossman, 1973.
    Includes bibliographical references and index.
    Contents: v. 1. From the seventeenth century to Mozart -- v.
 2. From Beethoven to the present.
    ISBN 0-931340-36-5 (v. 1). -- ISBN 0-931340-37-3 (v. 2). -- ISBN
 0-931340-38-1 (set)
    1. Violin and continuo music--History and criticism. 2. Violin
 and harpsichord music--History and criticism. 3. Violin and piano
 music--History and criticism. 4. Sonata. I. Title.
 ML894.L63 1991
 787.2'09--dc20   90-20922
                                                              CIP
                                                               MN

To Jill

Contents

𝕾𝕽 *Preface*

The first volume of this guide to the duo repertoire for violin and keyboard ended with a discussion of the mature sonatas of Mozart; I termed these a plateau upon which later generations of duo sonata writers would build their own efforts. It is a reflection of the musical riches that we all enjoy to find that this second volume can begin with another plateau in duo writing—a plateau that stands on a level with the Mozartian and extends its meaning and implication in a wonderfully fulfilling and individual way. I am speaking, of course, of the ten sonatas for piano and violin of Beethoven. In technical difficulty, for both instruments, in dynamic range, dramatic scope and intensity, in their brusque clowning and overwhelming poetry, their structural and thematic complexity, these sonatas never lose their capacity to challenge and reward, to surprise and satisfy.

It has often been pointed out that chamber music, unlike symphonic and operatic writing, offers the composer little cover. True enough, the untalented composer stands fully revealed even when surrounded by one hundred players or by the mammoth cast of the grandest of opera. But even the most gifted composer has—with due regard for the nature of the musical medium at hand—permitted himself to pad out his ideas with symphonic restatement by this or that choir of the orchestra, or by the exciting antiphony between the several protagonists or choruses of the operatic roster. On the other hand, in music for the small ensemble (and there is no ensemble smaller than the duo), repetition without growth of musical idea, without musical purpose, is nakedly and immediately boring.

In a number of works discussed or mentioned in the pages that follow, the lack of such growth and purpose seems apparent, at least to me. The absence of force and focus is made the more irksome in some instances by

the suspicion that matters are so contrived by the composer out of deliberate choice rather than from lack of talent or imagination. In other works,
the use of coloristic patches that seem more appropriate to the symphonic,
orchestrated piece strikes a jarring and bombastic note in the context of
ensemble sound. In still others, the flavor of regional, popular music, so
important a source of freshness in the serious music of any era, becomes
a substitute for, rather than a stimulus to, the individual thought of the
composer; the result is vapidity.

Nonetheless, emerging from the widely disparate musical styles and
idioms that have marked the past century and a half, there is more than
enough duo writing of incisive quality. It is in these works, whether by
Beethoven, Brahms, Debussy, Bartók, or Schoenberg, to name but a few,
that the ensemble will find the true lines of continuation from the great
sonata heritage of earlier times.

And even when choosing among those compositions of less imposing
artistry, the duo will still be interested, and its audience diverted, by the
individual qualities of the music at hand. One cannot function constantly,
either in the concert hall or in the home musicale, at the incandescent level
of concentration evoked by our most demanding composers.

Abram Loft
University of Wisconsin—Milwaukee
Spring 1973

Errata

Numbers = page/paragraph/line.

77/2/8	"two," not "fwo"
103/2/8	"4-12," not "4-11"
293/1/6	"5-7-7-8," not "5-7-8-8"
366/Note 22	No hyphen in Robbins Landon. Same error in Bibliography, with author incorrectly listed under R.
372/Note 180	Baron's book not published.

VIOLIN AND KEYBOARD:
THE DUO REPERTOIRE

1   The Ten Sonatas of Beethoven

ONE OF the most intriguing excerpts in the anthology, *Source Readings in Music History*, edited by Oliver Strunk, is that from *Hesperus*, by the writer, Jean Paul (Richter). Jean Paul (1763–1825), a popular novelist of his day and still a fount of inspiration to so young a contemporary as Robert Schumann, paints a highly colored scene of the hero, Victor, and the heroine, Clothilde, listening—transfixed and tearful —in the dark to a performance by Franz Koch, a virtuoso of the Jew's harp. If we are bemused by this picture of a chamber-music evening in the late 1790s, we may be even more taken by the following bit of information about Koch himself. Having been forced to enlist in the military service, Koch (and his artistry) was brought to the attention of King Friedrich Wilhelm II. What is more improbable still is that the king, hearing Koch perform, "ordered him discharged from his involuntary service in the army." This, from the same monarch, the target of the *King of Prussia* quartets, who was not sufficiently impressed by Mozart to offer that worthy a court post.

This is a roundabout way of approaching the point that, no matter how consummate the Mozart sonatas may seem to us today, they were taken in stride in the late eighteenth century as another manifestation, fine though it was, of contemporary composition. Even those composers who recognized the mastery of these pieces were not thereby inhibited

1

from trying their own hand at the medium. Just as well, from the music lover's selfish point of view, that the public was hard to convince, was unaware, was fickle, was curious to see yet newer things in music. Fortunate, too, that composers have the normal amount of vanity and self-conviction. In the years after Mozart's death, many tried their hand at sonata writing. In many cases, the results varied from middling to atrocious. But there have been enough men of genius to add significant works to the repertoire, in some instances worthy of comparison with the standards set by Mozart.

We begin this volume with a view of the sonatas that are fully the equal of the Mozart ideal; higher praise can be given no composer. These sonatas are the work of a man who, as a sixteen-year-old, was reportedly appraised by Mozart himself with the words, " . . . some day he will give the world something to talk about."[1]

A visit to Vienna, in the spring of 1787, brought the sixteen-year-old Ludwig van Beethoven to the Austrian capital for the first time. However, he was hastily recalled to his native Bonn to attend his mother, who died in July of that year. In November, 1792, Beethoven again set out for Vienna, which was now to be his permanent home. Early studies in composition with Christian Gottlob Neefe, coupled with experience as an active member of the musical retinue at the electoral court in Bonn, were now supplemented by studies with Haydn (who had removed from Eisenstadt to Vienna as a pensioned veteran of the Esterhazy court music), with the composer and theorist, Johann Georg Albrechtsberger, with the composer, Johann Schenk, and with the composer and imperial court kapellmeister, Antonio Salieri.[2] Beethoven did serious work with all of these men, though he was undoubtedly his own best teacher. But Salieri was, by virtue of his post, an important figure in the ranks of Viennese musical politics. As it happens, he is one of the few professional musicians to receive a dedication by Beethoven. The works so directed were Beethoven's first sonatas for piano and violin, the three of opus 12.[3]

In order to date these sonatas and to set them in context of the overall output, we present here a selective calendar of Beethoven compositions from the years in question:[4]

1796	Two Cello Sonatas, op. 5
1797–98	Three Violin Sonatas in D, A, and E flat, op. 12
	Three String Trios, op. 9
1798–99	Piano Sonata, *Pathétique*, op. 13
1798–1800	Six String Quartets, op. 18

1799–1800	Septet for Strings and Winds, op. 20
1800–01	Violin Sonata in A, op. 23
	Violin Sonata in F, *Spring*, op. 24
1801	Viola Quintet, op. 29
	Piano Sonata, *Quasi una fantasia* (*Moonlight*), op. 27, no. 2
1802	Violin Sonatas in A, C minor, G, op. 30
1802–03	Violin Sonata in A, *Kreutzer*, op. 47
1804–05	Piano Sonata, *Appassionata*, op. 57
	Opera, *Fidelio*, op. 72
1806	Symphony number 4, op. 60
	Violin Concerto, op. 61
	The three *Rasoumowsky* quartets, op. 59
1807–08	Symphony number 5, op. 67
	Symphony number 6, op. 68
	Cello Sonata, op. 69
1808	Two Piano Trios, op. 70
1809	String Quartet, *Harp*, op. 74
1810	String Quartet, op. 95
1811	Piano Trio, *Archduke*, op. 97
1811–12	Symphony number 7, op. 92
1812	Symphony number 8, op. 93
1812–13	Violin Sonata in G, op. 96
1815	Two Cello Sonatas, op. 102

It has been said that a remarkable fact about Franz Schubert was his ability to carve out for himself an individual musical style while standing in the shadow of Beethoven. It is no less astonishing that Beethoven was able to find his own musical way despite the awesome presence of the work of the recently departed Mozart.

As we play the Beethoven sonatas, the intensity of musical idea and the handling of it, the incredibly fertile inventiveness, the vividness of contrast—among successive phrases, movements, and entire compositions—the rigorous and yet flexible inner logic of the music is overwhelming. This must be the ultimate in sonata writing! Then one takes up again the Mozart examples, to be impressed anew with the utter grace and benevolence of those pieces. We are fortunate to have the legacy of both men: each complete in its own right; each quite distinct from the other; each a vital part of our awareness of what it means to be a sensitive composer, a compassionate human being.

In a general comparison of the two bodies of sonata composition, it may be said that the Beethoven works seem more huge, more difficult, more consciously grand in outline, more ready to storm the heights. To play these works is a severe challenge on every front. Whatever may be one's self-doubts, there is no question about Beethoven's sureness. He is never at a loss for a definite plan of attack in these compositions. If, as his sketchbooks show, his approach to composing required laborious trial and error, a great winnowing and sifting of possible ideas and treatments, he nevertheless had the indispensable gift of genius: to conceive of a challenging proposition and to recognize when—after much working and reworking of intermediate drafts—he had come upon *the* final result that is stamped with an air of inevitability, of consummate workmanship, and of unmistakable expressive purpose.

Sonata in D, op. 12, no. 1

Who wrote a movement 226 measures long, with one stop in the whole length of the piece? Or, if that is not impressive enough: what movement, 327 measures long, has only two stops, from beginning to end? The composer, Beethoven; the work, the opening Allegro con brio of his first Sonata for Piano and Violin, in D, op. 12, no. 1. We note that the original edition (December, 1798, or January, 1799) of the set of three sonatas that make up this opus, bore the description, "for harpsichord or piano, with a violin," but cannot take the words seriously.[5] Like its successors in the Beethoven output, the sonata is clearly conceived in terms of piano, definitely not harpsichord. Where the composer himself has generously larded the pages with crescendo, decrescendo, fortepiano, sforzando, and (seven times) fortissimo, harpsichord is unthinkable. To give the violin cursory billing in a work of this type is likewise unrealistic, a sop to the conventions of the closing decades of the eighteenth century; conventions rendered mere formality by the epoch-making sonatas of Mozart. The three sonatas of Beethoven's opus 12 are "with violin" as a mother is "with child"—the absence of the companion would be strongly noticed.

When the allegro in question opens, however, nobody is thinking about seniority in the instrumentation. You are looking, as measure follows measure, for a place to draw breath. Forget it; Beethoven is playing a special kind of game here. The eighth rests that divide the opening jets of melody from one another do not interrupt the line; the quarter rests in measure 3 do not stop the flow of sound, but simply give room for resonance.

Figure 1-1. Mm. 1-5

And after this, not a moment of silence, literally, until measure 46, where

Figure 1-2. Mm. 45-48

the lone eighth rest on the fourth beat is a gasp in a whirlwind. Not until
the cadence at the double bar do we get a short break:

Figure 1-3. Mm. 100-104

Until then, motion has passed constantly: from bass to treble, to violin,
and back from sixteenth to whole note and every value between. The runs
have come in every form of duple, and when that gave out, in the lope of
triplets. Just to prove that he meant every note of it, Beethovén has the
audacity to suggest (double bar, measure 101) that we go through the
whole marathon again by repeating the opening section from its very beginning. Those who have successfully weathered the first part of the movement (and possibly its repeat) are then led on into a new section—it is
in *F*, and its key signature is changed to prove it; but the idea is the same:
forward! Again, up hill and down dale. To make the development as ath-

letic as possible, its last passage, measures 126 to 137 (twelve bars out of the thirty-six allotted to the development) is given over entirely to a minefield of the

figures from the initial bars (with an overlay of the flowing eighth-note pattern from the first theme).

Figure 1-4. Mm. 128-129

I have stressed Beethoven's ploy of writing an "endless" piece, but it is just as much his gambit to have phrasing and contrast and flexibility within the continuous flow of notes. Consider three representative places in the movement: first, measures 19 to 21, where the force of the rolling eighths that has sustained the flow of the piece since the fifth bar is gathered and emphasized in the repeated C-sharp–D relationship:

Figure 1-5. Violin, mm. 19-27

Measure 20 must broaden under the weight of the emphasis, to spill over finally into the cascading sixteenths that follow. Or again, note the joint between "bridge" and second-theme area (another application of the eighth-note tide).

Figure 1-6. Mm. 42-44

To avoid poising on the fortepiano note of measure 43 (after the upward rush that leads to it) would be to override the necessary punctuation of the two ideas.

Finally, the transfer from the second-theme area to the closing portion of the exposition (measures 70 to 72): the triplets in the bass, the thirteenth consecutive bar of such figure, provide the rhythmic bond that covers the shift in material. The eighth notes of the closing material have already made their appearance over the triplet line. A broadening is not possible until the fortepiano of the downbeat of measure 71. Then, a stress and lingering is in order on that note in particular, on the first half of the bar in general, and even on the first three measures (71 to 73) of the close, with its hesitant responses. The full flow of tempo does not resume until measures 81 ff., with the sustained trill serving as a vibrant and quickening stimulus from measure 83 on. From here on, the pace goes ahead steadily, culminating in the exhilarating challenges, back and forth, of violin and piano in the flourishes of sixteenth notes that occupy measures 93 ff.:

Figure 1-7. Mm. 93-95

There is great force, coiling and uncoiling, in the legato eighth-note passages, first heard in measure 5. These must be played superlegato, sinuously, tenaciously, always building for the larger phrase (never less than the two-measure unit indicated by the slurring), and moving inexorably to the peak of the line (as in measures 11 and 12). The violin must use its sound-modulating ability to help this propulsion; in measures 5 and 6, for example, the sustained A needs a slight crescendo throughout, coupled with a vibrato that moves from paler to more intense, to climax in, and die away from, the F sharp in measure 6. Measures 7 and 8 should be treated in parallel fashion, but on a lower level of loudness, because the violin line is sinking, counter to the opposing direction of the piano part. Then both instruments (measures 9 ff.) join in the indicated crescendo.

Beethoven characteristically used the device of a sudden drop in dynamics, all the more effective because of its surprise and unexpectedness, at the peak of a rising surge in the music. A case in point is measure 12, downbeat: the crescendo of the preceding measures rises to a point beyond piano (say, to mezzo-forte), and the drop must be made emphatic by putting a very slight hesitation, a comma, into the music at the bar line between measures 11 and 12. This will stand out in retrospect when, at the corresponding joint between measures 18 and 19, the line moves through without hesitation. The sudden dynamic shift, then, is used for structural as well as expressive purpose, to define the role of specific occurrences in the course of the composition.

Beethoven's precise use of dynamics is seen in the aforementioned passage (end of development) where the eighth-note flow and the apparent interruptedness of the sixteenth-note fragment are combined. Here (measures 126 ff.), the placement of pianissimo at the beginning of the first, fifth, and ninth measures of the sequence, together with the swell-and-diminish markings, divides the continuous passage into three segments. Also, the fact that the segments begin (in the violin) on C sharp, D, and E, respectively, helps mark the divisions and (within the overall level) the general rise in intensity of the line.

In the recapitulation, Beethoven tightens the action by omitting the dialogue that occupied the corresponding space (measures 21 to 32) in the first portion of the movement. Instead, he moves directly from introductory fanfare and first theme to the flourishes that raise the curtain on the second theme. Finally, there is no special coda, or final area of thematic exploitation at the end of the movement. Beethoven closes here as he does in the exposition. He has made his point; take it or leave it.

Inspection of variation movements in Beethoven's string quartets (to cite one example) shows that the complexity of the individual variant as well as the overall size of the movement tends to increase in the later works. The same holds true in the violin sonatas, though the span of time covered by this output is much shorter than in the case of the quartets. A comparison of the variations movement of opus 12, number 1, with the corresponding movement from the *Kreutzer* Sonata, op. 47, just six years later, will show the great change in thickness and stature that takes place (see pages 47-49). Nevertheless, some of the same textural devices are used in the earlier example. Compare, for instance, the third variant of the opus 12 work with the first variant of opus 47; and the first two variants of the early sonata with the fourth variant of the *Kreutzer*. Not only will similarities of device and treatment be noticed; but it will be seen that practice of the earlier movement is good preparation for the more rigorous demands of the later.

In this early variations set, the duo will, for example, find its musicianship and dramatic sense thoroughly tested in moving from the rippling brilliance of the second variation (measures 49 ff.), to the tension of the third, minor one, and then on to the tranquil conversations of the fourth and last.

Returning to the idea of continuous motion, so much emphasized in the first movement of the Sonata in D major, we find some reflection of this in the work's finale, rondo. Last movements are entitled to move with some abandon, and this finale uses its franchise. Points of rhythmic suspension in the theme are the target of Beethoven's sforzandi, the impact (coupled with offbeat placing) helping to keep the ear from settling down to any real rest on these tones:

Figure 1-8. Violin, mm. 1-16

However—and this may be by way of compensation, at last, for the drive of the first and last movement—there are several points of more significant rest: measures 47 to 51, and again measures 162 to 167, offer actual spaces of silence and a fermata. And the idea of rest is extended, at the very end of the movement (cf. measures 196 ff., 217 ff.), into a dialogue where both instruments mark time, turning in place very quietly before making a short, two-measure sprint to the double bar. I am reminded, on a miniature scale, of the elaborate teasing used by the composer in the finale of the quartet, op. 18, no. 6, composed at almost the same time in Beethoven's career. For the performer, a prime concern in the sonata's rondo is to keep the 6/8 meter from showing its age; there must be no double-time thumping in each measure. Temper the athletic while avoiding the pedantic.

Sonata in A, op. 12, no. 2

Have you ever played *Chopsticks?* It is almost as infuriating to play as to hear, because it goes nowhere, either harmonically, melodically, or rhythmically. It sits on its tonic, makes a couple of small excursions, but really stays much at home; a drab experience.

We begin Beethoven's opus 12, number 2, Allegro vivace, and—despite the liveliness of tempo—find ourselves suspecting the worst: Beethoven got to *Chopsticks* ahead of all of us! What is the violinist to think when he plays his part in measures 1 to 8?

Figure 1-9. Violin, mm. 1-8

Just for the record, this doltish rhythm occupies at least 131 measures out of the 245 measures comprising this movement (fortunately, not all in the violin part)! There must be snickers from the other world and from this at such statistics; but the infernal thumping is pervasive, is drummed into us, so that, when it is absent, its omission hammers at the ear. Beethoven is deliberately creating a stable, almost static base, rotating in place with gyroscopic insistence:

Figure 1-10.   Mm. 1-4

From so solid a launching pad, he can propel the rocket of melody that eventually breaks free.

Figure 1-11.   Mm. 7-11

But he returns to his hurdy-gurdy again and again in the course of the movement. In the exposition, the clockwork runs insistently until measure 60. Measure 61 gives, not a breather, but a shock; it is a measure of complete silence, during which the ticking continues mentally. Then, as if intrigued by the experience of the silence, the music resumes in little ripples of sound in the piano, the violin chiming in coyly:

Figure 1-12. Mm. 58-63

And, a few measures later, comes blessed relief: a line that moves smoothly, flowingly,

Figure 1-13. Violin, mm. 68-76

releasing us for a time from the by-now-familiar hopping rhythm—which, however, returns in full force to close the section:

Figure 1-14. Mm. 84-87

For the players, the important point is to be aware of Beethoven's project in this movement: to exploit the idea of turning vigorously, jump-ingly, dancingly in place. But the movement cannot be reduced to a calis-thenic session; the inherent contrasts of the music must be emphasized. The basic jump should be handled with airiness and grace, with a view toward the longer, four- and eight-measure sway. The swirl of sixteenth-note motion (as in measures 9 to 12, and the like) needs sweep and upward lift. The contrasting, low-flying melodies (measures 31 ff., measures 68 ff., and so on) must be played with the requisite hush, hover, and mystery.

The development and its fireworks should be played incisively, force-fully, to make it stand out against the cuteness and lightness of the expo-sition. At the same time, the supercuteness—or is it accidental?—of the shift of slurred couplets from *on*-beat placement (generally true through-out the movement) to *off*beat response, as in measures 110 ff., must be marked in the playing.

Figure 1-15.   Mm. 109-114

The couplet (as portion of the triplet) is, after all, the theme of the move-ment. Its use in dialogue between high and low register, whether within the piano alone (see piano, measures 1 to 4, above), or more extremely, between high violin and low piano

Figure 1-16.   Mm. 16-20

is also part of the thematic treatment. And, at the end of the movement (measures 234 to end), the couplet and its attendant dialogue become the dominant factor, having completely won out against the accompanying, thumping figure.

Figure 1-17.   Mm. 239-245

The clearly exposed dialogue of the end of the first movement in the sonata carries over into the second. Here it is tearful, almost histrionically so, each instrument outdoing the other in quiet lamentation. The impact of the music comes not only from the theme (measures 1 to 8), with its quavering rhythm in the second bar, and its imploring sob in the third and fourth

Figure 1-18. Mm. 1-8

but also from the pacing of the dialogue between the two instruments. At the start of the movement, piano and violin answer each other politely, either player waiting for the end of an eight-measure speech by his partner before taking over the center stage (see measures 1 to 32). As the discussion continues, the ardor of the participants grows; now, neither instrument can wait its turn. The two (measures 33 ff.) take the thread of conversation away from each other on a measure-by-measure basis, then press on to a beat-by-beat interchange (measures 49 to 52, 59 and 60):

Figure 1-19.

a. Mm. 33-35

b. Mm. 48-52

When the opening material returns (measures 69 ff.), it has been affected by the preceding experience: the repartee is closer than at the start of the movement. And the instrument that has, for the moment, relinquished the theme takes up an obbligato commentary role; some of the episode is given over to quasi-canonic imitation between the two instruments, as though neither can now trust the other to express the musical thought completely.

This procedure—alternately imitative and synchronized handling of the two voices—continues through the coda of the movement (measures 108 to end), which is not so much a conclusion as a climax of despondency in this middle chapter of the sonata. All in all, the movement must be played as though wearing the pained mask. But—and especially after the teasings of the first allegro—the tongue must be slightly in the cheek of the mask, for the movement is just a bit too sad to be true!

Or is it? Much depends on the way the duo handles the movement. Not only its sounds, but even more importantly, its silences. Careful inspection of the score (or a playing thereof) will reveal more or less pregnant silences in measures 4, 8, 12, 16, 24, 32, 84, 98, 114, 116, 117, 118, 119, and the last two measures, 128 and 129. Not all are as important as the especially suspenseful break in measure 98; the players will have to gauge each one for effect. But an awareness of these silences and of their significance will have several effects on the interpretation of the movement: first, the instruction, Andante, will have to be read on the slow side (one can urge a speed of $\text{\musicquarter} = 44$ with conviction) in order to give the pauses their proper impact. Second, full allowance for the pauses as they occur will permit the resonance of the sounds just preceding the pause to hang in the air with due effect. Third, the easy and unhurried treatment of these pauses will set off, by contrast, those portions of the movement where Beethoven overrules pause by the overlapping of the several lines of the writing.

The finale seems innocent and straightforward after the lamentations of the slow movement. But the performers had better look out for at least a couple of surprises in the episode: first, the composed pauses in the first and last sections of the movement (measures 78 to 83; and measures 307 to 312):

Figure 1-20. Mm. 75-82

The accumulated effect of the successive pauses, along with the dynamic drop indicated by Beethoven himself, calls also for a retard over the sequence of three units of sound and silence, or at the very least, a stretching of the two-beat rests in measures 83 and 312.

Another significant item is the contrasting section, in D major, beginning in measure 120: although marked dolce, and coming from a previous mark of pianissimo, the passage has a thicker, more syrupy feel about it than the jaunty strains of the preceding section, as though a basso aria has been transposed willfully to a soprano register. The throatiness of the "original" should not be lost in the transfer. This will be specially noted in measures 168 ff. And finally, the brief flare-up at measures 206 ff., marking the transition back from the contrast section to the return of the opening idea (at measure 230), must be handled with the proper note of asperity, and with a nicely graded feeling of subsidence in the passage from measures 216 to 229.

Sonata in E flat, op. 12, no. 3

One need only look at the first movement of this sonata to realize what a lion of the keyboard Beethoven was. The piano part is black with showers of notes, a veritable concerto. The violin? Oh, yes, there are some chores for the string player, usually by way of responding to an outburst in the keyboard. But the essentially secondary role of the violin here is revealed in hilarious fashion at the beginning of the development section (cf. measures 68 ff., or even earlier, beginning in measure 64 of the exposition); here the piano sends out torrents of rapid sextuplets and triplets, while the violin shouts encouragement in a much safer sequence of quarter-note chords.

Figure 1-21. Mm. 68-69

This is an absolutely brilliant, pyrotechnic movement, of virtuoso difficulty for the pianist; it also demands a virtuoso violinist, but his wares will be displayed more reservedly. The emphasis of the movement does seem to be on display, and I am tempted to say that it alone, among all those in the ten sonatas, verges on the superficial. Even in this particular allegro, though, the *spirito* called for by Beethoven both in word and in melodic temper is so intense that any sense of surface flash and glitter is burned away. Even the quarter-note chordal commentary of the violin, referred to above, becomes more than that when played with bold, smooth, stentorian grandeur: the chords are the fuse that kindles the piano rocket; and they are at the same time the great bursts of light carried on the piano's fiery tide.

The incomparable vigor of the second theme (measures 29 ff.) and the rich solidity of the theme (heard only this once) that appears for but a few measures to usher in the recapitulation also contribute to the feeling that this movement bears its virtuosity with grace and conviction. A great joy for the players.

The same must be said for the third and last movement of the sonata, a Rondo: Allegro molto. From the first upbeat, the first sforzando downbeat, the dance is on, and the duo goes whirling down the page, never to stop until the peremptory flourish of the last two measures of the piece. Along the way, there are such felicities as the piquant sections, combining the boisterous, the bittersweet, and the shadowed, of measures 51 ff., and 194 ff.,

Figure 1-22.   Mm. 191-198

and the roller-coaster sweeps of the piano in measures 109 ff.

Again, this movement is more distinguished for its energy than for its profundity. What a rousing finale it makes, though, not only for this particular sonata, but for the entire set of opus 12!

As for the middle movement, an *Adagio con molt' espressione*, it is a lovely bouquet, fragrant with gracious melody and luxuriant turns and roulades, saved from frivolousness by the beauty of its lyric statement and especially by its tempo. The adagio instruction must be taken quite seriously, with a pacing of about $\flat = 58$. At this speed, which challenges the ability of the violinist to sustain individual tones and phrases, the music takes on a wonderful, timeless tranquillity.

On the whole, this third sonata seems most "market-minded" of all the cycle. It is engaging, attractive, and (though only at first glance) not terribly demanding of the intellect or emotions of the listener. It has everything that would suit it to the amateur music maker of Beethoven's day except ease of execution. If this is Beethoven writing down to his audience, they must have been musicians of considerable stature. The truth is, more likely, that Beethoven was really writing for himself. His bemused auditors, when they tried the score over in their own music rooms, must have had to use their imaginations as much as their fingers to recreate the effects of the master's performance of the work.

Beethoven's contemporary, the Bohemian composer and organist, Johann Wenzel Tomaschek, heard Beethoven play in Prague at the time of the opus 12 sonatas. He confessed himself so affected by the experience of the performance and by Beethoven's improvisations on a Mozart theme, that he himself could not play for some days.[6] What, then, must have been the feeling of the amateur?

Sonata in A minor, op. 23

If the finale of sonata number 3 suggests the friendly gaiety of social, ballroom dancing, the opening Presto of sonata number 4 (opus 23) takes us into quite another world. It may still be the world of dance, but now of the passionate, unbridled, utterly energetic, flamenco type. The sonata does not begin; rather, it bursts into view, its frenzy none the less apparent for the hushed dynamics of the opening.

Figure 1-23. Mm. 1-6

There is considerable stamping of rhythm in these measures, reinforced by the accentuation instructions (fortepiano and sforzando) of the composer. The surging energy of the movement must be realized by the players, as well as the occasional breaks that set this frenzy in relief. These can be brief, as in measures 14 to 16,

Figure 1-24. Mm. 14-18

or longer lasting, as in the flowing second subject that begins in measure 30. But always the turbulence lies in wait, flashing to the surface in scalding brilliance.

Figure 1-25. Mm. 56-61

Beethoven justifies the repeat of the exposition by making the first ending an easy turnaround, the second ending a telescoped, shouted pileup of the three lines—bass, treble, and violin (see measures 68 to 71). The composer also calls for a repetition of the second section, but this does not seem essential; better to press on to the coda. The second ending that opens this passage (measures 222 ff.) unites the violin and treble instead of having one leap in after the other. Before the end of the movement, however, there are to be a couple of elaborate teasings and interruptions of the hitherto almost constant racing of the music: first, the implied retard of measures 240 and 241; immediately after, the specified retard of the next two measures; and finally, the repeated arrests of the closing measures, almost as though Beethoven (already well on into the deafness of his later years) is listening to the resonance of each closing chord.

Figure 1-26. Mm. 245-252

After the unbridled directness of the first movement, the kittenish maneuvers of the Andante scherzoso, più Allegretto strike an astonishing contrast. The opening measures, where each sound is balanced by a corresponding silence, immediately suggests the possibility of jocular sequels.

Figure 1-27.   Mm. 1-4

And sure enough, when the violin enters, its glossing of the piano line (bass) stimulates the treble to fill in the spaces of the erstwhile silences:

Figure 1-28.   Mm. 8-12

The stage has been set, then, for delicate mimicry: of one hand by the other, of one instrument by the other. In measure 33, the piano quickly introduces a mock-grandiose fugal subject that is reflected first by the violin, then by the treble, until, in the quickening activity, all three lines rush toward the cadence, only to take up yet a third round of imitations; here is the junction in question:

Figure 1-29.   Mm. 49-53

The sauciest turn in the movement comes at the beginning of the second section, where both instruments are made to bow and scrape to each other with the most outrageous combination of demureness, sudden heroics, and mock piety:

Figure 1-30. Mm. 88-95

The incessant badinage, with every now and then a rushing to the brink as one idea is suddenly dropped for another, is exceedingly provocative. The more so because, at the end of the movement, the two protagonists saunter through the double bar without any great show of finality; we are left hanging, waiting for more (though a discreet broadening of pace at the very end will protect us from a completely raw drop-off):

Figure 1-31. Mm. 201-207

Beethoven's advice, that the character be more allegretto than andante, is to the point; the pace must be lively enough to set the alternations, the twists and turns, the near collisions, in bright relief.

The subtle contrasts of the middle movement in this sonata are mirrored, much more strongly, in the tumultuous flow of ideas in the finale, Allegro molto. A tour through measures 54 to 248 will impress the player with the rich array of episodes: the stern thrust of the initial theme (measures 54 to 73); the mincing conversations of the next episode (measures 74 to 94); the hushed reverie, enlivened soon enough by florid melodic embroideries, of measures 114 to 203; and the wild-eyed railings of measures 223 to 248. The finale is a musical panorama, one that, consistent with the tactics in the other two movements of the sonata, ends quietly, deliberately suggesting irresolution and exhaustion.

In no other Beethoven sonata will the duo find a greater challenge to its sense of drama, of timing, of musical repartee, than in this A minor work of the thirty-year-old composer. It is one of the most exciting pieces that amateur or professional can play.

Sonata in F, op. 24

The two sonatas, opus 23 in A minor and opus 24 in F major, were composed during 1800–01. Both were published in October, 1801, by Mollo of Vienna (who also brought out the opus 18 quartets); at first they appeared with the single opus number, 23. The engraver, however, mistakenly cast the violin parts of the two sonatas in different format. To save the expense of reworking the plates, the publisher split the two sonatas from each other and brought out the second with the opus number, 24. Both pieces were dedicated to Moritz von Fries, Viennese banker and renowned art patron.[7]

When we turn to opus 24, we see that, in contrast, for example, to the opening movements of opus 12, numbers 1 and 2, the Sonata in F pulls no special stunt in its Allegro first movement. This is simply an appealing work. Its lines are long: the first theme flows with only one minor break from beginning to measure 25. This immediately presents a player's problem: to keep the line from breaking before the composer intends it to. Partly, this involves a highlighting of important points in the line, and a subordination of lesser elements. On this score, a pertinent illustration is offered by the musicologist, Robert Donington.[8] Demonstrating the idea that ornaments, when added to a musical line, serve to decorate and surround existing points of significance in that line, he cites this example:

Figure 1-32.

And, to show its "ornamented" version, he gives us the finished version:

Figure 1-33.

This, of course, is the opening to the Beethoven sonata movement under consideration here. Beethoven has written the complete, unalterable mel-

ody, leaving nothing to our imagination in the way of "ornamental" addition to it. What Donington has done is what every player must do in
performing any musical passage: single out the elements of importance and
focus his and the listener's attention on them, first and foremost, in the
hearing of the work. The stress points in the entire opening violin melody
of the Beethoven would be shown as follows:

Figure 1-34. Mm. 1-10

The same would hold true for the piano version that follows (measures
11 ff.), except that the added ornamentation of the melody in this part
produces some new stress points as well.

Figure 1-35. Mm. 16-18

So also in the extension of the piano melody (measures 20 to 25): the G,
downbeat of measure 21, deserves stress; but its later counterpart, downbeat of measure 23, needs yet more, by virtue of the repetition of idea and
the cumulative force derived therefrom—an accumulation certified by Beethoven himself in the crescendo that he sets for the two closing measures
of the passage immediately after(measures 24 and 25).

The musical germ is the same in the next measures (26 ff.), but the
coloring is different: a fortissimo attack, followed by a prolonged descent
into shadowy regions and by some measures of groping in that gloom. A
certain brightness is restored (measures 38 ff.), but the light is darkened
fitfully, even so (measures 46 ff.). And the section is lulled to its close in
a gently tossing stream of sixteenth-note runs (measures 70 ff.).

In the passage beginning in measure 38, the pianist must avoid hack-

ing at the chordal clusters on each eighth. The shape should mold itself
to the two- and four-measure unit, thus:

Figure 1-36.   Mm. 42-47

And, in the next component of this area in the movement (measures 46 to
53), the motion must again be forward, to the momentary peak in the line.
In the billowing waves of sixteenths, measures 70 ff., the sforzandi must
be easy reinforcements of the notes in question, not so accented or percussive as to break into the surge and flow of the line.

   The development is introduced by a sudden, forte half-note: to emphasize as well as temper the shock, the note should be held a fraction
beyond its true value, and there should be a very slight pause immediately
after to let the sound settle. Then, the piano sixteenth-note line may be
taken up to get things going. We proceed in a broad dialogue between
violin and piano: first in the weighty ascents and descents, beat by beat,
over two measures answered by two,

Figure 1-37.   Mm. 92-96

supported, as the example shows, on the eighth-note pulsation already familiar from the first section of the movement. Then, the descending line
alone, repeatedly placed, is borne up by waves of triplet figures, a rhythm
used now for the first time. The broad span of the descents, and the complete arch-pattern of the triplets must be the targets for the players, not
the individual beats. And when the action simmers down to muttering
sixteenth tremolos, these must be played back and forth by the duo to
make a continuous chain, extending unbroken from measure 116 until the
quiet resolution in the return of the opening material.

The ideas and procedures in the recapitulation will be familiar from corresponding happenings in the opening section. Only the coda (measures 210 ff.) is new; and it, too, is reminiscent. It starts like the development, moves on to a very widely arched eighth-note trajectory, in chromatic and scalewise patterns, pauses suspensefully for a moment (measures 228 to 230), then launches into a closing peroration, looking back on the movement through the first-theme idea and the triplet motion derived from the midsection activity. To sustain the continuity of this expansive coda, to pace the dynamics (from pianissimo to fortissimo), and to arrive triumphantly, but not roughly at the loud final chords—that is the assignment.

The mood of the second movement, Adagio molto espressivo, is of a different order. The lowest dynamic level is again pianissimo; the peak, however, is a single, solitary forte, marking one measure quite late in the movement (measure 61). To the pianist falls the most difficult task, because some forty measures of that part contain—for one or both hands— an oscillating sixteenth-note pattern. Indelicately handled, these sixteenths will become an instant porridge, drowning the movement in a glutinous mass of sound. Properly played, these patterns will provide a constantly undulating, vibrant floor upon which the superstructure of the movement will float. It is rather simple: piano and violin, in turn, present an eight-measure tune; there follows a short diversion (measures 18 to 28); then both instruments again present the theme, but the violin chooses the tonic minor, leading the music into a short modulatory passage (measures 40 to 51). After this, the movement remains in the tonic, B flat, but instead of resuming the basic melody of the movement in clear-cut fashion, dissolves that melody into fragments or derivatives, and finally falls away through a series of thirty-second-note tremolos at the interval of the second or third (cf. measures 65, 67, 69).

Beethoven justifies the literal repetition of simple melodies in this movement by changing the ornamentation of the tune in its successive appearances. Compare the piano part, measures 2 and 30; and measures 4 and 32:

Figure 1-38.

a. Mm. 1-4

b. Mm. 30-32

In playing the ornaments in the movement, there can be no suggestion of the flashy, virtuoso performer. These are not frivolous decorations, but rather outpourings, a welling over of the emotional content of the melody. The line should be treated in the most sustained manner, singingly, with the most finely shaded dynamics. The ability to play easily, naturally, and with control will be tested by the ensemble tremolos at the end of the movement.

We have said something about the detail of this movement. What is extremely difficult to convey in words is the tremulous, clean-washed clarity of this music. To hear this Adagio sensitively played in the intimacy of the home or in the larger intimacy of a well-designed recital hall is to undergo one of the most moving experiences in music making. Tears come to the eyes of the most hardened music veterans when they are confronted with the devastating simplicity and directness of these lines.

As though to move to the opposite extreme from the Adagio, the Scherzo that follows is full of coquetry. In effect, the two instruments here are engaged in a dance; the piano leads off, and the violin swings into line in the second round of the dance. But alas, the violin almost immediately falls one step behind the partner; though the two occasionally move together thereafter, the violin is incorrigible, remaining stubbornly out of step until the final cadence. The occasional streamers of notes in the violin must be placed precisely, and downbeat quarter notes ended cleanly so as to leave clear room for the next attacks.

Figure 1-39. Mm. 14-20

The Trio, a breathless whirl, seems to have the two instruments locked into synchronization (on paper—in performance, it calls for studied abandon and precise pacing of the long melodic arches if the two instruments are to emerge unscathed). The eighth notes here require a light, rather dry treatment. The piano dynamic at the beginning of each section of the Trio must be meticulously observed, so that the rise to a contrasting, forte level can be achieved without roughness. The Trio is quickly over; it is the peg-legged gait of the Scherzo that frames the movement and brings it to a close.

The concluding Rondo's theme starts as though it is a duple-time, fleshed-out version of the Scherzo melody.

Figure 1-40. Violin, mm. 8-12

With less cause, there is some comparison with the theme of the first movement, at least in terms of general outline (see Figure 1-34). In any event, the finale has the same flow as the first movement, though with a greater sense of ease and humor. The more reason to play the Rondo with suavity and nonchalance, as though in the course of an enjoyable stroll. Keep your eye on the eight-measure phrase (at least at the opening) and on even longer—or shorter—units, as Beethoven dictates. Notes with dots should be played with an easy, rather broad spiccato. However, the dots for the figures in the violin part, measures 28 and 29, and all corresponding passages represent light *détaché* strokes, with the figure in question best played in slurred bowing, thus:

Figure 1-41. Mm. 28-29

The passage from measures 42 to 55 raises some points that will also apply to later episodes in the movement; they center on the simultaneous use of triple and duple divisions of the beat. Taking the situations in the order of their occurrence, in measures 42 and 43 we find triplets, slurred by the beat, against couplets, slurred *off* the beat to on, thus:

Figure 1-42. Mm. 43-46

The triplets should be played so that each beat is clear in itself, but also so the successive groups link up into one, larger chain. In the violin part, the couplets must indeed be bowed as Beethoven has shown, but without any fussy accenting of the on-beat eighths. The bowing should be articulate but smooth, the underlying shape of the quarter-beat melody showing through the rhythmic pattern. And the couplets must *be* couplets, clearly distinguishable from the running patter of the parallel stream of triplets.

In measure 44, the transition from triplet to duplet rhythm (see piano part) must be made naturally, so that the one seems only another facet of the other. So also the swing back and forth in alternate measures of this passage:

Figure 1-43. Mm. 47-51

And, finally, the response of triplet fragments (right hand) to the generating pulse of the bass line:

Figure 1-44. Mm. 52-54

The effect here must be of a triplet whose initial note carries through the entire beat, the linear pattern of the successive quarter notes dominating the bar.

The forte in measures 73 ff. is mild, not strident; of generous, easy boldness, not militant. And the triplets in the violin part here call for an easy, cantering feeling, as though reflecting—in miniature fretwork—the larger musculature of the piano lines. When the roles are reversed (measures 81 ff.), the characterization of the respective elements should carry on consistently.

This coolly shaded episode goes on at some length, finally running out into a composed accelerando (measures 108 to 111); this, in turn, into yet another rondo refrain—except that the refrain is in the "wrong" key: D major, instead of the movement's F major. But the refrain is played with some assurance, the violin providing a new, lilting countermelody to the pianist's statement of the tune. And when the composer sets matters right, in measures 124 ff., with proper key and all, the joke is passed over in quiet fashion, unless perhaps the violin's pizzicati, in these measures, is a wry comment on the goings-on.

There seems to be only one turbulent or less-than-relaxed point in this entire movement: the passage from measure 161 through 188. And that, only by its heightened intensity (greater length, higher harmonic and register level, and higher dynamic peak—to forte and fortissimo), as compared with the corresponding passage from measures 36 to 55. The outburst is concentrated in the passage, measures 171 to 180.

Figure 1-45. Mm. 178-181

From there to the end of the finale, it is as carefree a race to the double bar as a busy pianist and almost equally occupied violinist can contrive to make it. This coda is lavish with its episodes and assorted climaxes. Watch for these divisions and high points:

Episode (measures)	*Climactic points*
189-205 ⟶	195 downbeat; 203 and 205

```
206-223  ──────────────→  213-214;  222-223
224-235  ──────────────→  230;  235
236-end  ──────────────→  242
```

On the whole, opus 24 is a sunny sonata, in keeping with the picture we should like to have of Beethoven as a young, successful composer, and belied only by its own cooler and darker moments (and by the bitter complaints, in Beethoven's letters at this time, about his deafness).

The three sonatas of opus 30 were composed in 1802. The last movement to be written was the finale of the first sonata, which Beethoven composed to take the place of the original closing movement, later used as the finale for the *Kreutzer* Sonata, op. 47. The three works, published in May and June, 1803, were dedicated to Czar Alexander I of Russia, but earned Beethoven no specific reward until 1815, when, through the benevolence of Czarina Elisabeth, who was in Vienna with her husband for the Congress of Vienna, the omission was made good with a gift of one-hundred ducats.[9]

Sonata in A, op. 30, no. 1

In the urbane lesson in the art of seduction that is presented so convincingly in Mozart's duet for Don Giovanni and Zerlina, *La ci darem la mano*, the most delightful episode is that at the end, when, Zerlina having sighed her final and most willing "Yes!," the couple move toward the concealment of the arbor. It is then that the orchestra, ever the instigator and commentator in the Mozart opera, entwines the lovers in its melodic web, carries them liltingly and firmly toward the consummation of the Don's newest conquest. There is, of course, a fateful interruption, but we need not concern ourselves with that here. I am trying to draw an interesting parallel with the closing variation of the finale of Beethoven's A major sonata. For here again, at the end of a movement that has proceeded hitherto in various manipulations of a duple meter, the last episode turns to a swaying 6/8 to urge the movement and the sonata to its double bar.

Beethoven is in no hurry to wind things up. He actually turns aside, not once but twice, following his harmony down a by-lane until it brings him to the note, D, in the violin part, which he then proceeds to regard from every angle, as though he had never heard such a note before, while the piano chirps contentedly about, completely at ease.

Figure 1-46. Mm. 187-194

In a second such sally, the scrutiny of the repeated tone is even more intense in the quietness, so that the note oscillates with another self, alternately D and E flat.

Figure 1-47. Mm. 206-212

Beethoven does pull himself out of this dreaming to bring the movement to a close.

Before all this, it has proved to be quite a set of variations. To begin with, there is an innocent and graceful theme, set against a background of Schubertian, eighth-note murmurings in the piano. Then a variation that features the piano in flashing flights of triplets built on the solid pulse of the bass-line quarters. A second variation highlights the sinuous windings of the violin. A third variation locks the violin part and the piano treble into a quite jazzy, syncopated pattern. The fourth variation reduces the violin to crisp, terse chordal fanfares (we suggest that the violinist play the *quiet* chords all up-bow, near the tip of the bow, and with discreet, quickly negotiated rolling over the three and four strings involved). Next, a fifth variation that uses an adagio, gently exhaled cadence (measures 128 and 129) to divide itself into two subsections: the first, a minor-hued, fugal elaboration on the theme; the second, an episode where delicately snapped rhythms surround the quiet tollings of the chordal axis of the music. It is this tolling, concealed also in the rippling figures of the movement's open-ing, that finally unfolds into the bemused inspection of the note, D, referred to above.

This is a marvelous conclusion to the sonata; and it is preceded by the even more wonderful movement, the Adagio molto espressivo. Without undue reticence, let me suggest that this movement calls to mind a vision of Beethoven in heaven, with Verdi. The first part of the vision comes from the sublime tranquillity of the initial melody; the second, from the Italianate quality of the subordinate theme and of the embellishments that occur in the later portions of the movement. The presence of the florid runs and graces, however, must not mislead the performers into thinking that this Adagio is a display piece. It should be played for what it is: an ethereal, rather introspective movement, whose occasional melodic lush-ness is an unostentatious outpouring of the sentiment that fills the work. There are few loudnesses; the mood is low-key, but nonetheless warm and intense, and there is an utterly calm, suspended ending.

Figure 1-48.   Mm. 99-105

Turning, at last, to the first movement of the sonata, we find it con-sistent with its fellows: it has flashes of exuberance, of moderately brilliant technical display. But its essence lies in the warmly lyric tone of its prin-cipal theme, and in the coy dalliance of such passages as the following:

Figure 1-49.   Mm. 140-147

The A major is, technically speaking, not the most difficult of the Beethoven set; with regard to sensitivity, nuance, and restraint, however, it calls for the best the players can give. It is not for children (and not for all adults). The chamber-music literature holds few treasures to equal it.

Sonata in C minor, op. 30, no. 2

As usual, Beethoven states his premise forthrightly at the start of the C minor sonata. There is a short, swiftly falling fragment of sound; a second statement, higher placed; then a running off of the energy impounded in this two-fold declamation. In the opening phrase, the impact of each fragment is heightened by an ensuing pause—as though the composer would have us listen to the resonance of the sound.

Figure 1-50.   Mm. 1-10

As the movement continues, the silences are no longer literally observed in the thematic statements, but are filled with actual, composed resonance, either a deliberately nebulous rumble, as in measures 9 and 10, above, or a countermelody,

Figure 1-51.   Mm. 75-77

or even, still later on, by an echo of the fragment itself, as in measures 218 to 221. And, quite early, we find the fragment actually invaded by turbulent resonance:

Figure 1-52. Mm. 12-14

All of which indicates the dramatic tension of the fragment and of its first, sustained tone. The piano can realize the power of that tone by the molding of the surrounding resonance (cf. measure 75, Figure 1-51, where Beethoven himself calls for a swell). The violin can achieve the same result by swelling the sustained tone, as desired, even when no such shaping is stipulated by the composer.

The idea of the resonating sound is manifest in yet another form in this movement: the chordal response between piano and violin, followed by the momentary silence at the end of the third pair of chords.

Figure 1-53. Mm. 23-24

With or without the pause, this pattern of sound is used frequently during the movement, and at significant points. It marks the division between first and second theme (cf. measures 23 and 24, 27 and 28); and its march-like implication seems to spark the martial strains of the second theme:

Figure 1-54. Violin, mm. 29-32

It appears again (measures 72 to 74) to transfer us from the exposition to the development (which opens with the strain shown in measures 75 and 76, Figure 1-51). It returns once more, but in mollified, expanded, and espressivo manner, to close the development (cf. measures 131 to 137). During the recapitulation, it turns up at measure 153 and 154, 157 and 158, and 205 to 207, corresponding to its placement and function in the exposition. In the coda (measures 208 ff.), its derivation from the thematic fragment is at last certified by Beethoven himself, when the chordal flashes *and* the theme fragment are superimposed on one another (measures 218 to 220). And the chordal salvo alone, unadorned, without any apology and with violin and piano lined up rather than in staggered reply, is used at the very end of the movement in what would otherwise be regarded as a conventional cadential formula:

Figure 1-55. Mm. 251-254

In all cases, the chords must be played boldly. Note how Beethoven has, in measures 72 to 74, taken pains to mark each chord, in violin and piano, with fortissimo. Yet the idea of resonance must be preserved: the chords cannot be attacked so vigorously (particularly in the violin) that they become mere barking and scraping; they must ring out. The martial second theme, too, must be played with clarity and articulation, but still with warmth of tone and direction of motion:

Figure 1-56. Mm. 160-169

Passages such as that at measures 52 to 58, moving from piano to forte, can be messy at all levels unless played snugly, with clear stroke and touch, and with care to let the two lines of motion (violin and piano treble) come through with equal clarity. In measures 75 ff. and again at 208 ff., the theme (piano bass), and its violin countermelody must sing out clearly to each other around the central core of arpeggiated figures in the piano right hand.

The complete focus on the theme fragment, in unison repetition between violin and piano (measures 92 to 94), is unique in the movement and is cast in a range from piano to fortepiano. The passage must give a bold and ringing effect within its quiet level of sound. The same holds true for the peroration, measures 235 to the end. It is more difficult to bring off there, because the greater thickness of writing, the composer's crescendo marks and the occasional forte and more frequent sforzando indications are a temptation to force. Both players must exercise restraint in their bold-ness, closing the movement in the same resonant vein that has been domi-nant since the first measures.

The Adagio cantabile is written in "singing manner" indeed: the line is constantly long, sustained, plastic in its rises and falls. However, it re-veals in its placid waters two reefs of sound that stand out by their turbu-lence and loudness: the runs in measures 87 and 96. Here is the contrast offered in measures 86 to 88:

Figure 1-57. Mm. 86-89

The run, you will note, is written in 128th notes. There are sixteenths and thirty-seconds enough to be found in the rest of the movement. But 128ths! And placed, fortissimo, just before the return of the pianissimo quarter notes of the theme! Beethoven wants to shock, to jar us, to fling us from one end of the rhythmic and dynamic scale to the other, moving from extreme close-up to tranquil, distant view. The most distant of vantage points is taken at measures 33 ff., where first the violin, then the piano move in the most sustained, hushed, hovering line, to the accompaniment of equally quiet escalations of sixteenth notes.

Figure 1-58. Mm. 32-34

Other wonderfully quiet spots are the exquisitely delicate scalewise arches through which both instruments return to the opening melody, measures 50 to 52; the bass-register richness and clarity of the piano's passage-work in measures 60 to 68; the similar material at measures 76 to 83; and especially, the hornlike calls, heard through crystalline atmosphere, in measure 86 and again in measure 95. A musical reflection of this is heard in measures 103 to 106. And both the sustained line of measure 33 and the running passage-work of measures 60 ff. are reviewed in a nostalgic closing passage, measures 107 to the end.

The horn calls of the slow movement are reflected yet again in the sprightly Scherzo. Here they are changed into the trumpetlike flourishes of the violin part in measures 27 to 34.

Figure 1-59. Mm. 26-33

Note that the violin and piano are asked to hit the second and third beats of these measures. From early in the movement, Beethoven has been keeping us off-balance, in our hearing of the 3/4 time, by accents that suggest a duple rhythm within the triple context. (See, for example, the sforzandi in measures 5 and 6.) There are many *sforzati* in the Scherzo, and they must be incisively played, so that the rocking of the rhythmic boat can be felt. Also the figure of a dotted rhythm with preceding grace note must be played crisply, with short strokes and with resonant impact on the dotted note. When the figure occurs in the violin part, it should be started down-bow, as shown here.

Figure 1-60. Mm. 22-26

The dot in the Scherzo calls for crispness. In the Trio, on the other hand, the dot should be interpreted more easily, smoothly. For the emphasis in this section is on the flowing, long line, rather than on the sharp, incisive

figure of the moment. It will not be lost on the player, incidentally, that
the Trio melody is a modification of the Scherzo subject,

Figure 1-61.

a. Mm. 1-2

b. Violin, mm. 49-50

and that the distinctiveness of character of these two facets of the movement's theme should be preserved in the playing. Another carry-over from
Scherzo to Trio is the off-center sforzando, which crops up in all its bluff
vigor in the last measures of the Trio. The vigor must be made apparent,
and the music must charge right up to the double bar (measure 84) so
that the abruptness of the ending of the Trio can be heard as a consequence
of the sforzando hammering of the preceding measures.

The finale, Allegro, starts as though it too is building on the accented
thumping of the Scherzo. Certainly there is enough hammering in the
theme (see measures 1 to 3 in Figure 1-62, below) and its many later repetitions in the movement.

Figure 1-62.   Mm. 1-7

And the measures that react to the energy of the theme (see measures 4
to 6, above) seem to be a throwback to the significant and similar element
in the first movement (see Figure 1-53). If we play each figure at the appropriate tempo (♩ = 138 for the first movement, ♩ = 63 for the finale), we
find the two examples moving with almost the same swing!

We can make a good case for the idea that the entire finale is derived from the rather laconic opening subject of the movement. The anatomical parts of the subject are bracketed in Figure 1-62, above, and marked 1 through 4.

Reviewing the ideas to come in this movement, we may draw the following parallels:

Figure 1-63.

a. Mm. 33-34

b. M. 39

c. Mm. 179-180

d. Mm. 268-272

An inspection of the entire movement reveals nothing that is not shown above or that is not closely derived from these musical items. As if to crystallize the impression of economy of means and unity of idea in this finale, the Presto coda offers a whirlwind review of the melodic facets that have already been used in the body of the Allegro.

The Presto is also a summation in another way: its driving mood and tempo is an intensification of the character of the Allegro as a whole. The tempo of the Allegro is slower than that of the coda. But its nature through-out is one of drive, of tension constantly released and just as constantly regenerated, and of a certain degree of ominous foreboding. In this, too, the Allegro and Presto are at one with the first movement of the sonata, framing the work in that dark and tempestuous color that is so character-istic a side of Beethoven's personality.

From this it should be expected that my recommendation to the player in this finale is to play all as though in a state of pursuit or flight. Even such a moment of seeming respite as measures 73 to 80 is supplied by Beethoven with so seething an undercurrent in the accompaniment that it should not be difficult for the player to sense the continuing storm. And the violinist who can ease up in measures 244 to 252, coasting on his half and whole notes, and insensitive to the constant goad of the

in the piano part, must either sharpen his perception or give up the idea of playing this sonata. Chamber music is sometimes a relaxing experience, at least after the fact. This work is not relaxing, and it should take a con-scious effort on the part of the players and the listeners to unwind after hearing this piece.

Sonata in G, op. 30, no. 3

The first sonata of opus 30 is serenity epitomized; the second, glowering force; the third, energy in free flight. What an opening statement—a quick turnover of the melodic motor; immediate take off in a high-rising trajec-tory; direct arrival on a high target; and then, instead of rest, propulsion toward a second, lower, stronger target, followed instantly by its own, bril-liant, high-register reaction. All in the space of four measures, a masterpiece of distilled musical energy.

Figure 1-64. Mm. 1-4

This is repeated, immediately and more forcefully, to be followed by more tranquil measures where the seeds of propulsion still lie near the surface, to burst forth at last in a "closing" flourish.

Figure 1-65. Mm. 32-34

The motoric rumble of sixteenths forms an almost constant undercurrent in the movement. Only 98 measures of its 202 are quite free of the rhythm, and even then most of these bars have the eighth-note rhythm that is driven by the same basic force. The players must sweep through this Allegro with all possible bravura. Trills, as for example in the violin part at the upbeat to measure 32, should be played as simple turns, if need be—

—in order not to impede the tempestuous flow of the music. Sforzandi, though graded according to the context and sequence in which they are found, should be played with all due force, to lend impetus to the sound:

Figure 1-66. Mm. 50-53

Actually, despite the momentary lessening of excitement here and there in the movement, it does not really let down until the last two chords, piano; and they themselves are more in the nature of echoed resonances to the true close of the movement, the forte downbeat of the penultimate bar.

The second movement, *Tempo di Menuetto*, is enigmatic. It is cer-

tainly no "minuet," no matter what the title declares, if one is to judge by
the languidly graceful line of the opening measures:

Figure 1-67. Mm. 1-4

The composer himself qualifies the meaning of "tempo of a minuet" by
adding the subscript, *ma molto moderato e grazioso*. This performer finds
himself comfortable with the opening lines of the piece at a speed no faster
than $\rfloor = 80$. This seems at first thought to be a dangerous tempo, in view
of the considerable length of the movement (196 unhurried measures). To
play faster, however, brings with it a perfunctory air and robs the movement
of its function as the slow, meditative oasis in an otherwise exceedingly
energetic sonata.

At the speed we have suggested, this "menuetto" takes on an undulating, trancelike quality that is strangely convincing. This is especially so
because the haunting interludes, heard as if through the mists of time,
acquire a proper glow at this tempo.

Figure 1-68. Mm. 19-24

One might also speak of the distant, remote grandeur of another contrasting element in this movement, the dolce second theme that is first
introduced by the violin, except that it is accompanied, in this initial appearance, by a piano background all too reminiscent of the tootlings of a
street band:

Figure 1-69. Mm. 57-61

The oompahs here are actually not as blatant as those in the march episode of the final movement of Beethoven's Ninth Symphony. The pianist will, nevertheless, have to proceed with caution if the passage is not to become more vulgarized than enlivened.

For propulsion of the music, the principal theme should be shaped as shown in Figure 1-67. The following musical intersection, which occurs a couple of times, should be treated as shown:

Figure 1-70. Violin, mm. 138-142

And the entire passage from measure 162 through 176 should move freely, as though in an ever-increasing intoxication of rhythm, settling finally at the end of measure 176 and through 177 to the last statement of the theme, beginning in 178.

This last statement is quite something in its own right, an utterance that is presented, fragment by fragment, in alternation by piano and violin, the nostalgic reminiscence too much for either instrument to bear alone, until both finally unite in the cadential flourishes of measure 188 and 189, as well as in the repeated sighs that carry the final bars of the movement away into the distance:

Figure 1-71. Mm. 189-196

The concluding Allegro vivace is a perpetual motion and a rustic hoe-down, all in one. The piano leads off, the violin falls to willingly, and they're away. There are swaying moments of resting in place (cf. measures 20 to 23), and one much less restful pause, perched on the very lip of the canyon:

Figure 1-72. Mm. 172-178

Aside from such spots, it is all a persistent trot around the dance hall, carrying us through several steps, and to such remote harmonic fastnesses as E flat (cf. measures 177 ff.). There is more than one touch of vigor in the voyage, but much of the trip is characterised by the leggieramente the composer stipulates at the outset. The pace?—fast enough for excitement, continuity, and smooth phrasing, slow enough to convey an underlying ease. A stunning conclusion to a stunning sonata.

Sonata in A, op. 47 (Kreutzer)

Although this sonata's subtitle is known, even to those who have never heard the work, from literature and from perfume ads, it was originally not intended for its namesake at all. On the contrary, the sonata was completed for George Polgreen Bridgetower, for a concert that took place in Vienna in May, 1803.[10] The finale of the sonata had been composed in 1802, as the original close for opus 30, number 1.[11] As already pointed out, Beethoven provided a different finale for that work, and eventually used the first version to round out opus 47. Well that he did, for the rest of the composition was written very close to the deadline. Beethoven called his friend and assistant, Ferdinand Ries, at 4:30 in the morning of the concert day to copy the violin part of the first movement. Bridgetower had to read the theme and variations movement from Beethoven's own manuscript. And Beethoven himself played the premiere from a sketchy manuscript outline of the piano part for the first two movements. (Shades of Mozart!)

George Bridgetower was a mulatto violinist, son of a black father and a German or Polish mother, and was born in Biala, Poland, in 1779. He was concertizing in England as early as 1789, entered the musical service of the prince of Wales while still in his teens, and in 1802, took leave to visit the Continent. In Vienna, he met Beethoven through the good offices of Prince Lichnowsky.[12]

On the occasion of the first performance of opus 47, according to Bridgetower himself, the violinist improvised an imitation of the piano's grand arpeggio flourish in the early part of the Presto (bar 36). This (still according to Bridgetower) so excited Beethoven that he cried out, "Once more, dear fellow!"[13] The autograph of the sonata, not extant, is supposed to have had the joking title "Sonata mulattica" written on it. When the work came to print, however, it bore Beethoven's more serious title: "Sonata for piano and violin obbligato, written in a very concertante style [the word, "brilliant", originally placed by Beethoven after the word, "style", was removed by him], quasi concerto-like . . . "[14] Moreover, and possibly because of a quarrel between Beethoven and Bridgetower, the sonata was now officially dedicated to Rodolphe Kreutzer, composer, teacher, and virtuoso (now, alas, known to violin students chiefly for the awesome difficulties of his Etudes), and professor at the conservatory in Paris. Kreutzer had been in Vienna in the spring of 1798, and on October 4, 1804, Beethoven wrote to Nikolaus Simrock, the publisher of opus 47, that "This *Kreutzer* is a dear, kind fellow, who during his stay in Vienna gave me a great deal of pleasure. I prefer his modesty and natural behavior to *all the exterior* without *any interior*, which is the characteristic of most virtuosi . . ."[15] Whatever Kreutzer's endearing qualities, he was apparently not smitten with Beethoven's gift of homage. For, according to Berlioz, "the celebrated violinist could never bring himself to play this outrageously incomprehensible composition."[16]

In addition to the points made in our discussion of the first movement in our introductory chapter of Volume I, at least the following items should be covered here. Every violinist will have his own way of tackling the difficulty of the slow introductory measures. Let me suggest the following bowing and fingering, as my own preference:

Figure 1-73. Mm. 1-4

In measures 45 to 48, and so forth, the eighths *on* the beat (that is, representing the moving line) must be brought out more than the "drone" line. In measures 61 ff., the violin chords must be forceful, not harsh. And they must be played as part of a larger line, not as individual stabs of sound.

Figure 1-74. Mm. 59-73

Violin and piano have been dialoguing in eighth notes since measure 37. Now, measures 61 to 89, the piano takes over alone in this department, and the torrent of eighths, urged on by the chordal cheers of the violin and finally joined by that instrument in the last throes of the motion, must keep the pace unrelentingly until the release offered by the tranquil music of measures 89 ff.

Figure 1-75. Violin, mm. 85-94

Notice, here again, the extremes favored by Beethoven. From rushing streams of small notes to the striking contrast of series of whole and half notes. Note, too (as already seen in opus 30, number 2), that a device, once used in the movement, justifies itself by reappearing, with consistent function, at other points in the movement· the tranquil passage cited above poises finally on a very incomplete cadence, adagio, with the suspense of a fermata:

Figure 1-76. Mm. 115-119

The held-note gambit is used throughout the movement: at the end of the slow introduction (measures 18 to 20); in the Presto, at measures 27, 36, 116 (see Figure 1-76), measure 191 (the end of the exposition), measures 313, 323, 325, and 335 (the end of the development), measures 353,

437, 578, and 582 (end of recapitulation, beginning of coda). Clearly, the fermata is the boundary marker between the several sections of the movement, as well as a signal element of the opening of the exposition and recapitulation. And just as the performer must reveal his awareness and memory for melodic events as they occur in the course of the movement, so must he show a consistent and uniform treatment of these points of suspense, one after the other, even though they are widely separated by the rushing material of the movement.

The half-step motions, so prominent in the maneuverings of the slow introduction, remain important to the fabric of the Presto. If we tabulate the various melodic materials of the Presto, we note not only that they are distinguished from each other broadly along lines of note value, but also that they are bound to each other by the half-step-motif emphasis:

Figure 1-77.

a. Quarter note

b. Eighth note

c. Whole note, half note

d. Dotted rhythm

To a great degree, these are all manifestations of the one premise highlighted by the slow introduction. The whole movement is coordinated, integrated by this adherence to a central melodic idea.[17]

The storm center of the movement, comparable in its fury of spirit and sound to the notorious passages of the Great Fugue (Beethoven's original finale to the string quartet, opus 130, of the late years), lies in the passage from measure 226 to 257, where—to cite one small example—the two instruments have to navigate the following shoals:

Figure 1-78. Mm. 234-238

For the pianist, the hazards of creeping paralysis from the chore of playing myriads of eighths are at their worst when (beginning in measure 517, late in the movement), the performer has to lead into the final strains by first traversing a long sequence of figures, in octaves, from piano to pianissimo, thence to fortissimo:

Figure 1-79. Mm. 517-520

If the first movement looks and feels impressive to the player, the Andante con variazioni cannot hope to calm his fears. It begins with a richness of pianistic color such as another composer might have chosen to reserve for a much later point in the proceedings:

Figure 1-80. Mm. 1-8

And before the theme is completed, both instruments are joining forces to enrich the texture still further:

Figure 1-81.   Mm. 43-46

The first variant calls for delicate handling of textures that could become gummy at the slightest hint of sloppy articulation or overbearing touch (cf. measures 76 ff.). One of the most striking features of this variation is the great difference between the two parts—the luxuriant piano writing, on the one hand, and the monotone chirpings of the violin, on the other.

Figure 1-82.   M. 58

The pianist must combine incisiveness and delicacy in the playing of his truly predominant role in this section. Yet the violin cannot retire into self-effacing murmurings: for, if the seemingly static figures of the part are played *un*statically, as true responses to the piano, as reflections of the lyric statements of that instrument, the violin line takes on a cantabile role in its own right, and one that—because of the crystalline simplicity of the writing—assumes a unique beauty.

In the second variation, the violinist must pirouette through a thirty-second-note line that confines itself largely to the upper reaches of the E-string, and he must end the section with every appearance of enjoying a run up the tightrope to high F. Before this, he must have enough nerve to take his time, even to wax lyric, in measures 92 to 95:

Figure 1-83.   Violin, mm. 91-95

And both partners may find it effective to use a slight slow-up and turn-around at measure 100:

Figure 1-84. Mm. 99-101

Variation four, the longest, must have the refinement of a musical-clockwork performance, with such intricately geared measures as these:

Figure 1-85. Mm. 150-151

Both instruments are well occupied in these pages, with enough intricate rhythms, lengthy trill passages, intervallic stretchings, high-register melodizing for the violin, to fill out the rehearsal. Possibly the highest challenge will be to achieve the necessary delicacy in the playing of this passage, just before the end of the movement,

Figure 1-86. Mm. 225-228

and beyond that, the task of actually ending the movement, with both instruments drawing away from each other to finish, pianissimo, at the outer extremes of the register.

The finale, Presto, seems to begin with a reminiscence of the slow

introduction, from the very opening of the sonata, but reduced, here, to
one sustained fortissimo chord (in A, of course) in the piano. Then both
instruments are off and running, literally:

Figure 1-87. Mm. 1-6

The movement is a marathon, rolling along for the most part in the
snapped rhythm shown above, or in full triplet sequences, or in both simultaneously. Relief is given by the occasional appearance of this saucy tune
(derived from the snapped rhythm of the opening), which must be played
with the utmost grace and wit:

Figure 1-88. Mm. 61-69

Strangely, one of the difficulties of the movement lies in breaking stride
in order to enter and leave passages of the greatest relief, requiring a sudden
air of composure:

Figure 1-89. Mm. 125-134

As can be seen in the last measure of this example, Beethoven throws in
jolts of the basic rhythm of the piece to jar the performer and listener in

the midst of tranquillity. The entire movement is a tarantella of the possessed, a dance to death that is nevertheless filled with the highest of good
spirits and climaxed with the most triumphant of endings. The performers
who can develop the stamina and finesse to survive the movement and to
carry it off with an air of ease as well as temperament may well call themselves pros, whether in the living room or on the concert platform.

Sonata in G, op. 96

The last of the ten Beethoven sonatas for piano and violin was composed
in 1812 and dedicated to the longtime patron, friend, and pupil of the
composer, Archduke Rudolph of Austria.[18] The Linz *Musikalische Zei-*
tung in January, 1813, carried a notice of the performance of the work,
in Vienna that month, by the French violin virtuoso, Pierre Rode and
Archduke Rudolph. " . . . nothing more need be said about this work than
that it leaves all his other works of this type behind, for it excels over
almost all of them in popularity, wit, and invention."[19]

"Shall we do it?" "Shall we?" Violin and piano, respectively, seem to
be questioning each other at the start of the sonata. In this introduction
(unmarked, and very short!—measures 1 and 2) the question is posed, considered, and instantly decided. The two instruments *do* get under way,
and with great determination. So intense is their motion that it carries
them both (including the left hand of the piano) into treble register; and
the ensuing descent is to a series of cadences (cf measures 21 to 31) that
cannot close off the line, but can only try to stem its rush. The momentum
of the music is so forceful that it finally breaks into the quicker rhythm of
triplets (measures 33 ff.). This rhythm remains predominant for the rest
of the exposition. For a time, it underlies the second theme (measures 41
ff.), whose long-short-*long* figures contribute in their own way to the forward swing of the line:

Figure 1-90. Mm. 40-44

This in turn is swept (despite the momentary and partial barrier of a retard (measures 57 and 58) into a closing episode that combines the triplet motion and the initial questioning motive:

Figure 1-91. Mm. 60-63

Here the excitement culminates in the clamor of a long trill in the piano treble (measures 63 to 71); the triplets give way very briefly to duplets; the duplets rock under the impact of *sforzati* strokes, beat by beat (cf. measures 68 to 71). There is a matured reflection of the questioning motive,

Figure 1-92. Mm. 70-73

but the music rolls on inexorably (with a breath at the upbeat to 84), and, fading away, arrives at the double bar.

The questioning element comes to the surface for a time in the early stage of the development, at first within the piano part, then between instruments:

Figure 1-93. Mm. 108-112

In the process of question and search, both instruments are soon drawn into the rhythm of the triplet accompaniment line, and it is in this current that the development draws to its close, to poise for a moment on pizzicato and trill,

Figure 1-94. Mm. 136-143

and then, as seen, to move into the return of the opening. The recapitulation essentially traces the path of the exposition. At the beginning of the coda, the pace steps back from triplets to couplet eighths (unlike the opening of the development, where the triplet rhythms rush past the double bar to carry the music headlong into the doings of the middle section). The composed slow-up in the coda is deliberate, affording a last reminiscence of past events in the movement, and at the same time setting off the flurry of chromatically oriented sixteenths with trill (measures 260 to 267) that graces the final page.

It is interesting to compare this movement of opus 96 with the Quartet in F minor, op. 95, composed two years earlier (1810). The quartet's nickname, *Serioso,* deriving from Beethoven's own character-heading for the third movement of the work, is well chosen, and never more so than for the opening Allegro con brio of the quartet. That chapter is serious to the point of anger; and it shows a concentration of thought and force much akin, in its own way, to the single-mindedness of opus 96's Allegro. The ominous rumble of the opening figure of the quartet:

is all pervasive in the quartet movement, enforcing a sober tone throughout, even in the lyric second theme. In the sonata movement, the lilt of the opening subject and the constant easy rolling of the rhythmic current insist, just as surely, on a feeling of brightness and well-being. There is (fortunately) no nickname for this work, but the player will get his clues to the proper manner of delivery from the music itself.

Looking at the second movement, we are immediately struck by the significant amount of composed ornamentation in the lines of both violin and piano: runs in sixty-fourths, tremolos and arpeggiated figures in thirty-seconds, flowing phrases of sixteenths. The extended melody of the movement, twice stated (measures 1 ff., measures 38 ff.), and—at least the second time—with the instruction, semplice, is truly simple, of that innocence and sparseness that Beethoven can so well contrive.

Figure 1-95. Mm. 38-46

(One might think also of that paramount illustration, the Cavatina of the Quartet in B flat, op. 130, a movement that Beethoven himself especially prized.) The true purpose of the sonata melody is to flower into the elegiac rhapsodizing that we have just referred to. The movement is an exercise, of course, in naturalness, sobriety, and easy grace on the part of the players. How much more than this, can only be realised by the performers when they come to the actual playing. For they will then be aware (unless they should not be playing this music at all) that they are here as close to paradise as one can approach in this world. One does not perform this movement; rather, one uses it as an avenue, with Beethoven, to make a statement of personal faith and integrity.

Then, and without any pause, comes the Scherzo: Allegro. Is this a fall from grace? What organ-grinderish stomping have we here?

Figure 1-96. Mm. 1-7

Vienna in Beethoven's day was a hotbed of waltzing. Everyone danced, avidly, devotedly. It is the free-floating swing of the waltz that one must bring to this movement, tempering the sforzando-piano indications so that the respective tones are stressed, caressed, rather than thumped. Then the Trio, with its swirls of melody, will become another and appropriate aspect of the same impulse, rather than an extraneous episode.

Figure 1-97. Mm. 33-40

The coda of this movement is most effective if begun slowly, under tempo, then accelerating easily but irrevocably, to fling off triumphantly in the last fanfare.

The finale, even more than the Scherzo, wants to lead us through folkish byways, to judge by its opening measures:

Figure 1-98. Piano treble, mm. 1-8

This tune unwinds in a mood of such unbuttoned good humor that we expect the whole finale to be an easygoing lark. Even when we realize that

a process of variation is under way, the first variant (measures 33 ff.) seems
only a rather mild diversion:

Figure 1-99. Mm. 33-37

The temperature steps up slightly with the second variant (measures 48 ff.),
what with triplet rhythm, tossing of the melody into a double-voiced alternation, with trilled ornament, and with pounding accompaniment:

Figure 1-100. Mm. 70-72

Our expectations are heightened still more by the next segment, where the
bass line rumbles in a barrelhouse turn while the violin and the piano treble
slide quietly into a jazzy syncope:

Figure 1-101. Mm. 82-85

The lid finally blows off in the next variant (measures 113 ff.), immediately
is put back on with great delicacy, blows off again, and so on, repeatedly.

Figure 1-102. Mm. 113-117

What can remain to do? The most wicked trick of all: an Adagio espressivo, dripping over with the kind of written-out, *improvisando*-style ornamentation that we remember from the slow movement, but carried now to a length and degree such as to suggest the hilarious satires already observed (Volume I) in the cadenza measures of the finale of Mozart's Sonata in D, K. 306. Indeed, one might think that Beethoven was modeling himself here directly on the Mozart case. However, where Mozart turns everything to comic-expressive account, and very engagingly so, Beethoven chooses a more serious purpose. Here the piano and violin seem to strive to match, to outdo each other in flights of lyric fancy, in utter sobriety, and with every aspect of beauty:

Figure 1-103. Mm. 148-152

This is music in homage both to the finest human instincts, and, at the same time, to the essence of the chamber-music ideal—complete freedom, equality, and cooperativeness. The cadenza is a sublime oasis in the setting of a deliberately mundane movement (if one may still use the adjective in its literal, rather than its pejorative, sense).

But the secular aspect returns, tantalizingly and resolutely. The theme —in E flat—is suspended on teasing fragments (measures 169 to 173). Then a racing Allegro breaks out; in an intoxication of sound, the violin and piano vie with each other in splitting the melody up into a prismatic spate of sixteenths. The piano wins the day, working up a perfect frenzy of a two-fisted barrage (measures 205 ff.).

Nor is Beethoven finished, even now! A pianissimo passage, in eighths, is replete with murky chromatic wanderings, building yet again to a placid restatement of the theme. But now the floodgates seem to have opened irrevocably. The piano, first in the left hand, then in the right, is pouring out sixteenths; soon all three lines are racing toward the end. The violin spins off, solo, into a skyrocket of notes:

Figure 1-104.   Mm. 268-272

The fingering shown here, incidentally, is stipulated by Beethoven. Any violinist will know that it makes no sense at all. And if, as has been suggested, the fingering is applied to the corresponding notes in the pianist's reply, I can only conjure up a vision of Chico Marx playing the passage in his inimitable, stiff-fingered style!

A poco adagio interlude is mercifully short, because the listener has really been pulled this way and that enough already. And at long last, in eight presto bars, the piano shoots off into space, urged on by the cheerful thumping of the bass line and violin.

Concerning the last movement of opus 96, Beethoven wrote to Archduke Rudolph in December, 1812: " . . . in view of Rode's playing I have had to give more thought to the composition of this movement. In our finales, we like to have fairly noisy passages, but Rode does not care for

them, and so I have been rather hampered."[20] Not so that one can notice!
Paul Nettl, the distinguished musicologist, sees in Beethoven's comment
the thought that the composer was not smitten with Rode's prowess on
the violin. Moreover, he cites—from the same Linz review referred to above
—the comment that, in the January performance of the sonata at the Lobkowitz palace, Archduke Rudolph played better than Rode.[21] Be that as
it may, the work was duly composed, performed, and preserved for the
literature—a fitting capstone for Beethoven's writings for piano-violin duo.

2 *Some Lesser Efforts of the Beethoven Era*

AT THE END of Volume I and in the chapter just concluded, the duo has confronted two exceedingly taxing bodies of sonata literature. After the rigors of Mozart and Beethoven, a little relaxation is in order. In some of the pieces mentioned in the present chapter, the dexterity of the violinist and/or pianist will be well exercised. As a rule, however, the intellect and emotions of the players will be more easily used. The duo that tastes this music must be prepared to be amused rather than touched.

Niccolo Paganini

Between the years 1801 and 1804, the violin virtuoso Niccolo Paganini, then in his early twenties, lived in retirement, "devoting himself to practicing and composition." Part of his devotion was to the "lady of rank" with whom he spent this period of seclusion in Tuscany; and part of his practice was directed to the guitar. The compositional fruit of this interest were two sets of duets, opera 2 and 3, for violin and guitar. These pieces have been issued as sonatas with the accompaniment of the alternate to the guitar, the piano. Pianists who essay these works will find themselves, willy-nilly, sounding guitarlike, for the texture of the accompaniment is clearly written with the sound of that instrument in mind.

It makes little difference, though, which instrument is chosen; there is little contest against the violin. The first measure of the first sonata of opus 2, for example, contains a run of twenty-four notes for the violin; by the eleventh measure, Paganini has stepped his share of the spoils up to thirty-six notes. The lower lines of the score look bleak by comparison. A few movements in each set are the province of ordinary mortals. The rest are only for those violinists who have done all their homework assiduously. The melodies are quite handsome throughout, in a pretty, cosmetic sense. For the pianist in the duo, this will have to be sufficient reason to play the pieces. The violinist has other, though not necessarily more convincing, reasons for being interested in them.

Johann Ladislaus Dussek

He was applauded by audiences for his performance on the glass harmonica (graduated glass bowls, emitting sound when rubbed along the rims with moistened fingertips) as well as on the piano. In Holland he served as organist as well as pianist. He was for a time in the employ of a Russian prince in Saint Petersburg. In Paris, he played for an admiring Queen Marie Antoinette and lived to write a piece in her memory. In England he moved as a virtuoso in the circle of the great Clementi. As a failed music publisher, he took refuge on the Continent, where he served, in succession, Prince Louis Ferdinand of Prussia (whose death on the battlefield he also memorialized in music), and the diplomat, Prince Talleyrand, in Paris. All this in the fifty-two years from 1760 to 1812.

The composer in question is the Bohemian-born Johann Ladislaus Dussek, one of the more important pianist-composers of the early nineteenth century. If Dussek is not widely known today, it is significant that the great Haydn saw fit to write of the composer that he was "a most honourable and polished man who is a distinguished musician."[22] These words, it is true, were contained in a letter from Haydn to Dussek's father. Haydn, however, had occasion to know the work of Dussek, because the latter was a participant in the Haydn-Salomon concerts given during Haydn's triumphal visits to London.

Of Dussek's prolific output of works (mostly centered on the piano, either alone, in ensemble, or as concerto soloist), some sixty were sonatas for the piano and violin. Two of these are available from Artia, opus 69, numbers 1 and 2, ca. 1805.[23] (The third work in the opus is a sonata for piano alone.) Number 1, in B flat, is called Violin Sonata; number 2, in G, is entitled, Piano Sonata with Violin Concertante. There is no practical difference between the two works so far as relationship of the two instruments is concerned. The piano, Dussek's own instrument, is the predominant partner in the duo. The violin, however, is not reticent; it often serves as the support for the piano part, reflecting it in parallel motion as an undervoice. Just as often, it assumes and delivers thematic material in its own right, in full dialogue with its partner.

In sonata 1, the weakest movement is the middle, Adagio cantabile, titled, *Les Soupirs* ("Sighs"). It has the kind of treacly Romantic theme that is so difficult to deliver both seriously and effectively. The middle section of the movement offers formal, rather than dramatic, contrast; the reprise at the end is literal and, in consequence, a rather abrupt close to the movement. Matters would not be helped by the repetition of the last section.

One takes heart in the Rondo finale, which sets out in fine, galloping fashion, and, despite the apparent danger of boredom through rhythmic repetition, manages to sustain interest through a fairly long span. The contrast sections are a help in this regard, especially the *Minore*, bearing the composer's instruction, con fuoco. The first movement, Allegro molto con fuoco (again), has that duo parity mentioned earlier.

Like its companion work (which has only two movements, Allegro espressivo and Rondo), sonata number 1 is a respectable example of Mozartian-era music. It has nothing remotely like the inspiration, range, or intensity of a Mozart; Dussek here is too content with the role of virtuoso-composer to go beyond a superficial kind of classicism laced with touches of Bohemian folk style (see the theme of the B flat Rondo). The themes he uses are too facile, too flowing and self-indulgent in length to make pregnant material for elaboration.

If occasionally heard, these sonatas have a freshness and ingenuous appeal that—coupled with the craftsmanship of the writing—make them useful additions to the repertoire. They are not the kind of music that can be easily tossed off. The Bärenreiter string-music catalog lists them as of "intermediate" difficulty; they are rather more than that, for both the pianist and the violinist. Moreover, music of this facile nature must be played with all the more care and artistry (in the musical as well as technical sense) to make the experience a rewarding one. In short, they are fairly difficult and fairly enjoyable.

Johann Hugo Worzischek

The same higher purpose that brought four such names as Schein, Scheidt, Schildt, and Scheidemann (to say nothing of Jacob Praetorius, née Schulze, whose Germanic patronymic more than qualifies him for his place in this mellifluous quintet of organists) together as pupils of the seventeenth-century organist and composer, Sweelinck, probably also accounts for the fact that the early nineteenth-century pianist-composer, Johann Hugo Worzischek, studied in his early teens with the composer Johann Wenzel Tomaschek. Such rhymes are one of the minor delights of music history.

Worzischek, born in May, 1791, in Bohemia, and already of some public concertizing experience by the time he reached Prague University and Tomaschek's tutelage, in the early 1810's went on to Vienna, where his music was able to evoke the favor of Beethoven himself, and where he studied with Hummel. From service as the director of the Society of Friends of Music, he progressed in 1822 to the post of organist at the imperial court, only to succumb in 1825 to the tuberculosis that had for some time plagued him.

In the relatively small repertoire of pieces he produced during his short life, there is only one sonata for piano and violin, that marked opus 5. The editors of the modern publication of this sonata (the work dates from about 1819 or 1820, despite the "early" opus number) point out that the piano score of the sonata—as originally published in Vienna—is not a score at all, but presents only the piano part. "The violin part is never once indicated in small notes as is usual today. This is because the sonata was intended rather as a work for piano and violin than vice versa."[24] A curious argument, especially because the violin part retaliates by offering no piano cues to guide the violinist's reentry after rests.

More significant is William Newman's observation about eighteenth-century music-publishing practice: "the large majority . . . of chamber works appeared in separate parts rather than in score. Not a few of the optional violin-or-flute parts in accompanied sonatas are missing in present-day libraries that would be known had they been scored above the piano part."[25]

We may wonder, however, at the nature of ensemble performance in the late eighteenth and early nineteenth centuries, especially for works as complex as the Worzischek sonata. It must have taken an alert ear and some musical diplomacy for two or three players to stay together throughout the course of a performance. These prerequisites are still in force today, even with the refinements of modern publishing.

Is the implied isolation of the two instruments carried out in the nature of the piece itself? And is the technical demand of the work only intermediate (to quote again the Bärenreiter catalog rating)? No, on both counts. It would be an accomplished pianist indeed who could look on the piece as anything but a test of his keyboard abilities; and if the violinist is not called on as consistently and intensely for acrobatics, his part is still a demanding one, so far as some high-position playing, sureness of intonation in quick shifts, and bowing dexterity and warmth of tone are concerned. As for ensemble requirements, it would be possible to do without score and cues only after the work is memorized, or practically so, by the two players.

With the first two strains, we might suppose that we are to hear a work by Schumann (the sighing opening phrases) or even Bartók (the exotic intervallic coloring of the first measures in the violin part). The Allegro, moderato, with its showers of notes for the piano, its repeated rhythmic fragments pushing from dotted figure onto stressed quarter, reminds one of an amalgam of Weber, Spohr, and middle-period Schubert. The undeniable intensity of the movement is diluted somewhat by the feeling that a virtuoso has written a bravura keyboard part for himself and has become infatuated with the sound of his own bravura. A bit less of the voyaging through the middle and upper keyboard would permit more concentration on serious musical affairs.

The Scherzo shows some of this same keyboard flamboyance, but now placed at the service of a hushed, elfin effect. The pointed, laconic commentary of the violin, in this section, gives way to that instrument's quiet, flitting cantabile line in the Trio, thematically linked to the main body of the movement.

The Andante sostenuto is entirely the songlike province of the violin, the piano devoting itself for the most part to low, guttural commentaries on the action above. As matters turn out, the end of this short movement is marked to proceed without pause into the finale, which becomes the resolution not only of the Andante, but of the entire sonata. Here the piano is on display, racing with almost no letup through a rapid 12/8 part. Only occasionally, as at the beginning of the development section, does the violin have its chance at theme and prominence. Even in the *minore* section that closes the movement, the emphasis is on keyboard. We are treated to a perfect barrage of piano shrapnel. Much sound, some fury, and some of that sense of cheerful futility that suffuses this kind of movement in the Romantic repertoire. If the work merits such description, why bother to mention it at all? Because, if carried off with the necessary dash and pathos, the sonata is—despite all our hard-won sophistication and world-weariness—fun to play.

Ferdinand Ries

Ferdinand Ries (1784–1838), piano pupil of Beethoven in the early Vienna years and a close friend—and biographical reminiscer—of the master in ensuing time, was a concert pianist in his own right and a composer of some industry. Samples of his output published in recent season include three sonatinas for violin and piano (opus 30); crisp, light, inconsequential pieces of some brilliance, and not exceedingly difficult. They are well suited to the student duo, as sufficiently demanding preludes to such works as the Schubert sonatinas.

The *Grande Sonate*, op. 83, of Ries, is larger, longer, more muscular than the above works, but not really more important. It takes skilled hands, technically; musically, it can serve as a warm-up for the first Beethoven sonatas or, for that matter, for the middle Mozart sonatas. Even so, those works will feel like tall orders after this kind of fare.

Carl Maria von Weber

Carl Maria von Weber, in 1810, composed six sonatas for piano and violin (opus 10b). As published, they were called, "Progressive sonatas for the piano-forte with violin obbligato . . . dedicated to amateurs." They were written in Darmstadt, where Weber spent the better part of a year after his banishment from Württemberg and his dismissal from his post as secretary to Duke Ludwig of Stuttgart.[20]

These pieces are slight, and for student use primarily, as well as for the adult novice duo. The older player, however, may not take to this kind of writing, for the musical material is not very rich either in nature or in working out. In general, the technical requirements become a little steeper in the later works of the set, though never overly demanding. The piano is definitely the lion in Weber's handling of the duo; only in some movements and in some passages does the violin take on somewhat equal prominence.

The sonatas are a musical potpourri, mingling character titles (*Romanze*), exotic, folkloric references (*Caraterra espagnuolo, Air polonaise, Air russe*), and self-references (*Tema dell'Opera Silvana,* from his own opera of that name, premiered in Frankfurt that same year). The finale of sonata 3 is the Rondo, Presto, that has often been played in cello transcription as one of the lollipops of the concert repertoire.

These sonatas cannot pass muster on serious programs because practically anything else (including the Schubert sonatinas) will sound muscular and cerebral by contrast. Yet they are far better than the stuff ordinarily ground out for pedagogic purposes. Piano teachers, especially, should welcome the new and careful edition of this useful music.

3 ❦ The Sonatas of Schubert

FRANZ SCHUBERT was born in Vienna in 1797. He learned violin and piano at home, continued from this amateur instruction to somewhat more professional guidance, then, at the age of eleven, entered the court chapel as choirboy, with the attendant privilege of study at the Imperial-Royal Konvikt, the school that was part of the university in Vienna. As concertmaster and occasional conductor of the school orchestra, Schubert was exposed to the orchestral literature of the day. And also he had instruction from Antonio Salieri, kapellmeister to the court. These experiences, coupled with continued chamber-music sessions at home, acquainted the youth with the ways of performance and composition, nurturing the talent in this most natural of musicians—a talent that was soon to burst forth in a fury of productivity.

Schubert left the choir and its school in 1813 (his voice having already changed); and, after brief training in the teaching profession, took up that occupation for the years 1814 through 1816. During this time, he turned out symphonies, quartets, various dances and other works for piano, completed five stage works (one opera, four Singspiel), four masses and other church music, six cantatas, a fair number of choral pieces, and more than two hundred songs. Busy enough!

It was not until 1816, and the age of nineteen, that he turned to the combination of piano and violin. In that year he composed the Sonatas for Piano with Violin Accompaniment, in D, A minor, and G minor.[27] These were published by Antonio Diabelli (the same whose waltz tune served as

67

the nucleus of Beethoven's *Diabelli* Variations, op. 120, for piano) in 1836 under the title, Three Sonatinas for Pianoforte and Violin, op. 137. It is as "sonatinas" that these works have been labeled in many an edition since.[28] There is perhaps an unfortunate aspect to such a title, because it implies a work of slighter stature than "sonata," and has also been used for works intended for pedagogic purpose—though such purpose should surely not be at odds with high artistic standards.

Schubert's brother, Ferdinand, in a letter of November 29, 1829 (the year after the composer's death), turning over to the Diabelli publishing house the rights to a number of compositions of the late composer, lists the works in question in the following words: "Three easy, very fine Sonatas for pianoforte and violin."[29] These works are "easy" if compared, for example, with the rigors of a Beethoven sonata. But, as one who first executed these Schubert pages in his youthful years as a violinist, the author can testify to the fact that they are not quite as easy as Ferdinand made out.

Sonata in D, op. 137, no. 1 (D. 384)

This work[30] is often assigned to a young violin student as a good learning piece. It certainly is that; but one must be careful. Though *Gulliver's Travels* makes entertaining reading for a child, Swift would rage to see his biting satire sailing completely over the head of a young reader. Schubert in 1816 is no Swift. Nevertheless he has already had the insight to produce such settings as that of Goethe's *The Erl King*; also, we must be aware that Schubert has only twelve years of life left, and—in that short span— will move to such works as the Cello Quintet, the String Quartet in G major, and the "Great" C major Symphony. Even at the start of such a line of advance, it is not safe to assume categorically that a Schubert work is facile.

The D major sonata opens in unison (measures 1 to 12). Intonation is a problem, but a minor one. More difficult is the shaping of the four-measure unit, the ordering of the three sequential units into one melodic sweep (I cite the violin line alone here; the piano's right hand doubles the violin in unison; the left moves parallel, at the lower octave):

Figure 3-1. Violin, mm. 1-13

The suggested dynamic shadings must be carried out subtly and with restraint. Delicacy is needed, too, in the coloration of the violin line; vibrato must be on the cool side, adding just enough to season to taste.

The next measures are immediately enriched in texture: the bass line moves imitatively, a measure later than the violin; the piano treble sets up the shimmering arpeggiated ripple of eighths that is one of Schubert's most Schubertian traits. There is an air of motion and of mounting excitement. The goal? A fortissimo passage that summarizes in compact fashion the upward striving of the opening lines. With all the loudness and the sforzando emphasis, the rush is daunted, made apologetic just as it crosses the brow of the melodic hill:

Figure 3-2.   Mm. 29-36

Measures 37 to 49 are occupied with some fancy swinging in place, as Schubert toys with the definition of the dominant of the movement. Piano and violin move lazily around each other until at last the piano breaks out of the round (measure 45) to move into a definite cadence on A. Instead of a second subject, we must make do with a scrap of rhythm from the opening theme, applied now in a game of tease between the two instruments:

Figure 3-3.   Mm. 51-57

The entire section is short, so the composer's repeat sign might well be obeyed. But he ends the exposition with a forte passage that obviously wants to go forward into the development. It takes a catch of breath to pull up short at the double bar, drop from forte to sudden piano, and leap back to the temper and music of the opening measures.

All the more satisfying, then, is our eventual move, into the development. Forte follows forte, except that, only four measures into the development, we are brought up short once again, to find ourselves groping, in the quietest and stealthiest of piano, through a short but tightly wound labyrinth of harmonies, twisting and turning without interruption until we are released into the return of the opening material (at measure 102).

Here, the rippling-rhythm measures that follow the opening idea seem much more restless than they did in the first section of the movement. We are still unsettled by the memory of the harmonic maze. Besides, Schubert wants to find his way to, not away from, the D major tonic of the movement, so he takes another four measures of wave music to accomplish this. We are home safe. But before reaching the double bar, we have one last unison passage (a modification of the opening) to play neatly and in tune.

It's really a simple movement technically, and the musical problems are not so puzzling, either. But to play it trimly, to avoid pedantic hacking on the one hand and supercilious cuteness on the other, to be sophisticated enough to transmit one's pleasure at the innocent and happy tricks of this small chapter—it's not easy.

The Andante suggests a nostalgic Schubert, looking back to a courtly era that, by his lifetime, was already a thing of the past, blotted out by revolutions of people, ideas, and machines. In measured pace, and alternately stated by piano alone and the two instruments together, the elegant phrases unfold. Gracefulness and dignity must be mixed in equal measure for these lines. Then, in measures 31 to 60—a contrasting section, in A minor rather than the movement's A major—the mask is changed. The violin takes center stage now, pouring out a bittersweet melody to the quietly murmuring accompaniment of the piano. With roles reversed, the piano takes over in the third passage of this section, emphasizing the plaintive note and rising to a point of suspense (measure 60) from which the movement turns back to its opening strain. The piano holds forth as soloist almost to the end of the movement, with the violin weaving a sixteenth-note filigree around the melodic line. In the last seven measures, the violin breathes a hushed close; the entire episode is simple, quite unassuming, and perfect of its kind.

I have already pointed to the similarity in tone, figuration, and even melodic substance, between the final Allegro vivace of this Schubert sonata and the first movement of Mozart's K. 526. The similarity is so striking that I am drawn to assume an acquaintance on Schubert's part with the earlier work. Another parallel may be cited to reinforce this hypothesis. Compare Schubert, measures 57 to 60,

Figure 3-4.   Mm. 56-60

with Mozart, measures 75 to 92 (we cite here measures 89 to downbeat of 92):

Figure 3-5.   Mm. 89-92

And (a trivial similarity) the Mozart movement is 242 measures, the Schubert, 245 measures long. Of course, the player is *not* performing the Mozart here, but the Schubert finale. Unlike the Mozart movement, which has a certain intellectual, stern quality behind its gaiety, the Schubert has a singsong swing. Such temper is not to everyone's taste. And yet, properly handled—without undue metric pressures, with enough forward and upward lift on the rising scale of the third measure of the tune, with light-footed motion carrying through to the end of the eight-bar phrase, with deft takeover of the solo by the pianist in the ninth measure, and with equally suave assumption of the accompanying ripples by the violin in that measure—the movement can get off to a start that is irresistible in its good humor.

Figure 3-6.   Mm. 1-4

And always there are the sweetly melancholy shadows that fall across the countenance of the movement, saving it from saccharine sentimentality.

Going a bit farther, we find the mordant sting of passages such as that quoted in Figure 3-4.

Ensemble-wise, the two players have to be alert to the changing lineup and texture of the music: now one, now the other instrument in prominence, now suddenly both equally important,

Figure 3-7.   Mm. 73-76

or, just as readily, alternating with each other in close-order drill.

Figure 3-8.   Mm. 102-106

The fabric of the music is clean and open throughout. While care is needed to play the movement with appropriate clarity, the technical requirements are not overwhelming by any means. The dynamic grading and the sound contrasts of the closing lines of this finale, incidentally, reflect the similar arrangement for the ending of the first movement. All in all, this sonata is excellent training for the enterprising duo and, when well played, graces the repertoire without any need for apology.

Sonata in A minor, op. 137, no. 2 (D. 385)

Figure 3-9.

a. Piano treble, mm. 1-4

b. Piano treble, mm. 5-9

c. Violin, mm. 10-14

d. Violin, mm. 15-23

There are listeners in today's musical world who will insist, despite all reality, that music—*real* music!—ended with the work of Brahms, that up to and including his music, all is sweetness and light and expressive balm to the ear. What will such a music lover do when he realizes that it was the good, the safe Schubert, the kindly writer of mellifluous songs and *Trout* quintets, who concocted the rather horrendous sequences of tones cited above? At the age of nineteen! And at the start of the nineteenth century!

Taken in the musical context of the opening of the A minor sonata, these notes resolve themselves into harmonic relationships that are conventional enough. But it is clear that, first in the piano line, then in the violin, Schubert starts from rather easy intervals and progresses quickly to more rigorous aural terms, at the same time moving toward wider interval spans, as though stretching the mental and physical capacities of the ear. Consider the intervals in the piano treble, measure by measure: fourth; diminished fifth; minor seventh; minor second; fourth; minor ninth; diminished fifth; then two measures of descending scalewise steps (harmless enough, but with each step preceded by a stressed, on-beat leading tone that clashes with the harmonic accompaniment).

The five measures (5 through 9) contain, either in the melodic upper part or in the accompanying chords, eleven of the available twelve tones in the arsenal of conventional music: C, C sharp, D, and so forth; every note except G. Again, the musical circumstances are completely conventional, but a strange whiff of serial writing begins to fill the air! And the listener's chores are not yet over; for in measures 10 to 12 (just three measures, this time!) we have the same rich fare.

Figure 3-10. Mm. 10-12

At the same time our harmonic listening duties are compressed into a tight compass of time, our acoustic sensibilities are strained in the other dimension by having to hear, in measures 10 and 11, the intervals in the violin part of a minor thirteenth, a diminished tenth, and then a doubly diminished fourteenth (D sharp–C). We are allowed to taper off with simple double octaves (measures 15 to 18) and then with smaller and easier intervals—except for the passing splinter of a minor ninth in measure 19. If we pass basic training in this opening page of the Schubert score, we can breathe easier in the rest of the movement.

The performer has to make these intervals, wide or narrow, seem to be what they are: facets of a continuously growing and diminishing melodic line. And when, right after the demands of the opening lines, we are given *gemütlich* phrases such as this,

Figure 3-11. Violin, mm. 30-35

the compatibility as well as contrast of the two ideas must be made clear by the playing. The arpeggiation figures, in triplets, that make up the accompanying line in the piano under the statement of this secondary melody (presented by both piano and violin in turn) must be smoothly set forth, yet with special attention to those notes that require it:

Figure 3-12. Piano bass, mm. 33-34

The closing passage of the exposition calls for a light hand from both players in the touch and pacing of the ascending lines of tied, dotted triplets, and especially (in the piano) in the rapid succession of repeated, triplet chords:

Figure 3-13.   Mm. 43-47

The development of this movement is none at all, unless we choose to
regard a rather brief interlude of harmonic wandering on the half-note
rhythms of the opening idea as exploitation of musical material. The recapitulation begins in the "wrong" key (D minor instead of A minor:
measures 78 ff.), and persists in this until the contrasting theme has made
its expected reappearance (measures 115 ff.), in the home key of A minor.
The air of contrariness that has surrounded the movement from its opening measures is held to the final note: the last measures are again the
half-note rhythms, in restful intervals, but in pianissimo, diminishing yet
further, to triple piano.

The Andante is a study in sonority contrasts. A thickly and richly
written first section alternates with a contrasting, thinner-lined, more rapidly moving (a sixteenth-note line runs throughout) section, in A-B-A-B-A
sequence. The first B-section is in the key of B flat (subdominant to the
movement's F major). The second A-section, midpoint of the movement,
is in A flat; the following B-section is in D flat (again, subdominant to its
parent A-section). The second half of the B-section, however, leads us cir-
cuitously back to F major and the entry of the concluding A-section, which,
except for an added coda passage, is identical with the opening of the
movement. There are no special playing problems here, except perhaps for
the flowing delineation of the sixteenth-note runs, the observance of the
measure-by-measure alternation of forte and piano (as in measures 33 ff.),
and the hushed pianissimo where indicated (e.g., the harmonic wandering
passages at the ends of the two B-sections).

There is no problem with the Menuetto, either, except the obvious
point that the violinist should play the individual eighth-note passages in
broad spiccato, not on the string. The final Allegro, however, is another
matter; the opening lines already rely too heavily on unrelieved rhythmic
repetitions. The violinist must set a good example of phrase molding in
the opening statement:

Figure 3-14.   Violin, mm. 1-34

Most difficult is the passage beginning in measure 69, and the corresponding passage starting in measure 91. I might put some of these measures in
parallel with a passage from the finale of Mozart's K. 380 and again suggest
influence and imitation:

Figure 3-15.

a. Schubert, mm. 188-195

b. Mozart, mm. 108-114

If Schubert actually was guided by the Mozart example, he did not emulate the older master's economy. Mozart flares through a trajectory of seven measures, each bar having its own complete arch of sixteenths; Schubert moves in slower pace (eighth triplets), with but half an arch to the measure, and with a slower, more ponderous bass. Mozart has violin and piano moving in simultaneous octaves, whereas Schubert reserves the first action for the piano, has the violin continue the line (measures 82 ff.) for a time, then alternates the two instruments, measure by measure, in a long staircase pattern of triplets. With the entire complex of phrases covering fifty-one measures of the Schubert movement, it will take verve on the part of the players to avoid a feeling of anticlimax in the music; even more so, the second time around (measures 191 to 242).

The duo that has worked its way through the first two Schubert sonatas will be disconcerted now to be confronted with the English musicologist, J. A. Westrup's appraisal of the three compositions of opus 137 and the Duo in A, op. 162: "They are amiable works, sometimes formal in expression, sometimes charming, but without any pronounced characteristics."[31] Westrup goes on to indicate that there are some moments to treasure; and we have seen that there are more than a few surprises in the first fwo sonatas. Though I am not going to discuss the third sonata[32] here, I commend it to the ears and fingers of our readers. And we proceed directly to the fourth such work by Schubert.

Duo in A, op. 162 (D. 574)

The most engaging quality of the Allegro moderato that opens this product of Schubert's twentieth year is its generous gift of ideas. The initial piano measures are gentle curtain raisers, arousing our expectations:

Figure 3-16. Mm. 1-4

Against this background, the violin enters with a line marvelously unassuming, yet irresistible in its soaring expansiveness.

Figure 3-17.   Violin, mm. 1-20

Schubert makes his way through the entire exposition without repeating himself; by the time the double bar is reached, the opening idea has been followed by four others:

Figure 3-18.

a. Violin, mm. 29-31

b. Piano treble, mm. 40-41

c. Violin, m. 58

d. Violin, mm. 67-70

So naturally do they flow from one to the next that the movement seems more organized than it has any right to be! The development is scarcely more than a harmonic turnaround, designed to pass some time pleasantly while returning us to the first melody and to all its fellows, in proper order. The outpouring of tunes may be less surprising the second time around, but the movement will leave all concerned with a sense of well-being.

The Scherzo, Presto should be played at a tempo of ♩. = 92, so that each measure is touched only lightly. The first section (to the double bar) is one uninterrupted swing and moves directly into the second section, where quarter pulse takes over from eighth. Again there is no interruption until the short silence (prepared by the gaps that open up in the lines of the two instruments during the preceding measures) at measure 48:

Figure 3-19. Mm. 42-50

In the last measures of this example, the motor starts up again in the piano part, reintroducing the rhythm of the Scherzo's opening. The trio glides and hovers, progressing in hushed tone, finally poising on another of the by now characteristic silences of the piece,

Figure 3-20. Mm. 127-132

before sending us back for a last complete review of the Scherzo proper. The entire movement is quickly passed over in the sequence of chapters that make up this sonata. But its tautness and compression—qualities that Schubert achieves so well when he wants to—make an effective and necessary interlude in the composition.

The Andantino, moving at an easy ♪ = 84, promises a musical vacation after the Scherzo's racing:

Figure 3-21. Mm. 1-4

In fact, the mood of the movement is on the whole meditative, subdued, cool in color, framed in C, D flat, C, A flat, and C major, but punctuated with sharp chordal blasts at measures 9 and 10; 34 to 37; 60; 81 and 82. These chords should be stroked rather than beaten out of the instruments, applying in a new dimension the gathered force of the easy-flowing stream of the movement.

The material of this Andantino is made up as much from the luxuriant foliage of passages such as these:

Figure 3-22.

a. Mm. 22-24

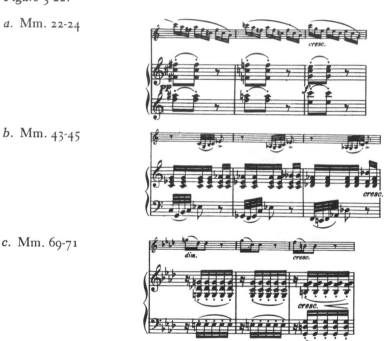

b. Mm. 43-45

c. Mm. 69-71

as it is of the specifically tuneful idea. The trick is to make these passages of embroidery seem melodic rather than interludes of nothing better to do. The stress points and indications of pacing I have written into the examples may prove helpful in keeping the movement filled with a quiet, yet vibrant life. One of the most touching points in the movement is its ending—not so much ending as fading out, the cessation of an ebb and flow that had already, in a rather short span of time, promised to be endless. If the players can evoke this feeling of unpressured timelessness, they will have captured the essence of this music.

The Scherzo, as we recall, began thus:

Figure 3-23. Piano treble, mm. 1-3

And the finale starts this way:

Figure 3-24. Mm. 1-4

Not only does this suggest the earlier movement, but the sweep of eighths, measures 5 to 7, seems to reflect a portion of the Scherzo opening:

Figure 3-25.

a. Violin, Scherzo, mm. 1-11

b. Violin, finale, mm. 5-7 (as reflected in mm. 171-173)

Even the tempi (Presto, and Allegro vivace, respectively) of the two movements are identical: both movements proceed very nicely at ♩. = 92. In short, the finale suggests a longer, bolder continuation of the Scherzo premise. The opening gun of the boldness, of course, comes from the resounding repartee between piano and violin in the chords of the initial measures (see Figure 3-24). To keep this dialogue resonant in its bluffness takes as much skill as (just a few measures later) for the two instruments to reverse roles and carry out their conversation now on a very quiet level:

Figure 3-26. Mm. 9-12

Hold your breath while striking key or string!

Part of the excitement of this movement comes from moving at break-neck speed while maintaining an air of nonchalant grace:

Figure 3-27.   Violin, mm. 33-40

The pianist gets his turn at running this melodic race; but he has first had the chore of moving the music from clamor to calm without letting the craft capsize (cf. measures 27 to 36).

Vienna, in Schubert's day, was wild about waltzing. The craze had spread from Germany, where, just before the end of the eighteenth century, it had already been found necessary to publish a diatribe entitled *Proof that the waltz is a main source of the weakness of body and mind of our generation.*[33] The duo that will keep in mind the heady whirl of a real, old-time waltz will find that passages in the finale such as this

Figure 3-28.   Mm. 73-80

will fly past with the appropriately intoxicated sparkle. And a passage such as *this*, played with the proper mixture of caution and abandon, will feel even more psychedelic than it looks on paper.

Figure 3-29.   Mm. 146-151

Mention of one other wonderful spot must suffice for this work: the end of the finale—a whole page of the most distant and sweet-toned conversation (or rather, communal musing) on the waltzlike strains, fading away, dying away, to be broken and cut off by a perfect barrage of the fanfares first heard at the beginning of the movement.

On June 7, 1828, the *Wiener Zeitschrift für Kunst, Literatur, Theater und Mode* (broad coverage) carried a notice of a new piece by Schubert —actually it had been composed in 1826, first played at the publisher, Artaria's, for Schubert by Slavik and Bocklet in early 1827, and published by Artaria in April of that year—Schubert's Rondeau Brillant for Piano and Violin, op. 70 (D. 895). In part, the review reads:

> Both the pianoforte and the fiddle require a practised artist, who must be prepared for passages which have not by any means attained to their right of citizenship by endless use, but betoken a succession of new and inspired ideas.[34]

If, after dragging such a bait along the trail, we do not pay specific attention to the slow introduction and long Allegro of the Rondeau Brillant for Piano and Violin, it is because the Fantasy in C major embodies all the devices and textures of the Rondeau and much more besides. The duo that has come to grips with the Fantasy will need no prompting in dealing with the Rondeau. (As for opus 160, Introduction and Variations, that work was originally written for flute and piano; for discussion of the composition, see the companion volume in this series, by Samuel Baron, on the flute repertoire.)

Fantasy in C major, op. 159 (D. 934)

The Schubert sonatas of 1816 may have had their easy moments. But the Fantasy, from 1827, is not easy; it is a long work in one movement, fraught with all sorts of technical difficulties. Let the duo be forewarned, and let it enjoy! For there is something for every finger and every ear in this work. The music was originally composed for a virtuoso violinist, the Czech, Josef Slavik, who became a member of the imperial chapel in Vienna in 1829.[35] On January 20, 1828, he performed the Fantasy in concert with the pianist and Schubert exponent, Carl Maria von Bocklet; the work had been composed the preceding month. One reviewer appraised the work as "a piece of music which . . . can be enjoyed as it deserves only in a smaller room."[36] Be that as it may, another commentator gave this sidelight on the occasion: "The hall emptied gradually, and the writer confesses that he too is unable to say anything about the conclusion of this piece."[37] The Leipzig *Allgemeine Musikalische Zeitung*, musical taste-maker of the time, pulled a

boner. Its reviewer, though unconsciously betraying the fact that he had
not been at the concert, ruled that "the favourite composer has in this
case positively miscomposed."[38] On the strength of this review, the Leipzig
publisher, Probst, in a letter of April 15, asking Schubert to send on manuscripts of his work, specifically rules out the Fantasy.[39] The work was not
published until 1850.[40]

The first reviewer praised the pianist, Bocklet, for his part in the proceedings. From the very start, the pianist is put on his mettle; for, at the
appropriate tempo of $\mathcal{J} = 72$, the opening three pages of score are a luxuriant jungle of tremolo, beginning with wide-spaced writing for both
hands,

Figure 3-30.   Mm. 1-4

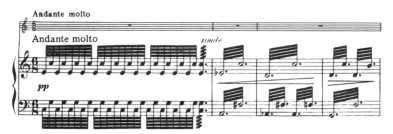

and soon relegating the shimmering chordal work, streamers of parallel
thirds, or what have you, completely to one hand or the other, leaving the
"free" hand to carry out more clearly lined activities. The violin has been
on the scene since the fifth measure, its sustained line heard above, and
through, the incredibly rich foliage of the piano part, as in measures 10
and 11:

Figure 3-31.   Mm. 10-11

The effect of this opening is quite magical. And I must confess that the
shock of transition to the second episode of the piece is correspondingly
great. For here, instead of spreading waves of musical color, is a faster,

cleaner, harder, stronger-rhythmed section. The melody here is poles away from that of the opening; there, everything was misty and lyric; here, all is brusque and militant.

Figure 3-32. Violin, mm. 35-42

The violin and piano treble are in duet with each other in these measures. And when (measures 81 ff.) the violin launches into virtuoso archings of sixteenths, the piano is quick to follow in kind.

Figure 3-33. Mm. 89-94

The elaborations of this section of the piece are long in the working out; it is not until measure 379 that the piano winds up the episode with a long, dwindling streamer of sixteenth notes. Then we come to the heart of the work, a set of variations on the melody of the song, *Sei mir gegrüsst* ("Greetings to Thee"), composed by Schubert himself in the year 1821.

Chamber-music aficionados will know that this is not the only self-borrowing by Schubert; call to mind the *Trout* quintet, with a variations movement based on the composer's song of the same title, and his Quartet in D minor, with its second movement a set of variations on Schubert's own song, "Death and the Maiden." The song, *Sei mir gregrüsst,* was in Schubert's mind owing, perhaps, to the fact that at some time during the months immediately preceding the composition of the Fantasy, he—along with the famed violinist, Schuppanzigh, the court cellist, Josef Merk, the court singer, Ludwig Cramolini, and one Capus von Pichelstein (the name is real)—repaired to the hamlet of Kahlenberg, near Vienna, to present a nocturnal serenade outside the home of Marie von Berthold, fiancée of Pichelstein (which gentleman performed on the harp in the serenade troupe). The purpose of the undertaking was to patch up a quarrel between Pichelstein and his betrothed. One of the items on the program was our song; happy to relate, the desired effect was achieved—the serenaders ended the evening over "light refreshments" in the Berthold household—and the lovers were reconciled.[41]

Dr. Westrup, writing about the relationship between the song and its offspring, the theme for these variations, points out that the "simplicity of the original is overlaid with a sentimental chromaticism," and that the "modifications are hardly an improvement."[42] But Schubert had already passed through the experience of the *Death and the Maiden* quartet variations (1824) on the original song (dating from 1817). The result in that case is definitely favorable; the textual and musical implications of the song are more fully, more explicitly, more strongly realized in the instrumental elaboration than in the original. It is scarcely conceivable that an older Schubert (the Fantasy is three years later than the quartet in question) would have been less sensitive in the reshaping of his own song in the Fantasy. Second, my hearing of the adapted theme induces no feeling of repulsion either by the harmonic or melodic detail, which only goes to prove that one man's sentiment is another man's sentimentality.

I might, however, take issue with Schubert over the variations themselves. In the case of the *Death and the Maiden*, the struggle between death and life dominates and unifies the shades of meaning so vividly explored in the quartet variations. The song, *Sei mir gegrüsst*, strikes a more innocuous note, both in word and tune, thus leaving the way open for Schubert to exploit the tune for showy and virtuosic purposes (which, after all, would have motivated him in the first place when writing for Slavik's concert).

In any event, a tabulation of representative measures from the several variants will underscore the point that these manipulations of the song melody call for dexterity from both players, sane and realistic tempos, and phrase-molding that takes the necessities of fingerings and string-crossings into account.

Figure 3-34.

a. Piano, mm. 380-3

b. Variation 1, mm. 414-415

c. Variation 1, mm. 421-423

d. Variation 2, excerpt from middle of second section, mm. 453-454

e. Variation 3, excerpt from first section, mm. 466-467

f. Variation 4, excerpt from closing phrase of variant, mm. 500-503

The two instruments must remain alertly and flexibly sensitive to one another, so that the exigencies of technique and the coherence of the movement—both within the individual variant and in the overall relationship of the variants to each other and to the germinating theme—can be well served.

Following the variations there is a brief revisiting of the shimmering opening measures of the fantasy, so arranged as to give a feeling of being in medias res, rather than of entering a literal da capo. This reminiscence, in turn, is interrupted by a brisk and positive episode, which begins thus,

Figure 3-35.   Mm. 520-523

and continues at some length, soon launching both instruments into passages of tempestuously rolling triplets and working the violin up into a perfect lather of sixteenths which, under the circumstances of tempo, must perforce boil up into a tremolo of extreme speed (cf. measures 682 ff.). First aid comes for the violinist in the very nick of time—in the form of nine and two-thirds measures of rest, at the beginning of a quiet Allegretto section that continues the thread of the variations episodes. Having recovered breath, the violin joins with the piano in the last half of this haven of tranquillity. Following this, both instruments enter a final Presto, the windup both for the triumphal section cited above (see Figure 3-35) and also for the Fantasy as a whole. The pianist contributes to the excitement of the final measures with a headlong ascending scale—much of it in fourfold octaves for two hands; but the violin has the very last say, with an upward arpeggio that leaves him poised for exit on a very high C.

Figure 3-36. Violin, mm. 751-757

Surely, a moment of truth in the performing experience of any string player!

The experience of these Schubert works will bear out, in the minds of the players, the truth—so far as it goes—of Robert Schumann's words about his recent predecessor:

> . . . Schubert will always be the favorite of young people. He gives what they desire: an overflowing heart, bold ideas, rash actions. . . . romantic tales, knights, maidens, and adventures. And he adds wit and humor —but not so much as to disturb the gentleness of the mood.[43]

4 ❧ Mendelssohn and Schumann

Felix Mendelssohn

Jacob Ludwig Felix Mendelssohn-Bartholdy was born, without the hyphenated conclusion, in Hamburg in 1809. His grandfather, Moses Mendelssohn, son of a Jewish scribe in Dessau, had moved to Berlin, withstood prejudice, and by hard work had risen to the position of partner in a silk factory. Friend of the poet, Lessing (Moses was the model for the protagonist in Lessing's play, *Nathan der Weise*), philosopher, active exponent of the cause of emancipation of the Jews, Moses Mendelssohn moved in Europe's highest intellectual circles.[44] Moses's second son, Abraham, became a banker. Abraham's wife, Leah Salomon, was also of a banking family; and both families traced back to Moses ben Israel Isserles, noted Polish rabbi and philosopher of the sixteenth century.[45]

Yielding reluctantly to the current tendency for Jews to convert in order to alleviate the restrictive laws and atmosphere that oppressed them, Abraham followed the example of his wife's brother, Jacob Salomon, converted, and (like Jacob) adopted the added surname, Bartholdy.[46]

Though the family sphere was generally interested in music and the other arts, it was a great-aunt of Felix, Sara Levy, pupil of Wilhelm Friedemann Bach and herself a harpsichordist of ability, who recommended that Karl Friedrich Zelter, the distinguished Berlin conductor, composer, and theorist, should be the music instructor of the young Felix. By the time he was seven, he—along with his older sister, Fanny—was on a taxing daily regime of general and musical studies (they began their "working" day at five in the morning).[47] Felix studied piano, violin, and voice, became an able performer on the viola, and also could acquit himself on cello.[48] And he was thoroughly schooled in the composer's prerequisites by Zelter.

One of Mendelssohn's earliest compositions, written at the age of fourteen,[49] was the Violin Sonata in F minor, op. 4, dedicated to his friend and violin teacher, Eduard Rietz. (Opera 1, 2, and 3 were also chamber works, three piano quartets, dedicated respectively to Count Radziwill, to Zelter, and to Goethe, to which last Zelter had taken Mendelssohn at the age of twelve; the aged writer and the young musician were equally impressed with each other.)[50]

One careful biographer of Mendelssohn ignores this sonata completely.[51] Another says this of the work:

> . . . the violin Sonata has one or two unusual touches, such as the opening recitative and the unexpectedly quiet end of the finale, but is on the whole the weakest and most colourless of all Mendelssohn's chamber works.[52]

A third biographer cites the appraisal of the sonata offered by a reviewer in the *Berliner Allgemeine Musikalische Zeitung*, 1825. The commentator complains about some of the progressions in the first movement, the part writing, the bridge passage, and the handling of the bass line.[53]

After such a buildup, one scarcely dares mention the work, let alone discuss it. True, it does not have the individuality, the inimitable melting tenderness of slow movement, the sparkling élan of scherzo (there is no such movement in this three-movement work) that are the hallmarks of the fully developed Mendelssohn. The sonata is, nonetheless, a good, workmanlike job, not overly difficult technically, and definitely a worthwhile addition to the arsenal of the teacher, student, and amateur. To represent Mendelssohn at fuller stature, whether in the informal program or in the concert hall, however, the later sonata, that in F major, is more appropriate.

"I am suffering, as I did four years ago, from complete deafness of one ear, and as I have to conduct and play in spite of it . . . you may imagine my agony, not being able properly to hear either the orchestra or my own playing on the piano!"[54] These anguished words may sound as though drawn from a letter of Beethoven. Actually, they come from a letter written January 20, 1838, by Felix Mendelssohn to his longtime friend, the conductor and composer, Ferdinand Hiller. Despite Mendelssohn's anxiety, the illness passed off, and in July, writing again to Hiller, he is in a much better frame of mind, at least when speaking of his five-month-old firstborn son, "who is fat, and merry," and of his work in progress, which included, among other things, "two sonatas, one with violin, the other [opus 45] with cello," and the String Quartet in D major, which was to bear the opus number 44, number 1.[55] Concerning the quartet, he said in a letter the following month (again to Hiller) that, "I like the first movement immensely, I wish I could play it to you—especially a *forte* passage at the end which you would be sure to like."[56]

The movement to which Mendelssohn refers is a curious piece. At first hearing, it delights the ear with its ebullience, and frustrates the intellect with its studied refusal to settle down and work out its ideas. Continued experience with the movement, however, brings the awareness that the motion and thrust of this music is its reason for being, both in the rocketlike propulsion of the initial theme and in the later treatment. And there is more than enough intricate and finely detailed contrapuntal interweaving of the four voices to satisfy the highest standards of craftsmanship; in addition, the frequent passages of rapid interplay between instruments lend an excitement of its own to the sound of this movement.

The quartet movement opens with a great, bustling sweep of tremolo from the three lower voices, against which the violin takes its starting leap. In the Sonata in F for Violin and Piano, the opening of the Allegro vivace offers less clatter, but maintains the same sense of buoyancy and expansiveness as its quartet contemporary; this can be seen in the first piano measures:

Figure 4-1. Piano, mm. 1-9

In the measures that follow, the piano provides a boiling-16th background, so like the quartet example, and over this the violin takes its turn at the theme.

Figure 4-2. Mm. 10-12

There is another point of similarity in this movement to the quartet example, and this feature is characteristic of Mendelssohn's instrumental writing: the tendency for the several voices to "challenge" each other in alternate presentations of the expansive themes, with a cumulative excitement that results from the handing back and forth. (Some of this way of writing seems to have rubbed off on Richard Wagner, though that worthy might not relish the suggestion, in view of his published expressions of dissatisfaction with the Mendelssohnian idiom.) Here is an excerpt from the "bridge" passage of the Allegro, just before the appearance of the second theme:

Figure 4-3. Mm. 24-31

This is a short, tightly spaced interchange; the second theme is an alternation in much broader placement, as can be seen from the length of the theme, completely stated in the violin before being taken up, with modified ending, by the piano:

Figure 4-4. Mm. 35-49

The contrast between broad and compressed alternation gives this kind of writing a feeling of depth and perspective even though the emphasis is on constant forwardness. The relief is written into the music. It is extremely important, however, not to be carried by this forward drive to the extent of sawing and pounding away in a state of autointoxication. This is very much players' music. It is so well written for each instrument that the player can easily fall into a feeling of glibness and slickness; the first thing to go is a sense of dynamic gradation. Exuberance becomes equated with loudness, shading and nuance are lost, and the effect degenerates into one of brashness and heedlessness quite unworthy of Mendelssohn's art.

A case in point is the violin part at the beginning of the recapitulation. Here are a few measures from that voice:

Figure 4-5. Violin, mm. 184-186

Now this is quite fiddlistic, as much so as its close counterpart, the cadenza of the Mendelssohn violin concerto. The left hand is fairly sedentary, and with an easy roll of the bow across the strings, quite a virtuoso splash can be made by the player. An overbravura emphasis of this line, however, would be quite out of keeping with the piano's statement of the opening theme (after all, the element of prime importance here) in bass register, under the accompanying violin figure. Mendelssohn himself calls for a crescendo paced from piano to fortissimo: the limits and grading must be nicely observed.

Throughout, robustness must be tempered with suavity and refinement, as in these ebullient measures from the closing page of the movement:

Figure 4-6. Mm. 293-295

Robert Schumann, writing in 1835, found these words to speak of an early piano sonata of Mendelssohn: "What touches and attracts us is not the exotic or the novel, but precisely the lovely and the familiar. It puts on no airs, nor seeks to astonish. It merely finds the right words with which to express our feelings, and in such a way that we think that we have found them ourselves."[57] We could apply this kind of comment to the slow movement of the F major sonata; it is simple and unassuming in its quieter moments, of Mendelssohn's inimitably elegiac tone in its more impassioned episodes. All carried off with an ease and directness that belies the charge of sentimentality so often leveled at Mendelssohn. Much depends on the players; if they interpret against a background of the usual suppositions about this composer, they may indeed squeeze out the saccharine and soupy from these measures. But this is to miss the sincerity of the composer's purpose; or, what Alfred Einstein sees, in speaking of Mendelssohn's chamber music, as "the originality and amiability of individual movements, usually the middle ones."[58] Or, I might add, the quite strong sweep of a moment such as this climactic point in the Adagio of this sonata:

Figure 4-7. Mm. 46-48

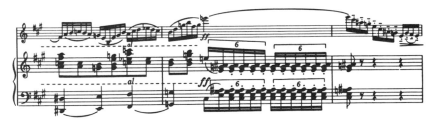

There is a curious correspondence between this sonata and the youthful F minor (opus 4). In the present Adagio, the violin philosophizes in full voice for several measures, thus:

Figure 4-8. Violin, mm. 85-90

If this is compared with the very opening of the F minor sonata—also an Adagio passage, for violin alone—a similarity in the rhapsodizing will be noticed:

Figure 4-9. Violin, mm. 1-5

Mendelssohn, in revisiting the medium ("trios, quartets and other pieces with accompaniment, genuine chamber music—is quite forgotten now and I feel a great urge to do something new of this kind"),[59] also turns to memories of his earlier work for the duo.

One more particularly felicitous passage in this Adagio deserves mention: the coda, which for a moment combines the principal melody of the movement (piano part) with flashes (in the violin part) of the rhapsodic passage just previously completed.

Figure 4-10. Mm. 99-102

The last movement, Assai vivace, of this sonata needs but one preparation on the part of the players: a rehearing of the *Midsummer Night's*

Dream music, and especially of its Scherzo, or of the second movement of the Quartet in E minor, op. 44, no. 2. That, and the determination and rehearsal to achieve the same elfin lightness, fleetness, endurance, and electric spirit that this most characteristic side of Mendelssohn's writing requires.

The same biographer who was quoted above as dismissing the F minor sonata out of hand is properly impressed by the F major. Speaking of the finale, he hails it as "brilliantly animated" and points to the distinction given it by the "constant interweaving of the violin and piano parts." Of the sonata in general, he says that it "is one of the best instrumental works of its period, and it is surprising that its composer apparently did not consider it worthy of publication."[60] The esteemed violin virtuoso, Yehudi Menuhin, rectified this state of affairs by bringing out an edition of the work from the composer's autograph in 1953.

Robert Schumann

In September, 1840, Robert Schumann married Clara Wieck. He was then thirty; she, twenty-one. Thus ended a five-year courtship, though the two had actually known each other for twelve years, since the time when Schumann had first met and—soon after—begun piano study with Clara's father, Friedrich. Wieck had vehemently opposed the match, possibly owing to dismay at losing control over the career and income of his talented daughter, who had grown from a piano prodigy into a young woman graced with a solid reputation in Europe as a virtuoso artist. Ugly courtroom scenes had taken place between parent and the young betrothed, not excluding a charge that Schumann was an alcoholic (and, truth to tell, he was as fond of spirits as of cigars). The father's objections were at length legally overruled, and the wedding took place.

Now an unrest of a different order arose to mar the bliss of the young couple—that of two strong artistic personalities being pulled by their respective ambitions. Schumann's pianistic aspirations had gone aglimmering with the muscular disability of his right hand, incurred in 1832. He had, however, thrown himself into his composing and music-journalistic activities with compensatory zeal. The time of which we are now speaking was no exception. In the months before and after the wedding, he poured out a torrent of songs. In January, 1841, he sketched his first symphony, and the work was premiered by Mendelssohn in March of that year in Leipzig (where Mendelssohn had been director of the Gewandhaus concerts since

1835). The first movement of the Piano Concerto and the entire D minor symphony followed soon after.

Now it was Clara's established status as a piano virtuoso that was threatened by suffocation under the domestic round. But not for long. Early in 1842, six months after the birth of their first child, Clara set off on another concert tour, with Schumann in attendance. He turned homeward before the end of the tour, and returned to active composing when Clara rejoined him there. The three string quartets were all written in the months of June and July, 1842. The piano quintet followed in September and October of that year. Also in October, came the piano quartet. And, late in the year, he composed the *Phantasiestücke* for piano trio.[61]

Schumann's preoccupation with composition for chamber ensemble did not, for the moment, extend to the duo. This was not forthcoming until 1849, when—in another one of his bursts of creativity—Schumann produced a torrent of music that included works for piano and, severally, horn, clarinet, oboe, and cello. Two years later, another stream of chamber music, including now the third piano trio of opus 110 (the first two trios, opera 63 and 80, had been written in 1847), the *Märchenbilder* for viola and piano, and the two violin sonatas, opus 105, in A minor, and opus 121, in D minor. The works were written in Düsseldorf, where, the previous fall, Schumann had begun service as orchestral and choral conductor. His experience in these posts, as in some earlier ones, was clouded by signs of his increasing mental illness, but his creative powers could still shine brightly, as these works prove.

The first measures of the piano part of the Sonata in A minor, op. 105, carry a flowing, undulating 16th-note pattern that is to be heard throughout the opening movement. The effect of surging and billowing fits the composer's instructive heading for the movement—"With passionate expression":

Figure 4-11. Piano, mm. 1-2

Through the foliage of these piano figurations, the violin and piano together weave a long garland of melody. This cooperation shows best in a composite line of the tune, extracted from the two instrumental parts:

Figure 4-12. Piano and violin, composite, mm. 1-26

The line is long; the length is made obtrusive by the harping away on the rhythm:

Or rather, it would be obtrusive except that the piano and violin are taking the action away from each other so insistently. The repeated snatching of the spotlight lends excitement to the repetitious flow. And (see measure 19) the violin breaks out of the pattern by stating the essential rhythm in even more unrelieved fashion (measures 19 to 21), finally to launch the duo into a tight-knit volley of the 16th-note pattern (measures 22 to 25). The sense of climax and resolution is the more satisfying for having been so long delayed. Because of the length of this opening episode, "passionate" should be equated in the performers' minds with "speed." There is need for drive, for a feeling of plunging through the waves of piano figuration, for a light, gliding approach to the broader rhythmic figures, so that the arrival at the resolution of measure 27 is made irresistible and inevitable.

Schumann's feeling for pace and contrast within a generally consistent texture is felt throughout the movement. The second subject, for example, harks back to earlier measures in its retention of the rolling piano-figure. But the brew is leavened by fanfares that break into the constant stream of sound:

Figure 4-13. Mm. 36-39

The second subject is another self of the idea that has preoccupied the
composer since the sonata's start. It is not surprising, then, that the development is equally single-minded. And, as often happens in an extended
Schumann instrumental movement, there is that feeling of confrontation,
over and over again, with one reiterated melodic fragment. The saving
grace is that the composer himself is completely convinced by his procedure. To demonstrate this point (while saving space), let us quote only
from the violin part, where it approaches the point of recapitulation. The
doggedly repeated rhythm culminates in—itself; for, just at the moment
of return to the opening idea, the basic idea is presented twice as boldly
as hitherto, in augmentation.

Figure 4-14. Violin, mm. 103-118

There is an ambivalence about this movement. The impassioned swing
of the minor melody has within its sobriety, by virtue of its very motion,
something exuberant. This was already apparent in the C major trans-
formations of the material in the exposition. Now, when the recapitulation
brings us to A major at the corresponding point, the effect is positively
radiant:

Figure 4-15. Mm. 145-150

It is the darker muse, however, that Schumann is wooing after all. He reverts to A minor, and to a positively ranting insistence on the germinal rhythmic pattern. The roles are reversed during much of the closing episode, as compared with the movement's beginning: now the violin has the sixteenth-note activity, the piano takes the broader line.

What the nineteenth-century critic, Eduard Hanslick, had to say of Schumann song settings seems appropriate to the movement we have been considering: "The music renounces its own substance and follows the visions of the poet like a shadow, now light, now dark."[62] The vision conquers all here: meter, rhythm, repetition.

It is a vision again, that unfolds in the second movement. We are transported into the middle of things. The players must help us make the transition from the bluster of the first movement to the reverie of the second. As much as possible, we must be kept in a state of suspense. Begin the Allegretto as though you have already been playing this kind of music in unheard, preceding measures. Live up to the implications of the offbeat, elliptic entry, and its enigmatic fermata pause:

Figure 4-16. Mm. 1-3

As it turns out, the fermata is of thematic importance; with or without its attendant retard (and sometimes in the form of the retard alone, the fermata existing then only by implication and association) the pause recurs again and again, dividing the movement into a whimsical series of fresh starts, of faster-moving snippets,

Figure 4-17. Mm. 8-10

generally palely washed by light, but in one episode transported to darker colors (measures 16 ff.). The movement does not really go anywhere, nor is it meant to. It is a rather tranquil conversation; more accurately, a soliloquy in which the composer permits his several selves to manifest themselves by turns. It was first in 1831 that he used (in a review of Chopin's opus 2, for the Leipzig *Allgemeine Musikalische Zeitung*) the names of Florestan, Eusebius, and Master Raro to personify the impetuous, the dreamy, and the judicious sides of his own nature.[63] These personifications seem still present in this sonata movement of his late years, and must be allowed to have their say, without pressure or urging.

Time enough for celerity in the finale: a marvelous will-o'-the-wisp fantasy, in *moto perpetuo* style, that suggests homage to the memory of Mendelssohn (whose passing in 1847 had been a severe shock to Schumann). It is a curious choice for finale; the presence of three clearly exposed chords at the very end cannot counter the impression that the sonata has evaporated into thin air rather than ended. And yet there is a logic to the overall scheme of the sonata. The first movement, darkly turbulent; the second, erratically contemplative; and the third, fleeting and questing. The change of mood is subtle and consistent, and it is just as well that Schumann did not choose to place an "imposing" fourth movement after the rather scherzando closer now in force.

Ferdinand David, born in Hamburg in 1810, came to Leipzig in 1836 to serve as concertmaster of the Gewandhaus orchestra under Mendelssohn. When the Leipzig conservatory, under Mendelssohn's inspiration and guidance, opened in 1843, David and Schumann were both members of the faculty. It was David who gave early readings of the three string quartets of Schumann.[64] It is understandable, then, that Schumann should have dedicated his Sonata in D minor, op. 121, to his good friend and colleague, even though, at the time of its writing, Schumann was resident in Düsseldorf, and David still at Leipzig (where he remained in office until his death in 1873).

The D minor sonata is a large work, in four extended movements. With the opening, slow introduction, we can see that we are in for some musical oratory, what with the recitativelike line of the violin and the accompanying punctuation from the piano. How expansive Schumann's mood remains in the movement proper can be seen in a compilation of the violin and piano lines for the second subject:

Figure 4-18. Violin and piano, compilation, mm. 57-79

Comparing this with the similar synthesis of the beginning of the first movement of Schumann's A minor sonata (see Figure 4-11) shows greater rhythmic variety in the present instance, but also a corresponding loss in concentration of force. The line woven by the two instruments is rhapsodic, but wanders too much and seems to lack a central and clearly denoted peak of motion.

By the same token, the development of this movement, ninety-two measures long, outlasts itself, dissipating some of its energy in broad sequential repetitions and excessive climaxes. And this, in turn, makes the recapitulation section not entirely welcome in bringing up the rear. Played with fire and conviction, the chapter can be brought off with effect. But the performer may find that he misses the pruning and editing that Schumann should have brought to the work.

The second movement, on the other hand, is completely successful. It bowls along at a fine clip, in an irresistible aura of energy and resonance

(and combines nostalgia and prescience at once, seeming to echo the tarantella movement of the Mendelssohn *Italian Symphony* as well as to forecast the finale of the Brahms Horn Trio). The electric rhythms of the
refrain sections

Figure 4-19. Mm. 1-6

must be played with strong, cleanly articulated strokes, so that the triplet
pulse is clearly heard within the governing duple swing. In the contrast
sections, it is the broad 2/8 figures that must predominate over the rippling
application of the triplet rhythm, which carries through (see measures 46
ff., 121 ff.).

An interesting moment arrives in measure 153, where the return of
the refrain section is varied by an oblique approach: through a momentary
(and quite distant) statement in C major; then a sudden drop into the
proper key of return, B minor. The result is a wonderful and unexpected
color play. Another fine spot in the movement occurs at measures 197 ff.;
broad fanfares, which have been part of the refrain tune since the start
of the movement, are heard again, as expected; but then, measures 205 ff.,
the rhythm of the fanfare—sturdy quarter notes—raised to fortissimo level,
becomes the vehicle for a stentorian premonition of the theme of the third
movement.[65] This forecast is in brightest B major, and it is in this mood
that the movement ends.

The third movement, slow, is a set of variations. When we get into
the movement, we realize that the very opening is already a variation. It
is the "preview," at the end of the second movement, that is really the
theme statement. The third movement, with quiet, triple-time rendition,
alternating between pizzicato violin strokes and equally short responses
from the piano (with soft pedal indicated), is—both in rhythm, dynamics,
and tone color—a transformation of the tune. The origin of the melody
is an old chorale, *Gelobet seist du, Jesu Christi.*[66] Here is the chorale phrase
as contained in one of four settings of this melody made by J. S. Bach,
and as presented by Schumann.[67]

Figure 4-20.

a. Bach, chorale, mm. 1-6

b. Schumann, second movement, violin, mm. 204-208

c. Schumann, third movement, violin, mm. 1-15

What we have in this *Leise, einfach* ("Quietly, simple") movement of
Schumann, then, is a chorale variation.[68] But this setting is more than a
view of the chorale alone; the fourth section of the movement, marked
"Somewhat more moving" and bearing the instruction that the sixteenth-
triplets be played to equal the eighth-note triplets of the second movement, is actually a flashback to the material of that movement. Woven
into this reminiscence is a pianissimo, ponticello(!) snatch of the chorale
tune (measures 78 ff.); and there are again some hints of the second movement at the very end of the third movement. The two middle movements
of the sonata, then, must be treated as a unit, and a rather dramatic pictorial unit, at that.

I cannot stir up much enthusiasm for the finale. This smacks even
more of that busywork that bothers the opening *Lebhaft* of the sonata.
Repeated hearings of this ditty

Figure 4-21.   Violin, mm. 1-4

do not endear the item to me, no matter how many transpositions are rung upon the tune. Even so, the end movements can lend a frame of motor excitement to the sonata; and they do enclose that fine middle pair.

Schumann does not yield himself to the performer too readily. Time and thought must be given to working out the nuances and details of phrasing and coloration in his music. It is too easy to gloss over his pages with a heavy hand; and it is perhaps this kind of performance, much more than any inherent fault in the music itself, that has enabled peppery critics such as Schumann's English contemporary, Henry F. Chorley, to deliver salvos like the following: "Opera, Cantata, Symphony, Quartet, Sonata— all and each tell the same story, and display the same characteristics—the same skill of covering pages with thoughts little worth noting, and of hiding an intrinsic poverty of invention, by grim or monotonous eccentricity."[69]

In the year 1843, the Hungarian violinist, Joseph Joachim, then a boy of twelve, gave his first public concert. It took place in Leipzig, with the great Mendelssohn himself at the keyboard. Joachim stayed on in Leipzig to study at the conservatory with Ferdinand David. Schumann, too, came to know and admire the prodigy.

Late in 1844, Schumann went on to Dresden, where he remained until 1850. That year, he transferred again, this time to Düsseldorf to take up the post of town music director, which he held until the final onset of the insanity that took him to an asylum for the last few years of his life (he died in 1856).

Joachim had meanwhile gone on to a performing career that gained him international renown. In 1853, he entered upon a long term of service as concertmaster of the royal orchestra at Hanover. In October of that year, he was scheduled to come to Düsseldorf for a first reading of Schumann's Fantasy in C for Violin and Orchestra, op. 131. (This work, as well as the Violin Concerto in D minor, composed this same year, were specifically for Joachim.) As Schumann awaited the arrival of Joachim, he had with him his pupil, the composer Albert Dietrich (1829–1908), and also Johannes Brahms, who, a young man of twenty, had just met the Schumanns through the recommendation of their mutual friend, Joachim. Robert and Clara had been impressed by the work of the young Brahms. And now Schumann suggested to Dietrich and Brahms that they join with him in the composition of a sonata to be presented to Joachim as a gift on the occasion of his visit. Each movement was to contain the motif F-A-E, to symbolize Joachim's motto, *Frei aber Einsam* ("Free but lonely"). Schumann provided the second and fourth movements (Intermezzo and

Finale), Dietrich the opening Allegro, and Brahms the Scherzo third movement.[70]

Joachim's concert took place on October 27; the next day, the F-A-E sonata was given to Joachim. The whole affair is reduced somewhat to a whimsy of Schumann, by virtue of the fact that he immediately set to work to compose another two movements to round out a full sonata of his own authorship. The entire birth period of his sonata extended from October 22 to November 1, according to indications by Schumann himself.[71]

It was in February, 1854, that Schumann threw himself into the Rhine, was rescued, and soon after sent to the asylum near Bonn where he ended his days. Joachim, in the year 1906, had the Brahms movement of the F-A-E sonata printed, but not the Schumann and Dietrich movements.[72] The entire collaboration sonata was published in 1935,[73] but the four movements of Schumann's own complete sonata were neglected in the wake of Schumann's tragic final years until, in 1956, the work was edited from the autographs by O. W. Neighbour.[74]

The haste with which the first movement of the sonata was written (between October 29 and 31, judging from Schumann's diary)[75] seems to show in the music. Its slow introduction is filled with histrionic flourishes and exclamations, portending dramatic happenings in the Lebhaft body of the movement. The fast portion, however, expends all its energy in an endless chase of up-and-down skirmishes by piano and violin. There is little relief, and the effect is one of hectic activity, kept at such fever pitch that almost no progress can be made of it.

The second movement, also Lebhaft, is cast in a small form of the kind that usually serves Schumann so well. In this particular instance, however, the movement, tight-knit as it is, becomes embroiled in far too many bar-by-bar upsweeps in the piano and too many repetitions of a seesaw rhythmic pattern in the violin. The contrasting middle section affords some change in the texture of the piano line, but the violin part is too close to the pattern of the main section to permit enough vacation from the prevailing rhythmics of the movement.

The Intermezzo proudly waves the F-A-E banner, and derives from it a melody of rather pleasing ebb and flow. It lives up to its title, however, and gives the impression of a passing vignette, wandering and humming its way to the finale.

The finale, in "Marked and rather lively tempo," clearly means business. The F-A-E is flung out bravely at the beginning, and there is a fine show of activity by both instruments, culminating in a grand contest in arpeggios for the duo over the course of the last two pages of the sonata.

But the edge has been dulled by the somewhat similar calisthenic air of the first movement. Joachim was no doubt exercising a critical sense when he neglected to have the Schumann movements of the F-A-E sonata printed even a half-century after composition. In any event, the third sonata throws an interesting sidelight on Schumann's mental and musical climate in the twilight of his life.

5 ❧ *The Brahms Sonatas*

J OSEPH JOACHIM was two years older than Johannes
Brahms. The two men met in 1853, Joachim already an internationally
renowned violinist, the twenty-year-old Brahms just starting to make his
way in the musical world. Brahms was in Hanover (where Joachim was
newly installed in the service of the royal court) in the course of a concert
tour in which he was accompanying the Hungarian violinist, Eduard
Remenyi. (It was Remenyi's gypsyfied view of Hungarian music that inspired Brahms in his writing of the *Hungarian* dances—for two pianos—
published in 1869 and 1880.) Brahms and Joachim took an immediate
liking to each other, which ripened into a friendship that lasted—with an
interlude of estrangement—until the composer's death in 1897. As we have
seen earlier, Schumann, Brahms, and Dietrich collaborated in the writing
of a sonata in Joachim's honor that same year of 1853. Brahms already had
to his credit the E flat piano Scherzo, the first two piano sonatas, and his
first three sets of songs for solo voice. But his first extant ensemble composition is the movement for violin and piano that he contributed to this
sonata.

Brahms was born in Hamburg and studied piano and composition
there. His first break was the tour with Remenyi, which took him outside
the confines of Hamburg and brought him into contact with Joachim, with
Liszt, and—the tour having ended with an estrangement between Remenyi
and Brahms over Brahms's coolness toward the music of Liszt—finally with

the Schumanns at Düsseldorf. Schumann was immediately taken with Brahms as a person and as a composer. In October, 1853, he dashed off a short notice for the *Neue Zeitschrift für Musik*, the publication he himself had founded, but for which he had not written in some time. It was the well-known tribute to Brahms, whom he hailed as "an individual fated to give expression to the times in the highest and most ideal manner, who would achieve mastery, not step by step, but at once, springing like Minerva fully armed from the head of Jove."[76]

The young composer must have been doubly gratified to join with the distinguished Schumann in paying musical honor to Joachim. The latter had already expressed himself most warmly about Brahms in a letter to the younger man's parents, in July, 1853: "His purity, his independence, young though he is, and the singular wealth of his heart and intellect find sympathetic utterance in his music, just as his whole nature will bring joy to all who come into spiritual contact with him."[77]

Unlike the F-A-E movements of Schumann, the Brahms Scherzo conceals its dedicatory motive so that one is forced to guess its hiding place in the movement. I think that the accented quarter-note chords in the piano, measure 8, contain the motto in the form of F, E flat, A; and if E flat does not serve, then at least E natural has been heard enough in the preceding measures to merge it in sonority with the E flat:

Figure 5-1.   Mm. 1-9

If one leafs quickly through the volume of Brahms's violin sonatas, the Scherzo stands out visually. It looks less thick on the printed page than any other movement in the score, even those that correspond in the other sonatas to the scherzo type of movement. For one thing, the piano figuration is quite unluxuriant, never progressing beyond such flourishes as the following:

Figure 5-2.

a. Mm. 154-155

b. Mm. 209-210

Partially as a corollary of this spareness of texture, there is much less of the friction of opposing rhythms in this movement than in the later works. The intersectional contrast offered by the trio portion of the movement is limited by the Mendelssohnian congeniality of tone in that episode. Everything is cleared for action, for propulsion; in this dynamism, as well as in the 6/8 meter, I am reminded of the finale of the Horn Trio, to follow twelve years later. A couple of writers have taken exception to Brahms's instruction, *sempre ff e grandioso*, for the cadential reminiscence of the trio section at the very end of the Scherzo. It may, however, be that Brahms was indulging in a little verbal fun at this point, in a piece intended for a colleague who was, after all, scarcely older than himself and of quite compatible outlook. In any event, Joachim thought enough of the piece to resurrect it in print, as we have pointed out, after Brahms's death. Players today find it a worthwhile addition to the repertoire and an interesting bit of Brahmsiana.

In the years after the composition of the Scherzo, Brahms progressed through terms of service at the princely court of Detmold; a year as conductor of the Singakademie in Vienna; a certain amount of concert touring; and several years as conductor of Vienna's Society of the Friends of Music.

He had also progressed through a passionate attachment to Clara Schumann, which cooled (we can only guess at the reasons), after Schumann's death in 1856, to a friendship that endured until the end of Clara's life (1896); and other warm, though perhaps less serious, feminine attractions. In the production of ensemble music, over the years, there were the first piano trio, the two string sextets, the three piano quartets, the first cello sonata, the piano quintet, the horn trio, and the three string quartets. Not until 1879 did Brahms turn again—and certainly in a more serious frame of mind than in the 1853 instance—to the duo of violin and piano.

The first sonata, opus 78, was composed in the summer of 1879, the third consecutive summer holiday spent by Brahms at the little Carinthian village of Pörtschach, in southern Austria.

Sonata Number 1 in G major, op. 78

Karl Geiringer, in his book, *Brahms: His Life and Work*, says that, as a result of his experience in the writing of the First Cello Sonata, op. 38, "Brahms may have realized that with an even treatment of the two performers the stringed instrument is at a disadvantage when opposed by a full piano part." And that, in approaching the writing of the G major violin sonata, the lesson learned is reflected in the fact that "here the pianoforte part is thin and transparent, and as the violin part generally has the leading melody, the balance is displaced to the advantage of the stringed instrument."[78] This view of the violin sonata depends on two things: where you read, and how you play.

Consider the opening of the sonata:

Figure 5-3.   Mm. 1-2

All is transparency and light, and the violin is indeed prominent. Read ten measures later, however, to see this:

Figure 5-4. Mm. 10-12

Here, even though the piano part consists of just two lines of sound, the visual (and aural) effect is one of some thickness because of the convolutions of the individual lines, the wide spacing between them, and the opposing motion of one to the other. There is another thickening agent at work: the friction of contrasting phrase lengths and rhythmic groupings heard simultaneously between the violin and piano lines. In the three measures in question, the violin statements occupy one and one-half measures each:

Figure 5-5. Violin, mm. 11-13

As we have shown, each statement divides its first six beats into three groups of two beats each, followed by a concluding group of three beats. At the same time, the piano—also proceeding in units of one and one-half measures—

Figure 5-6. Mm. 11-13

paces itself by the half measure (i.e., three beats), but divides each such group in half again; the result, especially as emphasized by the repeated opposite-direction playing in treble and bass, is an effect of tight, triplet eighth-note groupings, as opposed to the broader, dotted-figure rhythms of the violin.

The complexity of Brahms's musical clockworks is intensified by the fact that, from the very beginning of the page, he has emphasized the integrity of the measure by metronomic tolling of the piano part in the opening measures (see Figure 5-3, and note that this chordal counting by the piano continues through the first nine measures of the movement). The measures shown in Figure 5-6 are doubly intricate because, in phrase and rhythmic unit, they muddy the clear-cut pattern so briefly outlined by Brahms in the preceding lines of music.

Muddy is too strong a term, and applies only if the pianist slams into the eighth-note rapids with all-too-stolid digits. Brahms really wants that transparency that Geiringer mentions. Yet, at the same time he wants sinews of rhythmic conflict to run through the clearer tissue of the sound and give it vitality. The layers of motion in this kind of writing move with some freedom against and around each other, pull and rub and stretch in the process. A neat illustration comes just a few measures later on in the movement: the violin part moves from a steady, three-to-the-bar rhythm into a composed retard, or broadening, while the piano continues, seemingly implacable, with its four-to-the-bar pulse. Yet, both instruments meet at the musical crossroads.

Figure 5-7. Mm. 14-21

It is important to bring out the cross-grained rhythms, rather than to neutralize the differences between lines by playing for the unchanging 6/4 pulse. Any move in that direction will produce a lumpy, "counted" effect; for example, in measures 11 and 12, you should hear this:

Figure 5-8. Mm. 11-12

not this:

Also, you have to know when to count by the bar, when by the larger unit. For example, in measures 25 through 35, the phrasing scheme is cast in a sequence of 1-1-2½-1½-5[(3+2)] measures, as shown in the following marked example:

Figure 5-9. Mm. 25-36

Actually, the violin rarely has the melody all to itself. Consider, for example, the sequence beginning in measure 70; scanning the successive measures, you find that the melodic prominence is distributed as follows:

Violin and bass line	2 measures
Piano	2 measures
Violin and bass line	2 measures
Piano alone	1 measure
Violin alone	4 measures (ending measure 81)

I am trying to show the incredible richness of detail that Brahms builds into this music. No matter how swiftly it was composed, there is a fair measure of midnight oil in the brew. And in no other kind of music must the performers work as assiduously to keep the labor—the composer's and their own—from showing. The music must sound easy in conception and execution; it must sound as gracious as, indeed, it is.

As to whether the violin predominates, perhaps it does to a degree. But there are so many measures like the following,

Figure 5-10. Mm. 25-27

where the melodic line is obviously a team presentation. Or, immediately afterward (cf. measures 29-30), there is the passage where piano takes over the solo role, while violin assumes the accompanying voice that had originally been that of its partner. In some measures both instruments double each other, for the richer sonority that results:

Figure 5-11. Mm. 42-43

Or that most spectacular demonstration of equal rights for both instruments: the passage exactly midway through the movement where there is almost note-by-note interchange between the two instruments:

Figure 5-12. Mm. 123-124

As shown, the violin and piano treble account for a continuous braided line (it is difficult to call it two lines, even though there are continuous divergences, one from the other). And the piano bass supports the activity of the upper voices while adding a rhythmic-harmonic strand of its own to the musical web.

It cannot be emphasized enough that, in performance, this music must be brought to a simmer and not to a rolling boil. The linear aspect must be ever prominent, the percussive attack on chord or line held to the very minimum consistent with intensity. This movement—and the entire sonata —is based, not only in letter but in spirit, on Brahms's own song settings, the *Regenlied* ("Rain Song") and *Nachklang* ("Reminiscence"), op. 59, nos. 3 and 4.[79] Contained in a set of eight songs composed in 1871 to 1873, these two are set to poems by the poet and close friend of Brahms, Klaus Groth. In those poems, raindrops, tears, and nostalgic reverie mingle in parallel lines of imagery. Intensity and subdued musing move side by side. So it must be in the sonata inspired by the songs.

Histrionics and self-conscious declamation are clearly out of place here. Musically, our clue comes from such passages as that beginning in measure 60. Following upon a second theme in bright D major (the "regulation" tonality in a movement written in G major), this new episode, cast initially in a cool B major, then moving on to even more sober harmonies, puts a damper on any excessive fervor that may have been awakened by earlier experiences in the movement. The rather stationary rhythmic pattern of this passage contributes to the restful effect:

Figure 5-13.   Mm. 58-62

The development opens with piano in command (the violin, in pizzicato, shares with the bass line the chordal accompaniment originally handled by the piano alone). And surprisingly, the key is G major! It is as though we are starting to play a written-out repeat of the exposition section. Only gradually does Brahms move us, by the wash of harmony and by increasing density of texture and complexity of rhythmic interplay between lines, from a feeling of rest and security to the crush of activity already shown in Figure 5-12. There is some musical lightning to be dealt with in the development, concentrated in measures 107 to 133. The voltage, however, should be moderate, keyed to the realistic limits of violin sound in writing of this kind. Note, for example, how the violin's middle register is used in measures 115 ff.; the balance of sound must be gauged to let the violin be a truly audible third voice.

Figure 5-14.   Mm. 115-117

Immediately after the peak of activity (see measures 131 to 133) there is a fortepiano, a dramatic drop in excitement, the composer's instruction leggiero ("lightly, easily") in the score, and a long, ruminative transition back to the return of the movement's beginning. Throughout, the pianist should be guided by the kind of thinking discerned in Brahms's own playing in the decade that produced this sonata:

> He never aimed at mere effect, but seemed to plunge into the innermost meaning of whatever music he happened to be interpreting, exhibiting all its details . . . [80]

Violin and piano both have brilliant high registers. Thus, Brahms's deliberate choice of tonal palette, in the Adagio of this sonata, cannot be lost upon us. The emphasis is on the middle and low registers; and the brief episodes in the higher layers of sound are set off in relief against the prevailing sobriety of tone. The highest note touched in the entire movement is

(measure 41, piano part), and it is only a brief peak in the line, actually an octave doubling of a fanfare figure played in lower register by both piano and violin. Only in eleven other measures does the music reach peaks in the E-string register of the violin, and never higher than

Some of the high points come in the course of the fanfare motive referred to above. And the feeling for light and shade in the writing can

be seen in the different kinds of coloration of register and profile in which
that motive is presented to us (see also measures 42 and 49):

Figure 5-15.

a. Mm. 24-26

b. Mm. 61-62

Of course, there is one more version—the most important, because it is
the origin of the fanfare—the completely limpid and tranquil use of the
dotted-eighth-sixteenth rhythm in the principal subject of the movement:

Figure 5-16.   Mm. 1-4

For this writer, the ultimate clue to the performance of this movement comes in the violin part in measures 67 ff. Here, in the tone of the
beginning of the movement (Adagio, come prima), the violin takes up
the piano's original role and, in double-stops, carries out a thematic statement that had first been presented in multiple-stop chords by the keyboard.

The extremely clinging bow stroke needed to play this kind of passage on the violin,

Figure 5-17.   Violin, mm. 66-72

coupled with the mellow resonance of the violin's two lower strings, is a retroactive model for the pianist in measures 1 ff. If ever the pianist needed the "feel" of a bow rather than a key, with all the legato sustaining quality that that implies, it is in this movement; conversely, the violinist must, through artful use of the left hand, simulate the relative ease with which the keyboard can present two simultaneous, yet distinct, lines of tone.

For this performer, it is the richly colored restraint of a movement such as this, rather than more forcefully voiced chapters, that represents the most individual and characteristic side of Brahms. The critic, Hanslick, said about this side of the composer:

> There is no seeking after applause in Brahms's music, no narcissistic affectation. . . . But with Schumann's music it shares, to the point of stubbornness, a sovereign subjectivity, the tendency to brood, the rejection of the outside world, the introspection.[81]

The finale of this sonata, Allegro molto moderato, is—of all three movements—the most closely derived from the two songs that inspired the work. The opening violin strain is a direct quote from the voice lines of *Regenlied* and *Nachklang*; and the piano accompaniment is similarly a quote from the piano part of the two songs; there is a visual change, in that the note values have been halved (sixteenth taking the place of eighth, and so forth), and the music rebarred so that two measures of the song now occupy but one measure of the sonata. The tempo indication is faster than the "measured, restful motion" of *Regenlied*, or the "tenderly moving" pace of *Nachklang*. On the other hand, Brahms has qualified his allegro with the instruction, "very moderate," and it is in this frame that the movement should be played.

Figure 5-18.   Finale, mm. 1-2

The patter of the sixteenth-note accompaniment is rarely absent in this finale. And, as is usually the case with a well-contrived "accompaniment," the part serves as protagonist as much as in a supporting role. To put it another way, both violin and piano must play with such easy grace, and with such attentiveness to the parallel voice, that it should be impossible to decide whether the slower-moving violin line is the principal voice, resting against the foliage of the piano part, or whether, instead, the violin line is the structural frame upon which the thematically important piano part is draped. The two parts are actually of equal importance, for it is the blended texture of both that comes to the ear.

Brahms stresses this equality in a particular passage that recurs several times during the movement. Here, a quarter-note pulse, deriving from the violin line, is heard constantly; also constant is a sixteenth-note pattern that obviously comes from the piano voice. And, as is evident from the example given below, the two patterns are built up from a composite of piano and violin, intertwining with each other, interchanging roles in regularly alternating fashion:

Figure 5-19.   Mm. 9-11

Notice something else about this passage: each group of sixteenths leans toward, and resolves its motion on, the following quarter note. Thus, in addition to the beat-by-beat pattern, there is a larger pattern that arises from the overlapping of the two-beat units. A further result is that one gets a sensation of small wavelike motions in these measures; and this contrasts nicely, yet in kind, with the small-stepped pattering of the "raining" sixteenths in the rest of the movement.

In fact, a close look at the opening passage of the movement shows that Brahms is very much involved in a study in various wave lengths, playing with the liquid friction between simultaneously running and merging, contrasting ripples of sound. The piano part at the opening, for example, starts in broad waves, then moves to smaller shapes. The violin, at the same time, is moving in ways that reflect the changing pace of the piano part, but simultaneously—especially because of the longer note values in the violin line—sets up a melodic path that spans the entire length of the opening-phrase complex:

Figure 5-20.   Violin, mm. 1-9

The bass line of the piano part in these measures reinforces the motion of the violin, while the constant sixteenths of the treble emphasize the smaller details of that voice.

That Brahms, the pianist, is after all piano oriented, shows in the way a pianistic rhythmic figure is assigned to both piano and violin; in any event, the violinist must contrive to play the figure with the same ease and crispness that the pianist will naturally afford:

Figure 5-21.

a. Mm. 29-30

b. Violin, mm. 34-35　

Many a violinist will think unkind thoughts, especially when playing the last half of the second measure in this example. The pianist, playing the same figure in the corresponding spot of his example, is bound to sound the winner.

The main subject of the second movement reappears in the finale, both at measures 83 ff. and toward the very end of the movement, measures 149 ff. Look at the treble line of the piano part,

Figure 5-22. Mm. 149-150

and see that it is consistent with the sixteenth-note figuration that has been in force throughout the movement. Look again, and note that it also harks back to the accompanying rhythm in the second movement (see Figure 5-16); realize further that the rhythm actually goes back to the melodic-accompanying eighth notes of the first movement (see Figure 5-4). The attachment of the entire sonata to the precepts of the song models is apparent.

The last episode (Più moderato) of the finale does much to bind the several aspects of the sonata into one last, nostalgic summation. The feeling of quiet, yet yearning ease must be made apparent in these lines, especially at the hushed close:

Figure 5-23. Mm. 161-164

It is with mingled amusement and agreement that we append here some lines from the rather flowery biography of Brahms by the composer's younger contemporary, Richard Specht. The imagery is highly colored, but the thoughts will nevertheless be helpful to the performer:

> An essay ought to be written on . . . that tender magic with which the sweetly monotonous trickling of summer showers captivated the master's mind; . . . that warmly veiled, cosily melancholy mood engendered by the lulling music of raindrops on the window panes . . . [82]

Sonata Number 2, in A major, op. 100

Like its fellow sonatas, this work is a summertime creation. In the years since the composition of the first sonata (1879), Brahms had produced such works as the Piano Concerto in B flat, the Viola Quintet in F, the third and fourth Symphonies, the *Academic* Overture, the Piano Trio in C major, vocal ensembles, choral works, including *Nänie*, and a goodly number for solo voice. There were no compositions for piano alone during this period, nor would he turn again to such medium until the 1890s, in the twilight of his life.

The summer of 1886 was the first of three consecutive holidays that Brahms was to spend at Lake Thun, in the Bernese region of Switzerland. Here, near the home of his good friend, the Swiss poet and playwright, Joseph Viktor Widmann, and in the company of other close acquaintances, Brahms enjoyed the climate, the scenery of water, field, and mountain, and —composed. The output included a felicitous triumvirate: the Cello Sonata in F, op. 99; the Violin Sonata in A, op. 100; and the Trio in C minor, op. 101.

The A major sonata is sometimes nicknamed *Die Meistersinger*, because of the chance similarity between the beginning of the opening theme of the sonata and the melody of the Prize-Song from the Wagnerian opera. The similarity is obvious—and inconsequential. What *is* important is the beautifully imaginative treatment of the duo in this work. What can be more pleasurable for the violin than to respond, in succinct echo, at the end of each phrase in the opening piano statement? Rarely have so few notes been put to more effective use!

Figure 5-24. Mm. 1-5

And, of course, the pianist enjoys the same delight in his turn, though he has the more difficult task of assuming the echo role in midstream:

Figure 5-25. Mm. 24-25

Another fine thing about this movement is that it mingles with its tenderness such free and open gesture. The range and lift of the principal theme, seen in the outlines of Figure 5-26, are fulfilled, extended, and realized in the simple, yet wonderfully energetic, phrase that bursts forth in measure 31:

Figure 5-26. Mm. 30-34

The violin line combines stability (first two measures) with forward energy (last two measures). At the same time, the piano underscores the gesture of the violin part with the close chordal responses in each measure.

The faithful collaboration between the two instruments continues in the second subject (measures 51 ff.). The violin eventually takes over the lead, including (as had the piano) a rhythmic subepisode that will serve well in the middle section of the movement,

Figure 5-27.   Violin, Mm. 75-76

and both go on to introduce a codetta motive of similar importance:

Figure 5-28.   Mm. 77-80

In the development sections, the first and codetta subjects (but not the second theme) are utilized, not only in their entirety, but also with singling out of the component elements of each theme. (For example, the first theme yields two rhythmic ingredients:

and

,

each of which is given separate emphasis in the development.) Also, the pacing of intensity is very carefully controlled in the development process. In short order, we are moved from a quiet and contemplative musing on the first subject to a forte outburst on the broader rhythm of the theme,

Figure 5-29.   Mm. 108-113

and on into even more forceful exploitation of the codetta theme:

Figure 5-30.   Mm. 124-127

From this peak, and always on the codetta subject, we descend, through the rest of the section, but more in volume level than in density of texture (for both instruments—and all three lines—remain quite active until measures 149 ff., where the activity slows to a reflective walk), to the recapitulation in measure 158. That return, moreover, dispenses with the warm-up statements and echoes that marked the opening of the movement. Now, with the earlier experiences of the movement behind him, Brahms goes succinctly through the subject matter at hand. He extends himself, however, at the end of the codetta. Literally so, for a moment; the codetta rhythm is enlarged to ruminative proportions, as shown by the following excerpts:

Figure 5-31.

a. Mm. 211-212

b. Mm. 229-230

Then, in compensation, the music is driven on more quickly than ever, in a Vivace section that carries through triumphantly to the double-bar. One thing is not clear from the score, but should be read into the music of this episode: the passage from measure 259 to 267, introduced and closed

by a poco ritard, should not be taken at the Vivace clip. It is a momentary
and idyllic reminiscence of the opening and should be played at corresponding tempo. Where Brahms has indicated *a tempo*, measure 268, the
Vivace pace should be resumed and carried forward with mounting vigor
to the end.

Those who have heard or played the Hymn of Thanksgiving movement
of Beethoven's Quartet in A minor, op. 132, or the Quasi menuetto movement of Brahms's own Quartet in A minor, op. 51, no. 2, will know the
problem of relating alternating sections of contrasting mood and tempo
and meter within the frame of a single musical chapter. Brahms chooses
to follow a similar plan in the Andante tranquillo of the present sonata;
and the problems are the same. In A-B-A-B-A sequence, Brahms alternates
an Andante (F major—though the second A-section opens momentarily in
D major) and a Vivace (D minor) section. Brahms himself eases the transition from Vivace to Andante by composing a slow-up into the end of
each Vivace section:

Figure 5-32. Violin, mm. 62-71

More difficult is the handling of mood. The slow sections are actually the
radiant ones, though reflective and deliberate; the Vivace episodes, on
the other hand, are more bittersweet than gay, despite tempo and the
dancelike snap of the rhythmic pattern:

Figure 5-33. Mm. 16-19

Actually, the contrasting segments must be played as though there is some
cross-influence between them. For there is an enigmatic quality, an ambivalence about this kind of movement, compounded rather than resolved by
the way the final snatch of vivace moves suddenly and at last irrevocably
(in measure 165) away from D minor to F major:

Figure 5-34. Mm. 162-168

The final Allegretto grazioso (quasi Andante) is 158 measures long. It is not until measure 132 that the violin hits high G on the E-string. The upward progress is slow and measured:

E (i.e., "open" E pitch)   measure 38
A   measure 45
G   measure 78
A and C sharp   measures 93 and 94, 107 and 108
D   measure 128

The entire opening of the movement (at least to measure 34) is focused almost exclusively on the G-string. As in the second movement of the first sonata, Brahms seems intent—at least for the violin—in emphasizing the rich color of the low register, rather than the brilliant sound of the higher notes. Through much of this Allegretto, one has the feeling that Brahms is thinking of a trio setting, where the violin takes an often prominent role, but placed in the center of the trio sound, with the treble and bass lines of the piano providing a frame of sound around the violin line.

A difficulty with this movement is that it becomes embroiled in the thickness and richness of its timbre. The principal theme area recurs three times, framing the movement and alternating with two extensive contrast sections:

Figure 5-35.

a. Violin, mm. 1-5 (principal theme)

b. Violin, mm. 36-39 (first contrast theme)

c. Violin, mm. 90-93 (second contrast theme)

d. Violin, mm. 125-127 (first contrast theme, modified by elements from the second contrast theme)

Although the piano casts considerable coloration through the movement, and especially in its ascending pyramids of sound in the sections beginning measures 31 and 123,

Figure 5-36. Mm. 31-32

and the two instruments together whip up a fair pitch of excitement in the music around measure 90, the prevailing tone of the movement is ruminative rather than riotous. This must be recognized, and the warmth and lyricism of the movement played for all it is worth. When Brahms reflects, he is not to be jarred or stung into false frenzy.

Sonata Number 3, in D minor, op. 108

The last of the Brahms violin-piano sonatas was composed also at Thun, beginning in 1886 and ending in the summer of 1888, the last year of Brahms's visits to that city. This sonata is the only one of the three to bear a dedication: to Hans von Bülow, the pianist-conductor who had known

Brahms since 1854. Von Bülow had been a fervent supporter of Richard Wagner until that worthy won away von Bülow's wife, Cosima (daughter of Franz Liszt). Betrayed by the man he had revered, von Bülow found a new musical hero in Brahms.

In addition to his well-earned fame as a composer, Brahms enjoyed the comradeship of a warm circle of admiring friends. Brahms was, however, a mixture of the gruff and the considerate, at least in his later years. Even with the closest of friends, he could have fallings-out, sometimes through lack of perspective on his own part, sometimes through circumstances not of his own making. In the case of von Bülow, the dissension arose in late 1885, when Brahms conducted the Frankfurt premiere of his own Fourth Symphony, either not realizing or not caring that von Bülow was soon to bring his orchestra from Meiningen to Frankfurt to have the honor of presenting the work to that city for the first time.[83] It may have been in order to facilitate, or signalize the resumption of, cordiality between the two men that Brahms decided to dedicate the third sonata to his old friend.

Certainly the work would have appealed to von Bülow, the pianist. There is, at the opening of the sonata, a marvelous sense of space, of expectation, of infinite prospect; and this is largely the doing of the piano part—moving for most of the first page in interleaved rhythms (bass line on the beat, treble consistently in syncopation). Many of these measures, including those at the very start, achieve this effect with simple successions of parallel octaves between the two lines. And above this is the violin line, moving alternately in long breaths, then in short:

Figure 5-37. Mm. 1-5

The line, marked sotto voce by Brahms, and paced by him with carefully positioned swell marks, is remarkably long; despite sighs and gasps built into the music,

Figure 5-38. Mm. 16-18

there is really no breath of rest until measure 24. And then, breaking in like a crash of doom, the piano launches into an ominous metamorphosis of the opening idea. Step by step, the building of the musical structure is done by violin and piano in an indissoluble partnership. There is no need to exhort ensemble alertness from the duo in passages like the following; the lines are so interwoven by the composer that there is no way to play them but ensemble:

Figure 5-39. Mm. 35-38

When the violin is silent, it can still be heard! The piano has both theme and accompaniment in the second subject (measures 48 ff.); so lyrically is the theme contrived, however, so luxuriant the two-handed accompaniment—the pianist must weave around his own projection of the theme—that one easily loses sight of the violinist's absence. And when the violin takes up the theme, in measures 62 ff., it is more a new coloration of a familiar idea than the intrusion of a new instrumental voice.

Speaking about new sidelights on familiar ideas, the already effective device of the interwoven octaves in the accompaniment at the start of the Allegro (see Figure 5-37) is magically transformed by Brahms at the beginning of the development, simply by virtue of adapting the figure to the technical possibilities of the violin. Now, instead of the wide-spaced octave parallels, interleaved eighth notes march out in diverging lines from the starting point of an open string:

Figure 5-40. Mm. 84-87

So intriguing is the effect of the alternating resonance of the open A and the stopped color of the intervening notes, that Brahms contrives to reach a similar situation some measures later (measures 96 ff.), where he follows the same procedure around the open E-string. But the open-string resonance is a passing factor. The whole development is verdant, in any harmonic area, and equally on piano and violin, with the oscillating, undulating eighth-note patterns. The first theme, as we were introduced to it at the beginning of the movement, is present only in half-light, in snatches, in passing glimpses. It is the stream of eighths that carries us along; and in retrospect, we realize that the "accompaniment" at the beginning of the sonata was as much thematic as the more "melodic" violin part.

As if to signalize this fact, the recapitulation presents the theme to us an octave lower than its original statement, embedded now in the constantly twining eighths:

Figure 5-41. Mm. 130-132

I have spoken much of the eighths; but through these patterns, supporting them, can be heard the drumming pulse of the quarter beats. This was especially apparent at the beginning of the development (see Figure 5-40). And when, at the end of the movement, we are finally released from the hypnotic spell of the ever-tolling eighth notes, it is to find ourselves resting, narrowing our aural vision on the frame of quarters:

Figure 5-42. Mm. 253-257

Finally we are released from the quarter notes as well, rising to light and air through linear, then at last chordal, arpeggios:

Figure 5-43. Mm. 262-264

The Adagio of this sonata is one of those movements that defies description. I am tempted to call it a "simple song." Simple, because it is short; songful, because you feel like singing it. But it is too expansive, too continuous within its brevity to lend itself to any easy label. I have the feeling that there is no real break in all seventy-five measures of the movement. To write breathy, short-phrased musical doggerel is not too hard. But to write a long-spanned melody that keeps the ear in expectation until the last note: that takes doing. The peak of the movement should be placed at the area around measure 69; and the violinist should be careful that here, as well as at corresponding earlier passages leading up to this high point (measures 21 and 53), the forte is not raspy, but gauged to the sound capacity of the instrument, with the piano's dynamics adjusted to suit:

Figure 5-44. Mm. 59-60

In the discussion of the second movement of sonata 2, I referred to the Quasi menuetto movement of the A minor string quartet of Brahms. The same reference suggests itself now in relation to the third movement, *Un poco presto e con sentimento*, of the third sonata. Specifically, the point of comparison would be that of mood. The quartet movement alternates between slow passages of sober and nostalgic tone and Vivace sections that are fleet-footed and gay in effect. The sonata movement combines the sobriety, lightness, and swiftness all in one continuous movement (i.e., without the sectional changes in tempo). The gaiety is gone. This is a hushed, twilit movement, with a few outcroppings of louder sound that serve to intensify the effect of the returned quietness. The eerie effect of the quiet passages is dramatized by the way in which one instrument echoes each strong beat in the melodic pronouncements of the other:

Figure 5-45.

a. Mm. 1-3

b. Mm. 33-34

The consistent, "thematic" use of this answering device can be seen in the fact that one of the loud points in the movement retains this deployment of the two instruments:

Figure 5-46.　Mm. 63-69

Except for a certain thickness even in this airy movement, it might be counted—and certainly should be played as—one of Brahms's most Mendelssohnian moments. Especially the ending, where the music evaporates into nothingness:

Figure 5-47.   Mm. 176-181

There is a scene in Douglas Moore's opera, *The Devil and Daniel Webster*, where the ominous visitor, under the alias, Mr. Scratch, lives up to his name by his manner of playing the violin. The opening measures of the Presto agitato finale of the third sonata of Brahms can easily bring out the Mr. Scratch in any violinist. There is overwhelming temptation to lay into the eighth-note passage at the beginning with more vigor than care:

Figure 5-48.   Mm. 1-4

The very joy of swinging the bow in a hearty arc of string crossings encourages the meat-ax approach; more fury than sound is the result. Think not so much of individual double-stops as of linear motions that lead from one important tone to the next, as shown in Figure 5-48. A certain restraint is all the more necessary because the "chopping" eighth-note figure is thematic; it will recur so often, in various forms and in both piano and violin, right up to the end of the movement, that a forced and harsh manner of interpretation will quickly bore and annoy the listener.

Besides, it should be recognized that, in these first measures, the violin figure serves as an accompaniment to a more sustained piano line—itself an introduction to an introduction. The movement is in D minor; the opening revolves, not around D, but around the dominant of that key, A. The first four measures seem to spring from the middle of things, and to prelude the more definite stance taken by measures 5 ff. This entire passage, in turn, seems to take its reason for being from its drive to the restatement, in D, of the opening strain. But that restatement refuses to assert itself fully. It cannot, for its cadence (like that in measure 4) is so peremptory and has so much rhythmic pressure built up behind it by the preceding measures, that it must imply further action, rather than rest and stability. This is a hell-for-leather movement, which, even in its quieter moments applies the goad of rhythm to suppress any thought of complacent ease. The noble second theme, first stated by the piano, is in broad duple, but the lopsided rhythmic undercurrent creeps in to keep things at proper pitch:

Figure 5-49. Mm. 40-44

And when the violin takes over, there are three opposing lines of rhythm to lend a seething activity to the texture of the passage: duples in the violin, triples in the bass, and syncopated triples in the treble.

Figure 5-50. Mm. 60-62

To make this kind of writing sound "right" calls for combined insistence and appeasement: the pianist must work for rhythmic clarity in each hand, yet also the two lines must merge into a larger, continuous pattern; and so also the violinist must project his line clearly—after all, it is the continuation of the second subject—and at the same time mold it plastically to the rhythms of the piano, and especially to that of the bass line, whose pulse it opposes.

   Both players will gird themselves for a contrapuntal skirmish in the passage beginning (or continuing) in measure 107. For some measures, the violin has been jousting with the piano (at least with the bass line); now, what with the violin entering first (last beat of measure 107), and the piano entering in canonic imitation on the second eighth of measure

108, it would appear that the two are to remain locked in combat for a while. But Brahms has the piano change pattern immediately (second half of bar 108), so that, instead of fighting each other, the two instruments give the impression of a continuous, four-parallel-octave band of sound; a robust, impressive ending to the exposition.

Brahms's fascination with a jagged, angular rhythm sometimes carries him to daring lengths. In the development he quickly finds a low point of excitement: an understated sauntering sequence, measures 134 to 141, based on the first subject. This gives way to a long passage that exploits the opposition of syncope against calmer rhythms: at first the principal theme in extension, then a tighter, on-beat pulse pattern. This passage (from measures 158 ff.) carries us to a fortissimo peak; then can no longer contain the necessary energy, and so is supplanted by writing that almost —but not quite—matches the ferocity and the avant-garde quality of the pugnacious triplet passages in Beethoven's Great Fugue:

Figure 5-51.   Mm. 180-183

The vehemence of this passage is so great that it overshoots the edge of the recapitulation; not until the "bridge" passage (cf. measures 17 ff., 190 ff.) can the music break away from the rhythmic barrage. Otherwise, no special surprises; just more of the nourishing brew until the brusque and flamboyant ending flings its way out of the piece with a grand, piano arpeggio, still in the basic eighth-note pattern of the movement.

6   Some French Sonatas of the Nineteenth Century and a Twentieth-Century Hangover: Fauré, Franck, Saint-Saëns, d'Indy

If the artist (composer, painter, writer, or what you will) cannot drive himself, then neither time, place, nor circumstance will do the job for him. Again, as after playing the sonatas of Bach, Mozart, and Beethoven, we find after experiencing the three sonatas of Brahms that we have dealt with a composer who worked himself hard. In Brahms's case, the working can be overdone, with the resulting music sometimes too densely woven, too full of meaningful ingredients and cross-references, too unleavened for its own good.

I do not think that any player will be able to accuse the pieces in the present chapter of such density. Each work, according to the temperament of its author, will betray some element of flightiness, of intellectual self-indulgence, of frivolousness or superficiality, or of pedantic thinking. I have gathered the composers together in this chapter because they are all of the French sphere of activity in the nineteenth century. How much of the several qualities of their music is owing to their Gallic context I shall leave to the theorist-historians. In my own view, the appeal as well as the defects of these sonatas traces to the mind of the composer. When the pen touches paper, the composer is locked into the processes of the work at hand. The glory and the responsibility is then his alone.

Gabriel Fauré

Let us begin with a medley of opinions about Gabriel Fauré. Though taken out of context, these comments somehow begin to sketch a group impression of the man and his music.

Rollo H. Myers, English musicographer:

. . . the danger of lapsing into banality (to which a composer not possessed of Fauré's instinctive good taste and natural tendency to understatement would inevitably be exposed) is . . . miraculously avoided.[84]

William W. Austin, American teacher and author:

When harmony, rhythm, and counterpoint are fully mastered by performers, the economical piano writing turns out to be quite warm enough, and invariably grateful for the instruments, though at first it may appear dry and abstract.[85]

Debussy, in a review he wrote in 1903 of a Paris concert:

The *Ballade* is almost as lovely as Mme. Hasselmans, the pianist. With a charming gesture she readjusted a shoulder strap which slipped down at every lively passage. Somehow an association of ideas was established in my mind between the charm of the aforementioned gesture and the music of Fauré.[86]

Paul H. Lang, eminent musicologist and critic:

. . . Fauré, is a composer of the tamest old-fashioned romantic hue, whom the generation of Schumann would not have denounced for his progressivism.[87]

Martin Cooper, English critic and author:

Fauré . . . was no revolutionary, no theorist, but that *rara avis* in the musical history of the second half of the nineteenth century, a musician pure and simple, with no gospel, no *Weltanschauung*, no carefully formulated aesthetic.[88]

Roger Ducasse, composer and pupil of Fauré:

The scheme he follows is well known? Granted; but he was endowed by the muses with the gift of ideas full of youth and beauty. Be the flask of crystal, earth, or gold, what matters it if the imperishable scent be there?[89]

Florent Schmitt, French composer:

. . . the music flows on with the same unconstraint and the same graceful ease, yet never appears to lack invention.[90]

Eric Blom, Swiss-born English critic and author and the editor of the fifth edition of *Grove's Dictionary*:

His own taste in music was faultless, whatever else may have been deficient; he is thus not a musician for the masses, and never will be, nor is he quite a musicians' musician, for all the impeccable finish of his technique, as far as it goes, since it does not go quite far enough for those who like masters who, they fancy, can do everything. But for a cultivated and civilized minority his music will remain a precious possession.[91]

It will be seen, from this bouquet, that praise is tempered with reserve, that a good point is set in opposition to a drawback, that there is some searching for solid ground on which to appraise the work of this composer. Blom, author of the last excerpt, goes—perhaps unconsciously—to rather hilarious lengths to provide a niche for the special genius of Fauré.

All this is by way of preparing the reader for something he probably already knows: Gabriel Fauré's music, while not especially difficult to play, is hard to interpret. It's largely a matter of physical and mental touch. If you approach this music with gross abandon, if you try to inject into it an intensity false to its nature, it will crumble—"splinter" has too brittle a connotation for this kind of writing—into nothingness. On the other hand, it is just as much a mistake to treat Fauré's music with excessive fastidiousness and preciosity; there is in it something of robustness and sensuality, as well as delicacy. It can (as is often the case with the *Requiem*) be rendered with more otherworldliness than is good for it.

Born in 1845, Fauré revealed musical talent in early childhood. He studied from 1855 to 1865 at the Niedermeyer School of Religious Music in Paris, benefitting especially from his work with Saint-Saëns there. In addition to periods of service as church organist in Britanny, and, later, in Paris, Fauré became a teacher at the École Niedermeyer in 1872. At the time of composing his first violin sonata, he was courting Marianne Viardot, daughter of the famed operatic singer, Pauline Viardot. It was for Marianne's brother, the violinist Paul Viardot, to whom it is dedicated, that the sonata was written in 1876. The first performance of the Sonata in A major, op. 13, with Fauré himself at the piano, took place at the Trocadero, in Paris, during the exhibition of 1878.[92]

The work had the dubious distinction of being accepted for publication by Breitkopf and Härtel on condition that there be no fee or royalties to the composer.[93] This fact is a reflection of the reception the work had received. And yet, Saint-Saëns, Fauré's teacher, in an article in the *Journal de Musique*, hailed the sonata for its "formal novelty, quest, refinement of modulation, curious sonorities, use of the most unexpected rhythms," and for its combination of "charm [and] . . . the most unexpected touches of boldness." It is Fauré's pupil, Émile Vuillermoz, who quotes this appraisal; and he, in turn, acclaims the "new proportions and unsuspected balances" of the sonata.[94]

Playing the opening pages of this sonata reveals a couple of problems quite soon. For one thing, the distinctive rhythmic units are generously and repetitiously used: the figure of the first few measures—for piano alone—

Figure 6-1.   Piano, mm. 1-5

is deployed a few times in quick succession, so that the relief of the ensuing quarter-note motion (measures 14 ff.) is most welcome when it comes. As can be seen in Figure 6-1, the melody is set against a constant frame of eighth notes. Really "constant"; for, if you scan the movement, you will see that there is hardly a measure that does not brim over with running eighths, or triplets. So insistent is this rhythmic wash that its absence, in three passages—one long, two short—(measures 77 to 85, 226 to 251, and 347 to 355)—stands out like an island of rest in the waves of sound.

Figure 6-2.   Mm. 82-88

Visually, the motion is unrelenting; so one must take care to "play in" the needed breaths and pauses where they belong, even though not indicated, for example, at the end of measure 50, measure 56, and measure 81 (but not after measure 85, even though it like measure 81 is marked, *poco rit.*). Also the successive pairs of measures at the end of the exposition, representing as they do suddenly broken, ascending wave patterns, should be separated from each other by a breath:

Figure 6-3.   Mm. 94-97

As much contrast as possible should be made between the upbeat impulse of the first subject and the on-beat emphasis of the second theme:

Figure 6-4.   Violin, mm. 57-60

This distinction is helped for a time by the fact that the piano part changes from eighths to triplets precisely with the entry of the second subject. Schmitt calls this "a more peaceful and tender melody,"[95] but the description can only hold true if the piano executes the triplets truly pianissimo, as background ripple to the violin.

The opportunities for some fine outbursts should not be missed in the long passages at measures 138 and 210 in the development, the very brief salvo at measure 242, and the exhilarating return to the recapitulation, beginning its assault march from measure 250.

After the sometimes heady wine of the Allegro, the Andante will come as an easier experience; though perhaps not for the pianist, who has handfuls of notes enough. What might have been a serious overdose of

rhythm, which can readily become cloying and sticky, is counterbalanced by frequent injections of the sterner rhythm of the opening:

And where Fauré combines the two patterns simultaneously,

Figure 6-5.   Mm. 20-21

the friction between the two should be brought out, rather than a too easy surrender to the overall steady patter of triplets that might otherwise result.

The Allegro vivo *is* a good movement! And really surprising, in view of its date of composition; it has the dry, crisp crackle and electric rhythm of a later idiom (jazz?). The player may wonder why Fauré chose to write in so fussy a meter as 2/8 (1), with four sixteenths filling the entire measure. The clue lies inside the parentheses: by making each short measure a single unit of beat, the composer can assemble sequences of measures into changing lengths of phrase. Reading from the beginning of the movement, for example, we find these combinations: 3-3-3-3-2-3-2-3-3-3-3-3-2-6-6 and so on. In short, Fauré achieves the effect of a freely changing meter without having to write so radical an indication in his metric signature. The added fillip of the offbeat chordal jabs from the piano, or the similar, pizzicato punctuation by the violin lends spice to the pattern and the sound.

Figure 6-6.   Mm. 11-19

Several lengthy passages of 3/4 writing break up the uneven tenor of the movement. Fauré's instruction, "One beat [of the 3/4] equals one [whole] measure of the preceding [section]," gives the clue—these triple-time passages give breathing room after the somewhat puppetlike twitchings of the 2/8 sections. And in every case, the material of the broader passages is an adaptation of the principal idea of the movement. This Allegro is fresh, effective, and fun to play.

Look at this passage:

Figure 6-7.   Finale. mm. 1-4

This is the beginning (for piano alone) of the finale of the Fauré sonata. Well and good: it is in A major, the key of the sonata. And now, look at the sequence beginning in the fifth measure, when the violin makes its entrance:

Figure 6-8. Mm. 8-11

This is enough to show something curious: the piano part continues to behave (at least at first) as though it remains in A major; the violin part, immediately enigmatic, hovers around C sharp; by the time it touches the F sharp in measure 10, aided by the piano chord in the preceding measure (which chord certainly seems to be the dominant seventh—C-sharp chord with the added B—of F sharp), we are already torn between the desire to ascribe the melody to A major and/or its relative minor, F sharp. The whole exposition repeatedly and strongly suggests this key, with the parent, A, hovering only elliptically in the shadows.

Even having the initial theme return at measure 141 in the guise of the opening does little to calm our puzzlement; it is "out of place" in such an entry, and harmonically it doesn't stay put for long anyway. Soon (measures 175 ff.) a short development flits across the scene; the initial theme, in fragment, is combined—mostly in two-bar, short-breathed units —with the triplet rhythms of the by now familiar piano accompaniment line; and above this, the violin spins a new melodic pattern, provided solely for the development, and cast in a 2/4 meter against the piano's 6/8. To even the score, the two instruments switch these opposing meters for the last few measures of the section (measures 200 ff.).

To keep us guessing, Fauré introduces the recapitulation with the first theme in C major (though still with the built-in ambiguities of tonality and mode). The second theme, which originally appeared in F-sharp minor, now (measures 253 ff.) is cast in A minor, thus righting the harmonic plan of the work—so far as the old ways of sonata construction are concerned. As though to fasten things firmly in place, the principal subject itself appears in A at measure 329. But it only suggests itself in fitful flashes. Fauré has the final goal in mind: a vivacious dash to the double bar in, at last, an unequivocal A major (measures 345 to end).

There is a fine feeling of pace and suspense in this movement. It should go like the wind (or at least a zephyr), in accord with Fauré's quasi-presto instruction; fast and light, so that the elliptic harmonies can be viewed always in passing, the succession of tonal suggestions receding into the distance as soon as they have been recognized. This kind of blurred-image viewing, coupled with lines that, after all, are clear enough in rhythmic detail (and should be played with utmost clarity), and with the topsy-turvy harmonic scheme of the movement, gives a dreamworld vividness to the movement, in fitting conclusion to a most interesting sonata.

Fauré's Second Sonata for Violin and Piano, op. 108, was composed in 1917 and dedicated to Queen Elizabeth of Belgium. The composer was then seventy-two; for some years (beginning, ironically enough, in 1903, when he became a music reviewer for Le Figaro[96]) he had suffered from a deafness that was—by 1917—quite advanced. This affliction, coupled with age, brought on his resignation, in 1920, as head of the Paris conservatory, a post he had held since 1905.

Deafness need not—consider Beethoven—limit the aural perceptiveness of the imagination. In Fauré's case, however, at least as far as this work is concerned, and certainly in regard to the second piano quintet (1921), which Florent Schmitt unaccountably hails as one of Fauré's greatest works (I have found it an overwhelming bore), the condition seems to have heightened his innate penchant for rhythmic repetition. As one scholar has pointed out, Fauré is not concerned with conventional development techniques—the pitting of opposites against each other in dramatic conflict in the middle portion of the chapter—in this kind of movement, but seeks instead a steady and gradual rise in intensity from beginning to end.[97] The considerable length of the movement, coupled with the tendency of the several themes to extend themselves too long and to blur the clarity of their shape as themes, and the lack of sufficient differentiation between the themes, tends to rob the movement of impact.

The finale suffers even more from this feeling of diffuseness, of energetic rambling. Schmitt, indeed, is moved to speak of this Allegro as "irritating" in its harping on E major, and "overdone" in its "continual imitations."[98]

The middle movement, Andante, based on a theme drawn from Fauré's Symphony in D minor, op. 40, composed in 1884 (but unpublished), is—for this listener—the most effective in the sonata. The fine-grained, easy rhythmic propulsion of the theme and the ruminative quality that Fauré seems to be seeking here are perfectly matched to one another. The sense of rambling is not less here than in the end movements; it is simply more at home in the slower-moving Andante.

All this is by no means to speak in utter rejection of the sonata; it is, to be sure, a serious work, tending more toward comfort and pleasant restfulness than toward intensity. The same adjectives apply to the playing (the sonata is demanding, but not exceptionally difficult). But players and listeners should not be exposed to it too often. Its magic has limited potency. And, though much closer to us in time than the first sonata, it seems older, more remote, and rather anachronistic.

César Franck

César Franck was born in Liège, Belgium, in 1822. Early studies at the conservatory there were followed by the course at the conservatory in Paris, whither the family had moved when César was twelve. Paternal pressure was strongly in the direction of a piano career (his brother Joseph was groomed for the violin), but Franck's own aim was consistently toward composition. Unfortunately, his composing was to be relegated to hours wrested from a busy schedule as teacher and church organist (he was organist and choirmaster at Sainte-Clotilde, in Paris, from 1858 until his death in 1890, and professor of organ at the Paris conservatory from 1872).

In 1848, Franck married; his wife, though from a theatrical family, had strong ideas about music, at least her husband's. The result was not always happy for the domestic circle in later years. Léon Vallas, in his biography of Franck, recounts the following:

> . . . if the Master poured out sounds that seemed to her too complex or bold she would throw open the dividing door and call to him: "César, I do not at all approve of that piece you are playing."[99]

We may marvel at the patience, and grow suspicious of the sense of proportion, of the composer who would tolerate such interference.

In any event, one of the works that aroused Mme. Franck's ire was from the composer's relatively small chamber-music output: the Piano Quintet of 1878–79. The turbulence and emotionalism of that composition was troubling not only to the author's wife, but to others as well (including Saint-Saëns, who was pianist at the premiere). Franck stuck to his own line of progress, however. The Sonata in A for Violin and Piano, written in 1886, has some flashes of the same dark temper that marks the quintet. The duo work was written for the violin virtuoso, Eugène Ysaÿe, and the pianist, Léontine Marie Bordes-Pène, champion of contemporary French music. These two artists presented the premiere performances at Brussels in November and December of that year; the Paris premiere, with the same players, followed in May, 1887.[100] The sonata won instant success, and has remained a favorite of the concert repertoire, though I do not think it is now heard as often as was the case a generation or so past.

The Franck sonata has color, strength, a fair measure of fire, and enough whimsy to keep the listener on the alert. It also has enough rhythmic repetition and thematic consistency from movement to movement (Vincent d'Indy speaks of its "new and remarkable application" of the "cyclic type of construction"[101]) to make it not only an extremely cohesive work, but also a dangerous one. In careless hands, it can sound banal, histrionic, and tedious, all at once. Let the hands, then, be careful.

The opening measures of the piano part contain, in fragmentary suggestion, the material from which the entire sonata will be constructed:

Figure 6-9.   Mm. 1-4

When the violin enters, in measure 5, it spells out in its melody the implications already raised by the piano:

Figure 6-10.   Violin, mm. 1-6

The pace and temper of the melody in this movement is a matter for some nice adjustment. It is difficult to agree with Vincent d'Indy's view of the tune as being "calm and happy."[102] At the same time, he is right to caution against too slow a performance of it. Franck himself casts the movement under an *Allegretto ben moderato* heading; and a sense of motion (at about $\downarrow$. = 92) seems appropriate. Without any wrenching of speed, the player must try to respond to the alternate poising and going of the line:

Figure 6-11.   Violin, mm. 13-16

It is this very indecisiveness of the line, coupled with the hesitant quality of the cadences at the frequent moments of pause in the melody, that keep one from assigning too sunny a feeling to the music. Moreover, the tempestuous manner of the piano solo that takes over from the violin's fortissimo cadence in the dominant (measures 30 and 31) is not calculated to reinforce any feeling of calmness. In these lines, too, the rapid pace of modulation (a characteristic trait of Franck, who would exhort his pupils to "Modulate, modulate!"—with, as one result, the exit of an annoyed young Debussy from his class) sends ripples of color across the surface of the sound, unsettling to any complaisance of ear or mind. In any event, it is the task of the violin, when it reenters (measure 47), to lead itself and the piano back to a brooding lassitude, dolcissimo. Here (measure 63), unlike the beginning, the piano supplies a background that is at once quieter and more moving than at the beginning; the touch must be extremely delicate:

Figure 6-12. Mm. 71-72

The second outburst by the piano (measure 89) is interrupted, and its force broken, by the "premature" entry of the violin (measure 97). An attempted resumption by the piano withers away. From measure 108 to the end of the movement, there is a brief, retrospective coda, ending—consistently—with a forceful/languid trailing away in the closing measures. The movement is curiously and deliberately vacillating in tone.

The second Allegro, on the other hand, is predominantly fury and determination. Again the piano begins; and again it sets the stage in the opening few measures. But this time it responds to the introduction itself, supplying the initial theme of the movement. The eye of the player must seek out what the ear will quickly comprehend: the melodic strand tucked into the foliage of figuration.

Figure 6-13. Mm. 4-5

During and after the violin's turn with the theme, the music moves forward on the raging current of the piano part. As though spreading oil on the waters, the violin ventures to spin out a broader line, obviously derived from the theme of the first movement:

Figure 6-14.   Violin, second movement, mm. 28-33

For both instruments, however, a feeling of resolve arrives with the second theme of the movement (measures 48 ff.) which, in a rather vague way, still suggests allegiance to the theme of the first movement:

Figure 6-15.   Violin, mm. 46-51

Themes have a way of emerging from, and merging into, each other in this work. (Indeed, one sometimes feels that the themes of one Franck composition manifest themselves again in the themes of another Franck composition; possibly this is owing to the fact that he was accustomed to warm up for the act of composition by playing enthusiastically through some of his earlier products—and Wagner.) For example, a "traveling" theme, one that tends to carry us along in the time-space of the movement rather than to insist upon itself in its own right,

Figure 6-16.   Violin, mm. 68-72

suggests the theme we have just visited, and, in turn, seems to engender the next point of rest and propulsion (measures 80 ff.), leading in its turn, eventually to a more impetuous thrust:

Figure 6-17.   Violin, mm. 94-97

These manifestations of the basic material of the sonata suffuse each other in what amounts to the development section in this movement. In the course of this development, the turbulence of the above figure is rendered more so by fracturing into sixteenth-note rhythm:

Figure 6-18. Violin, mm. 112-14

Eventually, after regulation review of materials in a recapitulation, this excited rhythm returns to drive the coda that closes the movement:

Figure 6-19. M. 206

The movement ends, incidentally, in D major after all, throwing a rosy glow over what has been a tumultuous experience. And, by the same token, continuing the ambivalent tone already created by the questioning ending of the first chapter of the sonata.

The title of the third movement, Recitativo—Fantasia, simply confirms the mood that has characterised the sonata up to this point. The way the Recitativo opens suggests actual continuation of the preceding movement; for the initial measures (as d'Indy points out) are a very direct quotation of the principal theme of the second movement.

Figure 6-20.

a. Violin, second movement, mm. 14-15

b. Piano, third movement, mm. 1-2

Recitativo, of course, refers to the freewheeling oration of the violin part, completely alone or in response to statements by the piano, in the opening episode of the movement. The wheeling, by the way, should not be too free; the stretto, where indicated by Franck, should be as poco as he stipulates, otherwise a very erratic effect will be attained, what with the ensuing rallentando. Discretion is the watchword.

Figure 6-21. Violin, third movement, mm. 7-10

The Fantasia refers, I think, to the way in which the movement passes the ideas of the sonata in review, sometimes clearly recognizable as derived from earlier occurrences, sometimes representing new metamorphoses of familiar elements. This is a strangely appealing movement, even more unsettling and unsettled than its predecessors; its dreamlike sequence of visions makes it the center of gravity for the entire composition.

The incestuous breeding of theme from theme reaches a threshold almost of pain when one arrives at the finale. The theme there is distinct enough, yet has a rather cloying shred of connection to the nuclear cell at the sonata's opening. One can easily lose any sense of annoyance about this redundancy in a feeling of pleasure at having, at last, a completely radiant melody to deal with. However, through much of the movement, you will find yourself looking over your shoulder; for you are being followed —or are you following? Many a duo will founder in this movement, as they lock into a chained circle of follow-the-leader:

Figure 6-22. Finale, mm. 1-5

Sanity, and justice to the composer, demand that each performer play his line as though it is not a shadow to that of his companion. For in that direction lies the danger of breaking the individual line into one- or two-measure bits, with a resulting shortness of breath that is infuriating to the ear, stultifying to the mind, utterly childish in effect. If attention is given to shaping the melody for its longest possible line, there will be no temptation to quicken the movement beyond the Allegretto poco mosso indication given by Franck; for, in this instance, as in so many others, excessive speed is used by the performer as a false solution to unresolved musical problems.

It may also prove helpful to think of the theme not as treated in canon, but in *unison*; the piano ordinarily leading the way *by itself,* with the violin reflection heard as the other self of the same line, a brilliant resonance, an atmospherically delayed view, another perspective of the original statement.

The eighth-note passages, later in this movement, are peculiarly difficult in their own way. Both the violin and piano, when each is confronted with this writing, must at all costs avoid any finger-exercise quality in the playing; again, the longest possible line should be the aim—certainly no break at all until the end of the fifth measure of the sequence:

Figure 6-23. Violin, finale, mm. 34-44

There is an unfortunate marking in the music at the middle and end of the movement: the accents over each quarter note in the passage at measure 87 (and again from measure 223, at the end of the movement):

Figure 6-24. Violin, mm. 87-90

This brings out the beast in a violinist, and the bow is immediately applied to each note with a stolid and unrelenting whack. Rare is the melodic line that can survive such flogging. Again, season ardor with taste; temper the

right hand, add warmth with the left, and use both with flexibility, so that
the line can have a shape beyond that of the quarter-note lump.

Another danger spot follows immediately after this passage in the
middle of the movement. It is only ten measures of the following kind of
writing:

Figure 6-25. Mm. 100-101

Short as it is, it can be disastrous if there is the slightest sense of frenetic
oompah from the piano, or overbearing focus on the single bar by the
violin. Delicacy, please!

Beyond this (and again, immediately following), there is only the
danger of getting lost in the modulatory thickets that threaten to overrun
the midsection of the movement. The eight measures, 109 to 116, can
sound aimless unless the pianist subtly drives forward to the momentary
harmonic goal (marked by the change of key, measure 117). The same
holds true for the two solo piano interludes (measures 133 ff., 151 ff.). In
general, both performers will have to keep firm view of the musical compass until they emerge into the daylight of A major at measure 185 and
head into the final section and peroration of the movement.

Even then, they have to deal with what Norman Demuth calls "one
of those unfortunate codas for which Franck and his period were so famous.
The vulgarity of this is usually enhanced by the lack of restraint shown by
the pianist and the energy displayed by the violinist to keep his end up."[103]

I have arrayed my discussion of this sonata with so many cautionary
warnings and predictions of dire happenings that the reader may get the
impression that I myself feel dubious about this work. Not at all; I would
most certainly not relish playing a second-hand imitation of such a piece;
in its own right, however, and as one of the most successful efforts of a
unique musical personality, the Franck sonata is a most gratifying experience. Treated with sensitivity, and with a freedom to match that of the
composer's invention, this sonata is completely convincing and quite at
home with other worthy compositions in the concert or home repertoire.

Camille Saint-Saëns

One look at the First Sonata for Violin and Piano, op. 75, (1885) of
Camille Saint-Saëns is enough to give you the impression that it is both
hard to play and forgettable. Then, if you listen to the recording of this
work by Heifetz and the pianist, Brooks Smith (RCA Victor LSC-2978),
you will still find the piece extremely difficult to perform, but will now
feel definite respect for the work. This is especially so in the case of the
second movement, the finale. But only virtuoso playing of this caliber (from
both sides of the duo) will reveal the brilliant edge of the work.

In the Second Sonata for Violin and Piano, op. 102 (1896), Saint-
Saëns' customary skill is again in evidence. The music is agreeable in its
late-nineteenth century, slightly spiced harmonic style, though not memorable in its themes. It has the recommendation of being playable by ordinary, skilled mortals, in contrast to the inordinate demands of Sonata 1.

Vincent d'Indy

Franck was, by all reports, a modest and unassuming person. As so often
happens, his chief disciple, having a vested moral interest in propagating
the master's musical outlook, proved holier and more self-righteous than
the object of his veneration. This was the case with Vincent d'Indy; he
led the circle of those who supported and encouraged the work of Franck
in the later years and—meticulous analyst and zealous teacher that he was
—had a large hand in disseminating the theory and process of that style of
composition. In his own musical efforts, the spark did not always survive
the energy and efficiency of the man.

The Sonata in C, op. 59, of d'Indy dates from 1904. The opening
Modéré has a fatal case of rocking 9/8 motion. In the Animé the rhythmic
flight is more successfully applied; this is a will-o'-the-wisp, though the flame
is of giant proportion. The Très lent is meditative, with the inevitable section in which the piano garlands up and down the keyboard. The concluding Très animé suffers again from rhythmic hypnosis, but now in a dotted
figure marking the half measure in 2/2 meter. An aroma of age and preciosity surrounds this work. The Franck sonata, so admired by d'Indy, is
fresh and new by comparison with the apostle's effort.

7 ❧ Some Scandinavian Sonatas: Gade, Grieg, Nielsen, and Others

In THIS CHAPTER, again, I have grouped several composers by region as well as chronology: they are Scandinavians all, with everything that that attribution has come to denote in the way of espousal of local musical traditions, reaction to or adaptation of the dominant Germanic musical heritage of the eighteenth and nineteenth centuries, and so on. Some of the music is mentioned here to warn the reader off; some, to urge him to take up again pieces that have fallen into undeserved neglect in recent years; still others, to register my own agreement with a strong current of approval in the musical community. I do not feel that the player will make startling musical discoveries in any of the compositions discussed below. In the best of these works, however, he will earn fresh and enjoyable sensations, none the less valid for being accompanied by a feeling of nostalgia.

Niels Gade

Robert Schumann wrote in 1843 about the work of the Danish composer, Niels Gåde. The young man of twenty-six had just come to Leipzig to study, was soon to become professor at the conservatory and to assist Mendelssohn with the Gewandhaus concerts, then—after Mendelssohn's death —succeed him for a year as director of the concerts before returning to take up a dominant role in the musical life of Copenhagen. At any rate, Schumann said of Gade:

> One hopes that the composer does not succumb to his own national-ism . . . that he will focus his attention on other areas of nature and life . . . [will] achieve originality and then cast it off as a snake casts off its old skin when it begins to grow too tight.[104]

Curious advice, especially when coming from a man of the fantasy and imagination of Schumann's stamp. Gade, nevertheless, seems to have taken this kind of counsel too much to heart in his own work, shaking originality off before he found it.

His Sonata Number 1, in A, op. 6, published in 1843, is a voice from the past. It is not regionally individual, nor is it a good imitation of German Romantic writing. The Sonata Number 2, in D minor, op. 21, is more palatable. Although dedicated to Schumann, it stands more in the shadow of Mendelssohn, especially in the final movement. Mendelssohn came by the style first, and more naturally. Unfortunately, I have not seen the third Gade sonata, from the year 1887. The reader might find some progress there beyond the temper of the first two works. In my opinion, he will do better to skip Gade entirely and go on to Grieg.

Edvard Grieg

Edvard Grieg, after his studies at the Leipzig conservatory (1858–1862), returned to his native Norway for a year, and in 1863 and 1864, went to the then cultural metropolis of Scandinavia, Copenhagen, where he came under the influence of Gade. From him he acquired the ambition to work in larger forms; and in Copenhagen and elsewhere, he also met and was inspired by his fellow Norwegians, the nationalist-oriented Rikard Nordraak (founding with him and others the society, Euterpe, to propagate Scandinavian music), and the dynamic, roughhewn violin virtuoso, Ole Bull, whose interest and performance centered so much on Norwegian folk music.

There is obviously a time lag in the impact of these successive influences upon Grieg's work. His first violin sonata, as an example, is an attempt to fill the old forms in old and—to Grieg—apparently uncomfortable ways. Opus 8 was composed in 1865; the second sonata, opus 13, was composed in July, 1867, the month after Grieg's marriage to his cousin, the singer, Nina Hagerup. Between the two works, there is an amazing distance. Grieg has cast off his inhibitions and his schoolish ways, and breaks into his own paths as composer.

The Allegro con brio of the Sonata in F, op. 8, is an interesting movement in its harmonic color. At the very opening, for instance, the piano begins with a sighing warm-up in E minor; whereupon the movement takes up its first theme and its proper key. Also, its themes are engaging. The drawback of the themes—and of the movement as a whole—lies in Grieg's hypnotic fascination with the meter (6/8) and his tendency to let a see-saw pattern grow from the duple swing of that meter. This up-and-down motion, manifest in the opening theme,

Figure 7-1. Violin, mm. 1-12

and in its companions and derivations, as for example, the bridge material and the second subject,

Figure 7-2.

a. Violin, mm. 34-37

b. Violin, mm. 58-63

is pleasant at first, but soon palls. The development, imaginatively contrived at its opening, cast in Andante and presenting the opening theme in F minor, spoils its chances by relying almost entirely on harmonic transposition, idea alternation, and much sequential repetition, instead of providing the dramatic oppositions and conflicts this kind of movement needs.

The Allegretto quasi Andantino is a simple, neat movement, not difficult to play, that would stand quite nicely by itself as an encore, or a recital-program "lollipop." Its melodies have a nice lilt, especially the lightly tripping music of the contrasting middle section (measures 45 ff.). The phrase units are for the most part quite regular, but the brevity of the sections of the movement, and the way that the music shapes itself to fill the section with a sense of continuity and growth, relieves any feeling of squareness. A light hand will turn this delicate, scherzolike movement to good account.

Four hundred and thirty-four measures of the final movement are much too much. Grieg advisedly asks for fleet pacing (Allegro molto vivace); at any speed, though, the material of the movement just does not hold up well. Fingers moving at top speed, contrapuntal devices duly and smoothly delivered, one still has the feeling that the movement was written because a brisk closing chapter is de rigueur in this kind of composition. As with jogging, you may find the finale an enjoyable exercise.

When, in a letter of Grieg's to his friend, the writer, Bjørnstjerne Bjørnson, in 1900, the composer describes the three violin sonatas as belonging "to my best works," he should not really include the first sonata; though he is right in calling it "naive."[105] It *is* that, by turns in the best and worst senses of the word.

Dag Schjelderup-Ebbe, of the University of Oslo, gives this work careful and detailed analysis in his *Edvard Grieg, 1858–1867,* an expert study of Grieg's experiences and work during his stay at the Leipzig conservatory and the years immediately following. He finds much of interest to the theorist, praising Grieg for

> . . . providing melodic interest simultaneously in the violin part and in the piano part. . . . However, the freshness of melodic invention . . . is not so pronounced here.[106]

To this, one must agree: with the addition that the handling of the melody, once stated, is not inventive enough either. From the performer's point of view, the work could be more grateful than it is.

David Monrad-Johansen, in his older biography, *Edvard Grieg,* writes that:

> In the last movement, where many composers suffer from lack of material, how Grieg triumphs! Ideas and fancies crowd so thick on one another that they seem almost to fight for a place, . . . and stream as from an inexhaustible well."[107]

But this is a very hard sell indeed, smacking of overenthusiasm, chauvinism, or a little of both.

The Sonata number 2, in G, op. 13, opens with a lengthy, rhapsodic, Lento doloroso introduction. It has, in both instruments, a promising air of let-the-hair-down abandon. It comes as a shock to find the Allegro vivace devoted at first to a lively *springdans* (Norwegian 3/4-time folk dance) kind of tune:

Figure 7-3. Piano, mm. 26-29

The dance tune has actually been forecast in the melodic turns of the slow introduction. And the dance soon passes through a shadowed setting of its own before returning to its gayer version and to a rhythmic offshoot that is of continued importance in the movement:

Figure 7-4. Mm. 79-84

Best of all, in the opening pages of the sonata there is none of the fatally symmetrical phrase length that ensnared Grieg in the first sonata. Unpredictability governs and delights; never more so than in the second subject, with change in mood, texture, and pace:

Figure 7-5. Mm. 88-97

An arbitrary flourish by the piano marks the end of each phrase of this tune; and this, too, justifies its sudden appearance by prominent service later on:

Figure 7-6. Mm. 100-104

This figure, the snapped rhythm already seen in Figure 7-4, and other elements from the opening episodes are combined in a coda development at the end of the first section of the movement.

The actual development could stand more excitement; it follows the cue of the exposition, viewing a succession of extended contrasting episodes, without any real interaction between them. The timing and gradation of these episodes is good, nonetheless, and the total effect is of a long buildup to a triumphal (i.e., fortissississimo) return of the opening and a complete review of its ideas in sequence. Often we come upon interesting harmonic sonorities in this music. Schjelderup-Ebbe singles out the passage at measures 266 ff., where the melody in the violin part embraces tones from two chords, G major and its dominant (with the seventh) D major; and the piano, accommodatingly enough, plays both chordal clusters simultaneously, providing a rich and spicy setting for the violin line.[108]

Figure 7-7. Mm. 264-269

Two points should be made about the second movement (Allegretto tranquillo): the first and last sections, beginning with the quiet innocence of a slow, swaying dancelike round, are deceptive. They soon enough rise to sonorous, excited peaks, and should have (as in the following climax) some of the improvisational tone used in the sonata's first introduction:

Figure 7-8.   Mm. 34-36

The middle episode (measures 46 ff.) needs all the reverie and sunlit humor that the duo can provide. In itself, it is one of those musical vignettes that Grieg carries off so well; as a change of scene between the darker end-sections, its luminous quality can be intensely effective.

The last movement, initially and in its extension, is reminiscent of the very opening in theme:

Figure 7-9.

a. Violin, introduction, mm. 1-5

b. Violin, finale, mm. 1-10

c. Violin, finale, mm. 36-40

Despite passing contrasts in mood (compare Figures 7-9b and 7-9c, as examples), the finale essentially proceeds without real interruption throughout its first section: one grand, variable rush of music. Like the second movement, it focuses on the contrast between end sections and middle. And the midsection seems to reflect the corresponding portion of the second movement.

Figure 7-10.

a. Violin, finale, mm. 113-120

b. Piano treble, second movement, mm. 46-49

Again at the end of the finale, this contrasting idea is woven into the coda in review of earlier events (see measures 277 ff.).

The entire sonata is successful because Grieg puts well-constructed, coherently shaped, contrasting episodes in sequence; knits the whole together by semicyclic thematic material; and permits himself the use of the kind of tunes and rhythms familiar to him from distinctive regional music of his own land. The Sonata in G requires no little virtuosity, is well worth study, and deserves a firm place in the performer's repertoire today. It is old, but by no means obsolete.

Grieg was full of confidence when he wrote this sonata, yet aware of its strangeness in the musical circles of the time. In a letter written to a colleague at the time of this composition, Grieg states that he is awaiting his friend, Johan Svendsen (Norwegian conductor, violinist, and composer), to whom the sonata was dedicated, to have his new work played.

> He is really the only one to whom I dare give it—the other violinists all hate me from envy apparently. . . . Most people hate my compositions, even musicians.[109]

How like the complaints of Charles Ives, a generation later, in America!

Niels Gade himself, after the premiere of the sonata, came to Grieg and said:

> "No, Grieg, the next sonata you must not make as Norwegian." I [i.e., Grieg] had at that moment tasted blood and answered: "Yes,

Professor, the next one is going to be even worse." (However, that was
not the case, as you know.)[110]

The Sonata Number 3, in C minor, op. 45, was composed in 1886–87.
Grieg had now attained a position of prominence in the musical world of
the closing century. He normally divided his year into periods of composition, rest, and concert tours through Europe. But his periods of productivity in authorship were spotty, with sometimes long, fallow interludes.
The third violin sonata was his last finished composition of such large
scope. He completed it in January, 1887, but it was not premiered until
the following December 10, in Leipzig, by the Russian violinist, Adolf
Brodsky, and Grieg himself.[111]

Although the sonata won immediate and continuing general acclaim,
some voices were raised in attack. Eduard Bernsdorf, German critic in the
Leipzig music journal, *Signale,* laid to the new work the same faults he
found with Grieg in general:

> . . . lack of organic development, weaknesses of talent and invention
> that are only poorly concealed by all kinds of affectations (especially
> as concerns harmonic relationships), tasteless effects and buffooneries
> committed under the cloak of Norwegian nationalism . . . [112]

Obviously a prejudicial review—and one of unusual roughness, even to those
accustomed to the occasional excesses of criticism in our own time. Let us
turn to the sonata itself, and see what Grieg offers.

To begin with, a long and impetuous movement ("fast and passionate"). Within it, themes that tend to grow through sequential repetition,
but nevertheless have overall direction. Transitions that also move sequen-
tially, but, because they are in transition, tend to be disappointing in effect
(like taking a slow-moving escalator, when more definite and larger motions
would take us to our goal more quickly). The familiar, and not unwelcome
placement of very unlike episodes next to each other—as though a revolving
stage presents us with scenes from far-separated points in the action of
the play. A development section that transforms the opening motif by
inflating it:

Figure 7-11.

a. Violin, mm. 1-2

b. Violin, mm. 146-154

A musical mural painted by the sequential repetition of this inflated pattern against a shimmering background of piano arpeggios. A development episode where arpeggios are draped over descending scalewise passages and stepwise fragments (all derived from the role of the piano voice in the opening lines of the movement). A development that finally rises from the depths on a ladder of slightly augmented, tremolando settings of the opening figure:

Figure 7-12. Violin, mm. 232-236

A Presto coda that storms the heavens at last in chordal blasts of sound.

Aside from technical difficulties (which, after all, require endurance almost more than any special dexterity), the problem of this movement is primarily to keep the many sequences from sounding too obviously sequential. This is particularly true of the passages at measures 79 to 95 and measures 341 to 356, where—unless purest pianississimo and rare delicacy are observed—the performers will have the nightmarish sensation of playing a bad movie-score imitation of a bad Greig imitation of a mediocre imitation of Liszt:

Figure 7-13. Violin, mm. 79-86

In short, this is a dramatically ambitious movement, drawn on a large scale, concerned more with grand effect than with overly refined musical detail. To play it takes daring, conviction, and skill, for—played slovenly— its glow can become tinsel, its grandeur a threadbare mawkishness.

The second movement, a Romanza, is at the opposite extreme. It has no histrionics, no pretensions. Its simple melodic line, contrived with the expertise that Grieg displayed so often and well in his songs and short piano pieces, is presented first by piano, complete; then by the accompanied violin; and again, at the end of the movement, with an introductory harmonic transition, and with an accompaniment of greater rhythmic agitation, by the two instruments together. A fast middle-section, reminiscent of some Norwegian morris dance, provides a graceful interlude. With appropriate lyricism and lightness in the respective sections, this movement can be made to reveal itself as one of Grieg's most successful efforts.

As you start the third and final movement, believe it if it sounds familiar; there is more than passing resemblance between its theme and that of the central portion of the Romanza:

Figure 7-14.

a. Second movement, Allegro molto, mm. 1-4

b. Violin finale, mm. 1-6

Like the first movement, this finale is painted with an extremely broad brush. The scheme of things—a long first section, revolving around the leaping figure, shown above, and an obvious reference to the Romanza subject:

Figure 7-15.   Violin, mm. 63-66

Next, a contrasting section, in the submediant major, A flat, of the C minor key of the movement; the melody thereof suggesting an alliance to the contrasting subject of the first movement:

Figure 7-16.

a. Violin, finale, mm. 111-120

b. First movement, mm. 59-66

The first section is revisited. Thereafter follows the contrast section, now in the parallel major, C, and with great, arpeggiated waves of piano color as a backdrop (measures 319 ff.). A prestissimo peroration on the stamping-dance principal theme winds up the entire sonata.

The finale, all in all, is a bravura piece, of considerable—though not overwhelming—technical demand. What with the color washes that are required of it in large segments of the movement, the piano bears the digital brunt of the load. For the violin, the most taxing parts (aside from some high-register playing) are measures such as the following:

Figure 7-17.

a. Mm. 55-58

b. Mm. 101-103

c. Mm. 287-293

Is the sonata as a whole worth the time and effort of learning it? Monrad-Johansen, of course, cries the affirmative with all the enthusiasm of one who has a vested interest in Grieg.

> Because it was a question here of a struggle for life or death [I assume that the author refers to Grieg's need to test himself artistically, though, in view of Grieg's long history of respiratory ailment, Monrad-Johansen may be using the words in a physical, as well as figurative, sense.], this work . . . shows us the artist in a pure, noble and chastened form, . . . only possible when one has gone through the cleansing fires of suffering.[113]

Less poetic, but more to the point, is a review in the Paris *Le Matin*, 1890, quoted by Monrad-Johansen: "This brilliant composition seems to dispose completely of the reproach that has been leveled against Grieg, that he is not the man for works [of expansive breadth]."[114]

The individual duo will have to decide for themselves whether they want to traverse the spans of Grieg's structure with the composer. I suspect that they will so decide. And it may not be out of order to inject an extraneous note: namely, that Grieg spoke out, in his role of public prominence, in 1899, in protest against the renewed condemnation by court-martial of Captain Dreyfus in France. Grieg's stand on the matter stirred such enmity in France that, on his next visit there, in 1903, to conduct a program of his works in Paris, he had to withstand a torrent of abuse in the auditorium before finally winning his hearers over, by concert's end, to an unprecedented ovation.[115] A personality of such moral fiber could scarcely keep from making itself apparent in some degree in a work of the stature of the C minor sonata. I invite my readers to reacquaint themselves with the man and the composition.

Other Scandinavian Composers

Turning to the work of some lesser Scandinavian composers, there is first the Sonata in G minor, op. 83, published in 1888, of Johann P. E. Hartmann (1805–1900). This Dane, himself a third-generation successor in a family musically prominent in Denmark since the mid-eighteenth century, was the father-in-law of Gade. The sonata in question, the last of three Hartmann efforts in this vein, and the only one I have seen, is mentioned here only to warn off the reader. It would be ridiculous to play this sonata today except out of devotion to Danish music history; and that history can be better served by other examples.

A possibility in the sonata literature would be the work in G minor, op. 10, by the Danish violinist, trained by Joachim, Fini Henriques (1867–1940). This is a large work in four movements. The music is not without interest, but is discursive, a bit on the blowy side, and outdated.

Turning again to Norway, we have the sonatas of Christian Sinding (1866–1941). He was trained in Germany but spent almost his entire career in Norway, where he fulfilled a role similar to that of the somewhat younger Sibelius in Finland. Like Sibelius (who taught at the New England Conservatory in 1914), too, Sinding visited America to teach at the Eastman School in 1920–21. Of Sinding's four sonatas for violin and piano (opera 12, 27, 73, and 99), I have seen only the first.

That particular work, in C major, dedicated to Grieg, was published in 1892. If you can get past the opening Allegro moderato, you may be able to continue; but the movement is impossibly repetitive in its rhythmic waves, hard to play (for both instrumentalists), and threatens seasickness. The second movement, Andante, starts out promisingly in a simple, elegiac strain, but by measure 5 it is plain that we are back in the Romantic soup. The finale, Tempo giusto, is a bravura piece, mostly in that perpetual-motion vein that Sinding handles so well. Unhappily, it sounds like a frenzied treadmill. The entire sonata is obsolete. Hopefully the later efforts (though the fourth and last was published in 1909) might prove more encouraging.

Definitely not encouraging is the Sonata in E minor, op. 24, (the second of five such efforts) by the Swedish composer, Emil Sjögren (1853–1918). The work (written in 1888) requires mention because it is still available in the publishers' catalogs. Walter Cobbett, writing in the late 1920s, said of this work that it "is the only sonata which has won a permanent place in the repertory." If this was true then, it is apparently no longer the case. And inspection of the music gives no indication that matters should be altered.

Carl Nielsen

Carl Nielsen was born in 1865 near Odense (birthplace of Hans Christian Andersen), Denmark. Though of poor family, he was able to pick up some musical training in his early years, and—as he himself states—was "made a bandsman in the Danish army though only fifteen." From 1884 through 1886, he studied composition with old Niels Gade at the Royal Conservatory in Copenhagen. Years of service as principal second violinist in the Royal Opera orchestra were followed by a term (1908–1914) as conductor there. In 1915, he became a teacher and directing officer at the Royal Conservatory, continuing in that capacity until his death in 1931. His prolific output as a composer extended to many avenues of writing, and dates from his late teens to his last years. The catalog of his published works includes two sonatas for violin and piano: the first, from 1895; the second, from 1912.

Nielsen's countryman, Povl Hamburger, says of the first sonata that it counters

> . . . the myth of Nielsen as a pronounced "anti-romantic." . . . this youthful work which from first to last seems conceived in an effortlessly happy inspiration. . . . It did not arouse unqualified enthusiasm with the critics, but was thought to be too "learned," too "experimenting."[116]

The injustice of the critical attack will not be apparent to the musician who inspects this sonata by eye alone. It is more likely that such an investigator will be put off immediately by Nielsen's unusual choice of movement titles: *Allegro glorioso* (glorious!) for the first movement; *Allegro piacevole e giovanile* (juvenile!—youthful?) for the finale. Or if, taking these mastheads in stride, the reader proceeds into the body of the sonata, he will—unless he "hears" his way carefully and at length—quickly assume that this is another of those pieces that runs on a rhythmic treadmill. The second theme of the first movement, the beginning of the second and third movements, all threaten boredom:

Figure 7-18.

a. Violin, first movement, mm. 31-36

b. Second movement, mm. 1-6

c. Violin, third movement, mm. 1-19

But a live hearing of the work reveals that we are dealing with a composer who, though young, though giving some reflection of Brahms, of Grieg, of Franck, and (in the second movement) occasional flashes of a still undreamt of Gershwin, is obviously an individual and imaginative musical thinker. Far from seeming "learned," this sonata often delights with surprising turns of harmony, droll or affecting maneuvers in the handling of theme.

In the first movement, a sonata allegro, the second subject is introduced not once, but twice, first in C major (see Figure 7-18a.), and only after this in the dominant, E, that one would normally expect in an A major movement. Also, the meter of the movement is 4/4; but the second theme appears in 3/4 time; and, perversely, on its reappearance in the recapitulation, comes out in 4/4! Then there was the warning of the exuberant, kick-up-heels style of the sonata's opening (note the drumlike, "rim-shot" accompaniment of the piano):

Figure 7-19. First movement, mm 1-3

And late in the movement, the pensive and willful musing on rhythmic detail in the first measures of the coda.

As for the steadily pacing flow of the second movement, far from dulling the listener's sense, it will have a cumulative and quite moving impact upon him. The third movement is deceptive in its naïveté, for its open and disarming waltzing is the vehicle for music of considerable strength and direction.

There is, of course, something of a Nielsen cult abroad in the musical world of today. Those already enrolled will find little to dissuade them in this sonata; for newcomers, a rather effective inoculation. If this is followed by exposure to the second sonata, the virus may take lasting hold.

In Sonata Number 2, op. 35, Nielsen is the warmly lyric composer, expansive in idiom, but concise and well-organized in his thinking. To begin with, there is again a strange character-marking: *Allegro con tiepidezza*. When does a composer call for "tepidity"! A funny marking in this particular instance, because the movement palpitates with heat throughout, and not only in its loud passages. Have a look at the opening melody in the violin:

Figure 7-20.   Violin, first movement, mm. 1-13

Nielsen marks this opening to be played *senza espressione*, and piano (the violin is marked pianissimo in the full score), but he must have felt that the intensity in the melody would prevail against—or be brought to even more vital effect by—understatement rather than flamboyance. The line moves upward, colliding with the C flat and resting briefly; then moves up again to confront the A flat, and rests again for an instant before leaping with a great stretch to the high G. From there, it unwinds sinuously, until it flows away in the trill measures, only to end enigmatically with the little upward tag in the last measure. It's a good tune, well-shaped, and with strong drive; almost familiar enough to hum, but shot through with strange twists that save it from convention and triteness.

The key signature and the flavor of the violin opening suggest G minor, but the piano's initial measures do all they can to fight this impression, at the same time weaving added threads of motion against the violin line:

Figure 7-21. Mm. 1-4

The movement is a sonata construction of middling-long duration, yet tightly knit; its several areas are related to each other by thematic derivation, but are distinct enough in character to keep the movement alive. Compare transition, secondary, and closing subjects with the first theme (Figure 7-20):

Figure 7-22.

a. Transition, mm. 21-24

b. Second subject, violin mm. 43-45

c. Closing subject, mm. 74-76

Around and between these components, lines of sixteenths enliven the second half of the exposition. This liveliness, coupled with the complexity of the sounds that arise by the friction between the motion of the several lines, makes this sonata immediately a work for the more accomplished player, though even the less experienced should try the piece to benefit from its seriousness.

The faster rhythms dominate the development, interweaving with the broader thematic elements from the exposition and culminating in an agitato episode of (for the piano) truly bravura requirement; action and dramatic achievement in barely three pages of score. In a succinct recapitulation, the inherited thematic material is altered in the retelling so that a fresh view of familiar ideas is won. The bridge episode is set against a spiky piano part, with the curious instruction, *brioso* ("vigorously"), in pianissimo dynamics. The effect must be that of playing emphatically, but heard from a great distance.

At the very end of the movement comes a last quirk: the sound is dying, draining away; then, suddenly, in the middle of the very last note, an intense stroke:

Figure 7-23.   First movement, last 6 mm.

The second movement, Molto adagio, can best be described as incandescent. The opening is already at a fair boil; and matters progress, through measures of the most luxuriant, rhapsodic, and shadowy writing, to this (one measure!):

Figure 7-24.   Second movement, m. 19

This heightened temper quickens the events of the middle episode of the movement and colors the backward glances that crop up in the remainder of the Adagio. The closing measures taper away, lending a quasi-symmetry to the movement by the dying reflections of the snapped rhythms of the opening. This is one of those movements; it is inspired writing, conceived completely in terms of chamber music, yet holding those terms to new ways. The duo that wrestles through this Adagio will be the better for it.

We should now be put on our guard, for the finale, Allegro piacevole, starts almost too "agreeably," with swaying rhythm, clear texture, and unobstructed B flat, both in key signature and actual writing:

Figure 7-25. Third movement, mm. 1-4

The harmonic web does not remain all that clear, but the rhythmic swing goes on for what seems a suspiciously long time, even though aerated by patterns of staccato, then accented, eighths. The harmonic wanderings are such that the movement must eventually break out into a change of pace (alla breve), meter (duple), and key (E major, with signature to match).

Now we're in for it. By the time our piacevole triple returns, we are in an A major section; and when the signature of B flat returns, the tonality does not come with it. The next stop is at C major. By now, the texture of the movement has changed completely. The violin is still singing away in its broad triple rhythms, but the piano devotes itself entirely to a staccato eighth-note pattern that has come into the movement at an earlier stage in its progress. A further element, briefly touched on by the piano in the episode just preceding, is a hammered eighth-note pattern, in octave unison, extending through the measure. And now, for the entire closing page of the score, the piano bangs away passionately at B flat, as if in belated atonement for the harmonic infidelities that have taken us so far away from the movement's starting point. The violin finally dares to shout back, in a stentorian G:

Figure 7-26.   Mm. 248-253

This is strange, for we might assume from the sound of the combined instruments that we are getting, at long last, the G minor that flavored the very opening of the sonata. At the last possible moment, though, the piano suddenly abandons B flat for C, the violin completes its statement in a C-major progression, and the two instruments breathe out the last measures on C alone, dwindling away to a triple piano and suggesting some of that *tiepidezza* that Nielsen asked for, way back at the beginning. And could it be that, after all the harmonic roller coaster to which we have been put, the entire sonata was in C major?

The duo that is trying to set its aural compass for this movement may take counsel and courage from a thought advanced by Knud Jeppesen, Danish musicologist, composer, and pupil of Nielsen: "Nielsen did not set out to be a 'difficult' composer, though he did not mind being a controversial one."[117]

8 The Bohemian Sonata in the Later Nineteenth Century: Dvořák

Nationalism in music can be a troublesome thing, just as in world politics. For some composers, the use of regional folk music and dance as a source of musical idea can be a disguise for a lack of inventiveness; for others, it can serve as a springboard for fruitful musical thinking. Certainly folk, or folk-flavored, melody is not a substitute for the composer's ability to construct a work that has its own musical logic and coherence.

In the Bohemian sphere of Europe in the nineteenth century, the prime mover in musical nationalism was Bedrich Smetana. He wrote only one work for piano and violin, a Sonatina in D minor, published in the 1870s. The earliest example of Bohemian nationalism in the avenue of the violin sonata that I have seen is the Sonata in D of Zdenko Fibich (1850–1900), finished in early 1875. How early this is can be recognized by recalling that Grieg had written his first sonata only ten years before, with Brahms not to compose his first until 1879, and Dvořák to follow by a year later still.

Fibich had earlier written a first sonata, in C. Shortly before his death, Fibich destroyed the manuscripts of his youthful works. It is possible that he included both sonatas in this weeding out of his musical estate, for the compositions exist only in copies. Through the ministrations of admiring countrymen, Fibich's second sonata has been resurrected from one of these copies and published in modern edition.

Fibich was right; his saviors did him no service if they salvaged a work that he meant to suppress. The piece is a valiant, but hopelessly naïve, attempt to stir native, regional effects into the familiar sonata brew of his era. At least in this medium, and in the frame of Bohemian nationalist writing, the Fibich sonata shows what masters Dvořák and Janáček were to be.

In April, 1878, before leaving Vienna for another one of those enjoyable visits to Pörtschach, Brahms wrote to his publisher and friend, Fritz Simrock, following up an earlier recommendation of a composer he much esteemed. The kernel of the brief letter is contained in these words: "the best that a musician must have, Dvořák has. . . . I don't want to say more than to recommend Dvořák in general."[118]

So strong a reference from the knowledgeable, demanding—and laconic —Brahms was not to be taken lightly. Simrock soon became Dvořák's publisher, and did well by it. The ability and success of Antonin Dvořák is the more remarkable in view of his circumstances. Born in Nelahozeves, in Bohemia, in 1841, Dvořák was the eldest son of an innkeeper and butcher. He was apprenticed to a butcher in the town of Zlince and actually earned a certificate, in 1856, "entitling him to carry on the trade of butcher [and] to be recognized as a properly taught butcher's journeyman . . . "[119] At the same time that he was serving this apprenticeship, he had been studying music with a local organist-schoolmaster. This training was continued in Prague the following year, where he studied voice, organ, and theory and became acquainted with the older and contemporary repertoire. Though the early 1860s were spent as orchestral violist in Prague, his personal focus was on composing.

As Otakar Sourek, the Czech critic, author, and Dvořák enthusiast and cataloger points out, Dvořák started his serious composition in the field of chamber music, a fact that is especially notable because there was actually little concert market for such work in Prague when Dvořák began his writing career.[120] It is, nevertheless, a quintet and quartet, in A minor and major, respectively, that head his list of compositions. Dvořák went on to compose thirty-one ensemble works, including fourteen quartets, ten works for piano ensemble, six for string ensemble other than quartet, and one for two violins, cello, and harmonium. He persisted in his personal interest in chamber music, having completed nine quartets before any was heard in concert (late in 1878).[121]

Sourek divides the chamber music output of Dvořák into several groups, according to their chronology, and to their reflection of Dvořák's move from the derivative early works, through the stage of Wagner-Liszt influence, and on into the composer's development of his own, nationally colored style of music making. The chamber works span the time from 1861 to 1895. In the impressive sequence of these pieces, only two full-blown compositions are devoted to the combination of violin and piano: the Violin Sonata in F, op. 57, of 1880, and the Sonatina for Violin and Piano, op. 100, of 1893. Several single-movement works are excluded here because of their slightness or because they were originally intended for violin and orchestra. And the Four Romantic Pieces, op. 75, of 1887, are also not considered, owing to the fact that they were originally composed as a second terzetto (in sequel to that of opus 74), for two violins and viola. Performers will, however, welcome an opportunity to acquaint themselves with these graceful solos.

Sonata in F, op. 57

Sourek, who intimately knew the Sonata in F, op. 57, and the other compositions of Dvořák, says of that opus that it is "perhaps relatively less characteristic and musically significant [in Dvořák's current development] . . . a work of idyllic refinement and with Brahmsian colouring in the first two movements. It stands at the threshold of the next [most individualistic] phase of Dvořák's creation . . . "[122]

The Brahms allusion carries me to a relevant point made by Alfred Einstein:

> He [Dvořák] drew always from the sources of Slavic folk dance and folk song, much as Brahms had drawn from those of German; the only difference was that with Dvořák everything was childlike and fresh, whereas with Brahms there was always an overtone of yearning or mystical reverence.[123]

Which is better: the naïvely robust or the frustratedly yearning? In today's musical world, many are left uncharmed by both tendencies. Still, the labyrinthine maze of the Brahms musical psyche has probably intrigued more ears than the sunny ways of the Czech master.

Dvořák's sonata, op. 57, was composed in March, 1880, and published by Simrock that same year; Clapham suggests that the work was premiered in Bohemia in September, 1880.[124] Sourek describes the principal theme of the opening Allegro as of "faintly Brahmsian melodic colouring."[125] It has the expansiveness of a Brahms melodic line, but not quite the same cohesiveness. If we make a composite of the violin opening and the piano continuation, we can hear the graceful extension-by-echo relationship between the two:

Figure 8-1. Composite, mm. 1-22

Then, if we tabulate the successive ideas of the movement, we can see that the movement grows by emergence; one musical thought gives rise to the next:

Figure 8-2.

a. Mm. 1-5

b. Mm. 23-26

c. Mm. 38-42

d. Mm. 53-58

e. Mm. 63-65

f. Mm. 85-90

The skeletal frame represented by these excerpts is clothed with a fabric woven by the two instruments in X-fashion alternation with each other, or by isolated moments of imitation between the two voices. The weak link comes in the rhythm of the second theme. Where the first theme builds to and falls away from its triplet centerpieces, so that there is a feeling of rhythmic focus, the second theme tends to sway from tight sixteenth group to eighth leaps, to quarter swings, and back, with too much repetition of motion; the line doesn't seem to light anywhere. And the extension (measures 64 ff.) gives more of the same, too soon.

Fortunately, the development gives its attentions to the second subject only in the early measures (119 ff.), with the principal theme occupying the rest of the section. Both players will enjoy the switch in role and the resulting freshness of color in the thematic gathering-center of the development:

Figure 8-3.   Mm. 135-137

The recapitulation, by the usual nature of things, gives a fair amount of space to the ramifications of the second theme (measures 237 until at least 261, with a scattered droplet or two in succeeding lines). There is nice play of color, however, in the codetta interlude (from measures 291 to 302) and the equally gratifying closing lines, which allow the movement to drift airily away. Overall, the Allegro shows a curious mixture of direction and diffuseness; the players will have to keep their wits about them in order to make purpose prevail. The fitfulness of the movement is surprising in view of the sense of plan that Dvořák had so often displayed in the chamber works to this time. In any event, a good tempo (without too literal attention to Dvořák's admonition, *ma non troppo*) will help keep the bothersome second subject from putting sag into the Allegro's fabric.

For the second movement of this sonata, Dvořák originally started a Poco adagio in F. Apparently thinking better of the idea of having all three movements in F, he began again, this time writing the present Poco sostenuto, in A:[126] a movement with similar first and last sections, and a contrasting middle episode. The two end sections reveal a languidly falling theme, occasionally gathered up in folds of ascending faster notes, only to resume the floating descent once more. In the center of the movement we find two subsections; in the first, piano and violin alternate in upward arches, one in quarters, the other in eighths. Each instrument ends its momentary statement with a dotted-eighth sixteenth figure

From this comes the second subsection, wherein the instruments alternate in segments of sustained melody and garlands of the dotted-rhythm figures. The return section begins as a rather faithful reflection of its opening twin, but gives way to a closing episode that mingles, in quiet nostalgia, the melodic arches with the "lifting" elements of the principal theme. This movement is absolutely nonaggressive, even though one encounters a poco stringendo and even some fortissimi in its course. Throughout, one must try for a between-times mood, an interlude of ease and mental pallor far from the energetics of the surrounding movements.

The final Allegro is something else again. Here is the opening of the movement:

Figure 8-4.   Mm. 1-4

If, in these and the succeeding measures, the violinist does not feel like dancing (at least *inside* his shoes!), there is something wrong either with his diet or his moral fiber. As for the pianist, the notes pour from his fingers in challenge to his gyrating partner.

Turnabout! Now the piano dances while the violinist lets loose with a country-fiddler's virtuosity:

Figure 8-5. Mm. 19-22

A broader rhythmic step takes over for a time, with the sixteenth-note motion continuing—now in a more scalewise, but boiling, fashion—in the piano part. Then back to the lively step of the opening. This takes our perspiring duo as far as measure 77.

Now for a quick change of scene. Visions of peasant choruses, with all parts sung by the two lone instruments! Can't you see it?

Figure 8-6. Mm. 84-89

Series of looped eighths and snatched sixteenths appear to remind us of the gayer opening strains. And soon enough, the dance itself returns. But now (measures 142 ff.), we are not back at the beginning of the movement. Instead—and here Dvořák demonstrates his ability to combine the old and the new, the academic and the popular, all in one uniquely concocted brew—we have a full-fledged dance development, that careens through canon and counterpoint, through raucous forte and breathless pianissimo, through blatant rhythms and, finally, into these tickling measures that unleash the recapitulation of the dance:

Figure 8-7. Mm. 226-230

All goes according to plan in the recapitulation; the dance hall threatens to go up in flames. Frenzy is piled on frenzy in the coda; the concluding measures give only a hint of the whirlwind on the last page of the sonata:

Figure 8-8.   Mm. 355-361

My revered violin teacher more than once spoke of playing a work so effectively that there would be "not a dry seat in the house." When this movement ends, there should be none on stage, either. A superb Allegro, full of the fun that is all too rarely found in music.

Sonatina in G, op. 100

We confined our listing of works, earlier in this chapter, to Dvořák's chamber music. Dvořák had also been making his mark in the realms of choral, orchestral, and piano writing, and in opera as well. The works that Simrock had published at Brahms's urging were the various *Moravian* Duets; and the success of these was far surpassed by that of the *Slavonic* Dances, for Piano Duet, op. 46. Building on this response, and writing prolifically (he was happiest when working), Dvořák became a figure of great renown at home and abroad. His triumphs in England, for example, which he visited repeatedly, included the award of an honorary doctorate in music from Cambridge in 1891. And in the following year he went to America for what was to be a three-year term (divided into two journeys to and from Europe) as director of the newly founded National Conservatory of Music in New York. As everyone from grade school to grave knows, Dvořák composed in America the *New World* Symphony and the *American* Quartet (opera 95 and 96). There were other works, however, including the Cello Concerto, op. 104; and—the last chamber composition before returning home to Prague from the first American trip—the Sonatina in G for Violin and Piano, op. 100.

The Sonatina was dedicated by Dvořák "To My Children": on the sketch of the work, to Otilka (Otilie) and Tonik (Antonin), then fifteen and ten respectively, who had been with him during the entire stay in America; on the manuscript score were added the names of the remaining four children—who had come over from Europe to spend the summer holidays (principally at Spillville, Iowa) with their parents—Annie, Marenka (Magdalena), Otakar, and Zinda (Aloisie).[127] Dvořák assigned the opus number of 100 to the work for sentimental reasons, because he had not yet written opera 98 and 99 (which eventually proved to be the Piano Suite in A, 1894, and the *Biblical* songs, 1894).[128]

Dvořák composed the Sonatina in late November and early December of 1893 in New York. The following year, it was published by Simrock, to whom Dvořák wrote that the work "is intended for young people (dedicated to my children) but grown-ups, too, let them get what enjoyment they can out of it . . . "[129]

Dvořák was modest and accurate in his appraisal of the work. It is excellent training material for the novice or intermediate chamber-music player, of any age. The following measures represent about the most difficult technical material in the opening Allegro risoluto:

Figure 8-9. Mm. 98-102

The movement is a short, clear-cut sonata construction, without any really tricky ensemble problems, but with enough interplay between voices to exercise the alertness and musicality of the players.

The second movement of this sonata, Larghetto, will already be familiar to many readers from having played it as an independent work. Fritz Kreisler, for one, in his extensive series of short compositions and editions for the violin, has presented it under the title, *Indian Lament*. This title, along with others (all involving *Indian*, for good, salable local color), stemmed not from Dvořák but from Simrock, the publisher, who issued numbers of arrangements, without Dvořák's sanction, of this individual movement.[130] Sourek recounts that Dvořák "is said to have noted down [the first melody] while watching the impressive natural spectacle of the famous Minnehaha Falls beside the town of St. Paul, Minnesota."[131] Clapham places this visit in September, 1893, and states that Dvořák wrote the melody on his starched shirt-cuff, later reworking it in his sketchbook. Later that month, he saw Niagara Falls and said, "Damn it, that will be a Symphony in B minor!"[132] But this watery prediction never came to pass. He may have been wearing short sleeves.

In the light of the melody itself, the ways of musical inspiration will seem passing strange; the Minnehaha Falls must have been slowed to a mournful trickle when Dvořák visited them:

Figure 8-10. Mm. 1-8

In any event, the "Lament" is in fact a charming musical episode.

The Scherzo is a sprightly, rather easy third movement, remotely reflecting the sound and texture of the corresponding movement in the F major quartet, composed the same year. The finale is an Allegro; also, it is too long: 379 measures which, even in a fast 2/4 time, repeat too often melodies that are soon comprehended and accounted for. Also, despite interesting harmonies and key transitions, the fabric of the movement is made up too much of unrelieved series of statements and answers in four-measure units. The effect is a bit studiedly naïve for a composer of Dvořák's experience at age fifty-two. And if, as Sourek and Clapham both suggest, the American locale plays a role in the nature of the work, then the cause of "national" music must share the responsibility with Dvořák. In any event, the movement is a pleasant workout, a mild test of endurance, and a good study in the business of making the most of the available contrasts in the music. Besides, it has some perky tunes to light the way:

Figure 8-11.

a. Mm. 1-8

b. Mm. 62-69

c. Mm. 104-109

Best of all, the sonata is a work of (deliberately) modest difficulty written by a serious and knowledgeable composer. The combination of purpose and ability is all too rarely found in the easy chamber-music literature.

Some Sonatas Around the Turn of the Century: Strauss, Wolf-Ferrari, Busoni, and Reger

9

Here are grouped four composers all born within the span of twelve years and carrying us from the past into the present century. Each in his own way shared in the prevailing late-nineteenth-century musical taste for the massive sonority, the densely written texture, the highly colored harmonic palette. The works referred to often show the intrusion of this taste into the chamber composition, where the inherently delicate balance between the violin and the keyboard (especially the large and strong piano of recent times) is hard put to it to sustain the weight of such musical fabric. My own impulse is to reject this kind of inflation of the chamber style. But experience tells me that others, like myself, will be attracted to this music even while protesting that it is out-of-date. Through it, we look back to a time—not as remote as we would like to think it—when the opulent way in music was a norm.

Richard Strauss

Richard Strauss was born in 1864 at Munich; son of the principal horn player of the Munich opera, Strauss was trained from childhood for the musical career that, of course, he followed to worldwide renown. In 1885, he became assistant conductor at Meiningen under Hans von Bülow, the eminent musician who, since 1880, had led the orchestra there to a position as one of the leading symphonies of Europe. Von Bülow left the post that same season, with Strauss taking over the reins in his place.

At Meiningen, Strauss met Alexander Ritter, an ardent Wagnerite (he was the husband of Richard Wagner's niece) and member of the orchestra's violin section, who urged upon Strauss the new ways of music. To Strauss, who had been conservatively oriented in music by his father, the exposure to new music came with powerful impact. A trip to Italy in 1886 produced the symphonic fantasy, *Aus Italien,* which raised a storm of controversy at its premiere in Munich the following March. But for Strauss the course was clear: ahead lay a lifetime devoted to the orchestra and its adjuncts, to opera and (much less) to ballet, and to song.

Just at this fateful point in his career, Strauss added one more item to the small store of chamber-music compositions of his earliest years: the sole work for violin and piano, the Sonata in E flat, op. 18.[133] The sonata was written in mid-1887, except for the Andante slow movement, which was not completed until autumn of 1888 (the year of *Don Juan*), with the premiere following that October.[134]

Strauss produced a strange piece, more a duo contest than an ensemble. The following measures are typical of the textures in the opening movement; the full chords, the convoluted and interlocking melodic lines, make for a sound that is thicker than even the appearance of the notation would suggest:

Figure 9-1. Mm. 9-11

There is very little respite for the piano anywhere in the Allegro, either in the sense of rest or number of notes, so it takes great restraint indeed from the keyboard to give the fingerboard an even break. The violin is not bashful either, what with figures such as the following in its part:

Figure 9-2. Mm. 16-19

Though there is as much piano (and softer) as forte (and much louder) in this movement, the feeling—whether looking, playing, or listening—is of constant activity. And, rather than gazing nostalgically backward to his more youthful chamber works, it seems that Strauss is warming up here for the great orchestral works to come. The motivic germ of the piece, heard in the opening piano measures, has that unmistakable Straussian combination of opulence and nervousness.

Figure 9-3.   Piano, mm. 1-db. 3

Its inescapable rhythmic snap (the dotted figure followed by the triplet, heard either together or in separate extensions of the two patterns) is evident at almost any point in the movement, unless it yields the moment to the second theme or its offshoots:

Figure 9-4.   Violin, mm. 59-66

The movement is in sonata form; Strauss does fine things with the extension and combination of the musical ideas in familiar first-movement ways. But his exuberant figuration, harmonic excursions, chordal amplifications, athletic leaping from one end of the register to the other (in both instruments)—all on the foundation of ideas that seem basically plain and simple in their pristine state—produces a feeling of luxuriance run riot. One has the uneasy feeling that, at a moment's notice, the duo will find itself magically replaced by one hundred men and a conductor. The sonata is not so much a reduction of orchestral style (à la Strauss), but rather a compression of the orchestra into the frame of a twosome. As such, it cannot be entirely successful even in the most successful of performances.

The same holds true, in even greater degree, for the third and last

movement of the piece. The short, slow introduction, darkly set forth by
the piano, is one thing. But the Allegro, with a theme very strongly fore-
casting that of *Heldenleben,* absolutely cries out for orchestral forces. Instead, the piano sets up a veritable artillery barrage of notes, the violin
sings its heart out—the whole effect suggesting that of two actors trying to
simulate a cast of hundreds by running furiously onstage through all possible vents in the scenery. There are some more successful moments, such
as the quiet 6/8 episode where the piano and violin carry out elegant
traceries with a subsidiary theme of the movement. To offset this, however, there is an earlier, extended episode of busywork for both instruments,
with much thrashing up and down on keyboard and fingerboard, that must
be counted a waste of time.

The middle movement of the piece, which (under the title, *Improvisation*) has enjoyed a life of its own as a separate publication, has restraint
and eloquence, in the manner of the Mendelssohn *Songs Without Words.*
This is true, in any event, for the first four pages of the score and for the
last few lines of the piece. The middle episode of the movement, however,
marked by what Walter Cobbett calls "fluttering passages for muted violin," which elicit from him the evaluation, "strokes of genius," is deplor-
able, smacking strongly of the worst kind of cabaret music writing.[135]
"Improvisation" is, in short, a most uneven movement. And so, for that
matter, is the entire sonata of Strauss.

Strauss was a craftsman of stupendous order, of great imagination, and
of frequent inspiration. If he turned so definitely from this one effort at
duo writing to more abiding interests, we can but take our cue from him.
With stamina, agility, and the exercise of taste, one may explore the Strauss
sonata. In the words of the old saw about the crowded city, you are likely
to find it a nice place to visit, but no place to live.

Ermanno Wolf-Ferrari

Ermanno Wolf-Ferrari, born in Venice in 1876 (died 1948), was a successful opera composer before he reached the age of thirty. Most of us
will know him as the author of the *Jewels of the Madonna,* or more likely
as that of *The Secret of Suzanne,* and most probably only by the sprightly
overture to that work. His catalog includes no less than twelve operas,
almost all now unheard. His output in other avenues was minor, centering
on chamber music and including two violin sonatas, opera 1 and 10. I have
seen the second of these, in A minor (1901).

It is with a certain grand inconsistency that I commend the skilled duo (and none other) to this work. It seems written within the shadow of Richard Strauss. Several points, however, give it preference to the Strauss sonata; it is shorter (only two movements); less mawkishly sentimental (it is the middle movement that Wolf-Ferrari has omitted, and it is precisely there that Strauss met his downfall in his own sonata); and it is even harder to play. It is this very difficulty, with both instruments frequently involved in very rapid, intricate lines, full of chromatic runs and turns, that takes this score—for all its lushness—out of the orchestral sphere and keeps it in a kind of hothouse chamber-music atmosphere. The tight melodic detail would be lost in orchestral setting.

Like the Strauss, the Wolf-Ferrari is not a work you want to play or hear too often. But it is an experience that will linger in the memory of the duo and affect their way of playing, for the better.

Ferruccio Busoni

The Italian piano-virtuoso, Ferruccio Busoni (1866–1924), was also a prolific and gifted composer, though relatively little of his catalog is now performed. Among his early compositions were two violin sonatas, opus 29, of 1890, and opus 36a, of 1898. The first of these is now a dated work and need not be considered here. The second one, in E minor, is interesting, though not necessarily suited for concert programs today. It is a long and rather muscular piece, in three movements, played without pause. The finale is a panorama—one cannot call it merely a set of variations—on the chorale of Bach, *Wie wohl ist mir, o Freund der Seelen*. The scope and inflation of these variations, though not quite as woolly, have a touch of that same grandeur that colors the Reger *Variations and a Fugue on a Theme by Mozart*. One has a vision of the theme (and its composer) cringing in a corner of the auditorium before the onslaught that the later composer makes upon the borrowed idea. Busoni's comparative restraint is furthered by the limited sound-capacity of the duo ensemble.

The opening *Langsam* of the sonata, ornate, lyric, and energetic at the same time, unfolds at last into a Presto that makes room in its headlong rush for lines marked to be played, "tenderly, with some warmth," "with all force, without slowing," "always warmly"—and always applied to the same watery/lyric line. The same theme is preserved in an Andante section that closes this first complex of the sonata. Here the line appears again, "as a recollection." Thence we move directly into the Andante con moto that presents the Bach chorale in its first, plain version.

Max Reger

The extremely prolific Max Reger (1873–1916) was generous not only with time but with notes. The flood of tightly woven textures that characteristically fills his lengthy works tends to give contemporary ears—including mine—a case of aural indigestion. That his pen was not always gummy is demonstrated by his writing for violin and piano. There are more than a dozen works of his for this combination, mostly under the title, "sonata." Of these, I have seen six works, pieces that show him in contrasting lights.

Sonata 4, in C, op. 72, and Sonata 5, in F sharp minor, op. 84, are both fairly long, but number 4 seems longer still because of its square and repetitious rhythmics. The Fifth Sonata, in three movements, concluding with a *Variazioni*, is more interesting. To both of these, I prefer the two "small sonatas." The *Kleine Sonate* in A, *Hausmusik*, op. 103b, no. 2, consists of four movements, trim and piquant. Nor are they entirely domesticated house-pieces, either. They are rather demanding to play, but lighter in texture than the movements of the larger works. Somewhat easier in technical demands is the *Kleine Sonate* in D minor, *Hausmusik*, op. 103b, no. 1. Its three movements (ending with variations) again show lightness and sober humor, offering some of Reger's most appealing writing.

Turning to Reger's later, larger sonatas, opus 122 in E minor, and opus 139, in C minor, I find them again less pleasing than the *Hausmusik* pieces. The smaller works contain the essential Reger in more compact and delicate form, and fit comfortably in today's repertoire.

10   *Webern: Four Pieces for Violin and Piano, op. 7*

Both in playing and writing about music, it is easy to delude ourselves; if the music is familiar, conventional in structure and sound, we fasten on to the expected surveyor's marks. Subjects, harmonic goal points, accustomed sectional divisions, all make comfortable talking —and listening points. Attached to these islands of safety in the work, we may well slide over the details of musical composition in the vast no-man's-land beyond.

Even in dealing, in "detailed" fashion, with more particular elements of the music, we may evade difficulties of comprehension and communication by referring to extramusical symbols, pictorial allusions, personifications, and so on. In the playing, too, we can "milk" certain obvious effects from typical formulas in the music (or we can even impose hackneyed effects upon musical ideas that have freshness and individuality).

This has been possible, for the past few generations, because we have largely restricted our musical experience—whether as player or listener—to the music of the seventeenth to the nineteenth centuries. Despite all that has taken place in these centuries, despite all differences of style—on personal, national, or "school" level—the music is generally comfortable for us; we don't have to work hard to arrive at least at the impression that we understand it. When difficulties do arise in this kind of sound, we get around the trouble by dismissing the work as an aberration of the composer (was not Beethoven called mad because of some of the difficult traits of his late works?), or by concentrating on the less problematical areas of the piece. We complacently know all there is to know about this music.

To a certain extent, we ignore familiar music while listening to it. The attention wanders, or at least varies in intensity. With music written in the twentieth century, we reach a fork in the road. Some music of recent era has retained an air of familiarity, of comfort to ears accustomed to older ways. On the other hand, beginning quite early in our century, there have been avenues of composition that are new and different; where the concept of melody, of interval, of texture, and of structure has been extended so rapidly and suddenly that many players and listeners have not yet caught up.

In much of this music, the listener finds that stern demands are made upon him. So many aspects of the given work are unconventional, attached to that work, and that work only, that in-and-out listening becomes dangerous. Let the attention wander for a moment, and you are lost. You are now compelled to absorb a composition the way every worthwhile piece —of any vintage—should be: with complete attention to each consecutive step in the unfolding work.

The composer of new music today knows that he cannot make too many assumptions about those who will confront his work. The music is a new experience to him, thus is the further removed from those who have not—like the composer—lived through the process of its invention and working out. Accordingly, the author tries to limit doubts about interpretative points in the work by giving the most explicit instructions he can contrive in the written score of the work.

Among meticulous composers, none deserves the title more than Anton von Webern (born, Vienna, 1883; died Mittersill, 1945). He was by training, as well as instinct, of painstaking habit. Early instrumental and theory work in music was followed, from 1902 to 1906, by study in musicology under Guido Adler at the University of Vienna, with a doctoral dissertation on Heinrich Isaac, the Renaissance Flemish composer.[136] From his work at the university, his own broad listening experience, and his studies with Arnold Schoenberg (from 1904 to 1908), Webern was instilled with a deep respect for the craftsmanship of the master composers of the past.

Under Schoenberg's guidance, Webern moved rapidly (but, in his own view, inevitably) from the nineteenth-century reflections of his earliest work to his own way of musical thought. It is noteworthy that Alban Berg, who was studying with Schoenberg these same years, was, in 1910, writing the turbulent and thickly textured String Quartet of opus 3; while, at the same time, and under the same teacher, Webern had directed himself toward the extremely economical style shown by the Five Pieces for String Quartet, op. 5 (1909) and the Four Pieces for Violin and Piano, op. 7 (1910). The final version of this last-named work dates, according to a note on the autograph manuscript, from the summer of 1914.[137]

Friedrich Wildgans, in his catalog of Webern's works, says of opus 7:

> These highly concentrated pieces . . . already demonstrate the com-
> poser's conscious attempts to express every musical thought in the
> briefest possible form. They are, so to speak, the basis, as well as the
> point of departure, for those works of the middle period—without
> being built on the concept of a twelve-note structure—that finally
> break with the old tonal connections; they also finally do away with
> traditional thematic form. In their place motivic working appears, with
> extremely brief motifs of only a few notes, sometimes only highly
> expressive, isolated single notes acting as motifs.[138]

The Four Pieces are, respectively, nine, twenty-four, fourteen, and fifteen measures long. The dynamic palette tends overwhelmingly in the direction of pianissimo and pianississimo, with only sparing use of loud outbursts (electrifying in their sharp contrast to the prevailing quietness). Muted violin is used in the first and third movements (slow); brighter, open color in the two fast movements. The bowing techniques used extend the sound range of the pieces far beyond this basic contrast. "Softly drawn with the stick of the bow"; "at the bridge"; "soft pizzicato"; "with the wood of the bow, in slashing stroke"; "with the wood of the bow [i.e., tapped]"; "with the wood of the bow, softly stroked." There are further instructions, for both violin and piano, as the occasion dictates: "Extremely tenderly"; "lightly"; "very tenderly"; "very evenly"; "without crescendo"; "extremely short"; "scarcely audible"; "very expressively"; and, at the very end, "as though breathing out." Dynamics are carefully placed and indicated, both in letter signs and in swell and decrescendo signs. Tempo marks are specifically dictated, though the metronomic numbering is usually qualified with "about," a curious expression of leeway on the part of a composer so bent on indicating his precise wishes. Tempo fluctuations within the given movement are shown by character markings, calls for accelerando and ritard, and metronomic changes. The second movement (fast, and most active of the four) especially abounds with these changes in pace—no less than nine, not counting the connective time-transitions. The meter changes often, sometimes bar by bar. And there is never a key signature; each note in the composition bears its own accidental mark, to indicate which version of the tone is desired at the given moment in time.

The player who is new to this kind of writing (and many of us are, because it is only in recent years that the music of Webern has attained to some currency in the concert hall) will have only one purpose in mind at first: to learn to read the notes. No preconception about melody or harmony will serve here; all is cast new from the thought process of the composer. It will be well for the player, however, to keep firmly in mind that Webern, in his own way and the way of this particular work, has every composer's aim—to write a piece that will hang together, and will communicate itself as such to the attentive ear. The "meaning" of the work is inherent in the sounds it makes. In melodic interval, in the clustering of tones within the chord, or the resonance that rises from relationships between simultaneously moving lines, all is composed, in the true sense of the word; put together with art and purpose.

That Webern held the sound of the work to be all-important was evident not only from his music, but from his teaching, reports the English composer, Humphrey Searle:

> When I wrote exercises . . . he [Webern] invariably played them over on the piano, and he was as much interested in the actual sound of them as in their theoretical construction.[139]

In conventional music, a wooden performance can still pass muster. The listener—by past experience—supplies with his mind's ear the graciousness, the lyric sweep, the direction that the inept or heedless player fails to provide. The latter's deficiencies will be quite apparent but the listener will, by dint of some mental calisthenics, still have been able to salvage something in the nature of a musical experience from the ruins.

In a work such as the Four Pieces, almost nothing in the way of the performance can be left to the imagination. The gradations of tempo, loudness, color, and temper stipulated by the composer are absolutely essential to the inflection of the notes. The tones themselves, delivered with the utmost accuracy of intonation, are not enough. They must be connected—within the individual line and in the interplays between lines —in faithful accord with the composer's dictate.

Most important is accuracy of dynamic gradation. Triple piano must be defined, in the player's mind as a specific sound level, gauged on the quietest level that the pianist can evoke from the instrument. (Let him experiment, however, to be sure that he is playing his quietest!) To this, the violinist matches his pianississimo level, until in the estimation of both players (and, if need be, the appraising ear of a third party), the two have agreed on a dynamic "floor." From here, the way up the loudness ladder is taken, so that a controlled choice of *pp*, *p*, (*mp* is not used in these pieces), *mf*, *f*, *ff*, and *fff* is available to the players on demand. Then, for example, it will be possible to play the following measures (from the second piece), so that the left-hand commentaries—in treble, be it noted—are clearly heard, yet are subordinate to the duet between the right hand and the violin's pizzicati; and, at the same time, so that the pizzicati gradually take precedence over the piano treble, which yields ground by fading to a pianissimo:

Figure 10-1.   Second piece, mm. 5-7

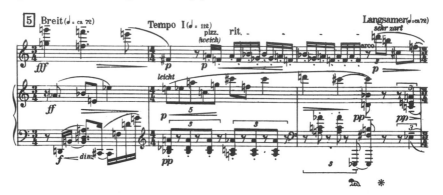

Rhythmic measure is also of the essence, so that changing pulse of activity in even the quietest moment of the piece can have its effect. Consider, for example, this excerpt from the third movement, where the floating quality of the first three measures gives way to the equally quiet eddy of motion in the fourth bar, then to settle again for a moment (marked by the indicated breath-comma) in measure 5. The three parts must fit together just so in measures 4 and 5 so that the interplay will give rise to a clear overall pattern, not an accident-seeming jumble of sounds:

Figure 10-2.   Third piece, mm. 1-5

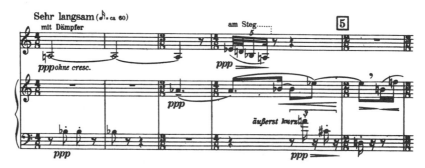

As for temper and color, try to imagine the range of "feeling" and inward gesture the violinist must exploit in these measures (9 to 12) from the second piece; observe also that the piano must at the same time be absorbed in remote triple-piano maneuvers, unmoved by the tigerish lunge of the violin in measures 9 to 11 (with the bow stick, *not* the hair!):

Figure 10-3.   Second piece, mm. 8-10

The range of temper that Webern is after is perhaps most apparent in the measures of the fourth piece. There, the violin part begins with roughly accented notes, flung across the three upper strings, only to recede from the topmost note in a swooning, legato descent to a dying away in the piano part.

Figure 10-4.   Mm. 1-5

And consider the last measures, where, following upon a passage of harmonics in the violin, the piano utters a very quiet, single line, while the violin, in ponticello, flutters away above it. The composer's instructions for the violin line there, "like a sigh" (*wie ein Hauch*), is typical. It is as though the composer himself is standing at the player's elbow during the rehearsal, telling him in the most graphic way possible the kind of sound he is after.

It is when the composer calls for such effects as legato playing with the *stick* of the bow, triple-piano, "softly drawn," that the player must wonder whether Webern knows what he is doing. But, as with every other effect he uses, Webern has carefully calculated his purpose. He *hears*; acutely. Listeners and performers have to live up to this acuteness. And they must recognize the ultimate purpose of the composer in all this. As with Beethoven's motto for the Sixth Symphony, this kind of writing is "more the expression of feeling than tone-painting."

11 § *The Sonatas of Ives*

CHARLES IVES was born in 1874, in Danbury, Connecticut, the son of the founder and conductor of the Danbury Band, George Ives.[140] Through the tastes and activities of his father and the life of the New England community, he was exposed to the broadest variety of music, from the various kinds and settings of hymns, to the popular music of the time, and on to a fair assortment of ensemble music by older composers. By actual instruction from his father and by practical experience, he was already familiar in his early teens with a number of instruments and with harmony and counterpoint. From the same sources he found encouragement to hear and think about musical sounds with an ear for the fresh and the untried, as well as for the conventional and "permitted" ways of music writing.

He went on to Yale University in 1894, earning his way partly by work as an organist, and continuing the composing that had already occupied him for several years. At Yale, he had instruction from the eminent Horatio Parker, who was friendly but not really sympathetic to the musical exoticism displayed by the boy. Upon graduation in 1898, he went to New York to learn—by working in—the field of insurance.

Over the years, through hard work, intelligence, and an imaginative and high-principled approach to the business, Ives became a leading figure in American insurance circles, building with a partner an insurance agency that became the largest in the country, and contributing to insurance practice ideas and methods that have become standards.

Every available free hour—evenings, weekends, holidays—was, with the approval of Ives's understanding wife, devoted to his composing. The Iveses did little socializing; Ives himself went to concerts only rarely, preferring to concentrate his energies on his own musical thinking and writing. A prodigious quantity of music of all kinds was turned out in the years up to 1917. In that year and the following, business and the exigencies of America's entry into the war kept Ives from composing; moreover, a serious bout of heart illness in October, 1918, and the weakened condition in which it left Ives, wrote an end for all practical purposes to his composing. Ives lived on until 1954, a keen supporter of the contemporary composer and of his right to compose in new ways. Also he found in his later years a belated but growing measure of professional and public response to his own music.

Ives's successful career in business made him financially independent; his training as well as his native instincts made him artistically independent, more so than most composers of past or present vintage. It is evident, now that Ives's music has achieved increased performance and dissemination, that his industriousness, his self-imposed musical isolation, and his conviction were all worthwhile.

The Ives catalog includes four published sonatas for violin and piano:[141]

	Dating in published edition	Dating in Ives's list	Dating encompassing manuscript sources and precedent works
Sonata number 1	1903–08	1903–08	1902–09
Sonata number 2	1906, 1909–10	1903–10	1902–10
Sonata number 3	1902–14	1902–14	1901–14
Sonata number 4 (*Children's Day at the Camp-Meeting*)	1915	1914–15	1902–15

The Ives sonatas must be learned, rather than taught. Only players of agile finger and alert ear can grapple with these pieces; even *Children's Day*, the least gnarled of the four sonatas, is *not* for children, though Ives's own note to the work explains its basis in the "children's services at the out-door Summer camp meetings held around Danbury and in many of the farm towns in Connecticut, in the 70's, 80's, and 90's." The sonatas are not mysterious; but they are difficult technically and in sound detail. Above all, they demand a sympathetic and patient attitude on the part of the duo.

One cannot be told to like this kind of writing. Only by wanting to hear through complexities, to adjust phrasing and balance so that niceties of melody and texture can be successfully conveyed, only then can these sonatas be effectively performed.

So far as the violin sonatas are concerned, we should be well past, even so far as the general audience for serious music is concerned, the stage where the sound of an accurately played Ives passage is repellent to the ear. Ives himself was sensitive to the frequent and incredibly ungracious comments of performers (to say nothing of listeners) about the presumed roughness and incomprehensibility of his music. We must wonder that, on the basis of sight-reading (!) this kind of music, a player would have ventured to speak categorically about the playability or musical worth of the composition. For most Ives episodes, sight-reading can only remotely approach the intent of the composer.

We have come a long way since the early years of the twentieth century. Much "worse" sounds than those of the Ives pieces are now the order of the day in contemporary music. The wiser and more experienced among us—young and old, player and listener alike—are no longer as quick to condemn a particular work or a style of writing. And when we do condemn a piece, it is more likely to be one of pointless or meretricious nature than was the case in earlier critical climes.

Thinking back over critical appraisals of music seen in recent years, I am not all that convinced of the truth of the above statement. But I know that music such as the Ives sonatas is now comfortably within the pale of acceptance by many knowledgeable ears. Professionals must master these works; capable amateurs should attempt them; and listeners are missing a rewarding experience if they do not approach these works receptively.

The lack of receptive response had definite impact on Ives. He might lash out against players' comments by writing, perhaps too broadly, "Why can't music go out in the same way it comes in to a man, without having to crawl over a fence of sounds, thoraxes, catguts, wire, wood, and brass? . . . The instrument!—there is the perennial difficulty—there is music's limitations."[142] This outburst makes good reading, especially in the light of the latter-day replacement of the performer and his instrument in those compositions that use only electronically generated tones. But the words are certainly intemperate, in view of the great sensitivity that Ives himself showed to musical sounds in terms of the instruments that make them.

Ives protested; but also yielded. He had some unkind things to say about his third and fourth sonatas, feeling that he had compromised his own standards of writing there, in deference to contemporary criticism. In listening to the finale of sonata number 3, for example, one is occasionally conscious of a strong suggestion of Franckian writing, and may take this to be one of the traits of surrender that bothered Ives about the piece. If these sonatas are "weak sisters," (to use Ives's own description), they are only comparatively so; one could not mistake them for the work of an earlier or less forward-looking mind.

In the violin sonatas, as in many another Ives piece, the ear is attracted (entrapped?) by the presence of familiar tunes. No less than nineteen hymns, popular tunes, or dance melodies, from *Turkey in the Straw* to *Jesus Loves Me*, are quoted in the four sonatas.[143] This could be a dangerous practice in lesser hands, especially because the quoted tunes are often used with insistence as the structural thread of a movement. But Ives is no lesser hand. He avoids the trap of writing a medley or potpourri kind of piece. The quotations are apparent, often stated by the piano and/or violin. Hearing these tunes so presented, even if he is not familiar with every source melody, the listener gets a feeling of security and nostalgia. But Ives never lets him sink into hibernation.

The tunes are set out of joint, take queer and unexpected turns, conflict—sometimes jarringly—with themselves or with other material in parallel voices of the music. Déjà vu, perhaps, but never quite as things were. The result is tantalizing; the ear is led on, enjoying again at each repeated hearing of the sonatas the things that happen to save the known phrase from the accustomed and sometimes trite inflections of its original. The parallel of the Ravel quartet comes to mind: its initial theme of horrendously insipid rhythmic doggerel is mysteriously transformed and beatified by its harmonization and by the progress of the accompanying voices.

A much closer parallel is that of the Bartók sonatas: there, too, the melodic ideas suggest regional melodies; but it is plain to the ear that the composer has had his own way with them. Where Bartók, however, builds musical structures that are often overwhelmingly clear-cut in their logical sequence of events, the Ives approach is more nonchalant; the elision, the sudden interruption, the alternation of ideas; the musical detours are just as important as the larger, cohering, formal outlines of the movement. The whimsicality, acerbly presented, is enjoyed by the composer.

Here and there, the ear will wonder why Ives chose to pursue a tangent line of exploration, moving out of a quotation, at such length. Such moments of doubt are few and far between, however. For the most part, there is only a sense of intense and varied sonority, or rhythms full of wit and surprise, with the jazz, or ragtime element a frequent but not exclusive ingredient.

The composer is fairly helpful in his instructions to the performer, as in page 11 of the score of sonata number 3, where he indicates the transfer of melodic lines between violin and piano treble, and the pyramiding, sustained-tone nature of the piano chords of the allegretto measures. In sonata number 1, the inclusion of the text to the borrowed hymn, *Watchman, Tell Us of the Night*, under the melody is unusual but is probably intended as a playing aid (page 24 of the score). Ives has been at some pains to mark the stress points in the quoted melody (using the signs ∧ and >, though not throughout). It is possible that he included the text to make clear to the violinist, who presents the tune, why the stresses are placed as they are, for they do reflect the important words of the hymn text.

The rhythm of the melodic quotation is not verbatim; the text stress is. Accordingly, the violinist can profit from the "explanation" offered by the text. An added benefit of both accents and text is that the player is prevented from placing a singsong stress on the first beats of the measures, though by this point, any such tendency should have been firmly put down by Ives's free way with rhythm and meter.

Some Sonatas from the War Years: Carpenter, Milhaud, Villa-Lobos, Sibelius, Janáček, Honegger, Respighi, Elgar, and Satie

12

T<small>HIS IS</small>, for the most part, an ill-tempered chapter. For a number of works mentioned here, I state my annoyance openly. In the case of others, my enthusiasm or acquiescence may puzzle the reader. In every instance, the judgment has been based on the work itself, and on what seems to me to happen between the opening clef and the closing double bar. It might be fairer to consider the music in context, specifically in the frame of the musical diet or the concert program, to see how the given composition would present itself in the company of other, more innately imposing works. Here again, the reader must be the final judge, by trying the piece in question for himself.

John Alden Carpenter

After we have been through the four sonatas of Ives, it is a curious experience to confront another American work of about the same vintage: the Sonata, copyright 1913, of John Alden Carpenter. It has an opening Larghetto, slightly "new" in sound, disjointed in idea; an Allegro that is, in its reserved way, unintelligible, noncoherent; a Largo mistico and a Presto giocoso that are equally baffling. Along with elements of musical nostalgia, this sonata has an innocent, trusting air about it that may be engaging to some. Those who prefer a feeling of compositional control in the music they play should look elsewhere.

Darius Milhaud

Darius Milhaud (born 1892) has proved one of the most prolific composers in the twentieth century, and also one of its most active and influential teachers. Two of his early chamber music products were sonatas for violin and piano. Both of them, for my ear, suffer from the composer's frequently and deliberately taken stand in favor of the simple and the naïve. Sonata number 1, of 1911, suffers from much repetition of thematic rhythm; and the great length of the first movement (carrying the rehearing of rhythmic pattern to great extreme) makes the work difficult to get into. Taken as a whole, this sonata is not vital to the contemporary repertoire. The Sonata number 2, of 1917, is easier to like, though the studied simplicity of the opening pastoral rhythm (again much heard) and the faster fixations of the second movement, Vif, and finale, Très vif, are still nettlesome. The third movement, Lent, is most likely to appeal.

Players can enjoy these pieces, because they are physically involved in them. Neither they nor their listeners can long bear with these sonatas if they are looking for much in the way of mental challenge. The music goes down too easily.

Heitor Villa-Lobos

Heitor Villa-Lobos (1887–1959), the fountainhead of contemporary Brazilian music—certainly in number, for the works simply poured from his pen during his long career—wrote four sonatas for violin and piano during the early years of his activity. These were four Sonata-Fantasies, from the years 1912, 1914, 1915, and 1918. I have seen the first two of these. Number 1, subtitled, *Despair*, displays more fantasy than logic; one may truly despair of hearing coherently through the work. The final blow, after the coloristic goings-on that mark the course of the piece, is to come upon the elliptically shaded C chord at the very close.

The First Sonata is in one movement, in many sections. Sonata number 2, on the other hand, is in three discrete movements. The thinking and sound is just as woolly and discursive here as in the first, however. The piano clatters a good deal, almost constantly. The violin is too erratic for words. These are baffling pieces, interesting in retrospective view of Villa-

Lobos's self-taught, experimental ways in his early writing, very difficult to use in concert.

The Third Sonata (1920), which seems to be next in line of the published works for violin and piano—I have not been able to find printings of the third and fourth Sonata-Fantasies, though these are listed in his repertoire—is a work in three movements, of considerable heat in its own right, but giving a more calm-and-collected impression than the two works described above. In the hands of a very competent duo (none other!), this sonata can be turned to good account. It is too bravura and oratorical, however, for the home music circle, and belongs comfortably only on the concert platform.

Jean Sibelius

Jean Sibelius wrote his Sonatine in D for Violin and Piano, op. 80, in 1915, the same year in which the Fifth Symphony had its premiere. The composer was then fifty and had long been firmly established as Finland's (and Scandinavia's) leading musical representative in the twentieth century. It is astonishing that the man who wrote violin music of the strength and color displayed in the Concerto (1903–05) should now permit himself to turn out the musical twaddle displayed by the opening Allegro of this sonatine: pastime music of the thinnest sort. The most exciting part of the piece is the two-page vivace dash to the double bar at the end. The most that can be said for the work is that it is a moderately difficult piece, suitable for the intermediate duo, though requiring the utmost deftness and clarity of performance to make it palatable to the listener. The Sonatine is a trifle, produced by a most able and uneven composer.

Leoš Janáček

The Czech composer, Leoš Janáček (1854–1928), composed his Sonata in D minor in 1913, reworking it several times to bring it to the form in which it was published in 1922.[144] The sonata is in "difficult" keys—D flat minor, C sharp minor, E flat minor, G sharp minor. It is also an unhurried work. The tempo is fast at various points, of course; but the pace of musical thought is deliberate. Broadly moving lines are set in frames and backgrounds of tremolando (thirty-second-note oscillations, either stepwise or in large-interval alternation), sometimes chordally arranged between the two hands of the pianist, sometimes reduced to short "warbles"—raised to ferocious levels in the finale—that are often revealed to be thematic crystallizations.

In the first movement, Janáček seems more intent on contemplating the little sonorous eddies than in making real headway; it is a nebulous, atmospheric chapter. Tune spinning comes in the Ballade, especially in an appealing passage where octaves (with the piano uppermost) outline the melodic line against the ever-present tremolo. Again the melody is digested slowly, repeated, shifted, regarded at ease. The third movement, Allegretto, has tripping end sections that are set against short, liquescent, chromatic runs in both instruments (another manifestation of the shimmering figure?). The finale is built of a number of small sections, arranged in an ascending and receding pyramid of speeds, and closing in a Maestoso—Adagio that emphasizes again the bubbling figurations from the sonata's opening. A strange work, and interesting.

Arthur Honegger

In the course of his long and productive career in composing, the versatile Arthur Honegger (1892–1955)—another of the composers included in the group of *Les Six* in Paris—wrote two violin sonatas. The first of these, from the years 1916–18, stands early in his catalog. However it may have been regarded in the era of the First World War, it must now be counted an inconsequential piece, pleasant and innocuous, its pattering rhythms made more irritating by the overextended length of the work (short though it is). There are three movements, the final Allegro assai putting on a cloak of newness with a 3-3-4 meter in slow quarters. This piquant touch is too mild to lend the sonata any pep.

The sonata number 2, only a year later in the writing (1919), does not carry us much further in enthusiasm. The first movement is almost all development, not through any dramatic opposition of ideas but rather through their recurrence and weaving around one another. The principal theme is lackadaisical in rhythm, a quality emphasized by frequent rehearing, either in direct quotation or in adapted form. The second movement again seems a loosely contained structure, framed by unaggressive, related end sections. Again, as in the first movement, the reminiscence is introduced in order to set the stage for a conclusion, not a full-dress review of earlier happenings. The final movement, rhythmically facile, melodically wandering, completes the impression of a sonata that makes a nice, but not musically memorable, workout for intermediate and advanced players.

Ottorino Respighi

Ottorino Respighi (1879–1936) wrote one sonata, in B minor, for violin and piano, in 1917. Its opening Moderato is filled with billowing rhythms and with a piano part that is of lacy textures, spun in various densities. The turn of phrase is vaguely Wagnerian/Straussian. The concluding Passacaglia, on a ten-measure theme, qualifies the sonata as a difficult piece. The busy duo should give other works priority.

Sir Edward Elgar

Aside from some variously titled pieces (including a sonata, suppressed) for violin and piano from early in his composing career, the prolific Sir Edward Elgar (1857–1934) produced the Sonata in E minor, op. 82, written in 1918. The opening Allegro insists too much on cross-stringed arpeggiations. They are violinistic, perhaps, but tedious when used for so long. Of the three movements, the second, *Romanze*, strange, moody, fitful, is the interesting one, worth playing by itself.

Erik Satie

In the first place, let us doubt that the work at hand is a sonata. A sonatine? Probably not; if it were, the composer would probably still hesitate to use the word. In all his list of compositions, there are no abstract musical titles, save for one piece, and there the qualifying adjective removes the curse of abstraction and replaces it with that of social criticism: the Sonatine *Bureaucratique*, for piano solo, of 1917. However, the work we are to discuss is the only ensemble piece he wrote, aside from a few piano duets. And his entire catalog of works is slight and spare.

Now for some instruction. Here is a list of the comments found in the score of Erik Satie's *Choses vues à Droite et à Gauche (Sans Lunettes)*, from the year 1912. First, there is the title itself: "Things seen to right and left, without eyeglasses." Then, the titles of the three component movements of the work: "Hypocritical chorale"; "Groping fugue"; "Muscular fantasy." Having pondered these, we progress to the detailed instructions offered by the composer in the body of the work; freely/literally translated by me:

> With hand on conscience.
> Slow down with benevolence.
> With silly but proper candor.

At the end of the back teeth.
Tranquil as a Baptist.
While winking the eye.
With tenderness and fatality.
With dry and distant bones.
Leave at one blow.
While enlarging the head.
With broad vision.
With bent back.
Lacquered like a candied green orange.
On fire.
With enthusiasm.
Quite crestfallen.
Coldly.

Some of these make sense. Then there is the comment of instant self-appraisal, at the end of the first movement (ten measures long): "My chorales are like those of Bach, with this difference—they are more unusual and less pretentious." By this time, we have all guessed that Satie is kidding. Is he? One often has a slightly uneasy feeling when in the presence; not because of the music, which is, after all, for the most part quiet and rather restrained, but because of the verbalizing. Satie says things so frankly and/or outrageously that we don't know for certain that he is joking. There Satie has us.

One thing is sure: the player who takes all the instructions in *Choses* as meaningful for the performance of the work is going to be so confused that he will not play a note. Only occasionally and by free interpretation can the words be applied in any real sense to the playing chore of the moment. The instruction that obviously does mean something is sometimes applied in a way that makes it almost impossible to execute. The last measures of the work, for example:

Figure 12-1. Violin, last staff

It takes a most pregnant silence indeed to get the mute on to the bridge (certainly the kinds of mute available in Satie's time, before the day of the piggyback, quickly emplaced mute) during the space of the one-sixteenth rest in the violin part.

Why bother to ask for such an awkward maneuver in the first place?

Because, having stipulated that the final sixteenths of the penultimate bar be played "coldly" (in pianissimo), it makes good sense to restrict the violin tone to the nth degree for the last, exhaled cadence. When you put the showy stage directions aside, the whole piece is sensible. The opening Grave is an unpretentious takeoff on a chorale, as you can see from this small excerpt:

Figure 12-2.   Page 1, mm. 5-6

The Fugue (homage to Satie's counterpoint lessons of 1905 at the Schola Cantorum, under d'Indy and Roussel?) does fugalize in a deliberately simple way on a "silly" subject:

Figure 12-3.   Page 2, mm. 1-6

At one point, the unhurried progress of the movement threatens to come to a complete standstill:

Figure 12-4.   Page 3, brace 4

It is at the end of the Fugue that the instructions "with swelling head" and "with broad vision" are given. This, in mock depiction, no doubt,

of the pomp and solemnity involved in delivering the skinny-massive conclusion of this movement.

As for the "Muscular fantasy," the muscles, such as they are, belong
mostly to the violinist, who is called upon to play some easy, but active,
crossing-four-strings patterns, artificial harmonics (in eighths, so not too
difficult), and so on. There is a short violin cadenza, beginning thus,

Figure 12-5. Violin, page 2, line 8

which is not as hard as it looks, of course—note the fingering to be used
for the three harmonics at the end of the example. The pianist's one claim
to the spotlight is in the "on fire" passage, a slide for life on triplets that,
if "fiery," is not too dangerous in the execution.

Figure 12-6. Piano, page 7, brace 4, mm. 3-5

The prime question: why play these pieces? The reason offered by
Rollo Myers, in his biography of Satie, smacks a bit too much of the musical shopkeeper: " . . . their charm is undeniable, and they can be recommended to violinists [not pianists?] on the look-out for something a little
out of the ordinary."[145] But it goes beyond this, as Myers himself and
other Satie scholars have indicated in their consideration of his person and
work. In his economy of means, his spareness of line, his slightly acidulous
use of harmony and tonal color, his sense of humor and of life's proportion
(evident in his music as well as in his overdriven literary glosses), he seriously reflects and indeed helps inspire the musical and social temper of
important currents in the world of the late nineteenth and early twentieth
centuries.

His life spanned the time from 1866 to 1925; in his personal output,
it extended from the quiet world of the piano pieces, *Gymnopédies* (1888),

to that more raucous era of the ballet, *Parade* (in collaboration with Jean Cocteau, Picasso, and Leonide Massine, 1916). If, because of modest talent, or personality, Satie does not rank with the musical greats—the Debussys, the Ravels, the Hindemiths, the Stravinskys—of his day, he nevertheless moved in their circle, and was thought fit so to move by his contemporaries.

Yet, one does not perform appraisals. In the last analysis, it is the music itself that is played. And *Choses vues* should be played, not because it is "out of the ordinary" but because, in a mild way, it is in the ordinary stream of our time. The music is good to hear, acts like an astringent tonic when included in an evening's reading, and—more important than its effect on its program mates—has a bracing effect on the sensibilities of the performer and the audience.

(Satie's piece has, I confess, had an undue amount of space here, because of the fun of dealing with his textual grace notes. Satie wins again! In any event, I salute his shade and apologize to the reader.)

13   *Debussy and Ravel*

Claude Debussy

Claude Debussy, at the height of his powers and—especially since the premiere of his opera, *Pelléas et Mélisande,* in 1902—regarded as one of the great leaders of contemporary music, both French and of the world, suffered a cruel blow. Beginning in 1909, he developed symptoms of the cancer that was to bring him to his end in 1918. Financial need forced him to create prolifically, nonetheless, and to undertake conducting tours for which, in temper, training, and physical condition, he was not suited. The onset of World War I, whose approach he had gloomily foretold, added to the circumstances that depressed the composer and inhibited his creative process.

Despite the growing torment of his condition, Debussy was not without plans for the future. In 1915, among other works, he composed the first piece in a projected set of Six Sonatas for Various Instruments: the Sonata for Cello and Piano. A crisis in his illness, coupled with a serious operation in December of that year, interrupted his attention to this project. During 1916, however, he completed the Sonata for Flute, Viola, and Harp, and began work on the Sonata for Violin and Piano, completing the finale in October of that year, and the first two movements in February, 1917.[146]

The first performance of the sonata took place in May, 1917, at the last Paris concert of Debussy's works during his lifetime. Debussy himself was the pianist, Gaston Poulet the violinist. A second playing by Debussy and Poulet was given at Saint-Jean-de-Luz, near Biarritz, France, in September, 1917, at Debussy's final public performance. He died in Paris the following March.[147]

Debussy's plans for carrying out his project are evident from the title page of the violin sonata: "Six Sonatas for Various Instruments, Composed by Claude Debussy, French Musician [a stylistic and political self-designation, reflecting his feeling for things and people French, as against the domination—especially in music—of the Germanic in preceding generations]: The Third, for Violin and Piano." Again, in the dedication of the work to his wife, Debussy specifically states, "Six Sonatas, for various instruments, offered in homage to Emma-Claude Debussy . . . "[148]

Lockspeiser relates the instrumentation that had been planned by Debussy for the remaining three works (never begun) of the complete set of six: number 4—oboe, horn, harpsichord; number 5—trumpet, clarinet, bassoon, piano; number 6—concert, with all the instruments of the first five works, plus a bass.[149] The roster, in usual score order, would therefore include: flute, oboe, clarinet, bassoon, trumpet, horn, harp, harpsichord, piano, violin, viola, cello, bass—so that the entire set of works would have constituted an apotheosis of the orchestra (old and new) and its component parts, but entirely in chamber terms. The colors and instrumental handling evoked by Debussy in the three extant works intensify our disappointment at not having in hand the remainder, especially the cumulative work, number 6.

Now let us turn to the Sonata for Violin and Piano, the last composition finished by Debussy before his death. There is a curious ambivalence at the beginning of the sonata: the piano declares G minor with both hands (measures 1 and 2), then ripples the harmonic waters with the E natural in the third and fourth measures. Despite this and other deliberate ambiguities to follow, however, the violin part, holding the opening solo (measures 5 ff.), clearly establishes G minor as the key of the movement. But rhythmically, too, there is something equivocal here. The piano begins alone. In its four solitary measures, there is nothing to reveal to the ear that the piano is playing four (rather than two long) measures. When the violin enters, it is still possible at first (measures 5 and 6) to think that the "long" measure (actually two measures) is the unit of meter; and, because the violin moves in three broad pulses in these two measures, we are led to believe, perhaps, that we are dealing with a piece written in slow 3/2 meter. The next measure (7) continues us in this belief; but measure 8 raises the possibility of question with the quarter rest—because it breaks the easily swinging thread of sound. The next two measures throw considerable doubt on slowness, because of the fast eighths and the immediate emphasis on a downbeat of a three-quarter unit (measure 10). And the teasing is prolonged both by the sustained, hovering tones immediately resumed by piano and violin (ending on the downbeat of measure 12), and the renewed driving motion of measures 12 and 13.

Figure 13-1. Mm. 1-14

All this is unsettling; it keeps us alert, expectant, unsure: good things to be when we are listening to music. The first section of the movement (to measure 63) takes us off guard—as we have seen—then keeps us on the move, sometimes on the run (though never at more than an eighth-note clip), throughout.

An interlude (measures 64 to 83) offers rest, confirming once again G minor, but containing within itself a quiet insistence on the rhythmic and metric countercurrents that mark the movement. Note the three levels of pulsation in this excerpt: a four-bar sustained chord in the bass, large triple units over a two-bar frame in the violin, similar pulsation in the piano treble, but out of phase with the violin part:

Figure 13-2. Mm. 72-75

The middle section of the movement follows next (measures 84 to 144). It is distant, both in tonality and material. The cool light of E major suffuses it; the piano figuration oscillates rapidly, in contrast to the much more static pacing of the part in the first section; and the violin moves—in flutelike tones, over the fingerboard—in 4/8 against the 6/8 pulse of the piano:

Figure 13-3.   Mm. 84-92

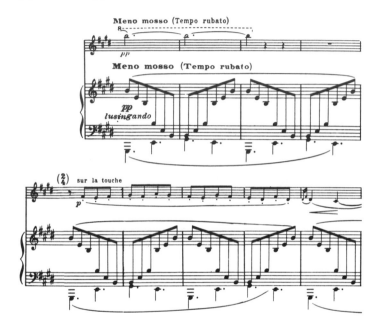

Toward the end of the section (cf. measures 132 ff.) we find another rhythmic mix, with the violin now moving in 3/4, to the piano's 5/8. The five-pulse is by way of carrying out a composed retard; for it replaces the prevailing 6/8 sweep that has marked the movement until now. The return of the opening material (tempo 1, measures 149 ff.) is somewhat hesitant (it takes two successive statements of the opening four measures of the melody, in piano and violin, to overcome inertia). And under the melody (with its occasional revelation of the old six eighths to the bar), the background now moves in the broader 5/8 pattern.

The slowing pulse dominates to the end of the movement. True, there is a spurt of energy, animando and appassionato, as seen in the violin measures from bar 185,

Figure 13-4. Mm. 185-188

but the pace cannot be kept up. The violin makes a couple of attempts, completely alone, to resume the melody, but the piano puts quietus to these with solemn tolling. As though the line is disintegrating, its several fragments are made the basis for further attempts to keep moving, on the last page of the movement. It won't work. A fortissimo, "with fire" ululation from the violin, to the accompaniment of great, bell-like chords from the piano, is a last frenzy—and perhaps the only false note in the movement, in view of the consistently shadowed color of the whole—before the flame is snuffed out by two final Gs.

If there is a suspicion of lassitude about the first movement, the same cannot be said of the Intermède, "capriciously and lightly." The description fits throughout, for this is—on the surface—a whimsical movement. But its fantasy is based on solid construction. The structural block that leaps to the eye is too simple to be true; but it appears everywhere in the movement, so insistently that it demands attention and must be brought out in the playing. Essentially, it is a chromatic downward progression of three notes. It may appear inverted, as an ascending progression, either in simultaneous opposition to itself or as an answer to itself, or as independent relief. It may also twist or somersault on occasion, especially when it appears in the form of an ornamental turn, but it is ubiquitous and will be heard.

It makes its bow at the beginning of the movement, with panache! Note the top line of the piano part (A sharp–A–G sharp); this is paralleled and reflected in the other three lines of the piano voice; at the same time, the violin splits itself into two, to carry out a double version of the ascending form of the progression: F sharp–G–G sharp and D–D sharp–E. And after a bravura high-dive (measure 3), the violin delivers itself, quite alone, of a mock-heroic, trilling-basso version of the actual fragment, A sharp–A–G sharp.

Figure 13-5. Mm. 1-4

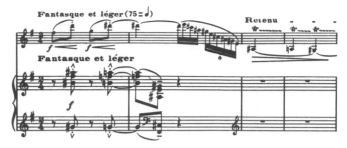

G sharp is not the goal of all this motion; the very next measures of the violin, a short and satiric cadenza, coyly offer us a choice between G sharp and G, finally centering on the G, and causing to coagulate around it (measure 7) a C-major chord, which is finally permitted to appear in root position—but only pianissimo, and topped with a shy whistle from the violin—as the goal of the whole opening process, in measure 8.

Figure 13-6. Mm. 6-8

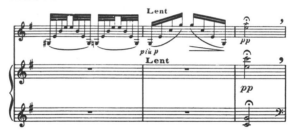

Is this movement in G (the key signature would so indicate), or is it in C? From the opening measures, one cannot be sure, for it all seems to be not only a grand opening fanfare, but at the same time a premature and rather final-sounding cadence on C. A nice puzzle. And, it would seem, a deliberate conundrum posed by Debussy. For he is still being sly about it at the end of the movement:

Figure 13-7. Mm. 130-135

You see how it is: everything undoubtedly revolves around C, including the fanciful arabesque of the violin. But somehow the violin overshoots itself, and—in the last two measures—finds to its surprise that it is settling on G. Not too positively, though; the movement is "dying" to a close, as the composer instructs, and because it started this procedure from a "più pianissimo" it is by now scarcely audible (shades of Webern!). Thus, when the piano slips in that bit of reinforcing evidence in the last measure— the cadence, D–G, in the bass—everything is so shadowy and oblique that it is almost by afterthought that we realize we have been left, after all, on G. A nice bit of musical sleight of hand.

But long before this, the duo will have enjoyed itself thoroughly while tripping Debussy's "light fantastic" (which, quite literally, is what he means by his subtitle for the movement), and playing chromatic chess. We won't spoil the fun by giving a roster of the guises assumed by the musical protagonist. Let the duo be on the lookout.

The iron will of the artist, Debussy, in writing a movement of this wit and temper in the time, circumstances, and place of his existence in 1917 is something else to contemplate—in awe.[150]

The third movement is also remarkable; not so much for its intricacy of thought as for its sheer energy. It is a robust, sensual, and thoroughly flamboyant closer for the sonata. It begins quietly enough ("Light and distant"), but there is immediately something fierce and strident about the piano, as though one is watching a storm or a battle scene through the wrong end of a telescope.

Figure 13-8. Piano, mm. 1-5

Against this turbulent backdrop the violin introduces a reminiscence— enlarged in retrospect as by the mists of time—of the principal theme of the first movement. But this is only a nod in the direction of cyclic struc- ture, for there is no further apparent reference to this idea in the rest of the movement. Compare the violin figure in measures 43 ff. with the closing figure of the second movement:

Figure 13-9.

a. Violin, mm. 45-46

b. Violin, second movement, mm. 134-135

Is this an accidental resemblance? Perhaps not more so than the link between this figure (in reverse, G–A–B) and one of the central ideas of the finale, the wild-eyed outcry of the violin, first heard in measures 29 ff. This is not a theme; it is more of an improvisation, an exultation:

Figure 13-10.   Violin, mm. 29-34

If this description seems too ornate, then Debussy's own comment on the subject must serve: "a theme turning back on itself like a serpent biting its own tail." As Debussy related to Paul Dukas, the present finale, and its theme, were chosen by him from among a number of attempts. Writing about the entire sonata, the composer cautions: "Beware . . . of works which appear to inhabit the skies; often they are the product of a dark, morose mind."[151]

In any event, the rebel yell appears several times again (measures 67, 146, and in peroration, in the last section, beginning in measure 172). Separating these framing episodes of the movement are: a quiet section in which the piano, and especially its bass line, holds center stage; a contrast section starting at measure 85, a somewhat extraneous, but pleasantly exotic moment of pirouetting by both piano and violin; more serious business, from measure 100, where the piano plays a tremolando and augmented setting of its curtain raiser for the finale. To this the violin adds its distant flutterings.

The last two sections have been in B minor and F sharp major, respectively; now, we launch into a quiet section that is a staging area for the

eventual recurrence of the principal fanfare. In hushed tone, and in a
moodily colored C major, the long journey back to the main subject begins:

Figure 13-11. Mm. 116-120

En route, and in the piano part (measures 134 ff.), a last, and newly
colored reminiscence of the first movement subject is heard several times.
It is swallowed in the last eruption of the finale's main theme. Some time
is taken for an augmentation of the tune, in E major, then in G major.
But the last windup of both tune and sonata comes on irresistibly, both
instruments making a clatter that suggests full orchestra and especially
the woodwinds, brass, and percussion, hard at work in the wings. By the
way, there is no question at this stage of the game. The sonata ends in
flaming G major. Any harmonic ambivalance we may have felt earlier in
the work was only illusory.

Maurice Ravel

In 1927, Maurice Ravel wrote *Bolero*: an obsessive crescendo for full
orchestra. From this same period (relatively late, because he produced
nothing after an auto accident in late 1932, and died five years later at
the age of sixty-two) in Ravel's career comes another, much more ingra-
tiating work, the Sonata for Violin and Piano. Completed in 1927, it had
been started in 1923. In writing it, Ravel had as technical consultant the
violin virtuoso, Hélène Jourdan-Morhange, to whom the work is dedicated.

There is a rather detached, objective, warm-cool attitude about the
piece that is completely identifiable with Ravel, coupled with that clarity
of texture and feeling for the sound of the instruments that is so distinctive a part of his equipment as a composer. Getting at the work, however,
calls for some discretion on the part of the duo. Especially so at the beginning of the piece.

In the first lines of his sonata, Ravel shifts moderately from 6/8 to 9/8 and back; later in the movement, this shifting broadens to include 2/4 to 6/8 to 3/4, back to 2/4, and so on. Behind these changes, however, there is a rhythmic pattern that is readily identifiable, and so often used that it constitutes a danger in the performance of the work. The opening phrase of the piano shows the pattern and gives some idea of its frequency:

Figure 13-12. Piano treble, mm. 1-4

The fragment,

is the troublemaker. Played too pedantically, it becomes sticky and acts as an irritating brake upon the motion of the melody; flippantly, the 16ths become a kind of rolling ornament, rushing on to the next 8th, an air of triviality settling upon the theme. Fast or slow, to plod through the theme is to make it one of the more trite concoctions of music.

Instead, try taking off from the first note in an airy, graceful manner, moving with continual sweep through the first two measures to pause briefly (and gently) on the two stressed points in the third measure; flit forward to the next stress, in measure 5—just *one*, this time; pirouette through the next measure and then hand the tune smoothly over to the violin. Here we have a musical relay of utmost charm and subtlety. The couplet of 16ths, far from sounding like an offhand twitching in the melodic line, becomes a lyric and indispensable facet of the musical motion.

Piano and violin alternate in presentation of ideas (often modified versions of those already heard) and in soloistic and accompanying roles. But the accompaniments are so finely wrought that both roles appeal. This passage, for example, from the violin part (there are similar passages for the piano) is clearly a filigree background to the partner line. Played at speed, the background turns into a rippling wave, its high points flashing against the more subdued parts of the line and arranging themselves into a separate pattern that draws our attention even as we hear the piano's important mutterings:

Figure 13-13. Violin, letter 1, mm. 1-4

When either instrument has the following figure (often heard in this movement),

Figure 13-14. Violin, letter 2, mm. 3-4

it should be played quietly, but resonantly, as though a flourish of drums is heard from afar.

The supreme test of the duo is offered by the passage from letter 3 to the return of the opening statement (twelve measures after letter 4). For thirty-two measures the violin glides through a line that proceeds unbroken—but with much melodic articulation. If the anatomy of the line goes unrealized, the treadmill will turn inexorably. If the player heeds the motion of the writing, a wonderfully supple and variegated tune unfolds, as in these few measures quoted from the passage:

Figure 13-15. Violin, letter 3, mm. 2-13

At the same time, the piano, in a quieter line that has a tranquil beauty of its own, proceeds individually, yet aware: sensitive to the violin line, the keyboard must outguess his partner's twistings and turnings, standing always ready to "catch" the violin line when it poises for a moment and, in the playing of the piano commentary at those points, giving the violin fresh impulse for the next flight of the line.

This kind of consummate interplay is needed constantly in this movement; never more so than in the grand review of principal ideas beginning at letter 11. Though this passage rises to forte level, the effect must never be hard, but always that of freely swelling and diminishing resonance. So also for the closing lines, where both instruments float quietly and regally up and away.

The second movement is marked, "Blues." If the player does not, from experience, know what a blues sounds like, verbal description won't help much. Most players have heard enough jazz to grasp Ravel's purpose in this movement; still, to deliver the lines with the appropriate cool-warm sultriness and nonchalance, to maintain the irresistible pulse of the music (whether played by violin or piano, the beat is constant throughout), while at the same time sliding the individual rhythmic beat this or that side of the metrically "proper" spot; all this, again, is not easy. Nor should the delivery be learned to such an extent that it will come out with complete predictability each time. Here, more than ever in art music, the effect must be one of improvisation on a known melody.

The pizzicato chords at the beginning of the Blues should be played well up on the fingerboard, where the strings offer less resistance and where they can be effectively brushed with the fingertip. The stroke should be applied evenly across the three strings, with no suggestion of swooping downward from the air into the strings. The occasional forte chord should be played with discretion, achieving loudness as much through more emphatic vibrato in the left hand as through increased force in the right.

Figure 13-16.   Violin, mm. 1-4

The piano version of these chords (beginning at letter 1), by the way, is marked with dots. The player should not be misled by this sign into making the chords too short and dry; rather, he should play them to imitate as closely as possible the sound and style already established by the violin in the opening measures.

Before this, and as a punctuation to the violin's pizzicati, the piano will have had this figure to play:

Figure 13-17.   Mm. 7-9

(Yes, there are two independent key signatures for a time at the start of the movement; the violin is in G, the piano, in A flat: a congenial, clashing arrangement.) Here again, the dots are not sufficiently informative in themselves; the eighth notes have to be played with enough length and resonance to establish the fact that the short note drives to the long, and that the final eighth is the most important of the entire figure.

At letter 3, 4, and 5, the piano introduces distinctive themes as counterfoils to restatements of earlier ideas by the violin. At letter 6, the violin presents a new line of its own, to the parallel commentaries of the piano. Throughout, the combination of jauntiness and ease is the important aim. The piano motive at letter 6 is an intriguing case in point; triplets must be distinct from duple rhythms; short notes must be snappy and crisp, without being dry, and must move to resolving long-notes with appropriate force. All this, while flicking out chords with either hand.

Figure 13-18. Letter 6, mm. 2-3

The violinist (though inevitably, and unfortunately, not the pianist) has slides marked at various points in the movement. These glissandi must be played with determination, the effect varying from easy to "dirty," as suits the mood of the player and of the musical moment.

One other violinistic point may be touched on, though it scarcely needs explanation: the up- and down-bow markings in the passages of strummed pizzicato signify the plucking direction. ⊓ = from G-string toward E-string; ∨ = from E-string across toward the G-string (this stroke, of course, being played with the fingernail of the index finger of the right hand). The entire motion is a rhythmic back-and-forth sweep of the hand. The glissandi in these measures are to be spaced out rhythmically, over four sixteenths:

Figure 13-19. Violin, letter 7, mm. 2-3

The last movement begins, in the piano, with an augmented version of the drumbeat of the first movement. The violin takes up the reminder with its pizzicato response in measures 4 and 5.

Figure 13-20.   Mm. 1-5

By dint of teasing repetitions of the motive, back and forth, between piano and violin, the idea of the grace-note figure is extended progressively through eighth couplets, triplets, a sixteenth-note pattern, and finally, into the "perpetual motion" figure that justifies the title of the movement:

Figure 13-21.   Violin, letter 1, mm. 1-6

The violinist may find it troublesome at first to master the rapid alternation of slurred and disjunct couplets. The slurring is thematically necessary, however, because it reflects the motivic origin of the line. Besides, the recurrent change from slurred to separate stroke gives the line its peculiar and welcome sonority.

Another difficulty is the composer's stipulation of the G-string for the first twenty measures of the perpetual motion. The rapid passage-work, moving as high as D (octave above middle C) calls for a combination of delicacy and strength in the bow in order to avoid an asthmatic tone. Here as always in this movement, the left-hand fingers must move incisively to keep the figures from collapsing into a gummy, indistinct mess. This is a peril that surrounds the entire movement, in common with other perpetual-motion pieces: the grain of the pattering rhythm must be kept transparent and clean, and the composite rhythmic and melodic patterns that want to emerge from the constant motion must be allowed to do so.

The movement for the most part favors a close-stepping line; passages of broader arc stand out in relief. The first of these, beginning at letter 4, reminds us of a passage in the second movement (see Figure 13-19). Elsewhere, the line reflects other thematic elements from the first movement, as in the following example (compare with Figure 13-14):

Figure 13-22. Violin, finale, letter 11, mm. 2-3

It is a fine Gallic frenzy that is whipped up for the end of the sonata, with the violin working through a crescendo of octave couplets to a final tattoo across four strings:

Figure 13-23. Finale, last 4 measures

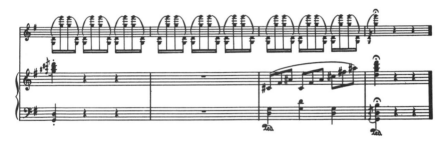

In the course of repeated performances of this movement, the player will grow past the feeling that his right arm will detach itself at the shoulder!

As for the pianist, he will have to show that his lines, too, carry reflections of earlier events: for example, the measures between letters 9 and 10 relating back to the first movement; those at letter 12, revisiting an idea from the blues. The pianist will be put on his mettle to deliver his lines with nonchalent incisiveness, so that the part is clear, fully equal to the violin line, but not overwhelming that busy element in the writing.

One writer after another, in discussing this sonata, cites Ravel's own intention of treating the two instruments so as to emphasize the difference in sonority and color between the two.[152] Because of the consistent contrast in texture of the material assigned to the two instruments in the finale, one can see the intent carried into effect there. In the first two movements, however, it is possible to believe that the two are more closely allied. In the opening movement, there is obvious sharing of musical material by both instruments. And even in the Blues, though the two instruments seem to go their own ways, in the improvisatory fashion of the jazz ensemble, the very fact that they are both involved in the same blues atmosphere gives them a community of purpose and sound that belies disparity. The ultimate challenge as well as listening pleasure in this piece is to have the distinct sonorities weave around each other in complete and unobscured clarity.

14   Some Sonatas from the 1920s: from Ernest Bloch to Ernst Toch

Tʜɪs ᴄʜᴀᴘᴛᴇʀ ʙᴇɢɪɴs with mention of two sonatas by one of the most forceful musical personalities of our time, Ernest Bloch, then proceeds to other music that seems distressing or interesting, as the particular case may be. The very existence of some of these works, now long unplayed, may come as news to readers. It my pique at this or that composition serves to stir the duo's curiosity as to the music still available from that distant decade between the two wars, then all will yet be well. Let the playing be the proof.

Ernest Bloch

The Sonata for Violin and Piano (why Bloch and/or Schirmer's decided to give the title in French, I cannot explain) of Ernest Bloch (1880–1959) was composed in 1920, the year that Bloch—who had been living in America since 1916—was named director of the Cleveland Institute of Music. In three movements, Agitato, Molto quieto, and Moderato, Bloch manages to achieve the panoramic, exotically colored, highly energetic, and equally languorous musical imagery that he often brought off so well. This is a difficult work to play, and just as difficult to describe. Perhaps I should content myself with saying that the effect is rather like that of the first piano quintet (1923), compressed, but only slightly, into the frame of the smaller instrumentation, which means that the violin has to do yeoman duty, and that the pianist has to be sensitive to balances.

Bloch himself spoke of the sonata as a "tormented work . . . written soon after the terrible war and the terrible peace." And a commentary sanctioned by him finds forces of immolation, monastic seclusions, savage rites, doomsday massacres mingled in the implications of this work. This probably accounts for my feeling that, though the work is definitely worth doing, the flavor and tone painting of the sonata is so dominant and so important to its sense that I would not dare hear the piece too often. The same holds true of the *Poème mystique*, the second sonata, composed in 1924. As determinedly optimistic as the first was pessimistic, this sonata is described (by the same spokesman) as an "expression of pure serenity," and of "the calm conviction that all the multitudinous protean faiths of man are one." Bloch refers to the fact that it encompasses a violin recitative of " 'jewish' [small letter Bloch's] character," as well as a Gregorian Credo (the text is printed in the score) and Gloria.[153]

Some Other Composers

Bloch's reflection of the war and its aftermath in his sonatas suggests the mention here of another work of similar vintage and reference: the Sonata in A (1919) of the Italian composer, Ildebrando Pizzetti (born 1880). The middle movement, entitled, *Prayer for the Innocents*, is a plateau between the turbulence of the opening and the victorious redemption of the finale. The sonata makes good ensemble, presents melodic lines that are clear and engaging. The events of the years since the writing of this sonata, however, inevitably affect our appraisal of the sonata's imagery (and, for all I know, the composer's own view of this work from his past). In any event, the musical postures that Pizzetti adopts here are no longer readily tolerable.

Sir Arnold Bax (1883–1953), one of the most prolific of the older generation of contemporary British composers, wrote three sonatas for violin and piano. The first was written in 1910, with the third movement dated 1915, the second, 1920, and the initial movement also revised by the composer. As it finally stands, the work is still behind the times. The trouble centers in the fact that Bax, like many another contemporary composer, simply refuses to construct a melodic *line*, one that—long or short, conventional or not—has direction and inevitability to it.

I have not seen the second sonata, from 1915, but have inspected the third, written in 1927. It is in two movements. The second of these is especially difficult, with much racing about. The composition is a turgid work, not essential to the contemporary repertoire and yet too late in style to serve as a throwback to the nineteenth century.

Germaine Tailleferre, the only female partner assigned to the nebulous (and journalistically titled) group of French composers, *Les Six*, is described as a pupil of Ravel. Tailleffere's violin sonata, composed in 1921, does not reveal in the disciple the master's control of line and color. The work is in four movements; the embarrassing naïveté of the first movement is often reflected in the ensuing chapters.

This sonata, coming late in the line of products of *Les Six* mentioned here, compels me at last to venture the opinion that, even though the members of the group may have sought, in varying degree, nonchalance, lack of pretense, and easy wit in their writing, the style now seems antiquated. No doubt it was a conscious musical stance, a response to the weariness with the old that came in the wake of the First World War. Regrettably, we are now compelled to regard these works not in their own time (the parent to our day), but in ours. Also, we have to play and hear the individual work as an isolated experience, without the aid of footnotes or parenthetic justifications. Whatever of inspiration is lacking or deliberately withheld from the compositional process in these pieces, the result is the same: futility. If instrumentalists held back in the same way, they would be quickly hooted off the stage.

Lest it be thought that woolgathering was the province only of some European composers in the 1920s, we should now behold such a chastening example as the sonata (opus 51) of David Stanley Smith (1877–1940), who was successor to his teacher, Horatio Parker, as head of the School of Music at Yale University. Smith's purpose in the work in question (copyright 1924) seems to be to cover the page with notes. It is not that the textures are so dense; but there is little other way of explaining the reason for being of this kind of sonata. I wonder whether composers always hear what they are writing.

For that matter, I wonder whether, once written, the music is really heard in the performance. For Smith's contemporary, the composer Arthur Shepherd, was able to write of the above sonata that "there are pages in this work . . . that set the 'high-water' mark for true expressiveness in American music."[154] It passeth understanding.

To even the score yet again, I mention here two Scandinavian works, from the 1920s, apparently still in print, to save the reader's time in scouting the repertoire. The Dane, Knudage Riisager (born in 1897 in Russia) wrote a sonata in 1923, made up of two movements, *Fresco con ritmo* and *Jocoso e risoluto*. The work is difficult, bravura, and unconvincing. The Norwegian flutist, Arvid Kleven (1899–1929), in his sonata number 1 (opus 10), has produced a tediously long effort. The effect is that of Strauss, without the good tunes. Much too much of two-handed arpeggiato ripples in the piano, the violin all over the place. Like the Riisager, this work is difficult and expendable.

The Italian composer, Mario Castelnuovo-Tedesco (born 1895), since 1939 resident—and later, citizen—of America, was a pupil of Ildebrando Pizzetti. Among other works for violin and piano, he has written a *Sonata quasi una Fantasia*, of 1929. It is a moderately florid, cyclic piece, technically in three movements (*Prologo, Intermezzo*, and *Epilogo*) but played without pause, so that the inter-movement references are heard in a continuous flow. As a tasteful and self-contained example of a musical style that is no longer part of the current scene, this piece has merit. It is of some difficulty technically, though still within reach of the proficient amateur duo.

Age does not necessarily bring discretion. Albert Roussel (1869–1937), student of Vincent d'Indy and musically much more adventuresome than his teacher, was sixty-two when, in 1931, he "revised" his first violin sonata, the one in D minor, op. 11 (1907–08). What the original version could have been like, I do not care to imagine. The approved later format presents us with three movements, each of them exceedingly long for the musical content. This sonata should be put by the side, and attention given only to the Second Sonata, opus 28, of 1924. Here we find a huge, sprawling first movement; an Andante in ternary form, with a boiling middle section; and a Presto finale, in alternating 6/8 4/8, that also alternates pizzicato and arco in the violin part. This sonata is a piece that keeps you alert and guessing. Recommended.

Georges Enesco

Georges Enesco (1881–1955), the best known of the Roumanian composers, a violin virtuoso in his own right and teacher of Yehudi Menuhin, wrote three violin sonatas. The first two, opera 2 and 6, date from the turn of the century. The former (1897) is a large work, too much like other music of its own or earlier period to require undue attention. The Second Sonata (1899), dedicated to Joseph and Jacques Thibaud (Enesco and Jacques Thibaud had both studied violin with Marsick at the Paris conservatory in the late 1890s), is titled "for Piano and Violin." There is no terribly good reason for giving the piano top billing, except that it is two hands to one; the musical interest is evenly parceled out between the two instruments. This seems more individual a work than the first sonata, though still exceedingly generous in its proportions. It has, by the way, a thematic resemblance to the opening subject of the much later Hindemith Viola Sonata, op. 11, no. 4. The Enesco second is an interesting work, not entirely up-to-date, but worth playing if the duo has the stamina, and the program, enough room for a work this size. The length is not a matter of time duration alone, but of the slow pace that Enesco allows himself in the unfolding of musical event.

With the Third Sonata, opus 25, from 1926, dedicated "to the memory of Franz Kneisel," and with the subscription, "in the folk-character of Roumania; A minor," we enter upon certain changes from the first two works.

The composer finds it necessary to offer at the start of the sonata a table of "explanation of some unusual signs." These include special markings for dynamic gradations; marks to guide tempo fluctuation; others to indicate sharping or flatting by intervals less than a whole or half step; and portamento signs. In addition to all this, there are many more signs governing bowing, character of interpretation, and so on, than in the other two sonatas. The Paris edition of the work carries special pedalling instruction and chord-arpeggiation rules for the pianist.

With all this apparatus, it would be a shame if the piece turned out to be more of the same old thing. But it is by far the most individual of the three Enesco sonatas, with three movements that bear out the implication of their titles: Moderato malinconico, Andante sostenuto e misterioso, and Allegro con brio. Whatever the character of Roumanian folk music, this sonata is full of enough color and aromatic sound to convince the listener; more so, I might add, than the familiar *Roumanian Rhapsody* by which Enesco is generally known in the Western world.

Ernst Toch

The Austrian-born composer, Ernst Toch (1887–1964) lived and taught for years in Germany, then briefly in London, removing to America in 1934. Here he taught first at the New School in New York, then transferred to Hollywood, where he spent the remaining decades of his life. In his prolific output, Toch included two violin sonatas. Of these, I have seen the second, opus 44, (1928). It is in three movements, all most neatly written. The opening, "Defiant, storming," for example, makes consistent and thorough use, in contrasting episodes, of the motive of a falling triplet followed by a still lower rhythmic resolution tone. The trouble lies in the hoped-for contrast between movements. The titles tell us that the Intermezzo is to be "dancer-like, gracious," and the finale, in an abstract Allegro giusto. But the sound tells the ear that all three movements are cut from similar cloth. The whole piece suffers, in a clean-lined way, from hyper-Straussian flush.

15   *Bartók: Three Sonatas*

Each of the sonatas considered in the last chapter—
even that of Bloch—stands as one of the slighter efforts of composition in
the 1920s. Two major achievements of the sonata literature, dating from
early in that decade, tower above the works around them: the mature
sonatas of Béla Bartók.

In the early 1940s, an evening of the music of Bartók was presented
in New York. Bartók himself was the pianist for this chamber-music concert. After the performance of the Fifth Quartet (with the Bulgarian
rhythms in its third movement), this writer heard a member of the audience say to another, "What did you think of those Bulgarian zoolaks?"
The comment was obtuse; and it reflected a way of hearing that was equally
obtuse. During his lifetime, Bartók was exposed to more than his share
of such listening. It did not divert him from his chosen avenues of musical
thought.

Bartók wrote two sonatas for violin and piano in the years 1921 and
1922, respectively. He was then forty—born in Nagyszentmiklós, Hungary,
in 1881—and already had fifty-odd compositions to his credit. Extending
back to the 1890s, these included a number of unpublished early works,
among them a duo-sonata from 1903. The published works begin in the
early 1900s. To them has recently been added the 1903 sonata.

Bartók's formal education in music was received at the hands of private

teachers, and, from 1899, at the Budapest Academy of Music. His exposure
to the music of Wagner, Brahms, Liszt, and Strauss must also be counted
part of his traditional musical training.

The fact of Bartók's musical descent from the nineteenth century is
made inescapably clear by a reading of the Sonata for Violin and Piano
of 1903. Where, in such a work as the First String Quartet (1908), derivative elements and colors have been absorbed into a personal style, they
are remarkable for their obviousness in the earlier work. Strauss and Tchaikovsky are heard in the principal theme of the first movement and one of
the melodic ideas of the third (final) movement:

Figure 15-1.

a. Violin, Allegro moderato, mm. 10-14

b. Violin, Vivace, mm. 129-138

What is most striking, though, is the prolixity that Bartók permits
himself in the early sonata. The First Quartet has its moments of self-
enjoyment (especially in some aspects of its finale). In the 1903 sonata,
redundancy flares out. The finale suffers particularly in this respect, parad-
ing its ideas too loosely and too often. Despite a successful premiere of the
sonata in early 1904, Bartók did not publish the piece. The editor of the
newly published (1968) issue of the sonata writes that Bartók "later made
changes in the end-movements, which reflects on his dissatisfaction with
the first version of the sonata." The only change apparent in the publication itself is the indication of a nine-measure cut in the Poco maestoso
section of the second movement. For the rest, one must assume that all
is shown according to Bartók's review of the work. From the present look
of the sonata, it would seem that Bartók did not have time to complete
his appraisal of the work in every detail, or perhaps, did not intend after
all that the work be published. The sonata is interesting more for its role
as an early work of the master than for its essential appeal to today's
listener. It does not approach the stature of the two sonatas of Bartók's
middle years.

From 1905 dates Bartók's scholarly study of the folk music of his native Hungary and the surrounding areas in Eastern Europe. These studies, conducted alone and in collaboration with his friend, Zoltan Kodaly, involved a great deal of recording, in the field, of the music as sung and played by peasants and townsfolk in their own habitat. Along with this went the greater labor of transcribing the music, determining its characteristics of melody and poetry, and classifying the pieces. Collecting, preserving, and disseminating the music of these native cultures, Bartók at the same time found in it inspiration for his own writing.

In 1907, Bartók became professor of piano at the Budapest Academy. It was as piano teacher that he spent the bulk of his professional career; he did not want to teach composition. And it was as a concert performer, rather more than as composer, that he was known to the general musical public during his lifetime. In composition, he found more recognition abroad than in his own country. Even so, it was not until after his death in 1945 (New York) that listeners at large learned to hear past the aural asperities of his writing to the warmth and compassion within.

There are some who still feel that Bartók is beyond them—or indeed, that he is beneath their consideration, "Bulgarian zoolaks" and all. The initiate may be inclined to shrug off such listeners as know-nothings. But Bartók's music tells us about ourselves and our world in a fashion so compelling that it can be compared only with that of a Mozart or Beethoven. To the extent that Bartók's "message" (especially in so bitter and telling a work, for example, as the Sixth Quartet, of 1939) still remains inaccessible to too large a segment of the world's people, to that extent are we all deprived and made smaller.

For many of us, the thread that carries us into the heart of Bartók's composing is precisely his use of the folk idiom, in the best and most honest sense of the term. Native music was a vital part of Bartók's experience. He could not cheapen folk music by using it either as a mere tincture to color conventional writing, or as a raw implant into his own composition. (Though arrangements of folk music do, of course, have an undisguised and important place in his output.) Knowing the anatomy of folk music as he did, he was able to use its rhythmic and intervallic traits, its structural patterns as part of his own musical thinking.[155] The works he built with that vocabulary, however, were unmistakably his own, inimitable, yet much imitated by those who followed.

For the Bartók performer, there is aid and satisfaction in this. There is security in the occasional folklike flavor and in the rigorous logic with which Bartók customarily unfolds his sequence of musical ideas. The player is sustained by a sense of familiarity, of knowing where he is bound. At the same time, he does not feel that he is wasting time, working hard to recreate something a folk artist could do instinctively, simply, and with less effort. The native, the old, is seen through the angular distortions of the new; the rigors of newness are softened, strengthened, supported, by the underlying, simple directness of the old.

The sounds evoked by Bartók are rich, colorful, often biting. In the two sonatas discussed here, the austerities are particularly great, the farthest that Bartók went in this regard.[156] It is no doubt true that Bartók "considered the First Sonata as in C♯ minor, the Second as in C major."[157] But the chromaticism, the interval patterns, the chordal structure all mask the tonal outlines of these pieces.

As a musical logician, Bartók is second to none. The clarity of his thinking is reflected in the very appearance of his manuscript, "the writing . . . neat and the layout careful in the extreme; a closer approximation to print can hardly be imagined."[158] The visual impact of even the printed Bartók page, all its clarity of instruction notwithstanding, is often more forbidding than the sound represented. I want to give the reader a road map through this Bartókian terrain, plotting out the chain of happenings in the music, giving some overview of the entire structure, and occasionally shedding light on notational features that might intimidate the hasty eye. If, in so doing, I seem more than ever to have my nose buried to the hilt in the score, reading myopically from one detail to the other, my pose will be matched by that of the player as he first picks his way through the music.

First Sonata for Violin and Piano

At the start of this sonata, the piano spends its first ten measures creating a shimmering background for the violin line. On the page, the piano part may look more important than its fellow, but the dynamic indications—forte for the violin, generally piano for the keyboard—give the clue to relative prominence:

Figure 15-2. Mm. 2-3

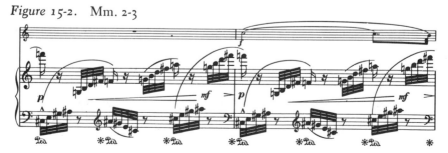

The pendulum of balance can swing just as readily in the other direction: to equal weight on both lines, as at letter 1,

Figure 15-3. Mm. 10-11

or to highlighting of the piano.

Figure 15-4. Mm. 74-76

The treatment of the violin is quite sensitive to the nature of the instrument. In Bartók's second string quartet (1917), he has the first violin, in the opening lines of that work, start with a little swirl of melody, then work its way outward from that center, sweeping in ever wider arcs through its range of sound. A similar purpose drives the violin line in this sonata. The initial violin statement starts in the middle of its range (C above middle C), then gradually reaches down to its lowest tone, G (measure 11), and upward to one of its highest, E flat (measure 16). It is not just seeking out limits of range. As the movement unfolds, the violin traces out various portions of its gamut so that a series of contrasting "envelopes" of sound are created, cells of tone in which—through faster or slower writing and changing amplitude of line, from high to low pitch—a great array of textures is set before the listener. Here are some examples of this variety.

The emphasis here is on the melodic line and its changing rhythmic detail:

Figure 15-5.   Mm. 3-db. 7

The line is shaped here so that its rapid trajectory suggests an enclosing, a capture of musical space:

Figure 15-6.   Mm. 11-12

A moving, but narrow and densely knit thread grows narrowest at midpoint, moves upward just as tautly, then breaks into a very wide amplitude:

Figure 15-7.   Mm. 13-20

A broad ribbon of sound places emphasis on its two outer edges:

Figure 15-8.   Mm. 29-33

A homogeneous ribbon of sound has its weight on the lower, motivating edge of the band:

Figure 15-9.   Mm. 60-62

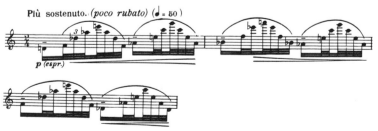

In this broad, densely packed band of sound, the emphasis is on the outer limits:

Figure 15-10. Mm. 66-67

Finally, here is a narrow thread of constant dimension and of varying compression in dynamics, rhythm, and speed (note the *ritard.* indicated):

Figure 15-11. Mm. 76-77

The piano is active in its own right, displaying the several sides of its nature as a keyboard instrument. There are:

a. Rippling washes of tone (see the beginning; letter 6; letter 20; and the last page of the movement).

b. Slower-moving, yet flowing, passage-work (area around letter 13; letter 25).

c. Softly textured, arpeggiated chordal playing (as at the *più sostenuto* before letter 11; and the four measures before letter 22).

d. Chordal playing of a more solid kind, but still softened by an out-of-phase relationship between treble and bass (three measures before letter 11).

e. Solid chordal playing (as at the *a tempo* before letter 2).

f. Percussive, angularly rhythmed chordal passages (as at measures 13 and 14; letter 3; letter 9; and so forth).

Conspicuously absent in the pianist's arsenal in this movement is the playing of simple, clearly exposed, single lines of melody. Bartók seems deliberately to avoid this one way of writing for the piano, so as not to encroach on the province of the violin—which, conversely, does no chordal playing whatever in this movement, but achieves its purposes only in terms of the single strand of sound. Note that, when the violin does occasionally hit a double-stop, the solidity of sound is mitigated by tremolo (letter 12, letter 25), or by a quiet dynamic level (see the closing measures of the movement).

Rhythmically, dynamically, in texture of sound, Bartók achieves variety by having the two instruments work against each other, either in complete integration, or with subordination of one to the other. Our earlier illustrations (see Figures 15-2, 15-3, and 15-4) show this; numerous examples can be found by the players, who must be alert to the flavor and context of each musical moment in this piece.

There is so much sound, and of such richly contrasting nature, in this movement, that the occasional silence, in either instrument, but especially in the piano, is quite noticeable. Significantly, the quietness is concentrated most at the structural dividing points of the movement: around and after letter 11, and so also around 22. The movement is in three parts, corresponding to the frame of the old sonata-allegro movement. Bartók himself certified his use of that form in the Third Quartet (1927) when he titled the third section of the work as "Recapitulation of the first section." In the present sonata, the first movement is made up of three sections, to which we may again apply the traditional sonata titles:

Exposition: from the beginning to meno lento, three measures before letter 11.
Development: from the meno lento forward to letter 20.
Recapitulation: from letter 20 to the end of the movement.

This is not a recapitulation in the usual sense. The original ideas are viewed, in their later manifestations, through the distance of the experience that the growing movement has itself provided. To conserve space, the following illustrations show only examples from the violin part, though similar correspondence (again with many a difference in detail and general shape) is found between interrelated passages in the piano part.

Figure 15-12.

a. Mm. 187-193 (compare with measures 3 ff., Figure 15-5, above)

b. Mm. 82-85

Mm. 245-250

c. Mm. 86-89

Mm. 251-253

d. Mm. 100-103

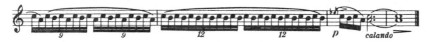

Last 4 mm. of the movement

The total shape of the movement, then, takes us from the wavelike opening of the piano, through lyric sweeps of the violin and piano together; on to the snapped rhythmic statements by the piano, and quiet murmurings by both instruments. Then into a middle section where these ideas are extended and played off against each other; and into a concluding section where the first section and its ideas are revisited, the entire movement closing as quietly as it began.

In this Allegro, as throughout the sonata, it is essential to make accurate observance of Bartók's dynamic indications, pedaling instructions, tempo markings, and rhythmic notation—especially the snapped pattern, whether *on* the beat,

Figure 15-13. Violin, mm. 53-54

or *off:*

Figure 15-14.   Mm. 38-39

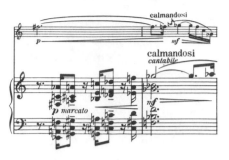

The second movement, Adagio, is also in three parts, the end sections closely related. At the opening, the violin is heard alone in a line marked by frequent changes of meter. The metric frame is only a general support for the melody, which chooses its own peaks and breaks (marked by Bartók with short, vertical dividing-lines), not always with regard to the bar-line confines of the writing. In the gradually building line, a series of initial falls, accompanied by subsiding dynamics, is prelude to an active rise toward the end of the solo, reaching high F sharp at tempo 1 (measure 16), where the piano makes its entrance.

Against the piano background, the violin continues its solo, floating gradually down from high C (letter 1) to middle C, its lowest point thus far (measure 28). From here it moves ahead in a second, shorter passage alone. Now its line is broken by frequent rests; moving portions alternate with more hesitant, yet still urgent measures.

Figure 15-15.   Violin, mm. 29-33

Once again, the end of the violin solo overlaps the piano entrance, which again provides brief, tolling background. The violin reenters, letter 3, from above (as at letter 1), moving from its highest takeoff point thus far, D, and making its way down to the "dying-away" tones of the measures leading to letter 4.

The section from letter 10 to the end of the movement corresponds to this beginning. The violin, at letter 10, takes on its initial solo role, though the piano now is heard along with it in simple background function. The violin part is much more ornate than at the first appearance:

Figure 15-16.

a. Mm. 1-4

b. Mm. 81-84

Again, at letter 12, the violin reflects its earlier second solo spot, complete with breaks, in more elaborate fashion; compare the following example with Figure 15-15:

Figure 15-17. Mm. 92-94

The passage in the last nine measures of the movement is a respelling of the music at letter 3, even to the extent of moving from the high D to the same middle-register C.

If the violin is prominent in the end sections of the movement, the duo is more evenly treated in the lines from letter 4 through 10. In this middle section, the texture is thickened by arpeggiations, linear runs, and octaves,

Figure 15-18. M. 67, first half measure

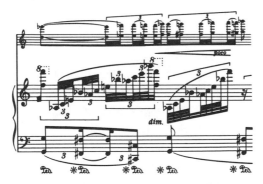

but always in restrained terms. The high point of the movement is reached in a very brief forte at letter 10 (where the violin solo returns) and again around letter 13, but the movement favors the quieter levels, with many a double- and triple-piano indication.

The last movement, Allegro, leans toward the other extreme, the loud and thick. The first fifty-three measures of the violin part are marked to be played on the G-string, often moving to its upper reaches, producing a guttural intensity. This beginning is a very energetic, stamping dance, marked by the percussive arpeggiated chords of the piano part and its occasional flashing swirl of sound:

Figure 15-19. Mm. 14-17

The opening episode extends until letter 8. Corresponding to this beginning is the section from letter 33 to letter 38. A contrasting, second section is found from letter 8 to letter 12. In these lines, the earlier motoric rhythms give way to broader paces, expressed by the violin in heavy quarter beats, by the piano in five-sixteenth groups. The heavy tread of the music is sparked by dotted rhythms in the violin, tightly snapped:

And again, this section has a later reflection, in the music from letter 38 to letter 40.

The third, middle area of the movement is introduced by the violin pizzicato chords (beginning at measure 122), pulled back drastically both in tempo and dynamics to become the accompaniment to the piano at letter 12. From here to letter 33, we are involved with various facets of the middle section. The first episode thereof, extending past letter 17, constitutes a wild development on the initial dance idea. This is essentially the pianist's show, Vivacissimo, with the violin offering a background of pizzicati chords, bowed arpeggiations, trills, and arpeggiated pizzicati. Shortly after letter 18, the violin takes up again its middle-episode line (cf. letter 8 ff.), combining with it some elements of the dancelike theme. This carries us as far as letter 22, where the opening of the movement, complete with piano introduction, is reflected.

The idea of such recurrence is reinforced by the appearance at letter 25 of the secondary episode (again, compare with letter 8). But, at the Meno vivo after 25, developmental maneuvers seem still to be in process. The principal dance idea is manifest in augmentation in the middle voice of the piano. And from letter 26 through letter 33, the several ideas of the movement's musical material are brought into play.

At letter 33, as we have already noted, the official recurrence of the opening of the movement actually takes place. There is a last respite in the measures leading into, and including the passage of, letters 44 and 45. And from 46 to the end, the final, unbridled run takes place. Never one to spare performance instructions, Bartók showers tempo indications upon the players during these last pages. From letter 33 to the double bar, the quarter note is progressively set at metronome speeds of: 66, 144-138, 152, 168, 112, 152, 168, 126, 96-92, 168, 152, 168, 72, and 168. You don't need a rally copilot to reach the successive mileposts on schedule! The point is, of course, that the movement, with all the structural interrelationships between successive ideas and sections, should unfold in freewheeling fashion; the many tempo fluctuations and the connecting tissue of accelerations and retards (beginning from the very start of the movement) are designed to ensure this mood.

The First Sonata (and the Second as well) was written for the virtuoso woman violinist, Jelly d'Aranyi. It was in March, 1922, in London, that the premiere performance of the work—it had been composed in October through December of the preceding year—was given, by d'Aranyi and Bartók himself. The Second Sonata was composed from July to November, 1922, and, again in London and with the same duo, was premiered in May, 1923.

Second Sonata for Violin and Piano

The piano begins this sonata with a long, low, sustained F sharp. There is a forte instruction, but the very act of sustaining the tone assures that, pianolike, it will constantly dwindle. It is this natural diminution of volume that Bartók elicits from the violin in the pulsating E assigned to that instrument's opening measures.

Figure 15-20. Mm. 1-5

The bow and vibrato must achieve a steady gradation downward from mezzo-forte to pianissimo. This dynamic shading is aided by the coloristic change: in measure 3, the composer calls for a shift from the A- (for certainly the initial E must be played stopped, rather than open!) to the D-string.

This is a curious way of starting a sonata—as though with a sigh of exhaustion before things have even begun. And it is a landmark for the initial episode of the score. In measure 5, reviving from the opening E, both instruments begin to move, each hovering and twitching by turns so that the partner's motion is left clearly revealed. The show of activity is circumscribed by the first event, however; for, at the next resting point (measures 19 and 20), we find ourselves again with the low F sharp in the piano, high E in the violin:

Figure 15-21.   Mm. 15-20

A comparison, too, of the piano notes in measure 5 with those in measures 16 and 17 will show that the first portion of this movement has been pivoting around a tonal axis, moving from G in measure 7 to D in measures 9 to 11; D sharp in measure 12; B in measure 13. And these plateaus of sound in the violin part have been quietly countered by opposing tones in the piano: F sharp against E; D sharp–E sharp against G; C–D sharp/ C sharp–D set against D; E–E sharp opposing D sharp; B flat paralleling B; and finally, F–F sharp set off against E.

The voyage of the violin is not through; its line continues on to a harmonic E, glides from there to the next higher E, exploring two octaves en route (measures 20 to 22). Against this, the piano—using three octaves to encompass its purpose—opposes low octave-touches on G, while the middle ground is dimly lit with murmuring, undulating figures. The searching out of harmonics takes the violin then to A, to G, and back to A.

The piano, now alone, reflects the upward octave sweeps of the violin in two measures of rising motion (31 and 32). But these are in 5/8 meter; and the bass, B, of these measures moves down to A sharp in the thirty-third bar. The scene is thus set for the next episode: in 5/8, and with the piano momentarily continuing its downward motion. It is the violin, how-ever, that takes up the 5/8 pattern, and not always confining its phrase within the frame of the measure. With a curious combination of inde-pendence and allegiance to partner, the piano moves its own way, in 4/8, returning only after a time to the 5/8 swing.

Changes in meter are frequent in this movement, often bar by bar. This is not an artificial complexity, but is actually a convenient and clear way of notating the progress of the music. Familiarity with the piece will make the metric changes seem quite natural to the player, and even simpler to read than would be a fixed barring, where the measure would fight the phrasing flow of the melody.

In any event, the momentary low-energy point, reached at letter 5, is marked also by a temporary, stable metric plane (5/8 enduring for some seventeen measures now, even though the piano moves for a time in quad-ruple motion). Then the pulse of metric change quickens again, along with a general increase in excitement. By letter 9, the violin has touched several new plateaus of sound: moving from A to E, to F, to G, to C, and (by the Vivo just before letter 9) to E again. And with the piano always in subtly parallel, yet opposing sonority.

From the Vivo onward to letter 16, the piano moves in more vigorous fashion: with arches of thirty-seconds (measures 73 to 75), rising sweeps (measures 79, 81), interlocking triplets (measures 83 ff.), and so on. The violin follows its own plateau-hopping routine, in broader steps for the moment, until letter 12. There, it switches to a new kind of sonority focus, that of touching on double-stop resting points, seeming in this to take up the kind of sonorities already well researched by the piano in earlier lines. For example, G, at measure 89, merges into F-G, A flat–B flat (measure 95), D–C sharp, E–D sharp, and G–F sharp. This chordal stress on the seventh is followed by melodic sweeps of the seventh (cf. measures 104 ff.) and, immediately after letter 15, a shaking-inside-out alternation between the tenth and the diminished octave. This is followed by a pulsation on the interval of the ninth, the piano insisting on F sharp–G, and C–C sharp, the violin on A–B flat (cf. measures 113 ff.). The middle episode of the movement closes with a strongly sustained, wide-spaced cluster of tones from both instruments: A sharp, (A)G, G sharp, (B flat), B.

From that last B, the violin returns us to the opening strain of the movement. This return centers on B, rather than on the axial E of the sonata's beginning. The rhapsodic turnings of the instrument bring us again (by letter 18) to the initial setting of the tune. But only momentarily so, for the line slips continuously, to end enigmatically on the remembered sonority of F-B in the piano and the actually heard sound of F sharp–G sharp in the violin (see measures 133 to 135).

The feeling of ambiguity is prolonged as the second movement opens. Here the piano stresses G (in the bass), but sets a cluster of tones (F sharp–F, G, A flat) against it. This solo clustering is replaced by the violin in a spelled-out, linear application of the cluster tones, with the addition of a stressed A. At the same time, it is apparent that the violin line is a new version—*undoubtedly the version intended by Bartók from the very outset of the work*—of the rhapsodic theme of the first movement. Here the melody takes on a stamped-dance character, quite in contrast to the aspect given it in the earlier chapter of the composition. Compare the following three examples:

Figure 15-22.

a. Second movement, mm. 1-12

b. Violin, first movement, mm. 1-6

c. Violin, second movement, mm. 63-68

To return to the event sequence of the second movement: the stage is now clear for the violin to present, again solo, the dancelike theme in plucked tones (measures 22 ff.). Note that (as in the first presentation), though the meter is a straightforward 2/4, the marked accents break much of the line into a cross-grained pattern of 3/8 units; this pattern must be clearly projected.

There is a tantalizing, double-life quality about many statements in this piece. Thus, when the piano reenters, letter 3, we are made uncertain whether the violin solo we have been hearing is really soloistic, or is rather the curtain raiser for material of more imposing melodic sweep, now presented by the piano. The uncertainty is heightened by the fact that the violin, now reduced to a drumbeat accompaniment, is instructed to play brusquely (*ruvido*) and at piano level, while the keyboard is told to make its appearance "from afar" (*lontano*), at pianissimo level. Musical-dramatic perspective is very much involved here, with the two instrumental sonorities making their way forward, from far to near, in the passage from letter 3 to letter 6. And the successive dynamic markings, which seem to favor the violin more than need be, are actually designed to keep the two instruments on a par with each other. In any event, when the duo arrives "downstage center," we are treated to a great, short barrage of resonance, with the several parts providing every tone other than E, G sharp, and C:

Figure 15-23. Mm. 58-60

Now, we are off into the first of an extended series of episodes that make up the heart of the movement. At letter 7, the violin undulates quickly and quietly against a backdrop of spiky eighths from the piano. (The violin rhythm is quite tricky, particularly in the accent-sparked groups of seven sixteenths, measures 206 to 209.)

At letter 8, the tempo lets down, but the pace steps up. The piano throws in groups of downbeat sixteenths in place of the steady punctuation of eighths. But we are not allowed to settle into any one swing for long. As in the First Sonata, frequent tempo change shapes and broadens the musical design. On these two score pages alone, from letter 8 to letter 12, we have this roster of tempo stipulations: ♩ = 104; 114; 86; 116-20; 132. And these segments are connected (or disconnected) by *accelerandi* and *allargandi*, or sometimes by comma or composed rest, or by sudden shift in pace. The overall effect is that of a dance moving inexorably forward, no matter what the passing direction in tempo may be. The breaks in pace render more vivid the general progress of events. An intensifying role is played, too, by the occasional deviations from the steady four-to-the-bar swing, as at measures 110 to 115, where a series of triplet figures (already familiar from the original violin pizzicato statement), some with off-center accents, are eccentrically superimposed on the regular flow of the measure:

Figure 15-24.   Mm. 111-115

Indeed, the remainder of the movement (and the sonata) becomes a complexly simple—and consequently, hypnotically effective—study in the various ways that the swiftly trotting figure can be maneuvered. The score shows the following events, among others:

Letter 13: violin in offbeat pattern, against steady piano pulse.
Letter 15: violin in solo paroxysm, against unobtrusive piano background.
Letter 16: three-man setting—piano on three staves, playing sustained

bass-tones, upper parts essentially in eighth-note motion; the violin above, in slurred-sixteenth couplets.

Letter 17: similar voice texture, but with violin now in descending triplet scale-runs.

Letter 19: activity essentially in the piano part, with a tattoo of accompaniment rhythm from the violin.

Letter 20: the piano still in the forefront, the violin whirling away in the background in a flurry of triplets.

Letter 21: violin moving in broad glissandi; piano in percussive tone-clusters.

Letter 22: violin sustains tone, piano plays quasi-glissando runs.

Letter 24: the measures around this letter present some horrendous-looking clusters for the pianist. The accidentals needed in our notation system make these chords look worse than they are. Essentially, we are dealing with patterns that have chordal tones moving in half-step oscillation. In the regular alternation of these tones, many of the accidentals are required only to cancel the effect of accidentals in the chord immediately preceding within the measure. Much more ferocious to the eye than to the hand!

Letters 24-27: the episodes contained herein are similar to the series of episodes between letters 21 and 24.

Letter 27: here is a passage in triple-weave texture—the violin above, in a line combining sustained, glissando, and rhythmic writing; the treble of the piano in eighth-note rhythm, with cross accents and some sixteenth-note impulses, and the "bass" line, moving next to, and sometimes through, the treble voice (some very precise hand crossing is involved here), races along in thirty-seconds, finally drawing the treble completely into its rapid orbit.

By letter 35, we have reached the climactic passage of the movement. From here to letter 43, the violin moves in rapid sixteenth couplets, paced by percussive eighth-note chords and runs in the piano. From letter 43 to letter 46, the roles are reversed, the violin now taking the percussive accompaniment function. From letters 46 to 48, the piano takes the stage alone, in an expansive and ponderous mood. At 48, the violin whirls back into action with scurrilous sweeps of sixteenths, the fastest version yet of the dance theme. Shortly before letter 50, the piano is drawn into the same frenzied pace. Its bar-by-bar sweeps eventually pull the violin into a similar pattern. This fragmentation of the violin line breaks the chain of excitement: the piano becomes intermittent, then falls silent, while the violin, continuing alone, thrashes its way down from its peak of frenzy. At letter 56, and from there to the end, the violin (now rejoined by the piano) states and restates—in a combination of fixation and nostalgia—the pervasive theme of the sonata, now again heard in much the same form it had at the beginning of the piece.

The work ends with a sense of fulfillment, release, and exhaustion, the violin floating very high on its harmonic E, the piano supplying, far below, a C and G to make all come right with a C-major triad!

And now that I have left the duo, road map in hand, in the harmonic Promised Land, how shall the players approach these sonatas? With mingled diligence, respect, and—above all—with a desire to move past the notes to a stage of performance where technical command is leavened with a quasi-improvisatory freedom (all the while remaining faithful to the composer's instructions). I cannot do better than to close this chapter with words by Bartók himself about the purpose of performance:

> We must realize that even performances of the same work of art music by the same performer will never occur twice in absolutely the same way. . . . This eternal changeableness gives life to music, be it folk or art music, whether the changes are considerable or scarcely perceptible. These intrinsic characteristics of music seem to be in contradiction with the contemporary trend of producing music more and more by mechanical means, according to which music would be compressed into a frozen and never-changing form.[159]

Obviously, both Bartók sonatas are for the accomplished player only. Those with lesser equipment can attempt them, but only for the increased awareness of the stuff of this music that slow and rather painful practice will gradually afford.

16 🎜 *Stravinsky:* Duo Concertant

Igor STRAVINSKY wrote his only piece for violin-piano duo in 1931–32, at the age of fifty. "I had formerly had no great liking for a combination of piano and strings, but a deeper knowledge of the violin [he had composed the Concerto for Violin, for the American virtuoso, Samuel Dushkin, in 1931] and close collaboration with a technician like Dushkin had revealed possibilities I longed to explore."[160]

The *Duo Concertant*, "a sort of sonata for violin and piano," was begun in late 1931, completed in July, 1932, and premiered in Berlin by Dushkin and the composer in October of that year. The composer says of this work:

> The spirit and form of my *Duo Concertant* were determined by my love of the pastoral poets of antiquity and their scholarly art and technique. The theme that I had chosen developed through all the five movements of the piece which forms an integral whole, and, as it were, offers a musical parallel to the old pastoral poetry.[161]

Stravinsky's references to literary and musical threads in this piece, and also his mention of inspiration by the book, *Petrarch*, of his friend, Charles Albert Cingria, has caused some strained interpreting on the part of musicographers. If, however, we take a simple definition of each title, and then make it secondary to an approach to the music itself, we shall fare well enough.

The musical process in the opening Cantilène seems to be that of

257

triggering one line by another, one instrument by the other. A rapid, low chiming of the piano (marked "let vibrate," with pedal, to give a briefly sustained resonance) sets the violin off on a series of sixteenth-note arches: eleven notes, another eleven, then fifteen. A silence; then another tintinnabulation in the piano sends the violin into longer and higher flights, extending as far as twenty-three sixteenths, and reaching (via harmonics) to high F sharp (measure 13). The piano has been supporting this activity with tremolo unisons. Suddenly, the trembling is enlarged and surrounded by chordal resonances; and the violin gives up its running and leaping to play more sustained, chordal progressions. The resulting texture is one of resting, of recharging of energy.

Now, to the continued double-stop support of the violin, the piano takes over the running sixteenths. In general, its flights, coming after those of the violin at the start of the movement, are longer; and the activity is furthered by similar agility in the bass part. This gives way to more sustained motion (paralleling the simultaneous movements of the violin part); after its longest-running sequence, more than two-hundred notes, the piano treble subsides into slower rhythms. Another brief rest, and the opening reappears, truncated and modified to end the movement.

If the word, *cantilène*, is to be taken to mean, literally, music of lyric and flowing character, or a tender, expressive song, then the lyricism in this movement is braced and made astringent by the angular passage-work in which it is framed and embedded. It is, in fact, hard to decide which aspect, which temper of the movement should be given predominance. The two aspects cross-influence one another. The sixteenth-note line, despite its active profile, should be played with some lyric grace; note, specifically, that the composer uses no dots or wedges for these figures. One may deduce, then, that the lines are to be played rather smoothly, legato. The absence of dynamic gradations or stress marks within the sixteenth-note melodies, however (there is, for example, only one poco accentuation mark in the first thirty measures of the violin part), should not be taken to mean that the figures can be played in absolutely level fashion. The peaks of the several rhythmic units are so strategically placed, in relation to each other, that it is clearly necessary to orient each unit around its own center of interest.

Figure 16-1. Violin, mm. 1-5

By the same token, the sustained-line measures also need the interpolation of dynamics, stress points, goals of motion.

Figure 16-2. Violin, mm. 17-22

In a way, the procedures of the first movement are taken over, modified, into the second movement, Eclogue I (an idyllic, pastoral conversation). The opening lines of the eclogue find the violin providing a backdrop: a long, sustained interval of the twelfth, analogous to the tremolos played by the piano at the beginning of the duo; and against this, the running sixteenths of the piano lines. The bass line of the piano is a written-out tremolo—a single, four-note sequence is repeated no less than seventy times. This forms the "floor" of a gargantuan measure (measure 5) that spans more than two pages of score. The piano treble, though varied in outline, contributes to the swiftness with similar running motion. The violin, abandoning its sustained humming, now duets with the piano-treble in the presentation of a simple tune, taking time also to imitate the running work of the piano.

The nonbarring of measure 5, so that sixty-nine beats run continuously, with not even a rehearsal letter to lighten the players' task, can only be for the purpose of encouraging free flow in the performance. But the patterns are not so eccentric that they could not be metrically grouped. Especially because, from measure 6 on, Stravinsky does use bars, in constantly changing meter.

The second half of the movement (measures 6 ff.) is given over to incisive, but reserved, jogging, by both instruments, in irregular sequences of meter (there is no readily apparent scheme governing the series of metric changes), and in dry, clipped resonance. The sound texture "opens" gradually, both instruments beginning low, the violin moving progressively higher and wider (in interval), the piano moving to a lesser high point, then returning to a deeper level for much of the last page of the movement.

Stravinsky's tempo indication, $\textstyle\rfloor$ = 76-80, is important. Even at the faster limit, the pace is elegant rather than frenzied. The figures of the violin part, at this speed, take on the jauntiness of the fiddler tunes in *L'Histoire du Soldat*.

Figure 16-3.   Violin, mm. 6-12

In Eclogue II, again, the preceding movement is reflected. This move-ment opens with sustained exhalation (measures 1 to 3). The violin melody is more "sustained" in rhythm than its opening episode (to measure 11). Then it moves insistently in snapped rhythms and in two voice-levels or more, with increased rhythmic mobility from measure 19 on. Framing, re-laxed, expansive lines carry us from measure 27 to the end.

The rather slow tempo set by the composer ($\mathsf{J} = 44\text{-}42$), combined with the continuously arching and winding melodic lines, makes for a sinuous, graceful effect. This is reinforced by Stravinsky's instruction, in the piano score: *sempre legato*. The notes should be very much bound to one another, so that the several lines audibly intertwine. The look of the printed page impresses the eye with the equal treatment of the two instru-ments and the three voices. Both partners must strive to approach each other's sound as much as possible (it *is* possible), so that a unified texture is presented.

Eclogue II is just long enough to speak its piece. As for the Gigue that follows, we wonder why there should be 251 measures. If shorter, the move-ment would still be a lot of fun, in a restrained, Stravinskian way. It is con-stantly touching its foot to earth, often with the "drummed" effect achieved by alternation of left-hand pizzicato and arco,

Figure 16-4.   Violin, mm. 19-23

as a resting point between flights of step. The predominant pace is light, with occasional flashes of brusquer writing.

The constant 6/16 patter is interrupted by the shuffling effect of the 2/4 section, midway through the movement. After this, the 6/16 resumes, spelled at one point by a passage in 12/16. In this area of the movement come the highest register-plays. There follows loud and low passage-work, and a closing episode that reflects the opening of the Gigue. Again, the composer's tempo marking is important. At a speed of ♪. = 120, Stravinsky is spinning a peasantlike dance of quiet endurance, rather than the more contained span of the courtly gigue-styled movement. In short, this is more jig than gigue; it must move steadily, briskly, but not hurriedly, and above all, lightly and with grace. For there is danger, even with the welcome changes of metric pace, that so long a movement can sag into tedium.

The finale, Dithyrambe, is another instance of psychological persuasion through notation. The page is dark with ink; thirty-seconds abound, and even sixty-fourths make their appearance. Then, belatedly, we look at the metronome mark: ♪ = 60. A slow movement, after all, deliberately cast in "dark" note values so that the visual thickness of the writing will add weight and plasticity to the ornamental turns that mark almost every beat. The swirls and undulations of motion make the progress toward the high-pitched, fortissimo climax the more intense: truly impassioned, as befits a hymn to Dionysus.

We wonder why the instruction, *e sempre legato*, in measures 7 and 8, was given in the piano score, but not in the violin part. Was it Stravinsky's (or the engraver's) assumption that the string player could be trusted to play legato, without reminder? If this were true, then the whole business of playing (and teaching) bowed instruments would be much simpler!

The lyricism in this work is indeed held within bounds. The impression that derives from this music (and that must also show in its performance), is one of precision and control, and ascetic—not to say aseptic—rigor. The warmth that attaches to this work will be brought to it by the duo from their experience with more extroverted music. By the same token, the *Duo Concertant* will show to best effect as an oasis of coolness and reserve, surrounded in concert or in the study repertoire by works of more outspokenly "Romantic" quality, whether of old or new vintage. A damning and heretic statement, to be sure, but one that the writer feels compelled to make, thereby placing himself directly in the line of that kind of fire that Stravinsky directed, deservedly, to denigrators of Beethoven: " . . . fools who think it up to date to giggle as they amuse themselves by running him down. Let them beware; dates pass quickly."[162]

17 ※ *Britten: Suite for Violin and Piano, op. 6*

THE SUITE for Violin and Piano, op. 6, was composed by Benjamin Britten in Vienna and London from November, 1934, to June, 1935, in the composer's twenty-first year. The title of the work is no doubt intended to bridge the assembly of labels given to the several movements of the piece. So far as the writing is concerned, the composition is a full-fledged sonata for the duo.

The Suite was Britten's second chamber-music offering, preceded only by the Fantasy Quartet for Oboe and Strings, op. 2, of 1932. Britten, a wunderkind in British music (and entitled to a place of considerable prominence in our musical hierarchy in general), demonstrated already in this suite the facility, musical imagination, and wit that has marked his prolific output in the years since.

The title page of the composition bears a subtitle,

Figure 17-1. Suite, musical motto

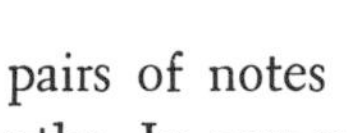

the musical motto, E-F-B-C. The successive pairs of notes in the motto can be viewed as seconds, or as inverted sevenths. In any event, it is the latter view that is taken for the opening statement, for violin alone, at the beginning of the introduction: G-F[E sharp]–D sharp–C-B. Literally, a succession of sevenths. The composer calls for the use of the high G- and D-string positions, to avoid slides in the playing of this series. The piano enters with the E-F-B-C (of the motto) as the upper edge of its double-stops in measures 3 and 4, hammering away at the idea. The violin mirrors the upward stepwise motions in its like progressions as it hurls itself downward from its pinnacle. Meanwhile, the piano crosses the violin, ascending, and ending topmost at the cadence.

The March seems to be based on the motto, still. By such devices as accent markings and bracketing of note sequences in the violin part, the composer emphasizes the upward second progressions, whether half or whole step, whether in linear or vertical interval. Aside from this, the march is properly brisk and pointed, with clipped repartee between the two instruments. Glissandi, at first single-, then double-stop, and harmonics in the violin part add color to the sound. (At least once, the harmonics introduce a motivic semitone.) The playing must have all the jauntiness and strut the players can muster.

The danger of such movements as the *Moto perpetuo* hinges on the endurance of both performer and audience. If one (and only one) player —either alone or in ensemble—has to keep a constant flow of quick notes going throughout the movement, he can grow tired; the listener, too, can be bored by the sound of one particular coloration. Britten solves both problems: he gives the players the motion assignment one at a time. Rarely is there an overlap or interjection by either instrument in the rapid work before the partner has finished with it. The violin begins the relay, playing sequences of downward stepwise couplets. Here and there a couplet is accented, the stresses projecting a rhythmic pattern of their own through the constant stream of sixteenths, but usually occurring in immediate response to a chord in the piano part (always accented).

When the piano takes over (after letter 8), it is with upward couplets (restoring the motion of the motto, if not always the identity of the upward half step). The violin takes the piano's original role, that of chordal commentator and stimulator. The piano's perpetualism is in terms of a broad ribbon of activity, both hands alternating with each other on successive sixteenths:

Figure 17-2. Moto perpetuo, mm. 35-37

In later installments of piano activity, the motion will be (respectively) alternate hand, but closely spaced—and with ascending or descending half step as part of the texture; alternating quadruplets or couplets; left-hand eighths, right-hand sixteenths, but in close spacing, so that half-step couplets emerge from the pattern; broader-spaced groupings in the right hand, with the second relationship emerging as sevenths (Animato, page 12); stepwise couplets in the right hand, with slower couplets in the left, the latter spelling out, leapfrog fashion, two lines of ascending minor seconds.

The violin has a similar variety of patterns, revealing the composer's intimate knowledge of that instrument's capacities. The passage from letter 14 to the Animato is the most striking example of this. Consecutive sixteenths alternate between harmonics on adjacent strings, spelling out, in expanded (but gradually quickening) sequence the interval relationships shown here in condensed form:

Figure 17-3.   Violin, letters 14 and 15, composite and condensed

To play the passages Britten has constructed calls for some intimate knowledge of violin technique; the quick, clean, precise shift, the arching of the fingers in order to clear adjacent strings, the precise and economical oscillation of the bow to touch only the required string, the straight, short, incisive stroke needed to evoke the harmonic sound clearly—all this in rapid-fire motion.

Another passage deserves mention: that of the Molto animato, before letter 16. Here the bow must touch adjacent pairs of strings (A-D, D-G, and so forth) in rapid alternation; first, second and fourth fingers must be held down throughout the figure, while the third finger is applied and released in order to effect the moving line in the writing:

Figure 17-4.   Violin, Moto perpetuo, Molto animato, page 7, mm. 1-3

As can be seen, the passage requires quick crossings, bow, fingers, and all, to a different set of strings (cf. measure 3). Later in the same passage, upward shifts carry the same kind of figures to the seventh position on the upper three strings.

The duo will enjoy, after all the arduous details in this movement, the diffident manner in which it ends (as though to say, "Nothing to it!").

The Lullaby is a strange one: are we lulling someone; or are we still, in quiet fashion, demonstrating the individual virtuosities of the violin and piano? The pirouetting, the high figure-work for both instruments, carried out pianissimo, dolcissimo by each instrument in turn, calls for control of a high order. Measures reaching as high a dynamic level as forte show that the title of the movement must be taken as a general, not literal, characterization. The accompaniment lines, incidentally, whether in piano or violin, retain the stepwise couplet motions already familiar from the first two movements of the sonata.

The concluding Waltz opens with a brief preamble, or invitation—and an energetic, leaping *alla valse*. Then, the leitmotiv. The Poco meno mosso section, after letter 31, brings back, in the violin, the half-step sequences we have come to expect. Here, they are G–F sharp, A sharp–B, C sharp–C, and so forth. They can appear elsewhere, and in completely casual guise, so that they are almost lost from view, as at the Animato molto subito, where the violin hammers out short arpeggios, and the piano, flicking out its responses "drily," as the composer instructs, presents the significant interval:

Figure 17-5. Animato molto subito, mm. 1-4

The duo will find, at every hand, the trail of the telltale intervals, guiding and illuminating their playing of the movement. I have an uneasy feeling that this is the kind of false statement made in written accounts (including this one) about music. The duo will actually be concerned with the variety of effects, the number of different "waltzes" that Britten offers in this concluding ball of the evening. Nevertheless, the composer himself seems to rule, paradoxically, on the importance of the underlying intervallic source of the music: in a footnote in the score of the last movement, he instructs, "If this movement is played separately [i.e., as an individual concert piece, and not as part of the entire sonata], a cut is to be made . . . " The omission shown in the score covers the Lento episode beginning before letter 43. It is precisely this section that reflects the statements made in the suite's introduction. It actually interrupts the thrust of the finale toward its conclusion in order to make time for its reminders.

The Lento, then, emphasizes Britten's preoccupation with the musical motto in this composition. In musical terms, it is the counterpart to the imprint on the title page.

18 ❦ The Hindemith Sonatas

In 1949 AND 1950, in a series of lectures delivered at Harvard University, Paul Hindemith touched on the fate of the stringed instruments in a world acoustically oriented by the strength of electronically amplified sound:

> After a few more decades, those fiddles that have not been killed by our unreasonable treatment [i.e., the loud, brilliant approach to playing] will survive merely as exhibits in a museum of sound, as part of the antiquated tool chest used for historic performances of those legendary composers of the nineteenth and twentieth centuries.[163]

It is now twenty years later. We string players have endured thus far, though the decibel ratings of the rock-bands-*cum*-amplifiers sometimes seem to be driving us all toward that brink that Hindemith envisioned. Hindemith was dramatizing; he had, after all, enough optimism to write yet another of his many works for stringed instrument (and piano) just the year before his remarks: the Cello Sonata of 1948.

Hindemith was an extremely prolific composer, one of those most generously endowed with skill and energy in our era. Of his many works, fully two-fifths were devoted to the realm of chamber music (though he himself sometimes stretched the chamber-music label to include so peripheral a setting as opus 46, number 2, a work for organ and chamber orchestra). In his chamber-music output, there are four sonatas for violin and piano:

267

Sonata in E flat, op. 11, no. 1   1918
Sonata in D, op. 11, no. 2   1918
Sonata in E   1935
Sonata number 4, in C   1939

At the age of twenty-seven, Hindemith wrote:

> . . . for people with ears my stuff is really easy to grasp, and so an analysis is superfluous. For people without ears, too, such asses' bridges are no help.[164]

We can hope that he would have taken a kinder view in later years, when he himself devoted much time to a distinguished career as teacher. In any event, we join the ranks of Hindemith's bridge builders herewith.

When he wrote the first of the violin-piano sonatas, Hindemith had just ended his years of study at the Hoch Conservatory in Frankfurt (near his native city of Hanau), where he had worked in composition under Arnold Mendelssohn and Bernhard Sekles. He had already served several years as concertmaster of the Frankfurt opera orchestra and had recently completed a short tour of duty in the German army. Before all this, in his early teens, he had made his way by his music, playing "in the movies, operetta, in the villages, in jazz-bands, and finally also in orchestra." Already well equipped as a violinist, he soon changed to the viola, his major instrument, and also gained fair competence on the entire roster of orchestral instruments.[165] His personal command of many instruments is reflected not only in the skill with which he treats them in his orchestral works, but also in the quite varied chamber-music output of the later years.

The list of Hindemith's early compositions includes a trio for piano and winds, a string quartet, and a piano quintet. A chamber work also heads the list of published compositions—the Three Pieces for Cello and Piano, op. 8, of 1917. He then turned to the violin-piano sonatas of 1918 before proceeding to other chamber music of that year and the next, followed in turn by opera (*Mörder, Hoffnung der Frauen*) and songs, from the years 1919 and 1920.

Sonata in E flat, op. 11, no. 1

Frisch it is labeled, and "freshly" it begins! So brazen and joyous a fanfare is rarely found at the head of a work so sedate as a violin-piano sonata. One almost expects this opening to raise the curtain on a triumphal march à la Verdi. But what a surprise! Turn the page, fall in with the marking, *Ein wenig ruhiger,* slowing the tempo accordingly; press the soft pedal, try to live up to the composer's call of quadruple piano in the keyboard part; scatter palm trees and sandy horizons in the background, and switch the mood to this quietly sultry scene:

Figure 18-1.   Mm. 20-22

If this is not sultry enough, there are juicier measures ahead:

Figure 18-2.   Mm. 49-54

Two short, Ruhig passages frame the next, Lebhaft episode, one that is not as definite in character as either of the opening two sections; instead, it seems to be in transit, generally giving a feeling of lift, abetted by a couple of crescendo waves, carrying us into a second Lebhaft. Here the sultry theme is given simpler and swifter orchestration than in its first appearance. And from here, in turn, we are led directly to a review of the opening fanfares to close the movement. This movement is open in plan, direct in tone, not too difficult for either instrument (harder for the piano than the violin), and certainly not difficult to hear. It is solid, serviceable, and—especially after the clangor of its opening—not too exciting.

In the second movement, or *Zweiter Teil*, as the composer has it (there are only two "parts" to the composition), the most noticeable structural element is a short-long unit moving upward a half step; the opening measures show that the rhythm alone can be made to serve in the accompaniment:

Figure 18-3. Mm. 1-5

The intervallic sequence, divorced from the original rhythm, can also be used, as in the more moving, *Bewegter*, passage beginning at letter D:

Figure 18-4. Mm. 48-51

It can be shoved over, rhythmically, even farther, as it is at least once, at letter E, during the most turbulent part of the movement:

Figure 18-5. Mm. 61-64

From the climax of the movement, which achieves its peak by rise in register and dynamics, rather than by any dramatic use of contrapuntal activity between the two instruments, there is a recession to the tempo and sound level of the opening of the movement. In sign of the symmetrical arrangement of this "slow, solemn" dance, the closing lines are to a great degree identical with the opening phrase (see Figure 18-3). Like the first part of the sonata, this movement is not difficult—if anything, it is easier, owing to its slower speed. And it, too, is pleasant, not overly challenging to either listener or performer.

Sonata in D, op. 11, no. 2

The Second Sonata, of 1918, is not too comfortable an acquaintance. Each of its three movements is clear enough formally, opening and closing with related end sections (including some literal repetition of material), having a developmental midsection in the first; a great rhapsodic outpouring in that of the second; and determinedly dancelike rounds in the body of the third. The finale, especially, seems to have the air of a necessary conclusion (all compositions must, after all, end), rather than of a convincingly rounded-out conclusion. All told, the work gives the impression of a somewhat forced, second experiment in the sonata vein. The duo will find more fruitful fare in the two sonatas from the composer's later years.

Beginning in 1935, Hindemith not only returned to the sonata duo after a lapse of some eleven years, but now seemed bent on touching all musical bases in a new series of works. From 1936 through 1943, he wrote a work with piano for each of the following: flute, oboe, English horn, clarinet, bassoon, French horn, alto horn, trumpet, trombone, violin, and viola. In 1948, 1949, and 1955, respectively, there followed sonatas for cello, double bass, and tuba. But the first in this entire series was the Sonata for Violin and Piano, of 1935.

Sonata in E (1935)

At first glance, the opening movement, *Ruhig bewegt* ("quietly moving"), of this sonata seems to have no reason for success or even likability. It has within itself rhythmic patterns that court disasters of boredom:

repeated throughout a movement, promise to leave the listener (and player) in a state of glassy-eyed stupor. Exposed to a student's plodding rendition of this music, I have myself been brought perilously close to just such a condition, wrenched from hypnosis just soon enough to read the riot act to the unwitting Svengali.

Properly played, the Hindemith melody, apparently full of repetitions, springs to life and reveals carefully engineered stress points, lines of force, goals. Consider the opening violin line:

Figure 18-6.   Violin, mm. 1-9

There is really no stress in the first measure, which serves as introduction to the weighted downbeat of measure 2 (weighted by reason of its faster-moving notes, its ability to drain its power into the second beat, and the force it has received from the three concluding notes of measure 1). The third measure's downbeat is also a stress point, but less so than the beginning of measure 2; even though at the peak of a swell mark, the third measure is simply coasting in the wake of the energy of the second bar. The downbeat of measure 4 is not stressed; it is a note of questioning inflection, shying away from any driving impulse contained in the third beat of measure 3. Moving into measure 5, the question is restated. We expect yet a third question, as we proceed to the next measure, because the third beat of measure 5 is simply an ornamented repetition of the corresponding beat of measure 4. But measure 6 surprises us by giving an aggressive pulse to the downbeat, and a sudden, unprecedented, and heavy stress to its third beat. Measure 7 is given over to an ebbing away of energy from this offbeat peak. At the bottom of the dynamic valley, in measure 8, we have two last surprises: the first beat, instead of a sounded stress (or arrival or release), offers a silent eighth rest, the first such downbeat treatment in the violin part thus far; also, instead of letting the line expire immediately, Hindemith has it rise briefly in departure, so as to blend with the overlapping action in the piano at this point.

I have dealt at some length with these few measures to give the reader an idea of the niceties in the violin line, subtleties that must be heard in the playing if the composer's intent is to be realized. Nothing has been said about the piano part: it begins simultaneously with the violin and not only supports that part but supplies a good deal of the motive force in the opening web of sound. To focus on the piano role, here are several of the piano measures, alone. The piano is as much soloist as accompanist here, and—even when in subordinate function—offers a satisfying vitality and motion of its own to intrigue the player:

Figure 18-7.   Piano, mm. 5-7

The second subject of the movement is distinct enough, yet so imbued with the same rocking rhythm of the opening subject that the two seem inextricably related.

Figure 18-8. Piano, mm. 13-17

Briefly extended, this theme brings us to the end of the first section of the movement. In structure, the *Ruhig bewegt* is a small sonata-form movement; the development, which extends from measure 32 through measure 47, continues the easy pace of the movement, without foisting any extraneous excitement on the material chosen by the composer, even though a couple of fortes crown the restrained climax of the section. The recapitulation is opened, in subject, if not in key, by the return to the second subject (see measures 48 ff). Coupled with the continued vagaries in harmony, this gives an overlapped feeling to the movement, as though development and recapitulation are going on simultaneously. It is not until measure 70 that an unequivocal return is made, to the first subject this time; and, except for a brief coda, this ends the movement.

In the second and remaining movement of the sonata, "slow—very lively—slow—again lively," the slow sections are scenes of stately games of leapfrog between violin and piano, though the second "slow" is a shorter, more active, compressed round than the first. The melodic subject of this game is designed for passing back and forth, and overlapping between, the two parts, for it is built in a wide-spanning arch, rising and falling twice in the course of the first *Langsam* (measures 1 to 19, 20 to 34). At the heart of the movement is a fast, jumping dance, with a melody that falls into phrases of varying length, most characteristically a seven-measure unit (or rather, a six-measure unit spread over seven bars):

Figure 18-9. Violin, mm. 30-41

The climax of the section arrives at measure 112 (letter N), where the theme of the *Langsam* is deployed, in enlarged, augmented form, against a background of the rapidly moving triplets of the Lebhaft. In measures 142 to 144, a portion of this melody is augmented yet again. From measure 151, the business of the Lebhaft proper is resumed, moving ahead now in quickened and compressed manner. Measures 193 ff. effect a transition back to the pace and statement of the lively music's opening, which actually returns at measure 210. This plows ahead long enough to establish itself, then moves into a composed retard (measures 228 ff.), bringing us once again to the *Langsam*.

This slow section is shorter than its initial counterpart because it is intent not on revisiting itself so much as building rather quickly toward the final appearance of the Lebhaft. And it is in this lively mood that the sonata closes—not, however, without a last clarion statement of the *Langsam* theme (measures 285 to end).

No mysteries, a certain amount of composer's sleight of hand, and above all, a sense of consummate control: of material, of form, of counterpoint, of dramatic pace. The work tends to emphasize the dry, rather than the flamboyant; but there is wit and sparkle in it, as well as solid sentiment. This sonata is not extremely demanding technically, and can be well managed by the duo of intermediate experience. If they do not seek out the pilot light, however, they will have a cold furnace.

Sonata in C (1939)

This work differs strikingly from its predecessor of 1935. It is longer, more aggressive, more bravura. Though it is, in the main, not overly difficult to play, a couple of passages mark it out for the virtuoso duo, especially as concerns the violin.

Some of this kind of writing occurs in the first movement, "lively"; moving at a clip of $\downarrow$ = ca. 120, the music progresses from sturdiness to Hindemith's hoedown-fiddler style of solo:

Figure 18-10.

a. Mm. 1-5

b. Violin, mm. 53-59

There are some quiet and sinuous interludes, but the movement is primarily an athletic, punchy opening for the sonata. Stimulating to play!

The second movement, slow, has a marking of $\flat = 80$. This may seem to the players a remarkably sedate tempo for the melody in question:

Figure 18-11.   Mm. 1-5

Two things must be considered, however. One, that the tune has enough sway and guile in it (note the way the phrase tips forward into the fifth measure, instead of ending, as one might expect, on the second beat of measure 4) to make the indicated tempo quite proper. Second, and most cogent, the movement has an ending that looks like this, for two full pages of score:

Figure 18-12.   Mm. 108-109

The piano, you will note, is replaying the old, familiar tune. The violin is running all over the sky, with higher flights yet to come. The thematic throwback dictates a tempo like that of the opening; and the violin line dictates that the basic tempo of the movement should permit clarity and grace in the execution of such devilments. The result has to be Hindemith's own choice, as shown above.

It will save confusion, incidentally, to think of the tempo relationships in this way, rather than according to the somewhat contradictory marking given by Hindemith in the score of this passage. The last section is imprinted: "Slow, as at first (the triplet-sixteenths equal the eighth-notes of the preceding 5/8 measure)." The first instruction relates to the initial tempo (i.e., ♪ = 80). If we follow the instruction in parentheses literally, we arrive at a tempo, for the final section of ♪ = ca. 66, which is not only slower than "at first" but also not quite as much fun in the playing.

The 5/8 section to which the instruction refers is a delight. It takes any possible sag out of the movement with devilish wit, combining a sing-song quality of melody and a 5/8 twitch:

Figure 18-13. Second movement, mm. 36-40

Also, the 5/8 is given added rhythmic diversion by the contrary groupings for violin and piano, one moving in 3+2, while the other counters with 2+3.

Incidentally, the Octet for Winds and Strings (1958), from the closing years of Hindemith's life, has a parallel, in the frenzied scurrying of the first viola at the end of the octet finale, to the similar carrying-on of the violin in the present movement.

The best way to give an idea of the finale, Fugue, is to show an excerpt from the start of the closing section of that movement:

Figure 18-14. Mm. 169-172

Seen in simultaneous combination here are the respective subjects of A, the first, B, the second, and C, the third sections of the movement. A and C serve as the material for four-part fugal settings; B is treated (pages 16-19 of the score) at first by itself, later (letter 28) in combination with A; and, as we have noted in the example above, the three elements are brought together for a grand finale. This kind of movement is especially difficult, of course, for the piano, what with keeping the several strands of musical material clear within the part writing for the instrument, as well as in relation to the strand that is woven at the moment by the violin.

19   *A Few Lesser Sonatas from the 1930s*

H<small>AVING</small> <small>DEALT</small> with music of substance, from Bartók to Hindemith, in the preceding pages, it is now time to turn, in extremely cursory fashion, to several less consequential pieces, all from the 1930s. It will be clear that my enthusiasm is lacking and that, in the case of the Furtwängler sonatas, I do not even comprehend the composer's purpose. With this word of warning, let the following works be testily considered.

Bohuslav Martinu

Bohuslav Martinu (1890–1959), Czech-born, who lived in Paris, then for some years in America, and again, in later years, divided his time between Europe and America, was a composer of prodigious output. It has been demonstrated often enough in music that quantity is a relative thing. For some, a huge output is barely enough to convey everything they have to offer. In the case of others, enough is sometimes too much. In Martinu's instance, thought did not always keep up with pace.

This applies to Martinu's two violin sonatas that I have seen (there is a third, from 1944). Sonata number 1 (1930) starts interestingly, with a long solo violin passage, unbarred and in free meter. A still longer violin solo occurs before the end of the opening movement. The Allegro duo sections placed around these solos are all too metric, their cut-time swing watered down into a jog trot. In the Andante second movement, there is more of the same kind of thing, though slower, and marked again by solo violin episodes, accompanied or otherwise. The balance is evened in the last movement, where the piano has more solo exposure than the violin. In this sonata, the interest lies in the cadenzas. The duo frame has an air of necessity, as though the composer is not yet comfortable with the medium he has chosen.

Sonata number 2 (1932) opens with a fairly good tune (it is too loose and expansive to be called a theme) that, despite the lack of key signature, strongly smacks of D major. A poco vivo section introduces a lockstep between the two instruments. On the whole, the movement presents rather obvious alternations and interpenetrations of the two principal ideas. There is some of what might loosely be termed development, but scarcely in the intellectual sense of the word. The Larghetto is written in a stream-of-consciousness style, with ambling rhythm, a wandering toward a climax, and a draining away of the proceedings.

The first page of the finale, Poco allegretto, presents us with the following sequence of time signatures: Alla breve, 3, 4, 3, 2, 3, 2, 4, 3, 2, 3, 2, 3, 4, 2. Why? The page piddles rather than moves, and the constantly changing metric frame emphasizes the weakness of the motoric drive of this thinly disguised perpetual motion. Moderately difficult—and disappointing.

A Sonatina, of 1937, opens with a Moderato and an Andante that are somewhat alike, both in melodic substance and in a (presumably) folkish tendency to build phrases slowly and with insistent repetition of idea. The last movement, Poco allegretto, has the same characteristic, but enlivened with dancelike verve. The work is rather brief, engaging for ensemble study purposes, and can hold a place in a concert program if well bolstered by more solid compositions.

Othmar Schoeck

Othmar Schoeck (1886–1957) lived a long and most fruitful life in his native Switzerland, his very sizable output tending mostly toward works for the stage, for choral groups, and song. Of his small body of chamber-music works, I have seen the second (of two) sonatas for violin, opus 46, in E, from the year 1931. The work is in three fully packed movements, Tranquillo, Scherzo, and Breit. The motion is more constant than calculated. The composer seems fascinated throughout (most obviously in the first movement, but not much less so in the later portions of the sonata) with the idea of pushing a melodic wave upward, then letting it cascade down. Even though the waves mount one upon the other, the similarity of motion is soon apparent enough to pall. The sonata is fairly difficult, and turgid.

Frank Martin

Another respected and industrious Swiss composer, contemporary with Schoeck, is Frank Martin (born 1890). Of two violin sonatas (the first was published in 1914) I have seen the second, composed in 1931–32. It impresses me as offering a curious combination of dense texture and diffuse thought. The most interesting of the three movements is the second, Chaconne. The work is also published in a version for cello and piano.

Wilhelm Furtwängler

Two sonatas by the conductor, Wilhelm Furtwängler, are included here as curiosities, and as illustrations of a fortunately rare disease in the sonata literature—extreme inflation. Whatever else one may think about the vicissitudes of Furtwängler's career, the place and time of publication of these pieces (Leipzig and Berlin, 1938 and 1941), and so on, one must be impressed by the statement, in the score of the second composition, the Sonata in D, that the three movements of the work have a "playing-time of 50 minutes." It takes courage and optimism, and a particular idea of what music is about, for a composer and his publisher to admit this fact in an edition. It takes more of these qualities on the part of the duo to find out whether the marathon is worth it.

I must confess that I am turned away by the prospect of such a lengthy musical bath, even if the score bids me to "Sing tenderly!" or again, "Diminish, but always singing!" The sheer unreality of thinking that a concert program will have room for so long a work is something to contemplate. The same must be said for Furtwängler's Sonata in D minor, of 1938. It gives no playing time, but also has ninety-six pages of score, so endurance is again indicated. Furtwängler was obviously born too late.

Bruno Walter

A somewhat happier example of composition by a virtuoso conductor is the sonata (1910) of Bruno Walter. You may come across a copy of the Universal edition of this piece. There is no rush; the music is much in the

Strauss vein, and does not cry out for restoration to the repertoire. It has, though, some sense of moderation, getting through its business in an un-Furtwänglerian forty-three pages of score.

Nikolai Medtner

Also under the heading of enlarged works (though no doubt of greater intrinsic value) fall two—of three—sonatas of Nikolai Medtner (1880–1951) that I have seen. The Second Sonata, in G major, op. 24, (1924), is already a work of respectable length—its three movements occupying fifty-nine pages of closely printed score—heroic phrase, and yeasty texture. With a title like *Sonata Epica*, the third sonata, opus 57, of the year 1936, promises to be no less generous and indeed expands to fill eighty-four pages. Here there are four movements, and it is an audience of ample mental and physical *Sitzfleisch* that will be able to deal with so large an assignment. The players will need as much stamina as technique. Perhaps they will want to climb these sonatas because, like Mount Everest, "they are there." There is incidentally, a recording of the Medtner *Epica*, by David Oistrakh and colleague, on the Russian Melodiya label, that can give prospective candidates an aural measure of the task involved.

20 ❧ The Copland Sonata

AARON COPLAND was born in Brooklyn in 1900 (four years later than his borough-mate, Roger Sessions). By his own statement, his decision to prepare for a musical career was tolerated, though not clearly understood, by his parents.[166] From 1917, he studied with Rubin Goldmark, pianist and composer, in New York. In 1921 he studied with Nadia Boulanger at the first season of the school at Fontainebleau. In 1925 he was given the first Guggenheim Prize, which he held for two years. The years since have brought to Copland's music the esteem of his professional colleagues and the acclaim of a broad segment of the general public. He is certainly among the best known of contemporary American composers.

Copland's Sonata for Violin and Piano, one of his finest and most representative pieces, was composed in 1943, when he was in Hollywood working on the score for the film, *North Star*.[167] It is possible also that Copland, "of the school of slow, careful workers," was at that time simply completing the final construction of a work that had already been some years in the incubation process.[168]

My colleague, pianist Armand Basile, and I played the sonata in an all-Copland program in Milwaukee in 1971. The composer was present and, after the concert, told us that he was somewhat surprised that we had elicited bell-like sounds from the piece, because he had not had that image in mind when he wrote the work. He did not argue against the idea, so it is to be hoped that he accepted this view of the work. If I recall correctly, the composer said that he had thought of an effect of space, of dryness, of distance. This, too, is in the work; and it does not seem incompatible with the idea of bell resonance, because that can also imply spaciousness and distance.

In any event, the bell sounds in the sonata were detected by Basile; the thought held up well in the rehearsal and performance of the piece, and I advance it herewith. The sonata begins with a slow section, Andante semplice: the piano plays several short phrases; the first two are five-part; the succeeding three are two-part, thinner in texture. The motion is simultaneous throughout. Each of the phrases ends on a sustained tone, as though the resonance of the phrase-ending is enduring; the rests between phrases let this resonance sound. To our ears, the sounding chords, the intervals used, the hovering resonances all suggest bell tones.

Figure 20-1.   Mm. 16-21

Bridging the resonance and the rest, as well as the space between the piano phrases, the violin projects phrases of its own that grow out of, reflect the melodic motions of the piano line. The harmonics indicated in the printed violin part for the Ds in measures 4 and 7 seem to contribute to this effect; the harmonic may be used again in measure 10, to continue the thought. In order to be quite consistent, one would suppose that the G in measure 14 should also be a harmonic; but I must confess that I play this as a stopped tone, but with rather "dead" vibrato. It will be noticed that the violin double-stops in measures 16 and 17 can also suggest bells; at least they do if the tones are played with separate bows and with very slight initial impacts, rather than with the slurring shown in the printed version.

In the Più mosso and Allegro that now take over the movement, a pedal-point (pedal bell?) G, sustained in octave, low in the piano, serves as the place of departure for the gradually accelerating violin line, and

several additional resonance pauses are touched on by both instruments
before the two are swept away in the increasing speed of musical events
in the ensuing measures. Even when matters are moving at a fairly high
clip, there are opportunities for the sustained tone to make itself heard
(cf. violin part, *Un poco più animato*).

The initial temper of the movement makes specific reappearances in
a lengthy middle episode, faster-moving, and again at the end of the movement (now slowest of all, though marked tempo 1). But even at the point
of highest excitement in this movement, in the section beginning in the
second brace of page 8, the trigger of the action is a bell-like clangor of the
violin and piano right hand. This ringing is continued and extended, fortissimo and marcato, in the very eye of the storm. The storm itself is made
up largely of rapid tintinnabulations on the eighth-note couplet first uttered
by the violin in its initial entry, back at the beginning of the sonata. One
of the most attractive things about the movement is the way in which this
particular motion, now a reminiscent tinkle, is brought back, under the
sustained tones, just before the final double bar. The reference is couched
in sixteenths, the only appearance of such note values in the entire movement, in order to give it a speed akin to that of the fragment back in the
climactic portions of the movement.

Figure 20-2.

a. Violin, mm. 1-4

b. Violin, page 5, mm. 4-5

c. Andante semplice, last five measures

The pedal tone continues on in the second movement, supporting the beginning and end of that Lento and appearing in many references and recollections: the moving piano line (as "analysed" by the slower, selective reflection, or quasi-augmentation in the violin part) seems to remind us, most quietly, of the climactic clangor and earlier parent phrases in the first movement. The piano's repeated figure, in the first four measures of the Poco più mosso, is clearly a tolling on the violin's first utterances, from the beginning of the sonata.

There is a very strong bell-like trait in the passage beginning in the fifth bar of the Poco più mosso: the piano plays soft chords, two pulses to the measure; above this, the violin plays its line with a time delay of one quarter-beat:

Figure 20-3. Poco più mosso, second movement, mm. 27-29

A footnote instruction says to "anticipate each half note [i.e., each entrance in the violin part] slightly." This proviso, coupled with the combined dot-and-line marking on the violin tones (a sign that I interpret to mean a slightly pointed stress on each note), creates an effect of broad, low resonances—the kind one hears from large, slow-vibrating bells—with the more prominent, more piercing tone of small, higher-pitched chimes. Our own duo chose to continue this effect in our playing of the next phrase, where the violin is thrown yet another octave up, and where the piano incorporates the on-beat pulse and the immediate aftersound in its right-hand part.

I can't very well extend the bell similes into the third movement of the sonata. Here, it is Arthur Berger's commentary, written in 1953, that is apropos:

> The expansive, uninhibited racing of strings over wide areas of pitch is also a gratifying new element in Copland's music. This device began to manifest itself in the Violin Sonata, its last movement in particular, where an almost classical continuity is achieved. . . . It is as if Copland, who had often hugged the ground in the manner of the "modern school" of American dancers, suddenly took flight like a ballet dancer.[169]

The violinist, at any rate, is very much "on point" as he follows the composer's uninhibited racing. It is a violin cadenza that starts this Allegretto giusto. The difficulty here is to maintain enough presence of mind to play in scherzando fashion, with sufficient poising on the many eighth-note rests that punctuate the line, while moving at the brisk pace stipulated by the composer (♩ = 144).

The bells still ring out, after all. Can they not be heard in the sharp impacts of the piano part, when it enters after the violin cadenza: fortissimo, in the bass, then mid-register, then high? So also the sforzando triple-octave retorts that spark the piano's line in its next page of music. And, further, the "change-ringing" episodes ("Twice as slow," page 25; Molto allargando, page 32).

There are musical back-references enough in this movement to sustain Berger's point about the "classical continuity." But there is one prime technical difficulty that none, other than the performer, would know about: the horrendous page turn in the violin part at the very brink of a presto, high A (violin part, page 10). Fervent inspection has shown that there are only three alternatives: break the pace of the movement grievously in order to make the turn; grow a third arm; or play the rest of the movement from memory.

At the very end, the last reference to the sonata's beginnings take the sound, not now of bells, but of that distance Copland himself spoke of. The final cadence is not a harmonic resolution so much as it is a shimmer-away of the music in the haze of atmospheric heat:

Figure 20-4.   Page 33, final brace.

Apologies are due both the composer and the reader if my bell ringing has seemed stubborn as well as arbitrary. The purpose was to give the reader an idea of an approach that seemed right and helpful to one team of players in performing an important contemporary chamber music work.

21 ❦ *Prokofieff: Two Sonatas*

SERGEI PROKOFIEFF was born on the large estate of Sontsovka, in the Ekaterinoslav province of the Ukraine, in 1891. His father, a trained agriculturist, was resident manager of the estate. His mother, a music enthusiast, recognized the boy's musical ability. Early studies with Reinhold Glière were followed by entry at the age of thirteen (at the suggestion, and with the recommendation, of Glazunov) into the Saint Petersburg conservatory, where he studied theory, composition, and piano with Liadov, Rimsky-Korsakoff, and Anna Essipova, and conducting with Tcherepnin. His compositions of the early 1910s startled the ears of many listeners, infuriating among others the very same Glazunov who had been his early sponsor at the conservatory.

In the wake of the revolutionary events of 1917–18 in Russia, Prokofieff left Russia of his own volition and without pressure, going eastward through Japan and on to the United States. He remained abroad for the next sixteen years: from 1918 to 1920 in America; from 1920 to 1922 in Paris (with tours to America—these were to continue until 1932—for recitals, premiere performances of his opera, *Love for Three Oranges*, and so on); during 1922 and 1923 at Ettal, in Bavaria; and returned in 1923 to Paris. In 1933, after two earlier visits to Russia, he once again made that country his home.

His life there in the two decades that remained to him was not without shadows, among the deepest being the violent attacks upon his style of composition in the musical inquisitions of 1936 and 1948. Prokofieff's output, however, despite the vicissitudes of political climate and the rigors of the war years, remained high. It was during his protective sequestering, along with a group of artists from various fields, in the cities of Nalchik, Tiflis, and Alma-Ata, during the years 1941 through 1943, that he worked, among other compositions, on the Sonata for Violin and Piano in F minor, op. 80, and the Sonata for Flute and Piano in D, op. 94, which was soon arranged also in the version known as his second Sonata for Violin and Piano, op. 94a.

The Flute Sonata was actually completed before the First Violin Sonata. Because, however, the latter composition traces back to sketches made in 1938, I shall consider it first in the discussion here.[170]

Sonata Number 1 for Violin and Piano in F minor, op. 80

This composition was not finished until the summer of 1946, at Nikolina Gora, a little town near Moscow, where Prokofieff spent much of his time from 1946 until his death in 1953. In January, 1944, Prokofieff had suffered a fall and brain concussion, and was in poor health for his remaining years; he continued to work indefatigably, nevertheless, and, as can be seen in this work, with all the vigor of old.

Here is the laconic description that Prokofieff gives of this work:

> In mood it is more serious than the Second [Sonata]. The first movement, Andante assai, is severe in character and is a kind of extended introduction to the second movement, a sonata allegro, which is vigorous and turbulent, but has a broad second theme. The third movement is slow, gentle, and tender. The finale is fast and written in complicated rhythm.[171]

Compare this with his Russian biographer, Israel Nestyev's, prescient and extended view of the workings of the piece, reading in part,

> . . . the meditation of an ancient bard on the fate of the motherland; . . . a scene of brutal encounter between warring forces; . . . a poetic image of a young girl's lament; and . . . a hymn to the might of Russia in arms, a paean to the people's freedom and strength.[172]

Between the Scylla of Prokofieff's own awareness of what he was doing, and the Charybdis of Nestyev's Russian feel for the inner meaning of the piece in the wartime context of its creation, I must be made of sheer brass to intrude the following performer's-eye viewpoint (and a Western tender-foot's eye, at that) of the composition. About the essential and utter seriousness of the work in the composer's own mind, there can be little question. David Oistrakh reports that, in suggesting the approach to various portions of the sonata, Prokofieff advised him and Lev Oborin, before their premiere performance of the work in October, 1946, " . . . one part of the first movement where the violin plays passages running up and down the scale . . . should sound 'like the wind in a graveyard.' "[173]

Prokofieff had that essential knack of the chamber-music writer: to make it seem that the instruments of the ensemble converse with each other. Such dialogue moves throughout this sonata. (A passage such as measures 23 to 27, where the violin and piano treble move in parallel octaves, is especially affecting because of its contrast to the generally disparate treatment of the two voices in the duo.) It is in force at the beginning of the opening Andante assai. Like the finale, this is cast in alternating meters (3/4, 4/4), giving the composer freedom to throw in an extra beat to the bar when the linear motion requires. The changing pulse gives the initial theme a sober jauntiness; and the theme, both in its steady fall to its ending and in its frequent recurrence in the movement, takes on the aspect of an ostinato:

Figure 21-1. Mm. 1-5

The violin interjection (at the very end of the example) of the off-center eighths and the accented trill is symptomatic. From this kind of impatient comment grows the other facet of the movement: the quickened, impetuous pacing that pulls against the phlegmatic main theme. The movement is framed by the slower theme; it is also dominated by it, for the subject —either in tonic or other key, complete or partial, verbatim or in derivative form—appears eight times in the course of this short opening chapter of the work. In the last third of the movement, the principal subject is garlanded with muted, cool, rapid runs by the violin, the "wind in a graveyard" that Prokofieff spoke of.

It is important that the contrast between the sober and active sections of the movement be brought out. Partly this is a matter of tempo, as indicated by the composer's specification (once) of Poco più animato, as well as a number of retards and A tempo marks.

Figure 21-2. Mm. 42-46

Beyond this, it becomes a matter of stress and phrase direction, and, in at least one instance, of preserving the individual quality of the two contrasting elements even though they are moving simultaneously:

Figure 21-3. Mm. 69-72

This "mutual isolation," each instrument concentrating on its own view of things, is most interesting toward the end of the movement; the piano makes the last utterances of the theme, while the violin carries on its own commentary (note that Prokofieff calls for a "reciting"—recitando—inflection of the violin part in the pizzicato measures):

Figure 21-4. Mm. 98-101

The conversation between instruments is strangest in the second movement, *Allegro brusco* ("brusque allegro"). Nestyev's view of the movement holds that its

> . . . march-like phrases, with their rigid, clipped cadences and strident harmonies, create an image of brutal military power. This has much in common with the music of the Teutonic invasion in *Alexander Nevsky.* . . . But later these coarse, mechanical images give way to a rich, soaring theme (marked *eroico*) sung out by the violin, which sounds particularly appealing after the harmonic and tonal harshness of the opening phrases.[174]

This may well be apt, especially because the sound of the movement—like the sonata as a whole—exudes seriousness and darkness. But as I see it, something wry and cynical lurks behind the orations of the two instruments. The dialogue of piano and violin takes on an aberrant, grimly hilarious quality. The two are engaged in a deadly sober debate, usually against each other, though sometimes the two upper voices join in opposition to the bass. But the debate is all carried on in terms of one theme; of two people saying the same thing, but out of phase with each other. This is not the consistent staggering of voices that one gets in a canon or round, but an unpredictable shifting, an arbitrary variability. Spurts of motion cut through the dialogue, only to be overwhelmed by the stubborn conversation once more:

Figure 21-5. Mm. 16-22

Just when the impasse promises to become intolerably prolonged, an equally curious solution is found; the violin launches into a "heroic" theme that is bombastic and completely—deliberately, one would think—out of place in the proceedings. (Nestyev sees these measures as a "rich soaring theme . . . sung out by the violin, which sounds particularly appealing after the harmonic and tonal harshness of the opening phrases.")[175]

Figure 21-6. Mm. 52-56

Again the passage in question can be played for Nestyev's effect. But let the piano treble be played with the slightest leaning toward the galumphing side of the off-stride couplets, and the effect becomes one of mock-heroics, caricature, rather than of patriotic vainglory. Carried away by the spirit of things, the two instruments move into a marchlike paroxysm, catch themselves short at a triple-forte peak, cover their embarrassment with a sedate two-step passage, and pretend to resume their original argument. But the exciting diversion cannot be forgotten; and so the movement works its rather winding way to the end by recurrent alternation and interplay of the debate, the heroics, and more fast-moving episodes. The violinist will enjoy the finish, which takes him, in two grand, upward flourishes, to the highest C available on the instrument. And the listener may possibly be forgiven for finding in this movement a wry musical editorial against confrontations in general, against military postures and other ingrained niceties of our civilization.

The third movement, Andante, is described by the score annotator, E. Lee Fairley, as "atmospheric—lyrical—subdued throughout, providing a lovely interlude between the rugged second movement and the brilliant finale . . . "[176] To this truth might be added the fact that the movement has its own interlude, a contrasting middle section beginning at letter 29, where the dense thread of triplet sixteenths that sustains the end sections gives way to an easier flow of 12/8 that winds its way between the three staves of writing. The gently yearning flavor of this music, the close interplay of legato line between piano and violin (sometimes parallel, sometimes in alternation), makes this one of the most demanding episodes in the sonata. To play the above-mentioned lines of sixteenths, too, is a challenge; in both instruments, these lines must ripple with the smooth continuity called for by the composer. (It is curious that, though the word *legato* is provided by way of instruction, slurs are shown for these lines only in the violin part, not the piano; the pianist may well add such marking to this part, as a psychological reminder of the desired effect.)

The finale is not quite as hard as it looks, despite an *Allegrissimo* marking and a fearsome metric signature: 5/8, 7/8, and 8/8. Actually, these signatures do not tell the whole story. The rhythmic-metric pattern of the principal theme of the movement goes this way, all pulses being counted in steady eighths:

Figure 21-7. Mm. 1-4

One readily comes to identify the four-measure complex of 5-7-8-8, complete with concluding "bump," especially because it recurs constantly with small separating islands of contrasting rhythm thrown in to break the stream. So comfortable does the pattern become that the passage from measure 46 to 82, cast entirely in 8/8, seems sedate by comparison.

Measure 83 seems to take us back to the initial rhythmic swing. Instead we find two statements with only the first three measures of the complex; then a number of measures cast in 5/8 only; at last, however, in measure 102, we are given the principal theme, complete. Not for long, though. For, in measure 122, things settle down to consecutive 5s (giving the effect of a speedup in tempo, but without loss of the interesting 5-twitch). Then the process reverses; there is a page in 6/8, followed by a page in 8/8: the pace broadens out. The violin, during much of the 8/8, devotes itself to runs in sextuplet sixteenths (and one measure of *sept*uplets). Which is by way of preparing us for the last section of the movement.

There, an Andante assai coda takes us back to the tempo of the beginning of the sonata. The violin is once again muted and moving in rapid thirty-seconds; the piano plays again the material it had at measure 79 of the first movement. There is no direct quotation of the principal subject of the first movement; instead, the violin, in its closing measures, hints at that theme obliquely. But the scheme is quite clear: Prokofieff has tied the package with a thematic knot to link beginning and end of the sonata to each other.

This sonata is by no means for the novice or even intermediate player. It does not present the kind of technical difficulties that, say, the Bartók sonatas pose for both violin and piano; yet it makes ample demands on the playing skill of the musicians. An even bigger difficulty lies in the matter of interpretative concept. The piece can be played in too unrelievedly serious a fashion. We have (perhaps inappropriately) pointed to a facet of caricature in the second movement. The finale seems more obviously boisterous and release minded (especially in the characteristic "bump" of the final note in the principal melodic unit—see the last quarter note in measure 4, Figure 21-7). It is certainly not levity or frivolity that I seek to press upon this imposing example of contemporary chamber music. But the bite and impact of this sonata will be weakened if the players seek the lugubrious tone too constantly, at the expense of that contrast in texture and spirit that the composer himself so clearly builds into the work.

Sonata Number 2, in D for Violin and Piano, op. 94a

David Oistrakh not only had the honor of being the dedicatee of Proko-fieff's First Sonata, but inspired the arrangement of the Sonata for Flute and Piano into the version that is called the Second Sonata for Violin and Piano. Oistrakh says about the preparation of this version:

> I had never believed it possible to work with such speed and efficiency. He sat me down at once and told me to jot down two or three versions of each passage in the score that required editing, numbering each one carefully. As I submitted the pages to him, he marked the version he considered suitable and made a few pencil corrections here and there. Thus in no time the violin version of the sonata was ready.[177]

Nestyev states that Oistrakh heard the premiere of the Flute Sonata on December 7, 1943, and that Oistrakh and Lev Oborin gave the premiere of the new version on June 17, 1944.[178] So things moved quickly in this transition. Curiously enough, the flute version was not published in Russia (at least up to the time of the publication of Nestyev's biography, 1957), whereas the violin version was published there in 1946.[179]

Because this sonata was originally designed for flute and piano and is a prominent item in the repertoire for that combination of instruments, I defer—in detailed consideration of the work—to the renowned flutist, Samuel Baron. He discusses the sonata at length in the forthcoming companion book in this series.[180] Suffice it to say here that the sonata is grateful in its violin version. The bite and incisiveness that is one aspect of the violin sound throws sidelights on the sonata that make for interesting comparisons with a flute presentation of the work. A sense of these comparisons is reflected in the changes made by Oistrakh-Prokofieff in preparing the violin version. Some of the changes are clearly for technical reasons only. Others exploit the peculiar sound characteristics of the violin. Still others seem designed to adjust the pacing of the music. (The following comparisons are derived from the Szigeti edition of this sonata, wherein the flute and violin versions are both given in the score. See Editions Used.)

In the first movement, the character title has been changed from Andantino to Moderato, though the same metronome mark has been retained. In measure 2, the second quarter-beat offers a triplet, instead of the four sixteenths of the flute version. This does not seem a desirable change, because the effect of the triplet is lazier, less thrusting than sixteenths. The octave grace note added to the violin part on the third beat is a characteristic violin device, but can still be retained with the sixteenths, especially in the moderato temper indicated.

Figure 21-8.   Mm. 1-2

The violin part from measure 21 to measure 29 has been set down an octave. This is not necessary, but was done apparently to set off the later recurrence, in minor, of this phrase. The violin figure in measures 81 to 83 has been changed from the more continuous arpeggio figure of the flute, probably to eliminate the repeated slides that would be needed in the violin treatment of the passage; also, the sonority of the open D-string drone can now be added. There is a further change from the sextolet figure to the four-sixteenths figure.

Figure 21-9.   Detail, mm. 81-82

The change at measures 119 ff. eliminates awkward string crossings. In the third measure of this sequence, the flavor of the flute passage is retained, while violin fingering is simplified in the new version, with the added touch of the double-stop sonority. The change, at the peak of the passage, from the flute's thirty-seconds to the violin's sextolets is simply a matter of choice.

Figure 21-10.   M. 121

In the second movement, the character marking is Allegretto scherzando in the flute, with a metronome mark of ♩. = 69. In the violin version, the inscription is Presto, and no metronome mark is given. My own feeling is that both the Allegretto scherzando and the original metronome mark of the flute version are appropriate to the pirouetting nature of the opening material as well as to the bluff strains of the contrast material in this movement. If the tempo is made much faster, the movement will gain in bravura, in violinistic flash, but at the expense of the humorous grace of the music.

There is a nice touch at letter 19 ff. Instead of the graces and sustained note of the flute figure, the violin's double-stop harmonics achieve the same flutelike effect, without the excessive snap that an exact duplication of the flute figure would entail.

Figure 21-11.   Letter 19 mm. 1-3

The modification (letter 25, measures 12 ff.) permitting a continuous sweep across all four strings, is more conducive to a bold effect on the violin. The pizzicato on the downbeat D flat (indicated as optional in the violin part) is not advisable, because it weakens the sound output of the violin line

precisely where needed most—in the low register and on the stressed pulse
of the measure.

Figure 21-12. Letter 25, mm. 12 ff.

In the third movement, the Andante is marked ♩ = 50 in the flute
version, ♩ = 69 in the violin version. Here the faster tempo indicated for
the violin seems more appropriate to the easy swing of the music.

In the flute version of the fourth movement, the metronome mark
of ♩ = 112 is given; it is omitted, for no good reason, in the violin version.
It seems a good tempo choice for both versions.

The changes in detail in this movement are chiefly designed to give
progressively greater sonority to the violin line as it moves toward the end
of the sonata. Here are successive versions of the violin figures, from early
and late portions of the movement.

Figure 21-13.

a. Fourth movement, m. 1

b. Letter 35, m. 1

c. Letter 39, 1 measure before, to 2 measures after

As already observed in the first sonata, so also in the flute-violin opus
there are bold, almost incongruous contrasts: from the languorous grace of
the first movement to the brusque militancy of certain passages (as at
letter 4). The coquettish whirl of the second movement has its opposite
in the brassy declamations heralded in the measures after letter 14. In the

third movement, the basically folkish tone is countered with the "blues-y" murmurings first introduced at letter 28. And in the brash hubbub of the finale, there are islands of ponderous grace in passages such as the Poco meno mosso, after letter 33. The duo must recognize these strong cross-currents in the writing and adapt themselves to the changing roles thrust upon them by the composer.

So far as difficulty is concerned, the Second Sonata is at least as hard as the First; for the violin, even harder, especially in the first and last movements. The piece can be tackled only by the proficient duo.

22 ✦ *The Shostakovich Sonata*

Dmitri SHOSTAKOVICH is regarded, by Russia and the West, as one of Russia's leading contemporary composers. His importance has been recognized at home by such positive tokens as the awarding of the Stalin Prize to his Piano Quintet, 1940; and, in negative vein, by the official rebuke administered in 1936 to his opera, *Lady Macbeth of Mzensk*, and the stern judgments of the musical inquest of 1948. It is a reflection of Shostakovich's checkered but illustrious career that he is described by commentators with such words as "enigmatic," "uncomfortably unbalanced," "remarkably consistent through all fluctuations of ideology," and (by Arnold Schoenberg—with obviously mixed feelings), "it is perhaps not his fault that he has allowed politics to influence his compositorial style."[181]

Shostakovich has written prolifically for various media and has devoted himself with almost special emphasis to chamber music, particularly to the string quartet. It is here, one would think, that the weaknesses of a composer would show up: in the pitiless transparency of the quartet sonority, without the blandishments of orchestral tone color to offer cover and diversion. I have specifically entertained some misgivings about the quartets of Shostakovich's recent years. Yet the chastening experience of hearing the Borodin Quartet, themselves Russian and closely involved with Shostakovich in the performance of his work, play the Eighth Quartet exquisitely and sympathetically, bore home once again the importance of looking at a given work without preconception, with a curiosity and freshness of viewpoint that would enable the player to seek out the essential qualities of the specific composition.

In 1969, Shostakovich published his only Sonata for Violin and Piano, op. 134. He had previously written only the Three Pieces (1940) for this duo. The sonata is dedicated to David Oistrakh on his sixtieth birthday.

The massive work is made of three movements, Andante, Allegretto, and Largo—Andante. The piano begins the composition with typically Shostakovichian marching, up and down the tone range. The march, however—and there is some surprise in this, coming from an official Russian composer—spells its way through a twelve-tone series up, and through the literal ("real") inversion of the series on the way down:

Figure 22-1.

a. Mm. 1-3

b. Mm. 5-7

(It will not be lost on the reader that much of this "row" is a stamping up and down the keyboard in fourths, as though the sequence represents a jocular hunt-and-peck improvisation at the ivories.)

The piano sticks to this path consistently until letter 3, then begins an augmentation of the series, only to skip part of it; and so also on the way down, there leveling off into extraserial tones.

The violin, meanwhile, has been crooning its own wandering line from letter 1. Roles and melodic materials are reversed at letter 6, the violin now taking over the dodecaphonic march. The sequence gives out, however, on the way down, and the idea of the march and its accompaniment now gives rise to snatches of reference in the music that follows.

The movement as a whole shows this scheme:

1. Opening to letter 3. Piano in "tone-row" march; violin accompanies.

2. Letter 3. Extension, quasi-development.
3. Letter 6. Review of opening, with violin/piano roles reversed.
4. Letter 8. "Stamping" theme, derived in part from aspects of opening theme.
5. Letters 9-14. Extension, quasi-development on jaunty outgrowth of the stamping theme.
6. Letters 14-16. Closing idea, spun off from previous melodies.
7. Letter 16. A "sneak" return of the opening, veiled in syncopations, augmentations, melodic ornamentation.
8. Letter 17. Analogous to letter 2 (entry of violin accompaniment line), with violin line emphasized and literal, the piano "march" only sketchily and freely suggested.
9. Letter 19. Analogous to letter 3, in altered texture (violin is now playing a filigree of sixteenths).
10. Letter 20. "Stamping" theme reintroduced, with modification.
11. Letter 20 plus 5 measures. "Second" theme, analogous to letter 9.
12. Letter 22. Analogous to letter 10. "Stamping" theme in relief.
13. Letter 23 plus 4 measures. Letter 19 (and letter 3) revisited, in muted color.
14. Letter 24. Closing subject (cf. letter 14).
15. Letter 26. Coda. Reminiscences of the second theme. Ends with quiet chimings on the interval of the fourth; i.e., a last reflection of the tone series.

The second movement is a vigorous scherzo, much brusquer than its Allegretto title implies. The (unmarked) "trio" of the movement extends from letter 34 through the sixth measure of letter 38. Though its material derives from that of the movement as a whole, it is set off by its swaying rhythm and by the fact that, unlike the end sections of the movement, it is in straightforward 3/4 time, without the meter changes (5/4, 3/2) that break repeatedly into the common-time course of those sections.

The movement is not symmetrical; a literal return of the opening (letters 28 to 30) is not to be found until letter 53, and then it is brought back in fortissimo, its heightened intensity justified by the delay in its appearance and by the events that have preceded. A first "return" appears before letter 39, in the sense that the 4/4 rhythm and the brusque stampings of the opening section are restored. And now the triple meter of the trio becomes an inherent part of a high-pitched, raucous reviewing of earlier material, lending a new swiftness and urgency to the proceedings. At the end of the first section of the movement, there was a long composed acceleration (letters 31 to 34). This writing returns here at letter 47, careening along in rapid triplets, three groups to the measure.

But now comes a reversal of procedure; at letter 49 (which corresponds to letter 33), Shostakovich applies the brakes by reverting to 4/4 time and by using duple-eighth rhythm in the piano instead of the triplets that originally had urged on the pace of the movement. This reversal sets the stage for the furious reappearance of the opening at letter 53. But not before the "trio" has had an equally frenzied last fling at letter 52.

The movement ends with its rhythmic brakes still partially set (duple figures instead of the racing triplets); otherwise, things are in a fine passion, with violin and piano flailing away, both crowded at last into the upper end of the register for much of the last page of score. The contrast from this ending to the impassioned dignity of the opening of the last movement could not be more striking.

The Largo begins with a warm-up preamble for the two instruments. The violin darts through its range, in figures suggesting the tuning (or at least touching) of adjacent strings, tries a few wide-flung intervals, a couple of four-string chords, finally lands, with the piano, on a sustained D. In their respective voyages, the two instruments touch the following tones:

Figure 22-2.   Largo, mm. 1-8

The sequence of tones at the end of the list is not certain, because they are embedded in the chords that are at that moment played by both instruments. It seems, though, that we have here a couple of tone-rows. We are only falsely encouraged to think of these sequences in this manner, for the body of the movement, beginning at letter 59, is not built according to the system of twelve tones (any more than is the first movement of the sonata).

Rather we are given another series of tones at letter 59, by the violin alone, in pizzicato—the simplest, driest, most honest possible declaration of materials. I show this melody here, because it is of central importance to the movement. In deference to my view of the preamble, and because the twelve tones are obtainable from the melodic line, I have stubbornly indicated yet a third "row":

Figure 22-3. Violin, letter 59 ff.

To find such a row is irrelevant, if not ridiculous, because it is the entire matrix of tones shown above, not the "twelve" that carries the ensuing musical events. The first treatment of the subject (letter 60 ff.) finds it presented in the bass of the piano, quietly, with the violin (still pizzicato) presenting a counterpoint to it. Moving through the movement, we find that each rehearsal letter marks a fresh reviewing of the subject; an ostinato, recurring stubbornly, over and over.

Until letter 68, the subject is untransposed. It always begins on G, presented in one instrument or the other, in different rhythmic or textural elaborations, and with changing treatments in the accompanying voice. The dynamic level is quiet throughout. Just as we reach 68, a particularly quiet, flowing tone has been achieved. But there, matters begin to tighten up. In only a few measures, the piano and violin have joined in a lockstep, with the violin shadowing its partner in a short, loud outburst on the subject. The stage is now set for the climactic sequence of events in the movement. From letters 69 through 75, we find the dynamic level rising in deliberate fashion, each repetition of the subject carrying us successively from pianissimo (twice) to triple forte. Among other changes, the section beginning at letter 74 is for piano only, with great chordal responses, involving both ends of the keyboard, woven through with bravura running work. Section seventy-five, the triple forte mentioned above, is for violin alone (it may be that the composer expects the violinist by now to be using a whip rather than a bow), exerting itself on melodic line and accompanying tremolo figures simultaneously:

Figure 22-4.   Violin, letter 75, mm. 2-3

Section seventy-six is marked *più fff* [!]; fortunately, the piano has now rejoined the violin, so there is hope of success in living up to this marking. The duo may experience some dismay, however, when they arrive at section seventy-seven. The piano has been set back to forte, but the violin must sail on into a triple forte espressivo!

This section is the peak of the movement, not only in loudness, but also for the fact that the subject now once again begins on G. Since seventy, it has been transposed successively to G sharp, A, F, C sharp, B flat, and D, its wanderings reflecting the turbulence of the musical events that have taken place. By section seventy-eight, things have simmered down to a forte espressivo, and from here to the end of the sonata, section eighty-two, everything moves toward quietness. By eighty, the violin is muted and is fluttering, pianissimo, against the brooding, chordal background of the piano's line:

Figure 22-5.   Letter 80, mm. 1-3

There are a couple of last accentuations in section eighty-two, but the whole fabric of the music has dissolved here, even the subject represented by no more than a few tentative intervals.

From the view we have given of the movement, it may seem more like musical engineering than composing; the entire procedure is guided by an ear keenly attuned to sonorous color and texture, however. The finale will be found a most convincing end to a convincing sonata.

23 ❧ Other Contemporary Russian Sonatas

VıоLıNısт AND MUSICOLOGIST Boris Schwarz closes his excellent volume, *Music and Musical Life in Soviet Russia, 1917–1970*, with a summation that includes the following comment:

> Western critical opinion concerning new Soviet music is often ambiguous and vacillating. There is an almost automatic rejection of music that suggests Socialist Realism, folklorism, or programmatic content. On the other hand, "advanced" music of Soviet composers is usually evaluated by the yardstick of the latest Western fashion; hence, it is often found either out of date or "imitative" of Western models.[182]

These are informed statements, made from the perspective of a Russian-born American scholar steeped in Russian musical achievement. It is against such a yardstick that the following appraisals of Russian violin sonatas must be measured. My comments are, in fact, colored by the awareness that some (by no means all) Western compositions of recent years meet and set standards of excellence that cannot be overlooked.

The duo ensemble, in building its repertoire, will want to devote itself to the more challenging musical products of our time, of whatever origin. The players will want to know of interesting Russian sonatas; at the same time, if they are willing to play their way through a representative cross-section of the Russian repertoire, they are bound to be disappointed in a number of the available examples of that literature. This would be true of the music of any region.

Of Russian sonatas for violin and piano (other than the Prokofieff and Shostakovich works already discussed), I have seen just one example by each of the following composers. The dates shown are those of publication, unless given in parentheses, in which case the date is that of composition.

A. Babajanian	1970
E. Botiarov	1966
B. Dvarionas	1968
A. Eshpai	1967
O. Evlakhov	1964
A. Goedicke	1959 (1899!)
E. Golubev	(1953)
R. Ibragimov	1967
K. Khatschaturian	1957
B. Kliuzner	1966
M. Kuss	1969
B. Liatoshinsky	1962
V. Laurusas	1967
A. Lobkovsky	1967
M. Milman	1969
A. Monasipov	1967
A. Niaga	1961
V. Salmanov	1967
B. Shnaper	(1964)
A. Shnitke	1963
G. Ustvolskaya	1966

Some of these sonatas are not discussed here because they did not prove sufficiently interesting to me (the Goedicke, for example, is as out-dated as others of its stamp and vintage—anywhere), or proved to be as self-conscious, bombastic, and consequently as unappealing as too many works of our time are. I have singled out some pieces for mention owing to their particular virtues or defects.

Evgeny Golubev's Sonata of 1953 abounds in swimming, or loping rhythms, invariably pursued too long. The work is too innocent to pretend to the grandiose quality it seems aimed at.

Karen Khatschaturian's (he is the nephew of Aram) Sonata of 1957 opens unfortunately: its first movement, Allegro—a race to nowhere on a melody of trite rhythm. The second movement, Andante, is also a study in long, not clearly articulated lines, this time of a rather blowy lyricism. The concluding Presto combines, in its episodes, the defects of the first two movements. The sonata is of moderate difficulty, and of little profit to the duo when measured against the riches otherwise available in the contemporary repertoire.

Alfred Shnitke (Sjnitke), in his Sonata number 1, published 1963, impresses me more than the other composers I have seen in the Russian repertoire. The work is in four movements, relatively brief. The piece uses the twelve-tone system, despite the "decadent" label so often attached to this kind of composing in Soviet circles. The devotion to the system is clear enough, for example, to show the piano part using the entire set of tones, already presented by the violin alone at the opening of the sonata, as the source material for its chord clusters at the entry of the keyboard part; and so that the piano part at the end of the movement is an inversion in transposition of the violin's opening twelve-tone statement.

The dodecaphonic way of writing at least helps this work break out of the mold of rambling diatonic motion found in much of the melodism of the other sonatas of recent Russian vintage, and makes it a refreshing change from convention and pomposity.

In the first movement, the players will note the balance of start and finish, the tight, concise attitude. In the Allegretto, a jaunty and peppery movement, there is a short cadenza for the violin, a two-page solo for the piano. Like the opening Andante, this movement ends quietly, but only as the outcome of a larger structure and the achievement of a greater climax.

The third movement, Largo, offers a sustained-tone line at the beginning and end. There is a correspondence here to the silence of the piano part at the start of the sonata (in itself a "sustained" effect) and to the held-tone line at the end of the second movement. The finale, Allegretto scherzando (very much so), presents the longest sustained ending of all. The composer has chosen an intriguing way of closing the work with a slowed-down, trailing-out version of the crisp theme of the movement.

B. Shnaper's Sonata, composed in 1964, is a florid, oratorical, agitated work, with some quieter relief passages in its train. There is in the latter part of the work too much and too obvious a play on orgiastic surges of line, but in a work of such brevity—perhaps ten minutes' playing time— this may be tolerated.

Boris Kliuzner has written a long Sonata (published 1966), in four movements. The Prelude and Toccata (the first two movements) are the best. The former is an impressive progression from muted murmurings by the violin, to a powerful climax and a tenuous ending. The Toccata is an exceedingly energetic and lengthy movement, also beginning quietly—but

with accentuations—in the violin alone. With the two instruments alternating in percussive and sustained lines, and with both given the opportunity to be heard alone at various points in the movement, the pressure
and excitement are relentless.

The third movement, Invention, is not imaginative enough to live up
to its title; a plodding essay. The finale tries to recapture the excitement of
the second movement; much sound, some fury, and a fair amount of wind
across the steppes.

The Sonata of Galina Ustvolskaya (published 1966) is strange in a few
particulars. To begin with, it has a metric signature of 1/4. The quarter
beat is certainly important in the work: every rhythmic unit the composer
uses is a quarter note or a multiple thereof; there is never a note value less
than a quarter. In its own right or as a counter-thread against longer
rhythmic spans, the quarter pulse is almost always in evidence. So reliant
is the composer on the quarter that she gives up the bar line in its favor.
Mechanical organization for learning and rehearsal purposes is taken over
by a rehearsal-lettering system that places a number at every tenth quarter-
beat in the piece. Further, the composer uses the quarter rest only, extending it to necessary multiples by showing (by number) how many rest beats
are to be counted in the individual musical line. This is not consistently
applied; sometimes a single quarter rest is used, apparently to finish out
a ten-quarter series before a rehearsal letter, followed immediately by a
group-rest number for the remainder.

To what purpose is this freewheeling metric? It does leave the composer free to choose whatever beat grouping seems desirable at the moment,
without the necessity of writing constantly changing metric signatures. The
players can, I am sure, accustom themselves to the barless score. But again,
to what purpose? What is visually a revolutionary piece is, aurally, not so
at all. A kind of free pitch/rhythmic ostinato is heard at frequent intervals
throughout the work. For the most part the ostinato oscillates between
G sharp and D sharp; about midway through the sonata, the sequence
shifts to C sharp–G sharp (there are other, transitory versions as well),
returning momentarily to the original ostinato, then insisting on the new
version with fresh and finally shrill vehemence for the remainder of the
sonata. Not quite, however; the final utterance is a col legno tapping of
the bridge. This tapping, appearing as one thread among several melodic
strands back at measure 193, actually traces its descent from a series of
D sharps in the violin part of letter 10, and is there revealed as an emphasizing of one "leg" of the familiar G sharp–D sharp ostinato.

Against this parade of ostinato figures, there is an equally obstinate drumming of "melodic" quarter-note series. In the 2,013 pulses that make up the sonata, one is hardly ever free of the confounded quarter rhythm, either as the sole musical factor or the dominant one. One welcomes oases of rest, of varied and sometimes considerable length, where the longer pulsation (but still a pulsation!) of the fermata takes over.

All might yet be well, but for the fact that "moving" quarter-note lines do not move with determination, but as though for the sheer sake of motion, dodging through sequences that suggest at times a free-fall flirtation with the twelve-tone system. The grid work of quarter beats is a cage. Even the prevailing fast tempo cannot save the piece; the sonata cannot be played fast enough to mask its innate weakness.

The Sonata (published 1967) of Andrei Eshpai is in one movement. It starts promisingly, though already with a dangerous hint of the epic. When it breaks into billows of broad triplets, the signs are clear. One over-extended episode of rhythmic wash follows another. The whole sonata is short, but long. There is a tendency to the unresting, the unrelieved; but mostly, to the self-indulgent.

The length and temper of R. Ibragimov's Sonatina (published 1967) befit its title: a little sonata, short, perky, fun. It has a folkish tang to its rhythms and melodies, with enough freshness of harmony to make the reference tangential rather than blatant. If a comparison may be drawn without any suggestion that the sound is similar, I may say that this sonatina reminds me of the *Roumanian Dances* of Bartók. Though there is some high position-work for the violin, the piece is not too difficult for the intermediate duo.

Also from 1967 is the Sonata of A. Monasipov. Its three movements are somewhat rambling and pastoral in quality. The music sounds as though it was written with a woodland instrument (panpipes?) in mind, then cast in the mold of the violin-piano duo. This is the kind of piece that is interesting more for its color than its content. I should not be recommending it, because it is rather too long and too lightweight to convince me. With these reservations, I call it to the attention of my readers for their own appraisal of a curious example of recent Russian writing.

24 ❧ The Sonata of Irving Fine

Irving fine was born in Boston in 1915 and died there in 1962. He did undergraduate and graduate work at Harvard, studying composition there with Edward Burlingame Hill and Walter Piston, and continued with Nadia Boulanger in France in 1939. His own teaching career included membership in the Harvard faculty from 1940 to 1950, and Brandeis University from 1950 until his death. The winner of many awards, grants, and commissions, Fine wrote a distinguished and varied repertoire, much of it for instrumental combinations.

His Sonata for Violin and Piano (1948) is a tightly knit and effective composition in three movements. The score's rehearsal numbers are placed at or near points of structural significance in the sonata. Examining the successive numbered segments, we find the piece goes together in orderly and logical fashion. The first movement grows by a process of accretion: basic ideas are stated, elaborated, provided with several counter-rhythm ideas, every element introduced clearly, then stirred into the musical amalgam before going on to the next ingredient.

The initial measures contain two basic components: the first motive, with its falling interval and the crisp rhythmic figure,

and the rising, quasi-triadic element stated by the violin.

The processes of the first movement may be tabulated as follows:

(Introduction.) Moderato. Statement of both elements; short extension on the rhythmic element.

Allegro moderato to letter 2 plus 4 measures. Constructed on the basic elements, cited above.

Letter 2 plus 5 measures, to letter 2 plus 9 measures. Clipped rhythm introduced.

Letter 3 to letter 4. Combination of the two preceding sections.

Letter 4 to letter 5. Eighth-note drumbeat emphasis in accompaniment.

Letter 5 to letter 7. Combination of the second and fifth sections, above.

Letter 7 to letter 8. Slower pulse in accompaniment.

Letter 8 to letter 9 plus 5 measures. Slower accompaniment takes over for itself, with rolling eighth-note arpeggiation derived from the triadic element as an added factor.

Letter 9 plus 6 measures, to letter 10. The drumbeat returns, with accentuation.

Letter 10 to letter 13. New, forceful version of the upward triadic motion under the subject. In slow and diminution form, with imitative treatment among the three voices.

still present. Also, especially after letter 11, the clipped rhythm is present. Broad, climactic, fortissimo rhythms after letter 12.

Letter 13 to letter 17. Thickly textured follow-through on the several thematic ideas. From letter 15, a letting-down; and at letter 16, a reminiscent and lyric backward glance.

Letter 17 to end. Coda: fast, delicate at first; then, a bravura finish.

The second movement, Lento con moto, is an extension on ideas derived from the first movement of the sonata. Again, the rehearsal numbers mark out structural episodes in the music.

Opening, to letter 1. The opening statement in the violin, pizzicato and arco, is reminiscent of the first movement subject. But now with sprightly, snappy rhythmic element added. Chimed, sustained accompaniment.

Letter 1 to letter 2. Rolling, legato texture, with broader-rhythmed version of the snapped rhythm, based on the opening idea.

Letter 2 to letter 4. Brusque extension of idea (with some clear reference to the rhythm ♩ ♫)
of the first-movement subject. Tapers off to couplet sixteenths, legato.
Letter 4 to letter 5. The couplet is made the basis for snapped rhythm, beginning on the beat instead of off, as originally heard at the beginning of the movement (see also section 2 of the first movement). Gives way to syncopation, in eighths and sixteenths.
Letter 5 to letter 6. Devoted to the snapped rhythm.
Letter 6 to letter 7 plus 6 measures. Almost the same as the first nine measures of letter 1, at first with violin and piano parts switched.
Letter 7 plus 7 measures to end. Coda.

The third movement, Vivo, still builds on ideas derived from the initial elements of the first movement; a strongly emphasized rhythmic element (which we shall label A ♫♩𝄾 ♫♩𝄾)
is added to the proceedings.

The first 8 measures of the movement: an introductory warm-up.
Measure 8 to letter 2 plus 6 measures. Lead-in to A, with rolling figure and A as accompaniment; then the lead-in figure (which is derived from the first movement) is used as the subject over the rolling figure.
Letter 2 plus 8 measures, to letter 3 plus 6 measures. Wide-rocking, slow figure set against tighter, triplet rolling figure.
Letter 3 plus 7 measures, to letter 4. Reminiscent of the snapped rhythm from the second movement, letter 2.
Letter 4 to letter 15. A returns at letter 5 plus 6 measures.
    Again, at letter 7 plus 4 measures.
    A now alternates with material elaborated from the ideas of the first movement.
    From letter 8 through letter 12, the flowering of these elaborations.
A again in prominence at letter 13 plus 7 measures.
Letter 15 to letter 19. Broad, slashing (*con slancio*) abstract from A, with alternate left-hand, right-hand drumming, changing to a triplet accompaniment. The fortissimo climax of the movement occurs just before letter 19. .
Letter 19 to end. Coda, with grand upward sweeps of the triadic element from the first movement.
A dominates the end of the sonata.

Though not ferociously difficult, the work is clearly meant for performers of high caliber. The amateur duo can profitably attempt the work,
but only with some diligence and alertness. Happily, the lines and textures
of the piece are as clean-cut as the format of the music, and will set no
unusual barriers for the performers.

25 ❧ *The Schoenberg* Phantasy

Music lovers who admit affection only for music of conventional stamp (usually interpreted to mean music up to the late nineteenth century, or twentieth-century imitations thereof), maintain that the sound of Arnold Schoenberg's music takes them into a no-man's-land. A territory where melodic line is discouragingly angular and disjunct; where rhythm is unpredictable and meter undependable; where the texture of interwoven lines compounds the agony already inflicted by the single, barbed strand of sound.

It is late in the day to belabor this point; composers, and many listeners with them, have progressed to musical fronts only dreamed of by Schoenberg in his day. But there are still many—perhaps especially among those amateur enthusiasts who play the chamber literature up to and including the late Romantic vintage—who deny themselves access to the musical sounds of today. So doing, they forbid themselves the pleasure of new and valid experiences. Often, too, they lose contact with music that is in its own way a closely related descendant of the very music that they treasure by habit.

This is definitely the case with the music of Schoenberg. As a teacher as well as composer, Schoenberg was most conscious of the fact that he derived from the heritage of older Western composers. In 1931, he wrote to his colleague, Anton Webern, about a course in composition the latter was drawing up: " . . . I could recommend your possibly arranging the analysis in such a way (by the choice of works) as to show the logical development towards twelve-note [i.e., Schoenbergian] composition."[183]

Schoenberg insisted his students base the development of their own way of composing upon an intensive study of the older repertoire. While he felt that older conventions could not be simply copied and duplicated by the contemporary composer, he recognized the vital importance of knowing how the musicians of times past thought, contrived, and wrote.

He was consistent in describing his music as, at one and the same time, new and yet to be considered in the same light as older bodies of composition: "the accent is on 'composing.' "[184] He wanted something really new, not merely the coloring of old ways with a surface film of pseudo-modern harmonies. And he wanted that newness built on solid ground: "In music there is no form without logic, there is no logic without unity."[185]

If we hear one of Schoenberg's most popular works, the early composition, *Verklärte Nacht* ("Transfigured Night"), op. 4, for string sextet, the line of descent from the two Richards—Wagner and Strauss—is quite clear. But the intensity and compression of material, the thickness of sound, is Schoenberg's own. Here again, frontiers are drawn. Many listeners can follow Schoenberg as far as the sextet, possibly even as far as the highly colored imagery of *Pierrot Lunaire*, of the year 1912, but no farther.

When Schoenberg made his way to the formulation—in the early 1920s—of the twelve-tone technique of composing, he traced a path that many followed in his wake. The principles of this way of composing have brought new dimensions of freedom and discipline to many composers who have espoused it. It has also served as the avenue for the creation of more than one stupendously boring composition. The technique—any technique—is only as good as the man who uses it. There is no substitute, in composition, for judgment, logic, a good ear, and a mind that has something to say.

Assuming this all-too-rare combination of attributes to be present in the composer, the twelve-tone technique affords him the means of organizing the given composition in close-knit fashion: by generating all happenings in the work, in all its voices and all its sections, from a particular ordering of the twelve tones familiar to us from conventional writing— the twelve pitches of the chromatic scale. The particular sequence of these tones, or "row," maintains its identity, and more important, that of the intervallic successions that characterize the various pitch-sequence fragments within the row, in any one of forty-eight manifestations: stated forward; backward; in the inverted position of either of these statements;

and in the twelve possible transpositions (i.e., starting on C, on C sharp, on D, and so on), of each of these four statements.

This can lend coherence to the writing. It cannot impart contrast, flexibility, appeal. Here the taste of the composer is again the essential factor. Rhythmic pattern, choice of register in which the successive elements of the row(s) are heard, tone color (instrumentation, dynamics, playing manner), texture (deployment of lines against one another, the density or openness of chordal clustering of tones, contrast in the rhythmic spacing of successive tones), all these factors depend on the composer's knowing what he wants to hear.

How effective a work can be produced through the twelve-tone technique is demonstrated by the *Phantasy* for Violin with Piano Accompaniment, op. 47, of Schoenberg. It is a challenging work, that Schoenberg described as "very difficult, but . . . technically very playable indeed . . . "[186] I can testify from performance experience to the truth of Schoenberg's assertion. Those who have heard the work will be able to agree that the piece is relatively accessible to the willing ear. Though Schoenberg wrote, with some diffidence, that the *Phantasy* "is said to sound very well. I haven't heard it yet,"[187] we must assume that he heard the work mentally in the process of composing it. Surely he would have known whether, by his own definition, the work would sound "well." Again, repeated performances of the work have substantiated his musical judgment.

Moreover, the work demonstrates the continuous "family" line leading from the nineteenth century to this composer. As it happens, the composition takes on a particular kind of significance by being the last composition of Schoenberg, written in March, 1949, when he was seventy-five (he died in 1951). What strikes one about the piece is the curious feeling of "old Vienna" that pervades it, an aroma of nostalgia and of familiar ways.

The generative material of this work is its particular ordering of the twelve tones. Here, they are set up as follows, each successive pair of notes constituting the interval of a seventh:

Figure 25-1.

In this sequence, the second half is an inversion of the first. That is, as can be seen in the following example, each interval of the second half of

the row is a reflection, in opposite direction, of the corresponding interval
in the first half:

Figure 25-2.

And the completed spelling out of the row begun by each of these halves
will show the two voices complementing each other in X-fashion. This
is interesting to contemplate; but it is not music until heard as the composer planned it—in actual sequence of rhythm and register:

Figure 25-3.   Violin, mm. 1-3

When viewed thus, the melody falls into two shapes roughly similar to
each other. One ends with a big leap downward; the other, with a big leap
upward; and each of these leaps is immediately preceded by an augmented
fourth. Each segment has a very active middle sequence; and each begins
with a short-long rhythm sequence. This pattern, translated into various
time values and placements throughout the composition, takes on special
significance because of its frequent recurrence:

Figure 25-4.

a. M. 1

b. M. 2

c. Mm. 13-14

d. M. 52

e. Mm. 63-64

f. M. 66-67

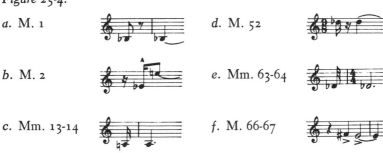

Taking the twelve-tone statement as a whole, its internal arrangement,
placement of the consecutive tones in their specific registers, and the rela-

tionship of the direction and spacing of leaps to each other follows, in rather close order, the tenets of conventional, good melody writing. The line moves with consistent plan (as we have shown above), exercises good contrast of fast and slow, high and low, and builds very effectively to a climax (in this case, at the end of the sequence, on the twice-touched high G flat). And, what with dramatic exploitations of vigorous bowing and string crossing, it is quite a violinistic opening shot!

The piano, for its part, is not less effectively used. Looking at the entire score for the opening measures, we see that the piano is active precisely in those spots where the violin is less so, and, in general, fulfills motions that the violin initiates. The two instruments are entirely complementary to each other. This is the more remarkable in view of the way Schoenberg tackled the composition of the work. In a letter to his brother-in-law, Rudolf Kolisch, in April, 1949, he wrote: "A week ago I finished a piece for violin solo with piano accompaniment."[188] His description is quite specific and is borne out by the fact that he wrote out the violin part competely before adding the piano part.[189] At the same time, he obviously must have had the relationship between the two instruments clearly in mind when he started, for the parts fit so well together in the finished product. Note the easy balance of the voices in the first four measures of the work:

Figure 25-5. Mm. 1-4

Note, too, that the piano part is actually the inversion of the violin part. Thus, in completing each its own set of tones, the two instruments "complement each other, X-fashion," just as shown in Figure 25-2.

The solo-versus-accompaniment roles of the two instruments in these measures dictates that the piano part is not spelled out in linear fashion. Instead, it gathers the tones of its row into chordal clusters, or into fragments of such quick sequence that they give a chordal effect.

We may now proceed a bit further into the violin part of the opening, to see that the line of that instrument adheres faithfully to the initial series and its manifestations. In measures 4 to 6, the violin plays G–F–B–C sharp–A–B flat, which is the reverse-order presentation of the pitch sequence of the first half of the initial row:

Figure 25-6.

a. Violin, from mm. 4-6

b. Violin, from m. 1

At the same time, the piano is playing the remainder of the series in reverse order, repeatedly:

Figure 25-7. Mm. 4-8

In measure 7, violin and piano together spell out the entire original statement, while in measure 8, the violin proceeds to play the reverse of the second half of its initial series, the piano offering the reverse of the first half thereof. In measure 9, the violin revisits the first half of its original series statement, but groups two pairs of the tones in simultaneous-sounding notes, while the piano groups the same tones in other fashion:

Figure 25-8. M. 9

Stop!—the command comes from the writer as well as the reader, by now distraught at such expounding of these details. The loudest call for a halt would have come from Schoenberg himself, who felt that the workshop process of judging and selecting the arrangement of tones into a finished composition was the affair of the composer, not the onlooker. Of the performer and listener, he wanted to know only that they reacted to his music as music. [190]

The eminent composer and theorist of serial music, George Perle, warns against the description of a serial piece through "tabulations of the notes of the set in their ramified course . . . on the assumption that the mere identification of the order numbers of the notes will establish their validity."[191] Yet even such a superficial approach, followed here, can indicate in the Schoenberg example a direction and control that many listeners (and players too, even today) may not otherwise suspect.

Of more immediate use to the player than the above approach is a view of the general plan of the composition. In the following table, Schoenberg's own titles and instructions from the score are at the left:

Grave	Measures 1 to 6, first episode.
	Measures 7 to 17, second episode.
	Measures 18 (with preceding sixteenth) to 24, third episode.
Più mosso, furioso	Measures 25 to 33; compare with closing, measures 161 ff.
Meno mosso	Measures 34 to 39, gliding episode.
Lento	Measures 40 to 51, augmented, keening episode.

Grazioso	Measures 52 to 63, waltzlike episode.
Tempo 1 (Grave)	Measures 64 to 71, stentorian interlude.
Più mosso	Measures 72 to 84, Grazioso revisited, but carried to point of boisterousness, intermingled with the stentorian element, and eventually flinging off.
Scherzando	Measures 85 to 92; compare with the second episode, measures 7 to 17.
Poco tranquillo	Measures 93 to 116, to some extent a scherzando reminiscence of the waltzlike mood of measures 52 ff.
Scherzando	Measures 117 to 134, a second look at the Scherzando.
Meno mosso	Measures 135 to 153; compare with measures 109 to 113.
Tempo 1 (Grave)	Measures 154 to 160, reference to first episode, measures 1 ff.
	Measures 161 to 166, closing, based on material and temper of the Più mosso section (measures 25 ff.), but now slowed down, pesante.

In approaching this work, it is important that both players follow the composer's instructions, specified and implicit. Tempi are given metronomically, and they are right. Dynamics, too, are given very explicitly, and they are an essential part of the musical pattern. For example, play measures 8 to 20 any old way; then play them with careful observance of the dynamic gradations given, and see the difference in dimension and perspective that the shadings of loud and soft provide.

Figure 25-9.   Mm. 18-20

Play measure 25, not only with the indicated tempo and dynamic range, but also with the furioso temper called for by Schoenberg:

Figure 25-10.   Mm. 24-25

Play measures 40 ff. with all the sense of yearning, never-never quality, and time-veiled color that the passage demands:

Figure 25-11.   Mm. 45-46

Play the Grazioso (mm. 52 ff.) truly graciously, with extreme fluidity. On the other hand, play the Più mosso (mm. 72 ff.) of that section with all the spice and sparkle you can muster:

Figure 25-12.   Mm. 73-74

Play measures 161 to 163 with clarity, but also with the fiery impetuosity of the bravura style:

Figure 25-13.   Mm. 161-163

End the work, at the very least, with the blazing flourish the composer has written into the music.

This work, for those at both ends of the living room or auditorium, will be an exciting experience, and one that will demand retelling. There is only one drawback: the duo (both members) will have to be of virtuoso grade in order to make headway with the *Phantasy*. But there is no harm in trying, even for the less accomplished. You owe it to your musical muscle tone and moral fitness! And let the first to cry, "Decadent music!" study until he sees the error of his ways.

26 ❧ *The Walton Sonata*

Sᴛʀ ᴡɪʟʟɪᴀᴍ ᴡᴀʟᴛᴏɴ was born in 1902. He made his first musical impact with *Façade,* for speaking voice and chamber ensemble, composed in 1922 to poems of Edith Sitwell, went on to those further successes, the highly esteemed Viola Concerto (1928–29), the oratorio, *Belshazzar's Feast* (1929–31), and the Symphony (1932–35). Walton's output in the years since has been diverted largely into film music, though he has also produced (among other works) several chamber pieces. These include the Sonata for Violin and Piano, from the year 1949.

Walton's own countrymen are rather put to it to describe his work. Thus, the English composer, Anthony Milner, writes:

> Although in his youth he was classed as a revolutionary, today many regard him as the musical embodiment of the national genius for compromise. He is truly neither rebel nor conservative . . . [pursuing] a strictly personal path in which innovation is incidental rather than fundamental.[192]

The consensus among English critics, musicologists, and the composing fraternity seems to be that Walton is a Romantic at heart, that his nostalgic style reached its apogee in the Viola Concerto, and that the romantic tendency in his work since then has become either overrelaxed, mannered, or all-predominant (depending on the particular writer's point of view).[193] Eric Blom mentions a further objection, raised outside England, that

325

Walton has no fixed allegiance to a "system," then goes on to ask, "Does it matter? He has what is worth more: style and maturity."

Walton's ability to use a system, or its trappings, for his own purposes is demonstrated in the Violin Sonata. The first movement, Allegro tranquillo, is quite controlled and orderly, to the extent that corresponding sections in the two halves of the movement balance even to the number of bars assigned them. The theme of the movement is expansive, winding its way through the first twenty-four measures without any real break. There are two melodic stepping-stones in this tune:

Figure 26-1. Violin, mm. 1-5

Because of their similarity to each other and the frequency of their occurrence in the melody in both instruments, a dangerously hypnotic effect is generated. Walton no doubt intends that this should be so, for the thickness of texture (from the interweaving rhythms) increases greatly toward the end of the opening passage, as though to engulf the ear.

The second theme is really a transitory rhythmic reaction to the final landing of the first:

Figure 26-2. Mm. 24-25

A rolling line, predominantly triplet, that occupies the succeeding measures (26 ff.) is the bed upon which are set further applications of the opening material. Elaborations in measures 25 to 49 are tightened, presented in snappier, faster rhythms, in measures 50 to 66. Measures 67 to 172 constitute a development, with peaks of excitement at measures 98, 114 ff., and 155. This is balanced, as shown in the chart below, by the section from measure 229 to the end; this last section corresponds, in the sense that it begins the same way as measures 67 ff., but it has its own concluding purposes. It is shorter, only one peak is provided for (measures 243 ff.), and that one is the apotheosis of the thematic element, which then manifests itself in broader versions (measures 254 ff., 261).

1. Opening to measure 24 ——————— Measures 173 to 198
2. Measures 25 to 35 ————————— Measures 199 to 209
3. Measures 36 to 49 (extension of material of
    section two) ——————————— Measures 211 and 212
4. Measures 50 to 66 ———————— Measures 212 to 228
5. Measure 67 to 172 ———————— Measures 229 to end

The tonality of the movement is an enigmatic B flat major.

As Colin Mason observes, the second movement is a set of variations built on a Tema of two subdivisions:[195] the first of these is stated twice by the violin (measures 273 to 280, and 281 to 289).

Figure 26-3. Violin, mm. 273-280

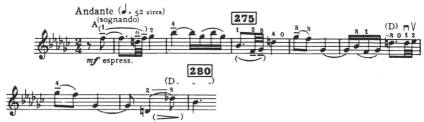

The second, proclaimed by the piano alone (again twice, measures 290 to 297) is a twelve-tone series. The tones are grouped in three sub-units of four tones each. Within each sub-unit, a descending fourth (or ascending fifth, as the melodic frame dictates) is followed by a second such interval, starting a semitone below the landing-note of the first interval.

Figure 26-4. Piano, mm. 290-294

The "row" is used, not as the basis for a twelve-tone structure, but as an ostinato that threads its way through the set of variations and that becomes a subject for those variations, at some points displacing the first of the two themes. Here is the scheme of the movement:

Tema: Andante. Two statements of each of the two subdivisions of the theme.

Var. 1: *A tempo poco più mosso.* Theme elaborated; ostinato stated twice.

Var. 2: *Quasi improvisando.* Theme more floridly elaborated; ostinato stated thrice, in both elaborated and compressed forms.

Var. 3: *Alla marcia molto vivace.* A still longer treatment of the theme; the ostinato, also in *marcia* version, stated thrice again, in successively shorter formats.

Var. 4: Allegro molto. This variation is devoted entirely to the ostinato. The fact that both the violin and piano are now involved in presenting the ostinato reinforces a suspicion that the theme, from the very outset of the movement, has itself contained allusions to the ostinato.

Var. 5: Allegretto con moto. The two instruments having coincided with one another in the previous variation in the pronouncement of the ostinato, now pass beyond each other, exchanging former roles. Here the piano presents the theme in very rhapsodic fashion, while the violin provides (pizzicato) accompaniment. And, conversely, the violin presents the ostinato at the end of the variation. Actually, the violin (with some participation by the piano as well) treats incipits of the ostinato, rather than the entire melody, and these become fragmentary and closely spaced, especially in measure 490.

Var. 6: Scherzando. The theme setting is treated in airy fretwork by both instruments. The peak of intensity in the variations occurs in the statements of the ostinato (by the violin, with piano accompaniment), measures 513 ff.

Var. 7: Andante tranquillo. The choice of adjective in the title of this variation and its instrumentation suggest the opening of the first movement (Allegro tranquillo) of the sonata.

Figure 26-5. Mm. 523-525

The piano again takes up the presentation of the ostinato; it does so twice (measures 545 ff.) and then is joined by the violin in the presentation of fragments of the series.

Coda: Molto vivace. There are seven statements of the ostinato series, by both instruments, in the space of fifteen measures, with an effect of rhythmic acceleration and thickening of texture. The impression of gathering speed is aided by the fact that the first four statements are complete, the last three (by violin with accompaniment), abridged (the last one most of all).

Presto. This concluding section toys with the intervallic tag that is left after the shortening process that began at the end of the Molto vivace section of the Coda. It is as though the composer puts on a display of impatience with the subject that has dominated the movement so long.

The transposition scheme chosen by the composer in the sequence of presentations of the ostinato series is interesting in its own right. The following table shows the plan; it should be added that, at the end of each variation's statements of the ostinato, the first note of the series is added; and that tone becomes the first tone of the next variation. Like the *custos* in early notation, which gives warning, at the end of each staff, concerning the placement of the first note of the next, this "added note" carries the ear from one section of the movement to the next.

Tema.   B♭ F E B C G F♯ C♯ G♯ D♯ D A
Var. 1.   B F♯ F♮ C C♯ G♯ G♮ D A E E♭ B♭
Var. 2.   C G F♯ C♯   and so forth
Var. 3.   C♯ G♯ G♮ D and so forth (second and third statements begin D♭)

Var. 4.	Db	Ab	G	D	and so forth
	A	E	D♯	A♯	and so forth
	D	A			
Var. 5.	D	A	G♯	D♯	
Var. 6.	E	B	Bb	F	and so forth
Var. 7.	F	C	B	F♯	and so forth
Coda.	Bb	(seven times!)

(Though present throughout the variation, the series is stated only incompletely, or in allusion, toward the end.)

There is no doubt about it. The sonata ends (as it begins), firmly in B flat major.

27 ❧ Some Other Sonatas of the 1940s

In the wake of a number of rather detailed descriptions of individual compositions, I now give brief mention to several works by prominent American and European composers. At beginning and end, there are works by three stalwarts of American music in this century: Cowell, Piston, and Riegger.

Henry Cowell

Henry Cowell (1897–1965), one of America's most energetic champions of new music, himself an extremely prolific composer, open to the many currents of contemporary music and—both in his writing and his work as pianist—an interesting and experimental contributor to that stream, wrote a Sonata for Violin and Piano in 1945. Its five movement titles suggest that we are about to play the arch-American sonata da camera: Hymn, In Fuguing Style, Ballad, Jig, and Finale.

All is well, except that the second and last movements go on too long. The jig is rousing, and fun. The finale is energetic, its length somewhat relieved, just before the end, by a short passage in which the piano displays the only instance (in this work) of those unusual manipulations of the instrument that Cowell experimented with in his writing. Here the pianist plays a line composed of the four tones, F-A-B-C, while at the same time

331

pressing "the fingers of the right hand firmly on the open strings" of the same tones, "right next to the bridge (of the piano) near the tuning pegs . . . the resulting tone will be muted in quality, bearing in general the same relation to an open piano tone that muted violin tone bears to the open." At the same time the violin is playing pizzicato and then pianissimo bowed tones against this piano background.

Walter Piston

Walter Piston (born 1894), one of the grand older men of American music, as productive of good students as he has been of well-built compositions, has written two sonatas for violin: one, with piano, from the year 1939; the other, a sonatina for violin and harpsichord, from 1946. The Sonata of 1939 opens with a Moderato in easy 6/8 swing, of a clearly tonal idiom, overlaid with enough dissonant melodic and harmonic tones to give it a tart, slightly acidulous flavor, without any danger of being banned in Boston. So also for the metric situation, where the episodic introduction of a five pulse gently ripples the otherwise unmarred duple progress of the movement.

The middle movement is an elegiac 5/4, the constant flow of its line carried almost to the point of surfeit. Its lyric beauty is impressive, however; a most satisfying episode and, for me, the high point of this piece. The Allegro finale is neatly constructed, offering equal and well-planned activity for both instruments. Unfortunately, the melodic and rhythmic sequences of the movement sound like New England busywork; inevitably an anticlimax after the second movement.

The Sonatina for Violin and Harpsichord avoids indication of crescendo or diminuendo in the keyboard part; so much for the harpsichord, unless the election to emphasize linear, rather than chordal, texture is another reflection of the choice of instrument. The use of accent marks and stress (duration) lines shows that the piano is more than a parenthetic suggestion for this piece.

The Sonatina is not too different from the Sonata; a somewhat easier version of the same kind of music, again in three movements, again with an active finale. This is good Piston, clean lined, adroit, and not extremely exciting. The work is dedicated to Alexander Schneider and Ralph Kirkpatrick. For a duo of such caliber, the work is an easy jaunt; for the less accomplished ensemble, an exacting workout. It is only fair to say that a piece of this kind can sound well only if played with some ease and pointedness. Labored, heavy-handed performance will make the lean textures sound strained and skinny.

From the year 1946 come sonatas by a member of the middle generation of contemporary American composers and by one of the younger and best known of today's German musicians. I do not find either work very stimulating. Nor will the composers necessarily feel that these are still representative pieces. The sonatas should be mentioned here, nonetheless.

David Diamond

David Diamond (born 1915), prominent and active in American music since the early 1930s, wrote his Sonata from 1943 to 1946. It is in four movements, beginning with an Allegro moderato of bucolic effect. The Allegretto con moto moves at a fair pace, but the constant emphasis on one-to-the-bar (in accord with the composer's instruction) makes for the impression of a slower pulse. The impression is one of a lullaby or slow waltz, pleasant for a time, but carried on too long.

The Adagio respirando is more successful than the second movement, but too stark and prairie flat for my ear. The final movement, on the other hand, with accented on- and off-rhythms, gets to seem twitchy and aimless in its jiggery.

Hans Werner Henze

Hans Werner Henze (born 1926) would almost certainly think his Sonata of 1946 to be out of the advanced musical currents that he has followed since then. It does not, in any event, seem a felicitous work. Its Prelude is energetic, but suffers from a rather ungainly, peg-legged rhythm, too much heard and giving the appearance of emotion without any real substance. The moonings (no pun intended) of the two instruments in the Nocturne seem unconvincing. If the Intermezzo is short and fragmentary, the Finale, to compensate, is long and tedious, with the piano spending too much of the movement in a texture-background role for a not very interesting violin line. The piece does not reach me.

Boris Blacher and Gottfried Einem

The German composer, Boris Blacher (born 1903), has written a moderately difficult work in his Sonata, opus 18 (ca. 1947). It is clear, short, bracing (but not very impassioned) in style and has lightly spiced, conventional harmonic writing; a good, safe, "progressive" piece. The most difficult part of the sonata, for the violin, is the Allegretto middle section of the second movement. There the combination of arco and left-hand pizzicato is demanding. And perhaps the most enjoyable movement of the four is the finale, a Rondo: Allegro, which, in its rather dry, wry wit, is a Stravinskian romp.

Blacher's pupil, the Austrian, Gottfried Einem (born 1918), is less impressive in his Sonata, opus 11, written in 1949. The work is acceptable, but not outstanding. The first movement proceeds in wavelet motion and is short-breathed in effect. The Larghetto is not only nocturnal and pallid, but a little dull. The finale has much and constant activity, but gives a mushy and rolling, rather than an incisive impression.

Wallingford Riegger

A fine, short work for the proficient duo is the Sonatina, opus 39 (1948) of Wallingford Riegger (1885–1961). Its brevity comes from the laconic tendency of this excellent American composer. He had the admirable quality of writing only enough, of saying much in little. The effect in this work is a marvelous blend of the dry, the lyric, the quizzical. In two movements, Moderato and Allegro, rising at a few points to fortissimo, but for the most part in understated tones, this work is ideal concert material. It will make its presence and wit felt against the most flamboyant program mates.

28 ❧ Kirchner: Sonata Concertante

LEON KIRCHNER was born in Brooklyn, New York, in 1919, and—from the age of nine—was raised and educated in California. There he studied with Schoenberg at UCLA, and at the Berkeley campus with the composer-theorist, Albert Elkus, and with Edward Strickland, coming also within the influence of Ernest Bloch, at that time a member of the faculty. His undergraduate years completed in 1940, he studied with Roger Sessions in New York, returned (after military service) to Berkeley for graduate work, then served successively as faculty member at Berkeley, the University of Southern California, Mills College, and since 1961, as professor of music at Harvard.

A career rich in honors and in productivity has seen Kirchner writing in many musical avenues; in his chamber music output, there are two works for violin and piano: the Duo, of 1947, and the Sonata Concertante, written in 1952. The latter work, termed by the musicologist, Alexander L. Ringer, "Kirchner's first completely 'settled' composition, [representing] a crystallized style all his own,"[196] is (like the earlier duo) cast in one continuous flow. The twenty-two-minute length of the piece has an implicit division into two movements, if we judge from the use of the word *attacca*, that separates the Adagio molto from the Grazioso, two-thirds into the length of the work. One is, however, more conscious of the integration of the entire piece than of separate structures, as our schematic diagram of the sonata will indicate.

335

There are some thirty metronomic markings in this short work, carrying the quarter-beat pulse from values 40 to 224. This, coupled with the larger metric groupings (some of the metronome marks govern units as large as the dotted half-note), ranging from 2/4 through Alla breve, 3/4, 6/8, 7/8, 4/4, 8/8, and on to 6/4, and with the shifting emphasis in predominant rhythmic motion from long to short notes, makes for a musical texture of great variability. In these matrices, wide-ranging melodic lines are either accompanied or answered by lines that rock back and forth, or move in more directed fashion, but in small intervals. These recurring space and time patterns, free though they are in their combinations, account for the cohesive progress of the piece.

The composer's care in guiding the flow of the piece must be matched by the performer's attention to the speed instructions. It is essential, too, to follow the "connective" indications: the acceleration and slowing-down transitions between successive areas in the piece. So also for dynamic and coloristic gradations (e.g., *senza vibrato*, marcato, and so forth), shown with equal nicety.

All these requirements are part of the flesh-and-blood vitality of the work, as is clear from the character markings of the sonata: Andante maestoso, Calmo, Grazioso, A tempo resoluto (sic), and so on. The temper of the music means something to the composer, who says of his purpose that:

> An artist must create a personal cosmos, a verdant world in continuity with tradition, further fulfilling man's 'awareness,' his 'degree of consciousness,' and bringing new subtilization, vision and beauty to the elements of experience. It is in this way that Idea, powered by conviction and necessity, will create its own style and the singular, momentous structure capable of realizing its intent.[197]

The point is made more strongly still by Aaron Copland in his appraisal (written in 1950) of the Kirchner style:

> Kirchner's best pages prove that he reacts strongly [to today's unsettled world]; they are charged with an emotional impact and explosive power that is almost frightening in intensity. Whatever else may be said, this is music that most certainly is 'felt.' No wonder his listeners have been convinced.[198]

Clear-cut correspondences appear in the course of the sonata; compare, for example, these two passages:

Figure 28-1.

a. Score, page 1, brace 3

b. Score, page 7, brace 4

Note, however, that the half note in the first example = M.M. 88, in the second, ♩ = 112, en route (via an allargando) to a faster tempo. This sounds like a contradictory statement, and it is. The apparent speed-up in the second example is seen, rather than heard. The eighths in the second bar, and following, are marked to equal the sixteenths of the preceding measures. In effect, then, the tempo is now ♩ = 224. From here, the allargando does indeed slow us down to the next tempo designation, ♩. = 72 (in this time-frame, ♩ would equal 216—you can check with your metronome), at the passage beginning at the ¾ shown at the end of our example. That passage, tempo and all, corresponds to an earlier one, heard as a Presto, beginning in the thirty-sixth measure of the sonata. As can be seen in Figure 28-1, the shift in tempo makes it possible for the composer to preserve graphic, as well as thematic, relationship between corresponding musical passages.

The related areas of the piece may be broadly mapped as follows; other, more detailed correspondences abound.

(Numbers refer to pages in score. Arrows and braces indicate obvious or inferred correspondence of sections.)

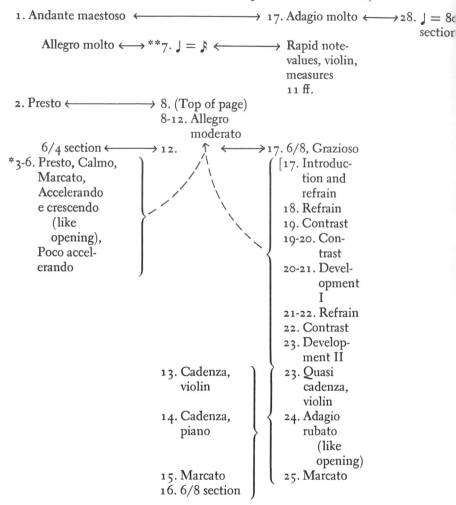

1. Andante maestoso ⟵——————————⟶ 17. Adagio molto ⟵——⟶ 28. ♩ = 8c
                                                                              section

Allegro molto ⟵——⟶ **7. ♩ = ♪ ⟵——————⟶ Rapid note-
                                                     values, violin,
                                                     measures
                                                     11 ff.

2. Presto ⟵——————⟶ 8. (Top of page)
                       8-12. Allegro
                              moderato

6/4 section ⟵———⟶ 12.   ↑   ⟵——⟶ 17. 6/8, Grazioso
*3-6. Presto, Calmo,   [17. Introduc-
    Marcato,   tion and
    Accelerando   refrain
    e crescendo   18. Refrain
    (like   19. Contrast
    opening),   19-20. Con-
    Poco accel-   trast
    erando   20-21. Devel-
                                            opment
                                            I
                                      21-22. Refrain
                                      22. Contrast
                                      23. Develop-
                                            ment II
13. Cadenza,   23. Quasi
    violin   cadenza,
                                            violin
14. Cadenza,   24. Adagio
    piano   rubato
                                            (like
                                            opening)
15. Marcato   25. Marcato
16. 6/8 section

* Page 5, più accelerando, relates to page 10, ♩ = 112.
** Pages 6 and 7 constitute a development area.

Technically and musically, this is a quite difficult work, calling for players of virtuoso caliber who can stand off against one another in a manner reflecting the concertante roles assigned to the two instruments by the composer, as in the following excerpt:

Figure 28-2. Score, page 11, brace 3

We have encountered such treatment, including individual cadenzas, before this in the duo-sonata literature (recall the Mozart and Beethoven examples, among others). Kirchner, like his predecessors, is able to contain the bravura element within the frame of the sonata, drawing excitement and heat from it without destroying the sense of intimacy and sincerity that is essential to the chamber work. The Kirchner Sonata Concertante is an indispensable item in the twentieth-century duo repertoire.

29 ❧ Ben Weber: Sonata da Camera

Bᴇɴ ʙʀɪᴀɴ ᴡᴇʙᴇʀ was born in Saint Louis in 1916. After studies at the University of Illinois and at De Paul University in Chicago, he moved to New York, where for years he earned his livelihood by copying music in a meticulous hand (refusing to teach composition, for the reason that he thought it unteachable—possibly reflecting the fact that he was to a certain extent himself an autodidact). In his own right, he has won a place as one of the important American composers of our time. This is reflected in the significant awards, grants, and honors that have come to him and in the performances that have been given his music by major soloists and symphonies—including the New York Philharmonic —in America and abroad.

For the player, the proof of Weber's skill comes in the combined sense of organization and freedom, intensity and basic gentleness that has, from early in Weber's career, informed his music. The twelve-tone way of composing is his by habit and conviction, used with ease and flexibility. My own feeling about this, inspired by performing years ago his First Sonata for Violin and Piano, is reinforced by acquaintance with the composer's Sonata da Camera, of recent provenance, published under the auspices of the Fromm Foundation.

Much of the first movement of this three-movement work is dominated by a tolling effect, in both instruments. Each sonorous line, whether in violin alone, in keyboard alone, or in some combination of the two, lends its share to the pulsing, both in the large (on the bar line), or in the smaller units of the half-note beat. If we examine the movement section by section, according to the following tabulation, we find scarcely a measure where every beat is not marked by a massive note or a shorter, accented one.

Measures 1 to 8.	Tolling, loud, with crescendo to fortissimo, and with the motion quickening toward the end.
Measures 9 to 12.	Tolling, loud and massive. Culmination in the peal of measure 12.
Measures 13 to 17.	Tolling continues in piano. Violin turns to lacier windings, with glissando to connect its most wide-ranging intervals. Dolce and piano.
Measures 18 to 23.	Here there is interweaving of the tolling and winding, from one voice to another. This is the fastest rhythmic passage of the movement. Ends fortissimo.
Measures 24 to 29.	This section gives contrast to the preceding measure. The passage is quiet, slow.
Measures 30 to 37.	Marked *come prima*, this is almost throughout a literal repetition of the opening measures of the movement.
Measures 38 to 40.	A quiet version of measures 9 to 11, and without the windup of a measure 12.
Measures 41 to end.	This is analogous to measures 13 to 17, but slower paced. Its *molto delicato* corresponds to the dolce, piano treatment of the earlier passage. And the instruction, *e sentimento*, is appropriate to the lacy piano treatment in these measures.

The second movement, Moderato, is an ostinato piece. The line, E–G–B flat–C–D flat–C–B flat–G–E, E flat–A flat, that is, a rising and falling, archlike series, followed or attended by a two-note suffix,

Figure 29-1.

is traceable throughout the movement, in complete or truncated or embroidered form. See, for example, the passages beginning as follows:

Measure 1.   Piano, bass and treble
Measure 6.   Violin
Measure 10.   Violin
Measure 15.   Piano, treble
Measure 17.   Violin
Measure 19.   Piano, bass
Measure 27.   Piano, bass
Measure 51.   Piano, treble
Measure 52.   Violin
Measure 57.   Violin
Measure 67.   Violin
Measure 76.   Piano, treble
Measure 77.   Piano, bass

The movement is framed in two closely related end sections: measures 1 to 38 and 150 to the end. The final section is a close, but not literal, restatement of the opening; also, it veers off on a closing pattern of its own. A "preview" of the return is offered in measures 91 to 96. The poco meno mosso, beginning in measure 97, is like the opening, but with embroideries, *delicato*, in the violin part. From measure 109 on, these embroideries are shared by both instruments, and the remainder of the section carries out a development of ideas already well used in the movement. This includes not only the ostinato, but also an element of sprightly eighth-note rhythm and attendant wide-range legato swoops, introduced at measures 39 ff., again at 60 ff., 73 ff., and so forth.

The whole movement has the air of a gliding waltz, with the sections from measures 39 to 150 constituting a quasi-trio/development. A delicate touch, even for the points of loudness in this movement, is very much in order. This comment holds true, indeed, for the entire sonata, which is as distinctive for its charm as for its intricate detail.

If we can imagine a sprightly J. S. Bach (and we certainly must, on the evidence of many a Bach movement), the Allegro con spirito of Weber's sonata makes one so imagine. As in the Bach violin-keyboard sonatas, there are only two instruments at work, but the independence of the bass and treble in the keyboard part produces a three-voiced ensemble. Throughout the movement the three parts act in the most congenial kind of rivalry. Look at the first brace of the score:

Figure 29-2. Allegro con spirito, mm. 1-5

Where one voice sounds, the other answers. A sforzando in the bass can find a like response in the treble (measure 2), or again (see measure 4), the emphasis in one part can be highlighted by a reticence in the parallel voices. Sometimes the composer separates the voices by distinct textures:

Figure 29-3. Allegro con spirito, mm. 15-18

In general, though, the movement progresses from texture to contrasting texture, carrying all three parts simultaneously through the given changes. The first section (measures 1 to 65) is subdivided as follows:

Measures 1 to 10. Essentially disjunct, articulated motion.

Measures 11 to 20. Legato arabesques (in sixteenth notes), against articulate sounds.

Measures 21 to 45. Slower (eighth note) motion, but again combining legato and detached writing.

Measures 45 to 65. Admixture of sixteenth-note filigree to the basic eighth-note pulse, the rhythmic pace gradually quickening and thickening.

The second section, measures 66 to 79, is marked L'istesso tempo; but it is in 3/8 meter. The *effect* is that of a slowdown, because three eighths now take the space previously held by four eighths. Together with the angularity of some of the writing and the emphasis on sixteenth-note motion in the last nine measures of the section, this makes for a combination of elegance (Weber calls for leggiero and secco playing) and boisterousness.

The third section, measures 80 to 100, is Poco meno mosso. This brings us, then, to something slower than the pace of the first section of the Allegro. We are especially aware of the parallel because the part writing of the opening of the movement is now brought back, verbatim, for a few measures—except for the fact that it is now barred in 3/8 instead of the original 4/8 meter, a simple yet intriguing jog in the rehearing of the remembered music. Though shorter than the opening section, this episode again moves from thin-and-slow to thicker-and-faster texture.

The concluding episode, Poco moderato, of this finale (measures 101 to the end) begins with a tolling bass reminiscent of the opening treatment of the first two movements. The violin part is a lyricized modification of the motto already familiar from earlier portions of the finale:

Figure 29-4.   Violin, mm. 104-109

Except for a brief cadenza of the violin (against the sustained resonance of pedaled piano chords, measures 130 to 139), the two instruments maintain fairly equal activity through this close, with a last show of togetherness in the ebullient "curtain call" that ends the piece.

30   *Some Other Sonatas of the 1950s*

HERE AGAIN, by virtue of the dating of the compositions included, is gathered as variegated a group of musicians as might be imagined. Disparate though the provenance, style, and successfulness of the pieces may be, there is one thread that runs through almost all of these works: they are serious, sometimes to the point of solemnity. Is this a sign of the times and is it still a sign of today's time that I, willy-nilly, tend to pay my respects to the more sober works, even while gazing with some affection at the one or two lighter examples? It's a grim world.

Peter Racine Fricker

Peter Racine Fricker (born 1920), English composer and teacher, product of the Royal Conservatory of Music and of later study under the composer Matyas Seiber, preceded his teacher in the writing of a work for the violin and piano duo. His Sonata, op. 12 (1950) is in three movements, Allegro, Allegretto, and Adagio. The two instruments are equal in prominence throughout, projecting in the first movement sinuous, constantly extending lines that suggest—in their convolutions and chromatic windings—a serial concept. This energetic movement is followed by the scherzando, thinner, lacy textures of the Allegretto. The muted, "distant waltz" stipulated by the composer is drawn dynamically into the foreground; the sense of space and dimension is kept alive by alternating sound levels thereafter. The finale is a ruminative one, with related end sections and more vigorous

345

central area. To my ear there are reflections here of the musical material of the opening Allegro. This sonata is a difficult work, of almost unrelieved seriousness. It will amply reward the efforts of the skilled duo.

Julien-François Zbinden

The Swiss-born, Swiss-trained Julien-François Zbinden (born 1917), now officer of Radio Lausanne, composed a Sonata for Violin and Piano, op. 15, in 1950. The first two of its four movements seem to me the most successful. An opening Preludio presents the two instruments in dialogue, or rather in a pair of solos, responsive to each other, deferring to each other (to the point of falling silent several times in order to let the partner have his say), beginning boldly and moving through several climaxes, but ending in very subdued fashion. All four movements, for that matter, end quietly. The Scherzo is written in moderately mixed meters and is perky and driving. It presents the surprise of a subdued largo middle section. The Romanza is short but wandering, the least felicitous of the four chapters. Both instruments, and especially the piano, have a brilliant display in the finale. This seems to be an apotheosis of a ponderous theme that itself refers back to the opening thematic elements of the entire work.

Henk Badings

One of Holland's most prominent contemporary composers is Henk Badings (born 1907), student of the equally distinguished older Dutch composer, Willem Pijper. Badings came to music relatively late, but has composed prolifically since the 1930s. I have seen his three sonatas for violin and piano, dating from 1933, 1940, and 1952. The first two are rhythmically trite, to an extent that outweighs the coloristic and thematic interest in the music. The third sonata is more interesting than the others. The first two movements, Allegro and Adagio, are dark, brooding; the finale, Rondo giocoso, is intoxicated rather than jocose, suffering from its attempt to achieve its effect by singsong patterns. It is a weak spot in a sonata that is on the whole intriguing. The piece is difficult to play.

Malcolm Arnold

Malcolm Arnold (born 1921), one of England's more modestly productive composers, has provided the repertoire with a pair of sonatas that are pleasant, if not stirring, to work on. His Sonata number 1 (copyright 1947) can be summed up as crisp. The piano part in the first movement is filled with opposing rolled and articulated thirds, accented syncopes, short driven fragments of melody. Other sections match piano staccato to violin pizzicato. In the Andante tranquillo, the violin lyricism is countered by dryly articulated chordal pulses in the piano (with a brief, "angry" section where both instruments hit out in fortissimo strokes). The 6/8 finale is full of rousing, brash rhythms and swinging melodic arcs, rather like a combination of drinking-song and dance-hall tune. The sonata is clean-cut, entertaining—and that's it.

The tone of the one-movement Sonata number 2 (copyright 1953) is wry and acerb. The material has a popular air to it, as though—but for the sophisticated vagaries of line—the writing could devolve into musical stage. The piece ends Adagio molto, suggesting more than achieving an end; somehow the work seems a musical vignette rather than a movement. The sonata is too inconsequential to study, yet entertaining enough to be included in a program, in relief from its serious fellows. A more paradoxical appraisal I cannot give.

Giselher Klebe

Giselher Klebe (born 1925), one of the prominent, avant-garde composers to emerge in Germany after World War II, has an interesting short Sonata op. 14—copyright 1953—in three movements, written in the twelve-tone system. There is little attempt to make the work approximate a conventional sound (as some twelve-tone composers have contrived to do). The duo will have to play, and enjoy, the sonata for its own coloration, largely determined by the stress on major and minor seconds, heard both linearly and vertically. Recommended to the proficient duo.

Marcel Mihalovici

The Roumanian composer, Marcel Mihalovici's (born 1898) Sonata number 2, op. 45, is copyright 1954. It is a long work, very long, especially when one hears the rhythms of the first and third movements repeated ad infinitum like some kind of sick march-waltz. The score is expensive, and deserves a wide berth.

Bernard Heiden

Bernard Heiden, born in Germany in 1910, studied there with Paul Hindemith. Like his teacher, Heiden eventually came to the United States. Like

Hindemith, too, he combined here the careers of composer and teacher (he is professor of music at the University of Indiana). The halls of academe are, for that matter, one of the few havens for the composer in America today.

Heiden's Sonata for Violin and Piano dates from 1954. The work is not prolix—its four movements total no more than about sixteen minutes of playing time; they are concise and well contrasted. The first movement, in rather slow 4/4, has the violin moving in rhapsodic, fast-note line, with the piano left free to provide a cantabile foil and counter-voice. In the Andante third movement, as well as in the final Allegro deciso, both instruments share similar textures.

In its own way, the finale is as much a perpetuo as the second movement. Because its ♩ moves at 132, as contrasted with the ♩ = 132 of the Molto vivace, its running eighths move as fast as the sixteenths of that earlier movement. The stress on continuous motion is such that the page turner for the keyboard is instructed at one point (measure 106) to turn for the violinist as well.

The tone of the work is dry, witty, crackling. This is a sonata of challenging difficulty, but not so forbidding that it need frighten off the duo of moderate proficiency, willing to work toward clarity in their playing.

Ralph Vaughan-Williams

Ralph Vaughan-Williams wrote prodigiously during his long lifetime (1872–1958), but never a violin-piano duo sonata (or for any other duo either, for that matter) until near the end. In 1954 came the lone sonata, in three good movements: Fantasia, Scherzo, and *Tema con Variazioni*. The piece is difficult, for both instruments (especially in the rapid and active second movement), but—like much of Vaughan-Williams' music— solid, meaty, and satisfying to hear. The sonority of the duo is wonderfully exploited, in lines, passage-work, and harmonies that suggest an English Bloch. Like Bloch, too, the composer tends here to make his points more insistently, more repetitiously than actually necessary. The entire work, though, is twenty-five minutes long, so the feast is manageable. There is a certain poignancy about the nostalgia of the music, tasteful and contemporary in tone though it is.

Ross Lee Finney

The American composer, Ross Lee Finney (born 1906), uses twelve-tone writing to passionate and lyric effect in his third sonata (copyright 1957).

This piece is definitely worth the attention of the proficient duo interested in trying a sensitive, well-crafted work by an American moderate who has added dodecaphonic composition to his already acquired taste and training. As usual, it is not the system that makes the composition, but the man. This is a no-nonsense, effective sonata.

Jean Martinon

The eminent French conductor, Jean Martinon (born 1910), who—as composer—was a student of Roussel, has written ably in a variety of avenues. Two of his works for violin and piano that I have seen are the Second Sonatine, op. 19, no. 2, published in 1944, and the Duo, *Musique en forme de Sonate*, op. 47, published in 1959. Both works show the composer's intent (he is himself a violinist) to treat the two instruments in completely equal fashion. The Sonatine is in one movement, opening with an Adagio that recurs in brief reflection later in the work; the body of the movement is fast, moving from Allegro through the returned Adagio and into a concluding and extended Presto with Coda. In the full-fledged Duo (as in the Sonatine) the composer again favors a winding line. This work is in four large movements; the first and last are "in sonata form"; the second, a Molto vivace, cast in scherzo-with-trio outline; the third, a Lento, separates the two instruments in function, the piano presenting predominantly angular and brusquely rhythmed lines, the violin, a more smooth-flowing countermelody in which the piano at times also participates. The Duo is a solid work, rather reserved but forceful, and of some brilliance in its effect. It deserves the attention of the concert ensemble. The Sonatine is perhaps too slight for the concert program, but will certainly serve well as material for study.

31 ❧ *Seiber and Others of the 1960s*

I CLOSE THESE DELIBERATIONS with a brief view of yet another trio of intently serious pieces, and even briefer mention of three recent Hungarian works. It is a pleasure to be able to end with a cluster of sonatas that seem, in their several ways, to be equally appealing and deserving. Among them, and along with many other works that have not been included in these pages, they indicate that the art of writing for the violin and keyboard duo is still most viable.

Matyas Seiber

Matyas Seiber was born in Budapest in 1905 and died in Cape Town, South Africa, in 1960. A student of Zoltan Kodaly in composition, Seiber was already esteemed for his composing in the 1920s by no less a figure than Béla Bartók. In 1928, Seiber became a teacher at the Hoch Conservatory in Frankfurt, which some dozen years earlier had been the training ground of Paul Hindemith. Seiber was active, during the years that followed, as conductor and cellist as well as composer. In 1935 he came to London, where he spent the rest of his life. In the decades that remained, he was active in the furtherance of new music, his own as well as that of others.

His repertoire encompassed stage and film music, choral and orchestral works, concerti, chamber music (both instrumental and vocal), songs, piano music, and so forth. Seiber wrote a Concert Piece for Violin and Piano in 1954. In 1960, in response to a commission by the BBC, he produced his last chamber composition, the Sonata for Violin and Piano (1960), which was given its premiere in July of that year at the Cheltenham Festival.

Seiber was fluent in the many musical styles of his time; an especially strong influence in his work was that of the twelve-tone system. The violin sonata is a serial piece and is based on the row,

Figure 31-1.

which is first heard in the violin. It will be noticed that, in close-order outline (as shown above) the series divides into three groups of four tones, the interval relationships of the first group being reflected, in inversion, by those of the second, and at first also by the third group, with the final tone veering off. In the course of the work, Seiber adheres to the series or to its transpositions, inversions, and so forth, but also feels free to alter the sequence of tones within the several groups, though preserving the succession of the groups themselves.

There are three movements in the sonata, progressing from lively (*Appassionato e rapsodico*), to light (*Grazioso e danzato*), to restful and sober (*Lento e rubato*) in an overall span of less than eighteen minutes. The first movement divides into two major portions, the first ending with a quasi-recitativo section; the second, with a corresponding section labeled, *Senza misura quasi improvisando*. Amounting to a cadenza for the duo, this section concludes with fifteen to twenty seconds of aleatory improvisation on note groups that have already been presented by the two instruments in the preceding measures. The movement ends with an inversion of the lines presented at the beginning of the sonata, before a *Violente* passage carries us to the double bar.

In the opening measures, the two instruments carry out lines that leap energetically and that supplement each other closely:

Figure 31-2.   Appassionato, mm. 1-3

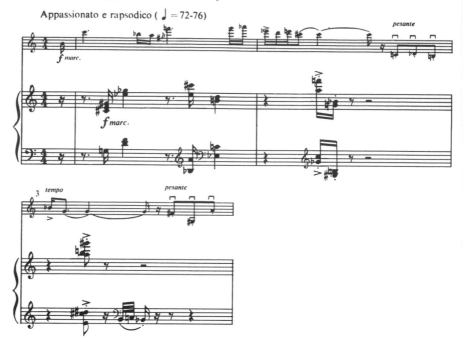

The rhythmic sequence marked, *pesante, tempo*, recurs significantly in the movement. The outline of the movement, then, is as follows:

Marked by angular, leaping motion:

1. Measures 1 to 6.   Violin leaps are responded to by those of piano. Stringendo, with increased density of rhythmic motion.

2. Measures 7 to 13.   Reflects music of opening measures. Measures 9 and 10, the stringendo element; measures 11 and 12, a holding action within the stringendo.

Marked by smoother motion:

3. Measures 13 to 34.   Quasi recitativo, rubato.
    Measures 13 to 27, essentially an accelerating passage.
    Measures 21 to 27, the basic rhythmic fragment is in the violin, with swirling figures in the piano.
    Measures 28 to 34, *movendo*, but in slower

rhythmic motion, marking the end of the first area of the movement.

Resumption of turbulence:

4. Measures 35 to 41.   *Energico, violente*, angular motion.

5. Measures 42 to 54.   *Andante, lirico*: this corresponds to measures 21 to 27, even to the presence again of the swirling figures in the piano.

Quasi-recapitulation:

6. Measures 55 to 69.   Lento (measures 55 to 57) and *movendo* (measures 57 to 69), bring us back to the initial idea, with swirling figures, and so forth, effecting the transition.

The opening rhythmic fragment returns in measures 61 ff.

The più mosso (measures 64, ff.) corresponds to the passage, measures 7 to 13.

7. Measures 69 to 83.   (Cadenza) *Senza misura quasi improvisando*. This ends with the aleatory passage in measures 82 and 83 (which is described, not notated).

8. Measures 89 to 95.   Tempo I: the violin and, initially, the piano, present inversions of their respective lines from the beginning of the sonata.

9. Measures 96 to 100.   *Violente*: corresponding to the *Energico, violente*, of measures 35 to 41, this passage, and the movement, ends with a hammering, accelerating insistence on one chord.

The second movement, *Grazioso, danzato*, is quite logical in its proceedings, no matter how airy and tripping the gait of the music may seem. An initial thought is presented; a second is propounded. The latter is concentrated and intensified in the next passage. All preceding events are surveyed in a fourth episode. Then, a third proposal is advanced. This, together with elements one and two, is reviewed in a last passage of summation; and the movement then (sonorously speaking) evaporates.

1. Primary idea, measures 1 to 30.

Measures 1 to 9, violin has the solo line. Measures 10 to 18, piano takes the prominent role.

Measures 19 to 20, cadential rush, both instruments equal. Measures 21 to 30, violin again in solo.

2. Second idea, measures 31 to 43.
   Airy, extremely "open" writing, with constant alternation of the
   two instruments.

3. Concentration of the second idea, measures 43 to 54.
   The rhythmic pulse of the second idea is solidified, thickened in
   a massing of the two instruments, then again somewhat thinned
   out.

4. Résumé of sections 1 to 3, above, measures 54 to 65.
   Tempo I.

5. A third idea, measures 66 to 70.
   Marked più lento, and moving toward a tremolo, this is a relatively static and hovering passage, giving respite from the maneuvers of the earlier happenings.

6. Conclusion, measures 77 to 103.
   Tempo I: elaboration and extension of the earlier résumé, now
   including the element of the più lento (as represented by the
   tremolo texture). Everything boils away to one tone, E flat (measures 120 and 121). In this, there is some reflection of the procedure at the end of the first movement. The last two measures,
   marked "in exit," carry the movement away in a wisp of sound.

It is apparent from the first two movements that Seiber has, as one
of his compositional devices in this piece, the alteration of open and dense
textures. This is born out, again, by the procedures in the third and final
movement.

1. Measures 1 to 9.	*Lento e rubato*: violin, in a moderately wide range, interwoven with and surrounded by the piano writing. There are only two loud notes in the passage, in measure 8.
2. Measures 9 to 22.	*Andante, molto calmo*: again, this passage is soft, except for three loud notes in measures 18 to 21. Though marked in slower metronomic pace, the rhythmic motion of the violin part is more "going." Note that the violin part of measures 15 ff. is an inversion of that in measures 5 to 8.
3. Measures 23 to 29.	*Molto calmo*: canonic writing in three parts. The resulting texture is thicker than that of the preceding areas.

Figure 31-3. Mm. 21-24

4. Measures 29 to 33.　Tempo I. Corresponding to the passage, measures 9 to 22, this version reverses the roles of the instruments; now, the violin has the slower, wide-ranging line, as against the couplet motion of the piano part.

5. Measures 34 to 42.　Corresponds to measures 15 ff. (and measures 5 to 8).

6. Measures 43 to 49.　*Calmo*: again, a three-way canonic texture, but with the violin part now in tremolo.

7. Measures 50 to 59.　Tempo I: corresponds to measures 29 to 33 (and 9 to 22).

8. Measures 60 to 74.　Closing area: Molto lento—Calmo—Molto più lento. A fragmentary kind of writing, marking the final decay of the textures of the piece. It will be noted that both the violin and piano are here using the original row, with the clear intent of viewing again the beginning of the sonata, from the experience of the entire piece.

As is true of other music of Seiber that I have heard, the effect of the Sonata is one of great warmth and sensibility, couched in terms of strict compositional control. Seiber's musical stance is very much akin to that of Bartók, without in any sense making him an imitator of that master.

Easley Blackwood

The formidable pianist, composer, and professor of music at the University of Chicago, Easley Blackwood (born 1933), wrote his Sonata, op. 7, in 1960. Blackwood is not a man to trifle with; he knows his piano, his music, his composing, his own mind. A case in point is his admonition at the start of the sonata: "Metronome indications give exact tempos: any deviation greater than five percent is a distortion of the composer's intentions."

Other specific instructions include: avoidance by the violin of stopped-and-open unison on certain tones (fiddlers love to grab for the extra resonance), and the directed combination of both in others; wide-reach chords for the piano, "not arpeggiated, if possible"; double-stop "Pizz. with two fingers, not arpeggiated"; and, "not the harmonic."

The three movements to which such comments are attached include an Allegro rigoroso, extremely vigorous, with chunky rhythms and chords to match, punctuated by, paralleled with, running chromatic passage-work. Next, an A-B-A movement, with the melodic line of the concluding A-section set an octave up and modified in outline, the angularities of the whole softened by the Adagio tempo. And a final Allegro molto whose very dense textures are created by closely crenellated lines and accompanying voices. This closing movement is fiercely difficult, especially for the piano. The ensemble coordination, too, is hard to bring off. Blackwood enjoys stern challenges in his own performance and doesn't mind putting his interpreters to similar test.

Roberto Gerhard

Roberto Gerhard was born in Spain in 1896 and died in England in 1970. His studies took him from Enrique Granados to Felipe Pedrell, and to Schoenberg. His professional career included teaching, composition, and editing in Spain until 1938, when in the wake of the Civil War he left his homeland to settle in England. His output, not extremely large but varied and meticulous, stems in large part from his English years, and he is counted among that country's more important contemporary composers.

Gemini, or Duo Concertante for Violin and Piano, is one of the last chamber works of this composer and was premiered in London in 1966. The composer's own annotation for the piece states that:

> The work consists of a series of contrasting episodes, whose sequence is more like a braiding of diverse strands than a straight linear development. Except for the concluding episodes, nearly every one recurs more than once, generally in a different context. These recurrences are not like refrains, and do not fulfill anything remotely like the function of the classical refrain. Rather might they be compared to thought persistently on some main topic.[199]

One of the most persistent strands in the piece is that of the sustained resonance. This is presented in various ways: in the piano, in the form of tone clusters, widely spaced intervals, combinations of clusters and single-tone sounds, sustained "pyramid" chords, sustained simultaneous chords, long trilled tones, gently touched rhythms that articulate a sustained interval. These sustained resonances occur in every dynamic level, from soft and delicate to (initially) brusque and fortissimo. They are also colored (in the piano) in various ways, such as by stopping portions of the struck chord by damping the strings with the hand, the stipulated use of pedal or maintained key-pressure to sustain the chord, clustering consecutive or white-only keys, sustaining tones elicited by strumming a glissando on the strings with "plectrum or nail-file (using the broad end)," and striking a tone cluster with the palm of the hand or (for a cluster spanning an octave and a fifth) the forearm.

The violin, of course, is limited to single- or double-stop sustained strands, either of natural or harmonic sonority, in various registers and spacings, with the added resonance of the glissando and trill on occasion.

Against and between the recurrent bouts of sustained resonance, there are arpeggiations and pyramidings of tones through one or both instruments; sharply punctuated tones and chords; many-leveled webs of tones, set off by abrupt dynamic and accent changes; running, quasi-tremolo passages (sometimes in ponticello effect); pesante chords and double-stops; running webs of eighth notes; pointillist spotting of chords; rapid-fire passage-work; and so on.

These passages seem to be as much an outgrowth of the sustained-tone strand as contrasts to it. They are, in their various ways, exploitations of sound and resonance. A case in point is the passage at measures 100 ff., where the forte-fortissississimo chord of the piano is held with the pedal and allowed to die out over a span of fourteen measures, while the violin

goes through a parallel, simulated "decay" period, moving from loud ponticello to quiet and ordinary tone in a rapid sixteenth-couplet rhythm:

Figure 31-4.   Mm. 97-107

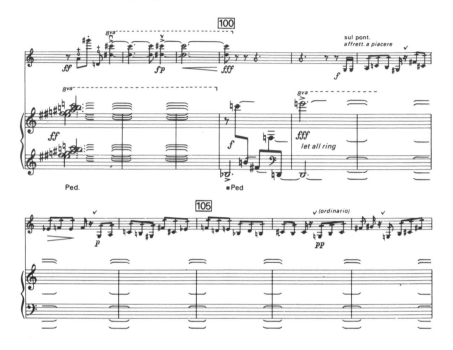

Gemini, then, is a short (twelve-minute), difficult, and interesting
experiment in duo sonority, treating the two instruments in truly "twin"
equality. It is a colorful listening experience, a welcome relief from the
vacuity or just plain dullness sometimes found in the sonata literature,
and a worthwhile addition to the study and concert repertoire.

Other Composers

Of several works from the 1960s by Hungarian composers that I have seen,
the following seem to me to merit attention. All are published by Editio
Musica of Budapest, and the composers in question all trained at the
Academy of Music in that city: Béla Tardos (1910–1966) and Pál Kadosa
(born 1903) with Kodaly; István Loránd (born 1933) with Ferenc Szabo
and Ferenc Farkas.

Kadosa, who is dean of the piano faculty at the academy, has written
several works for violin and piano, including two sonatas, the first from

1925, the second, opus 58, from 1962. Of these, I have seen the last named, which opens with an interesting and rhapsodic *Preambule*, and attracts also with the similar sostenuto sections that alternate with the vivacissimo dancelike portions of the third, Finale movement. The middle Scherzo, though light and brisk enough, is somewhat overlong and diffuse, lacking the intensity of the end movements—though its trio makes up for this with some vigorous flashes of its own. In all, the sonata is one of the more rewarding possibilities in recent sonata literature.

Béla Tardos was, from 1955 until his death, the director of Editio Musica. The Sonata (1965) is the last of his chamber works. This is a quasi-cyclic piece, of two long end movements with a shorter, intervening slow movement. The Lento is the most attractive portion of the work, what with its expressive dialogue between the two instruments. The finale, a motoric movement based on a rhythmic sequence of some triteness (at least when repeated as often as Tardos sees fit to do), is overextended and spoils the sonata. Rather difficult, especially for the violin in the broken chromatic runs of the opening Allegro.

István Loránd has served in teaching posts and, for a time, at Editio Musica. His sonata, from the year 1967, is an attractive work in three movements. The first, Appassionato, is angularly rhapsodic, mildly dissonant, with the emphasis on drive. The Scherzando is short, with just enough recurrence of the opening material at the end to frame the movement. The theme, Semplice, moderato, of the third movement is the most relieved portion of the work, but the textures thicken again radically in the course of the five variations. The piece has good sounds and is suited to the professional-caliber duo.

Postlude

Many sonatas are described and appraised in these pages. Even so, I have left unsung a disconcertingly large number. In the Preface to this survey, I hinted at my misgiving at omitting such a work as the Sessions Duo. Now at the close, my uneasiness is all the stronger over this, as at the fact that I have not included other such vital works as the sonata of Stefan Wolpe, the characteristic sonata of Virgil Thomson, and many another piece by composers from both hemispheres. The most difficult of these overlooked works (the Sessions and Wolpe among them) will be attempted only by the most proficient duos. For such players, the composer's own measures will offer more guidance than might be forthcoming from words of mine. For these and other compositions in the duo repertoire that space, energy, or arbitrariness have excluded here, the reader may refer to the various publishers' catalogs, the listings of such composer-representing agencies as Broadcast Music, Incorporated (BMI), and American Composers' Alliance and similar agencies abroad—for example, Donemus in Amsterdam for contemporary Dutch composers, and the Centre Belge de Documentation Musicale in Brussels for Belgian composers—and the catalogs of such large dealers and/or publisher's representatives as Blackwell of Oxford, England, or C. F. Peters of New York. A ready avenue to a detailed roster of duo music in print is the appropriate section in Margaret Farish's *String Music in Print*; the second edition of that work is now in preparation.*

With all these resources, and assuming the duo will already have

* Margaret K. Farish, *String Music in Print* (New York: R. R. Bowker, 1965; Supplement, 1968).

made sufficient use of the repertoire offered in the present volumes, players will scarcely find time hanging idly on their hands. More than that, they will be confronted with an amazingly rich and varied body of music literature. In scanning this literature, players will undoubtedly note that pieces for duo (as in other musical categories) have tended to become larger and more difficult over the decades and centuries. There has been an intensification of the technical demands on each instrument in the duo and of ensemble requirements as well; this is true, however, only in a limited sense. A work establishes its own frame and can be quite difficult therein, even though its technical rigors are inherently not as taxing as those in a later work. Bach is not always easier than Mozart, nor are either of these necessarily less demanding than Beethoven or Brahms or Bartók. To interpret any work in a manner satisfying to the general intentions of its author, to the specific traits of the work itself, and to the expectations of the listener will challenge the duo.

With the passing of time, composers have proved less and less interested in writing for the amateur duo. This is partly owing to the fact that every composer, in his own presumably new and personal way, is trying to live up to the highest models of the music that has gone before. It is due, also, to the fact that the emphasis on the training and presence of a professional class of musician, especially since the beginning of the nineteenth century, has led the composer to write for that caliber of player, in the hope that such instrumentalists would take up his music and present it to the public under the most promising circumstances.

The difficulty of the music written and the very existence of the professional performer has forced the amateur increasingly to the sidelines, there to listen, to admire, and to criticize. The situation has been aggravated by improvements in travel and communication. The finest artists perform the world over, preceded and followed by recorded, broadcast, telecast, and cinematized reflections of their work. If this immediacy of the best that our era has to offer in performance has been a goad and benchmark to the professional fraternity, it has been all the more a source of self-appraisal and frustration to the amateur player.

Amateurs, however, are a hardy breed; they are not easily dissuaded from their enthusiasm. Besides, it is their enjoyment—not their livelihood —that is at stake in their music making. So the amateur has kept active, after all, alongside the professional. In ensemble terms over the years, it is of course the string quartet that has accounted for the most visible part of amateur playing. I am encouraged to think, however, that the quantity of duo playing in the home circle has not lingered far behind.

It is important that this activity continue and flourish. Though the gap between composer and amateur may be widening constantly, I believe that the composer would more willingly alienate the amateur's hand than ear. Paradoxically, it is through the actual manipulation of the stuff of music, through the playing of it, that the amateur can help his ear move toward familiarity with the sounds the composer sets before him. The amateur must grapple firsthand with the wonderful array of duo music from the past and present, and thereby equip himself to approach with confidence and curiosity the newest writing for his ensemble.

For both the amateur and the professional, the greatest gift is freedom from complacency and from devotion to the musical status quo.

Notes

References to music editions are given in abridged form. For complete bibliographic listings, see Editions Used.

ABBREVIATIONS:

Cobbett's Survey	=	*Cobbett's Cyclopedic Survey of Chamber Music*
DTÖ	=	*Denkmäler der Tonkunst in Österreich*
Grove's Dictionary	=	*Grove's Dictionary of Music and Musicians.*

1. Alexander W. Thayer, *Thayer's Life of Beethoven,* rev. and ed. Elliott Forbes (Princeton: Princeton University Press, 1967), p. 87.
2. Ibid., pp. 139 ff.
3. Georg Kinsky, *Das Werk Beethoven: Thematisch-Bibliographisches Verzeichnis seiner sämtlichen vollendeten Kompositionen,* completed and ed. Hans Halm (Munich: G. Henle, 1955), p. 29.
4. Ibid., pp. 743-750.
5. Ibid., p. 28.
6. Thayer, *Life of Beethoven,* p. 207.
7. Ibid., p. 59.
8. Robert Donington, *The Interpretation of Early Music,* 2nd ed. (New York: St. Martin's Press, 1963), pp. 95-96.
9. Kinsky, *Beethoven Verzeichnis,* pp. 76-77.
10. Kinsky, *Beethoven Verzeichnis,* p. 111; Thayer, *Life of Beethoven,* p. 333.
11. Thayer, *Life of Beethoven,* p. 333.
12. Ibid., p. 332; and Emily Anderson, *The Letters of Beethoven* (New York: St. Martin's Press, 1961), I, 91, footnote 1.
13. Thayer, *Life of Beethoven,* p. 333.
14. Kinsky, *Beethoven Verzeichnis,* p. 111, quoting from the Simrock edition, April, 1805.
15. Anderson, *Letters of Beethoven,* I, 120.
16. Kinsky, *Beethoven Verzeichnis,* p. 112, quoting in the original French from Hector Berlioz's *Voyage musical en Allemagne et Italie,* I, 261.
17. For a rather extreme view from the same premise, see Rudolf Reti, *The-*

matic Patterns in Sonatas of Beethoven, ed. Deryck Cooke (New York: Macmillan, 1967), chapter 14, "The Thematic Pitch of the Kreutzer Sonata."

18. Kinsky, *Beethoven Verzeichnis,* p. 269.
19. Quoted in the original German by Gustav Nottebohm, *Beethoveniana, Aufsätze und Mittheilungen* (Leipzig: C. F. Peters, 1872), p. 29. Kinsky, *Beethoven Verzeichnis,* p. 270, relates that the first performance took place at the Lobkowitz home on December 29, 1812, and that it was repeated there on January 7, 1813, a day after Rode's first public Viennese concert.
20. Anderson, *Letters of Beethoven,* I, 391.
21. Paul Nettl, *Beethoven Handbook* (New York: Frederick Ungar, 1967), p. 202.
22. H. C. Robbins-Landon, trans. and ed., *The Collected Correspondence and London Notebooks of Joseph Haydn* (London: Barrie and Rockliff, 1959), pp. 130-131, letter of February 26, 1792.
23. The edition is listed below under Dusík, the Czech spelling of the composer's name.
24. Jan and Bohumír Stědroň, Vorizek, *Sonata,* "Editors Notes," p. ix.
25. William S. Newman, *The Sonata in the Classic Era* (Chapel Hill: University of North Carolina Press, 1963), p. 77.
26. For details about the circumstances that brought about the banishment, see John Warrack, *Carl Maria von Weber* (New York: Macmillan, 1968), pp. 70-72.
27. Otto E. Deutsch, *The Schubert Reader: A Life of Franz Schubert in Letters and Documents,* trans. Eric Blom, 1st ed. (New York: W. W. Norton, 1947), p. 894; and Gerald Abraham, ed., *The Music of Schubert,* 1st ed. (New York: W. W. Norton, 1947), pp. 264, 99-100.
28. Schubert, *Sonatinen,* prefatory note.
29. Deutsch, *Schubert Reader,* p. 901.
30. The opus numbers attached to many Schubert compositions are confusing. They do not necessarily give a picture of the chronological ordering of the works. Rather, they were assigned, often arbitrarily, to the compositions by the publishers. To make order in the Schubert oeuvre, Otto E. Deutsch, the eminent Schubert scholar, has catalogued the works along chronological lines according to the best available information. The "D." number refers to the ordering of the composition in Deutsch, *Schubert, Thematic Catalogue of All His Works in Chronological Order,* in collaboration with Donald R. Wakeling (New York: W. W. Norton, 1951).
31. Abraham, *Schubert,* p. 99.
32. Sonata in G minor, op. 137, no. 3 (D. 408).
33. Curt Sachs, *World History of the Dance,* trans. Bessie Schönberg (New York: W. W. Norton, 1963), p. 432.
34. Deutsch, *Schubert Reader,* pp. 781 ff. See also, same, pp. 599, 629.
35. *Grove's Dictionary,* VII, 836.
36. Deutsch, *Schubert Reader,* p. 715.
37. Ibid., p. 716.
38. Ibid.

39. Ibid., p. 767.
40. Deutsch, *Catalogue*.
41. Deutsch, *Schubert Reader*, p. 715.; *Schubert: Memoirs by His Friends*, coll. and ed. Otto E. Deutsch (London: Adam and Charles Black, 1958), p. 262.
42. Abraham, *Schubert*, p. 101.
43. Leon B. Plantinga, *Schumann as Critic* (New Haven: Yale University Press, 1967), p. 222, quoting and translating from *Neue Zeitschrift für Musik*, 8 (1938), 177-78. Cf. same, Appendix, I, 115, for original text of quotation.
44. Eric Werner, *Mendelssohn: A New Image of the Composer and His Age*, trans. Dika Newlin (New York: The Free Press of Glencoe [Macmillan], 1963), pp. 2-4; and Heinrich Eduard Jacob, *Felix Mendelssohn and His Times*, trans. Richard and Clara Winston (Englewood Cliffs, N.J.: Prentice-Hall, 1963), pp. 16, 18, 21.
45. Werner, *Mendelssohn*, p. 7.
46. Ibid., p. 33; and Jacob, *Mendelssohn*, p. 29.
47. Philip Radcliffe, *Mendelssohn*, rev. ed. (London: J. M. Dent, 1967), p. 5.
48. Werner, *Mendelssohn*, p. 15.
49. Radcliffe, *Mendelssohn*, p. 9, indicates the year of composition as 1823; *Grove's Dictionary*, V, 703, lists the sonata as "finished" in 1825.
50. *Grove's Dictionary*, V, 702; Werner, *Mendelssohn*, p. 19.
51. Werner, *Mendelssohn*, p. 19.
52. Radcliffe, *Mendelssohn*, p. 89.
53. Jacob, *Mendelssohn*, quoting on pp. 48-50.
54. G. Selden-Goth, trans. and ed., *Felix Mendelssohn, Letters* (New York: Pantheon, 1945), p. 275.
55. Ibid., pp. 277-278.
56. Ibid., p. 279.
57. Henry Pleasants, trans., ed., and annot., *The Musical World of Robert Schumann, A Selection from His Own Writings* (New York: St. Martin's Press, 1965), p. 89.
58. Alfred Einstein, *Music in the Romantic Era*, 1st ed. (New York: W. W. Norton, 1947), p. 127.
59. Selden-Goth, *Letters*, p. 279, letter to F. Hiller, August 17, 1838.
60. Radcliffe, *Mendelssohn*, p. 167.
61. See Joan Chissell, *Schumann* (London: J. M. Dent, 1948), pp. 55 ff.
62. Henry Pleasants, trans. and ed., *Eduard Hanslick, Music Criticism, 1846–99* (Baltimore: Penguin Books, 1963), p. 52, quoting from an 1856 review of a concert by Clara Schumann, which included performances of *Schön' Hedwig* and *Der Heideknabe*, two Schumann settings of ballades by Friedrich Hebbel.
63. Pleasants, *Schumann*, p. 17, footnote.
64. Chissell, *Schumann*, p. 58.
65. Ibid., p. 179.
66. Ibid.
67. Chorale as given in *Christmas-Oratorio*.

68. Manfred Bukofzer, *Music in the Baroque Era* (New York: W. W. Norton, 1947), p. 266.

69. Norman Demuth, ed., *An Anthology of Musical Criticism* (London: Eyre and Spottiswoode, 1947), pp. 219-220, quoting from Henry F. Chorley's *Modern German Music: Recollections and Criticisms*, 1862.

70. Prefatory note by O. W. Neighbour, in Schumann, *Sonata number 3*.

71. Ibid.

72. Karl Geiringer, *Brahms: His Life and Work*, 2nd ed. (New York: Doubleday Anchor Books, 1961), p. 205.

73. See Editions Used, Brahms-Dietrich-Schumann, *F.A.E. Sonata*.

74. Neighbour, Schumann, *Sonata number 3*.

75. Ibid.

76. Pleasants, *Schumann*, p. 199.

77. Geiringer, *Brahms*, p. 30.

78. Ibid., pp. 216.

79. Ibid.; and Walter Niemann, *Brahms*, trans. Catherine Alison Phillips (New York: Knopf, 1929—6th printing, 1947), p. 257.

80. Quoted by Niemann, *Brahms*, p. 192, from Florence May's *Life of Johannes Brahms* (London: Arnold, 1905).

81. Pleasants, *Hanslick*, p. 83, quoting from a review of 1862.

82. Richard Specht, *Johannes Brahms*, trans. Eric Blom (London: J. M. Dent, 1930), p. 298.

83. Geiringer, *Brahms*, p. 147.

84. Rollo H. Myers, "France from the Age of Fauré and Debussy," in Arthur Jacobs, ed., *Choral Music* (Baltimore: Penguin, 1963), p. 325.

85. William W. Austin, *Music in the 20th Century from Debussy through Stravinsky* (New York: W. W. Norton, 1966), p. 153.

86. Quotation from a review of a concert performance of Fauré's Ballade for Piano and Orchestra, op. 19, cited by Léon Vallas, *The Theories of Claude Debussy, Musicien français*, trans. Marie O'Brien (New York: Dover, 1967), pp. 55-56.

87. Paul H. Lang, *Music in Western Civilization* (New York: W. W. Norton, 1941), p. 1024.

88. Martin Cooper, *French Music: From the death of Berlioz to the death of Fauré* (London: Oxford University Press, 1961), p. 79.

89. Quoted in Florent Schmitt's article, "Gabriel Urbain Fauré," *Cobbett's Survey*, I, 388.

90. Ibid., p. 387.

91. Eric Blom, "Gabriel (Urbain) Fauré," *Grove's Dictionary*, III, 41.

92. Schmitt, "Fauré," pp. 386-387; Cooper, *French Music*, p. 83.

93. Blom, "Fauré,'" p. 39.

94. Émile Vuillermoz, *Gabriel Fauré*, trans. Kenneth Schapin (Philadelphia: Chilton, 1969), pp. 59-60.

95. Schmitt, "Fauré," p. 387.

96. Blom, "Fauré," p. 39.

97. Max Favre, *Gabriel Faurés Kammermusik* (Zurich: Niehans, 1948), pp. 223-224.

98. Schmitt, "Fauré," p. 390.
99. Léon Vallas, *César Franck*, trans. Hubert Foss (London: Harrap, 1951), p. 242, reporting an anecdote verified by the composer's granddaughter, Mme. Chopy Franck.
100. Ibid., pp. 195-196.
101. Vincent d'Indy, "César Franck," *Cobbett's Survey*, I, 424.
102. Ibid.
103. Norman Demuth, *César Franck* (New York: Philosophical Library, 1949), p. 138.
104. Pleasants, *Schumann*, p. 193.
105. Dag Schjelderup-Ebbe, *Edvard Grieg, 1858–1867, with special reference to the evolution of his harmonic style* (London: Allen and Unwin, 1964), p. 245, quoting letter of January 1, 1900.
106. Ibid., p. 248.
107. David Monrad-Johansen, *Edvard Grieg*, trans. Madge Robertson (New York: Tudor, 1945), p. 74.
108. Dag Schjelderup-Ebbe, *A Study of Grieg's Harmony, with special reference to his contributions to Musical Impressionism* (Oslo: Johan Grundt Tanum, 1953), pp. 76-77.
109. Letter of July 30, 1867, quoted by Monrad-Johansen, *Edvard Grieg*, p. 101.
110. Letter to Gerhard Schjelderup, May 11, 1905, quoted by Schjelderup-Ebbe, *Grieg, 1858–1867*, p. 244.
111. Monrad-Johansen, *Edvard Grieg*, pp. 279-280.
112. Translated from German quotation, ibid., pp. 280-281.
113. Ibid., p. 278.
114. Ibid., p. 279.
115. Ibid., pp. 352-354.
116. Povl Hamburger, "Orchestral Works and Chamber Music," in Jurgen Balzer, ed., *Carl Nielsen, Centenary Essays* (London: Dobson, 1966), p. 26.
117. "Carl Nielsen," *Grove's Dictionary*, VI, 86.
118. Richard Litterscheid, ed., *Johannes Brahms in seinen Schriften und Briefen* (Berlin: Hahnefeld, 1943), pp. 356-57.
119. Certificate reprinted in translation in Otakar Sourek, *Antonin Dvorak, Letters and Reminiscences*, trans. Roberta Finlayson Samsour (Prague: Artia, 1954), p. 22.
120. Otakar Sourek, *The Chamber Music of Antonin Dvorak*, trans. Roberta Finlayson Samsour (Prague: Artia, n.d.), p. 12.
121. Ibid., p. 13.
122. Ibid., p. 18.
123. Einstein, *Romantic Era*, p. 302.
124. John Clapham, *Antonin Dvorak, Musician and Craftsman* (London: Faber and Faber, 1966), p. 194.
125. Sourek, *Chamber Music*, p. 169. Clapham, *Dvorak*, p. 194, also feels the Brahmsian shade here and in the slow movement of the work as well.
126. Clapham, *Dvorak*, pp. 193-194; he points out that the F major sketch was later used for the Quartet in C major, op. 61, composed the following year.
127. Ibid., p. 209, footnote 2; Sourek, *Chamber Music*, p. 172.

128. Clapham, Dvorak, p. 20.
129. Sourek, Chamber Music, p. 172.
130. Ibid., p. 175, footnote.
131. Ibid., p. 174.
132. Clapham, Dvorak, pp. 20, 209.
133. Biographical information is from Richard Strauss: A Critical Commentary on his Life and Works by Norman Del Mar (Philadelphia, Chilton, 1966), Vol. I, and Wilhelm Altmann, "Richard Strauss," Cobbett's Survey, I, 460-461.
134. Del Mar, Strauss, p. 46.
135. Altmann, "Strauss," editor's (i.e., Cobbett's) postscript to the article.
136. Webern is the editor of the second part of Isaac's Choralis Constantinus, DTÖ XVI/1 (1909).
137. Anton von Webern, Perspectives, comp. Hans Moldenhauer, ed. Demar Irvine (Seattle: University of Washington Press, 1966), p. 127.
138. Friedrich Wildgans, Anton Webern, trans. Edith T. Roberts and Humphrey Searle (London: Calder and Boyars, 1966), "Critical Catalogue of Works," p. 24.
139. Ibid., p. 9, Translator's Preface, in which Searle quotes from his article on Webern as teacher, in the Sunday Telegraph, April, 1961.
140. Biographical information about Charles Ives in this chapter is drawn from Henry Cowell and Sidney Cowell, Charles Ives and His Music, (London: Oxford University Press), 1969.
141. The chronology of the Ives sonatas is compiled from information given in the editions of these pieces and also in Laurence Perkins's "The Sonatas for Violin and Piano by Charles Ives" (M. M. thesis, Eastman School of Music, University of Rochester, June, 1961), p. iv.
142. Charles Ives, "Essays Before a Sonata," Three Classics in the Aesthetic of Music (New York: Dover, 1962, from the Knickerbocker Press publication of 1920), p. 168. Originally written as a Preface to Ives's Piano Sonata number 2, Concord, Mass., 1845, the essays open with a dedicatory paragraph whose wit clearly reflects the man and his music:

> These prefatory essays were written by the composer for those who can't stand his music—and the music for those who can't stand his essay; to those who can't stand either, the whole is respectfully dedicated.

143. A comprehensive table of the borrowed melodies, as well as a "traditional version" of each, fully written out, is given by Perkins in his thesis, pp. 150 ff.
144. Hans Hollander, Leoš Janáček, His Life and Work, trans. Paul Hamburger (New York: St. Martin's Press, 1963), p. 186.
145. Rollo Myers, Erik Satie (London: Dobson, 1948), p. 94.
146. Edward Lockspeiser, Debussy, His Life and Mind (New York: Macmillan, 1965), II, 300.
147. Ibid.
148. Debussy, Sonate.
149. Lockspeiser, Debussy II, 214.
150. Debussy himself refers to the entire sonata as an "example of what may

be produced by a sick man in time of war," in a letter to his friend, Robert Godet, of June 7, 1917, excerpted in translation by Lockspeiser, *Debussy* II, 218-219.

151. These several points are drawn from material cited and translated by Lockspeiser, *Debussy*, II, 214.

152. Ravel's statement on this, carried in his "Esquisse autobiographique," *La Revue Musicale*, December, 1938, p. 215, reads as follows (my translation):

> The *Chansons Madécasses* seem to me to bring a new element, dramatic —or even erotic, introduced by the very spirit of the . . . texts. It is a sort of quartet where the voice plays the role of principal instrument. Simplicity dominates. The independence of parts [affirmed there] will be found more markedly in the sonata [for piano and violin].
> I imposed that independence on myself in writing a sonata for piano and violin, essentially incompatible instruments; far from minimizing their contrasts, the work emphasizes that incompatibility.

153. The comments, by Bloch himself and by his British exponent, the violinist and writer Alexander Cohen, are quoted in the annotation, by David Hall, for the recording of the two sonatas, by Rafael Druian and John Simms, Mercury, MG 50095.

154. Arthur Shepherd, "David Stanley Smith," in *Cobbett's Survey*, II, p. 433.

155. For a detailed and imaginative investigation of this aspect of Bartók's music in general, and including a consideration of the two violin sonatas, the reader is referred to the dissertation of the American composer, John W. Downey, "La Musique Populaire dans l'Oeuvre de Béla Bartók" (Centre de Documentation Universitaire, Paris, 1964).

156. Ibid., p. 346: " . . . all the harmonic progress acquired during the preceding years is exploited to the limit of possibility, falling just short of atonality and dodecaphonism." Halsey Stevens, *The Life and Music of Béla Bartók* (New York: Oxford University Press, 1953), p. 49: " . . . the trajectory [away from conventional tonality] was to reach its vertex in the two Sonatas for violin and piano, and then turn back toward a stronger affirmation of key." For insights into the melodic and harmonic procedures of these sonatas, see this and the Downey study.

157. Stevens, *Béla Bartók*, p. 205.

158. Emanuel Winternitz, *Musical Autographs from Monteverdi to Hindemith* (New York: Dover, 1965), I, 144, is the source of the quotation, where Winternitz is speaking of the autograph manuscript of the Fifth Quartet.

159. Béla Bartók and Albert B. Lord, *Serbo-Croatian Folk Songs* (New York: Columbia University Press, 1951), p. 20.

160. Igor Stravinsky, *An Autobiography* (New York: W. W. Norton, 1962), p. 169.

161. Ibid., pp. 170-171.

162. Ibid., p. 118.

163. Paul Hindemith, *A Composer's World: Horizons and Limitations—The Charles Eliot Norton Lectures, 1949–50* (Garden City: Doubleday Anchor Books, 1961), pp. 179-180.

164. Quotation from Hindemith's article for *Neue Musikzeitung* (1922), as

translated in William Austin's *Music in the 20th Century* (New York: W. W. Norton, 1966), p. 398.

165. Biographical detail from Heinrich Strobel, *Paul Hindemith*, 3rd ed., (Mainz: Schott, 1948).

166. Stated in an informal introduction, by the composer, to a program of his music, Milwaukee, January 28, 1971.

167. Arthur Berger, *Aaron Copland* (New York: Oxford University Press, 1953), p. 32.

168. Arthur Berger, "The Music of Aaron Copland," *The Musical Quarterly*, XXXI (1945): pp. 425-426, footnote.

169. Berger, *Aaron Copland*, p. 77.

170. Israel V. Nestyev, *Prokofiev*, trans. Florence Jonas (Stanford: Stanford University Press, 1960), p. 385.

171. Ibid., quoting from Prokofieff article, "What I am Working On."

172. Ibid., p. 386.

173. From reminiscences by Oistrakh on Prokofieff, contained in S. Shlifstein, comp. and ed., *S. Prokofiev, Autobiography, Articles, Reminiscences*, trans. Rose Prokofieva (Moscow: Foreign Languages Publishing House, n.d.), p. 242.

174. Nestyev, *Prokofiev*, p. 387.

175. Ibid.

176. Preface to sonata I, International Music Co., N.Y., edition, 1960.

177. Shlifstein, *S. Prokofiev*, pp. 241-242.

178. Nestyev, *Prokofiev*, pp. 348-349.

179. Ibid., catalog of works, p. 511.

180. Samuel Baron, *Chamber Music for Wind Instruments* (New York: Grossman Publishers, in preparation).

181. Erwin Stein, ed., *Arnold Schoenberg: Letters*, trans. Eithne Wilkins and Ernst Kaiser (New York: St. Martin's Press, 1965), p. 219, letter of October 17, 1944, to Kurt List. In typically wry fashion, Schoenberg adds, " . . . there are heroes, and there are composers. Heroes can be composers and vice versa, but you cannot require it."

182. Boris Schwarz, *Music and Musical Life in Soviet Russia, 1917–1970* (London: Barrie & Jenkins, 1972), pp. 495-496.

183. Stein, *Schoenberg: Letters*, pp. 146-147, letter of January 22, 1931, to Anton Webern.

184. Ibid., p. 267, letter to G. F. Stegmann [music-lover, South Africa], January 26, 1949.

185. Arnold Schoenberg, *Style and Idea*, trans. Dika Newlin (New York: Philosophical Library, 1950), p. 143.

186. Stein, *Schoenberg: Letters*, p. 270, letter of April 12, 1949, to Rudolf Kolisch, famed violinist and Schoenberg's brother-in-law.

187. Ibid.

188. Ibid.

189. Josef Rufer, *The Works of Arnold Schoenberg, A Catalogue of his Compositions, Writings and Paintings*, trans. Dika Newlin (London: Faber and Faber, 1962), p. 74.

190. Stein, *Schoenberg: Letters*, pp. 164-5, letter to Rudolf Kolisch, July 27, 1932. Kolisch has been working out the row and its treatment in the third quartet (opus 30, 1926). Schoenberg points out, in part, that, "I can't utter too many warnings against over-rating these analyses, since after all they only lead to what I have always been dead against; seeing how it is *done*; whereas I have always helped people to see: what it *is*! . . . The only sort of analysis there can be any question of for me is one that throws the idea into relief and shows how it is presented and worked out."

191. George Perle, *Serial Composition and Atonality*, 3rd ed., rev. (Berkeley: University of California Press, 1972), p. vii.

192. Anthony Milner, "English Contemporary Music," *European Music in the Twentieth Century*, ed. Howard Hartog (New York: Praeger, 1957), pp. 135-136.

193. See Ernest Bradbury, "Modern British Composers," *Choral Music*, ed. Arthur Jacobs (Baltimore: Penguin, 1963); Frank Howes, *The English Musical Renaissance* (New York: Stein and Day, 1966); and Ernest Walker, *A History of Music in England*, 3rd ed., rev. and enl. by J. A. Westrup (London: Oxford University Press, 1953).

194. Eric Blom, *Music in England*, rev. ed. (Middlesex: Penguin, 1947), p. 269.

195. For the clue to this structural thread, I am indebted to the discussion of the work by Colin Mason in *Cobbett's Survey*, III, 86-87.

196. Alexander L. Ringer, "Leon Kirchner," *The Musical Quarterly*, XLIII (1957): 11.

197. The composer, quoted in the biographical-sketch leaflet, "Leon Kirchner" (New York: Broadcast Music, Inc., n.d.).

198. Aaron Copland, review of the Duo for Violin and Piano, in Music Library Association's *Notes*, VII (1950): 434.

199. "Composer's Note," from Roberto Gerhard, *Gemini*.

Bibliography [*for Volumes I and II*]

Biographical data about composers and details about their works (date, opus number, editions, and so forth) have been drawn from information given in the editions used, in *Cobbett's Survey, Grove's Dictionary,* and *Die Musik in Geschichte und Gegenwart,* unless specifically attributed to other sources. Particular articles from the encyclopedic sources are specified only where direct reference or quotation of material has been made. References to music sources are given in abridged form. For complete bibliographical listings, see Editions Used.

ABRIDGEMENTS OR ABBREVIATIONS:
Cobbett's Survey = *Cobbett's Cyclopedic Survey of Chamber Music*
Grove's Dictionary = *Grove's Dictionary of Music and Musicians*
MGG = *Die Musik in Geschichte und Gegenwart*

Abraham, Gerald, ed. *Handel: A Symposium.* London: Oxford University Press, 1954.

———, ed. *The Music of Schubert.* New York: W. W. Norton, 1947.

Altmann, Wilhelm. "Richard Strauss." *Cobbett's Survey* II, 460-461.

Anderson, Emily, ed. and trans. *The Letters of Beethoven.* 3 vols. New York: St. Martin's Press, 1961.

———, ed. and trans. *The Letters of Mozart and His Family.* 2 vols. 2nd ed., edited by A. H. King and M. Carolan. New York: St. Martin's Press, Macmillan & Co., Ltd., 1966.

Austin, William A. *Music in the 20th Century: From Debussy through Stravinsky.* New York: W. W. Norton, 1966.

Bach, Carl Philipp Emanuel. *Essay on the True Art of Playing Keyboard Instruments.* Translated and edited by William J. Mitchell. New York: W. W. Norton, 1949.

Johann Sebastian Bach's Werke. Bach-Gesellschaft edition (Breitkopf & Härtel).

Vol. 3, *Clavierwerke*, Band 1. Reprinted by Farnborough: Gregg International Publishers, Ltd., 1968.

Badura-Skoda, Eva, and Badura-Skoda, Paul. *Interpreting Mozart on the Keyboard*. Translated by Leo Black. London: Barrie and Rockliff, 1962.

Balzer, Jurgen, ed. *Carl Nielsen: Centenary Essays*. New York: Dover, 1966.

Baron, Samuel. *Chamber Music for Wind Instruments*. New York: Grossman, in preparation.

Bartók, Béla, and Lord, Albert B. *Serbo-Croatian Folk Songs*. New York: Columbia University Press, 1951.

Beckmann, Gustav. *Das Violinspiel in Deutschland vor 1700*. Leipzig: Simrock, 1918.

Berger, Arthur. *Aaron Copland*. New York: Oxford University Press, 1953.

————. "The Music of Aaron Copland." *The Musical Quarterly* XXXI (1945), 420-447.

Blom, Eric. "Gabriel (Urbain) Fauré." *Grove's Dictionary* III, 38-42.

Boretz, Benjamin, and Cone, Edward T., eds. *Perspectives on American Composers*. New York: W. W. Norton, 1971.

Boyden, David D. *The History of Violin Playing from Its Origins to 1761*. New York: Oxford University Press, 1965.

Brainard, Paul H. "Giuseppe Tartini." MGG XIII, 130-137.

————. *Die Violinsonaten Giuseppe Tartinis*. Ph.D. Dissertation, University of Göttingen, 1959.

Brown, Thomas A. *The Aesthetics of Robert Schumann*. New York: Philosophical Library, 1968.

Buelow, George J. *Thorough-Bass Accompaniment According to Johann David Heinichen*. Berkeley: University of California Press, 1966.

Bukofzer, Manfred. *Music in the Baroque Era: From Monteverdi to Bach*. New York: W. W. Norton, 1947.

Burney, Charles. *A General History of Music: From the Earliest Ages to the Present Period (1789)*. Edited by Frank Mercer. 2 vols. New York: Dover, 1957.

Calvocoressi, M. D. "Maurice Ravel." *Grove's Dictionary* VII, 55-60.

Chissell, Joan. *Schumann*. London: J. M. Dent, 1948.

Clapham, John. *Antonin Dvorak: Musician and Craftsman*. London: Faber and Faber, Ltd., 1966.

Cobbett's Cyclopedic Survey of Chamber Music. Compiled and edited by Walter Willson Cobbett. 2nd ed. With supplementary material edited by Colin Mason. 3 vols. London: Oxford University Press, 1963.

Contemporary Hungarian Composers. Budapest: Editio Musica, 1970.

Cooper, Martin. *French Music: From the Death of Berlioz to the Death of Fauré*. London: Oxford University Press, 1961.

Copland, Aaron. Review of *Duo for Violin and Piano*, by Leon Kirchner. Music Library Association *Notes* VII (1950), 434.

Cowell, Henry, and Cowell, Sidney. *Charles Ives and His Music*. London: Oxford University Press, 1969.

Dart, Thurston. *The Interpretation of Music*. New York: Harper Colophon Books, 1963.

David, Hans T., and Mendel, Arthur, eds. *The Bach Reader: A Life of Johann Sebastian Bach in Letters and Documents*. New York: W. W. Norton, 1945.

Del Mar, Norman. *Richard Strauss: A Critical Commentary on His Life and Works*. 2 vols. Philadelphia: Chilton, 1969.

Demuth, Norman, ed. *An Anthology of Musical Criticism*. London: Eyre and Spottiswoode, 1947.

———. *César Franck*. New York: Philosophical Library, 1949.

Deutsch, Otto E., ed. *Handel: A Documentary Biography*. London: Adam and Charles Black, 1955.

———, ed. *Mozart: A Documentary Biography*. Translated by Eric Blom, Peter Branscombe, and Jeremy Noble. 2nd ed. London: Adam & Charles Black, 1966.

———, ed. *Schubert: Memoirs by His Friends*. London: Adam & Charles Black, 1958.

———, ed. *The Schubert Reader: A Life of Franz Schubert in Letters and Documents*. Translated by Eric Blom. 1st ed. New York: W. W. Norton, 1947.

———, in collaboration with Wakeling, Donald R. *Schubert: Thematic Catalogue of All His Works in Chronological Order*. New York: W. W. Norton, 1951.

Dolmetsch, Arnold. *The Interpretation of the Music of the Seventeenth and Eighteenth Centuries Revealed by Contemporary Evidence*. With an introduction by R. Alec Harman. Seattle: University of Washington Press, 1969.

Donington, Robert. *The Interpretation of Early Music*. 2nd ed. New York: St. Martin's Press, 1965.

Downey, John W. *La Musique Populaire dans l'Oeuvre de Béla Bartók*. Publications de l'Institut de Musicologie de l'Université de Paris, No. 5. Paris: Centre de Documentation Universitaire, 1964.

Einstein, Alfred. *Mozart: His Character, His Work*. Translated by Arthur Mendel and Nathan Broder. London: Oxford University Press, 1945.

———. *Music in the Romantic Era*. New York: W. W. Norton, 1947.

Eppstein, Hans. "Zur Problematik von J. S. Bachs Sonate für Violine und Cembalo G-dur (BWV 1019)." *Archiv für Musikwissenschaft*, 1964, 3/4, 217-242.

Farish, Margaret K. *String Music in Print*. New York: R. R. Bowker, 1965. *Supplement*, 1968.

Favre, Max. *Gabriel Fauré's Kammermusik*. Zurich: Niehans, 1948.

Forkel, Johann Nicolaus. *On Johann Sebastian Bach's Life, Genius and Works* (1802). Translated by Mr. Stephenson, 1808, reprinted in *The Bach Reader*. Edited by David and Mendel, pp. 293-356.

Gal, Hans. *Johannes Brahms: His Work and Personality.* Translated by Joseph Stein. New York: Alfred A. Knopf, 1963.

Geiringer, Karl, in collaboration with Geiringer, Irene. *The Bach Family.* New York: Oxford University Press, 1954.

———. *Brahms: His Life and Work.* 2nd ed. Garden City: Doubleday Anchor Books, 1961.

———, and Geiringer, Irene. *Haydn: A Creative Life in Music.* 2nd ed., rev. London: Allen & Unwin, 1968.

Geminiani, Francesco, *The Art of Playing on the Violin (London, 1751).* Facsimile edition edited and with an introduction by David D. Boyden. London: Oxford University Press, 1952.

Gérard, Yves, ed. *Thematic, Bibliographical and Critical Catalogue of the Works of Luigi Boccherini.* London: Oxford University Press, 1969.

Grove's Dictionary of Music and Musicians. 5th ed. Edited by Eric Blom. 9 vols. New York: St. Martin's Press, 1954. Vol. 10, *Supplement,* published 1961.

Händel, Georg Friedrich, *Elf Sonaten für Flöte und bezifferten Bass.* Edited by Hans-Peter Schmitz. Realization by Max Schneider. Kassel: Bärenreiter, 1955. [Hallische Händel-Ausgabe, Serie IV, *Instrumentalmusik,* Band 3.]

———. *Jephtha, An Oratorio. The Works of George Frederic Handel,* vol. 42. Edited by Friedrich Chrysander. Republished Ridgewood: Gregg Press, 1965.

———. *Solomon, An Oratorio. The Works of George Frederic Handel,* vol. 74. Edited by Friedrich Chrysander. Republished Ridgewood: Gregg Press, 1965.

Hartog, Howard, ed. *European Music in the Twentieth Century.* New York: Praeger, 1957.

Hausswald, Günter, and Gerber, Rudolf. *Johann Sebastian Bach, Werke für Violine, Kritischer Bericht, Serie VI, Band I,* Neue Ausgabe Sämtlicher Werke. Kassel: Bärenreiter, 1958.

Hawkins, John. *A General History of the Science and Practice of Music [1776].* 2 vols. New York: Dover, 1963.

Hemel, Victor van. *Voorname Belgische Toonkunstenaars uit de 18de, 19de en 20ste eeuw.* 4th ed. Antwerp: Cupido, n.d.

Hertzmann, Erich. "Mozart's Creative Process." *The Musical Quarterly* XLIII (1957), 187-200.

Hindemith, Paul. *A Composer's World: Horizons and Limitations—The Charles Eliot Norton Lectures, 1949–50.* Garden City: Doubleday Anchor Books, 1961.

Hoboken, Anthony von. *Joseph Haydn: Thematisch-bibliographisches Werkzeichnis.* Vol. I. Mainz: Schott, 1957.

Hoffmann, E. T. A. "Don Giovanni." Translated by Abram Loft. *The Musical Quarterly* XXXI (1945), 504-516.

Hollander, Hans. *Leoš Janáček, His Life and Work.* Translated by Paul Hamburger. New York: St. Martin's Press, 1963.

Howes, Frank. *The English Musical Renaissance.* New York: Stein and Day, 1966.

Hubbard, Frank. *Three Centuries of Harpsichord Making*. Cambridge: Harvard University Press, 1965.

d'Indy, Vincent. "César Auguste Franck," *Cobbett's Survey* I, 418-429.

Ives, Charles, "Essays Before a Sonata." Reprinted in *Three Classics in the Aesthetic of Music*. New York: Dover, 1962.

Jacob, Heinrich Eduard. *Felix Mendelssohn and His Times*. Translated by Richard Winston and Clara Winston. New York: Prentice-Hall, 1963.

Jacobs, Arthur, ed. *Choral Music*. Baltimore: Penguin, 1963.

Jeppesen, Knud. "Carl (August) Nielsen." *Grove's Dictionary* VI, 85-86.

Kinsky, Georg. *Das Werk Beethovens: Thematisch-Bibliographisches Verzeichnis seiner sämtlichen vollendeten Kompositionen*. Completed and edited by Hans Halm. Munich: Henle, 1955.

Knocker, Editha, trans. and ed. *Leopold Mozart: A Treatise on the Fundamental Principles of Violin Playing*. Preface by Alfred Einstein. 2nd ed. London: Oxford University Press, 1951.

Kolneder, Walter. *Antonio Vivaldi*. Translated by Bill Hopkins. Berkeley: University of California Press, 1970.

Köchel, Ludwig R. von. *Chronologisch-thematisches Verzeichnis sämtlicher Tonwerke Wolfgang Amadé Mozarts*. 6th ed. Edited by F. Giegling, A. Weinmann, and G. Sievers. Wiesbaden: Breitkopf & Härtel, 1964.

Koole, Arend. "Pietro Antonio Locatelli." *MGG* VIII, 1075-1079.

Krause, Ernst. *Richard Strauss: The Man and His Work*. Translated by John Coombs. London: Collet, 1964.

Lang, Paul H. *George Frideric Handel*. New York: W. W. Norton, 1966.

———. *Music in Western Civilization*. New York: W. W. Norton, 1941.

Liess, Andreas. "Heinrich Ignaz Franz Biber (von Bibern)." *MGG* V, 1828-1831.

Litterscheid, Richard, ed. *Johannes Brahms in seinen Schriften und Briefen*. Berlin: Hahnefeld, 1943.

Lockspeiser, Edward. *Debussy: His Life and Mind*. 2 vols. New York: Macmillan, 1965.

Maczewsky, A. "Georg Philipp Telemann." *Grove's Dictionary* VIII, 370-371.

Mishkin, Henry G. "The Solo Violin Sonata of the Bologna School." *The Musical Quarterly* XXIX (1943), 92-112.

Monrad-Johansen, David. *Edvard Grieg*. Translated by Madge Robertson. New York: Tudor, 1945.

Moser, Andreas. *Geschichte des Violinspiels*. Berlin: Max Hesse, 1923.

Mozart, Wolfgang Amadeus. *Streichquartette*. Edited by Ludwig Finscher, in *Neue Ausgabe sämtlicher Werke*, Werkgruppe 20, Abteilung 1, Band 2. Kassel: Bärenreiter, 1961.

Die Musik in Geschichte und Gegenwart. Edited by Friedrich Blume. 14 vols. Kassel: Bärenreiter, 1949–1968.

Myers, Rollo H. *Erik Satie*. London: Dobson, 1948.

Nestyev, Israel V. *Prokofiev.* Translated by Florence Jonas. Stanford: Stanford University Press, 1960.

Nettl, Paul. *Beethoven Handbook.* New York: Frederick Ungar, 1967.

Newman, William S. "Concerning the Accompanied Clavier." *The Musical Quarterly* XXXIII (1947), 327-349.

————. *The Sonata in the Baroque Era.* Rev. ed. Chapel Hill: University of North Carolina Press, 1966.

————. *The Sonata in the Classic Era.* Chapel Hill: University of North Carolina Press, 1963.

————. *The Sonata Since Beethoven.* Chapel Hill: University of North Carolina Press, 1969.

Nielsen, Carl. *Living Music.* Translated by Reginald Spink. London: Hutchinson, 1953.

Niemann, Walter. *Brahms.* Translated by Catherine Alison Phillips. New York: Alfred A. Knopf, 1947.

Nottebohm, Gustav. *Beethoveniana, Aufsätze und Mittheilungen.* Leipzig: C. F. Peters, 1872.

Oldman, C. B. "Wolfgang Amadeus Mozart." *Grove's Dictionary* V, 923-983.

Perkins, Laurence, *The Sonatas for Violin and Piano by Charles Ives.* M.A. thesis, Eastman School of Music, The University of Rochester, 1961.

Perle, George. *Serial Composition and Atonality.* 3rd ed., rev. Berkeley: University of California Press, 1972.

Pincherle, Marc. *Corelli: His Life, His Work.* Translated by Hubert E. M. Russell. New York: W. W. Norton, 1956.

————. *Jean-Marie Leclair l'Aîné.* Paris: La Colombe, 1952.

————. *Vivaldi: Genius of the Baroque.* Translated by Christopher Hatch. New York: W. W. Norton, 1957.

Plantinga, Leon B. *Schumann as Critic.* New Haven: Yale University Press, 1967.

Pleasants, Henry, trans. and ed. *Eduard Hanslick, Music Criticisms 1846–99.* Rev. ed. Baltimore: Penguin Books, 1963.

————, trans. and ed. *The Musical World of Robert Schumann.* New York: St. Martin's Press, 1965.

Pohl, Carl F. "Regina Strinasacchi." *Grove's Dictionary* VIII, 146.

Prokofiev, S. *Autobiography, Articles, Reminiscences.* Compiled and edited by S. Shlifstein. Translated by Rose Prokofieva. Moscow: Foreign Languages Publishing House, n.d.

Radcliffe, Philip. *Mendelssohn.* Rev. ed. London: J. M. Dent, 1967.

Raguenet, François, "A Comparison Between the French and Italian Music." Translated by Oliver Strunk. *The Musical Quarterly* XXXII (1946), 411-436.

Ravel, Maurice. "Esquisse autobiographique." *La Revue Musicale,* December, 1938 (Numéro special, *Hommage à Maurice Ravel*), pp. 211-215.

Reti, Rudolph. *Thematic Patterns in Sonatas of Beethoven*. Edited by Deryck Cooke. New York: Macmillan, 1967.

Ringer, Alexander L. "Leon Kirchner." *The Musical Quarterly* XLIII (1957), 1-20.

Robbins-Landon, H. C., trans. and ed. *The Collected Correspondence and London Notebooks of Joseph Haydn*. London: Barrie and Rockliff, 1959.

Romain Rolland's Essays on Music. Edited by David Ewen. New York: Dover, 1959.

Rothschild, Germaine de. *Luigi Boccherini: His Life and Work*. Translated by Andreas Mayor. London: Oxford University Press, 1965.

Rufer, Josef. *The Works of Arnold Schoenberg: A Catalogue of his Compositions, Writings, and Paintings*. Translated by Dika Newlin. London: Faber and Faber, 1962.

Sachs, Curt. *World History of the Dance*. Translated by Bessie Schönberg. New York: W. W. Norton, 1963.

Schjelderup-Ebbe, Dag. *Edvard Grieg, 1858–1867: With Special Reference to the Evolution of His Harmonic Style*. London: Allen & Unwin, 1964.

————. *A Study of Grieg's Harmony: With Special Reference to His Contributions to Musical Impressionism*. Oslo: Johan Grundt Tanum, 1953.

Schmieder, Wolfgang. *Thematisch-Systematisches Verzeichnis der musikalischen Werke von Johann Sebastian Bach. Bach-Werke Verzeichnis (BWV)*. 3rd unrev. ed. Wiesbaden: Breitkopf & Härtel, 1966 (original copyright, 1950).

Schmitt, Florent. "Gabriel Urbain Fauré." *Cobbett's Survey* I, 386-392.

Schmitz, Hans-Peter. *Die Kunst der Verzierung im 18. Jahrhundert: Instrumentale und vokale Musizierpraxis in Beispielen*. 2nd ed. Kassel: Bärenreiter, 1965.

Schneider, Max. "Zu Biber's Violinsonaten." *Zeitschrift der Internationalen Musikgesellschaft*, VIII, 1906/07, 471-474.

Arnold Schoenberg: Letters. Selected and edited by Erwin Stein. Translated by Eithne Wilkins and Ernst Kaiser. New York: St. Martin's Press, 1965.

Schoenberg, Arnold. *Style and Idea*. Translated by Dika Newlin. New York: Philosophical Library, 1950.

Schwarz, Boris. *Music and Musical Life in Soviet Russia 1917–1970*. London: Barrie & Jenkins, 1972.

————, "Pietro Nardini." MGG IX, 1264-1267.

Selden-Goth, G., trans. and ed. *Felix Mendelssohn: Letters*. New York: Pantheon, 1945.

Seroff, Victor. *Sergei Prokofiev: A Soviet Tragedy*. New York: Funk and Wagnalls, 1968.

Smith, William C., assisted by Humphries, Charles. *Handel: A Descriptive Catalogue of the Early Editions*. London: Cassell, 1960.

Smith, William C. *A Handelian's Notebook*. London: Adam and Charles Black, 1965.

Sourek, Otakar. *Antonin Dvorak: Letters and Reminiscences*. Translated by Roberta Finlayson Samsour. Prague: Artia, 1954.

————. *The Chamber Music of Antonin Dvořák*. Translated by Roberta Finlayson Samsour. Prague: Artia, n.d.

Specht, Richard. *Johannes Brahms*. Translated by Eric Blom. London: J. M. Dent and Sons Ltd., 1930.

Philipp, Spitta. *Johann Sebastian Bach: His Work and Influence on the Music of Germany, 1685–1750*. Translated by Clara Bell and J. A. Fuller-Maitland. 3 vols. in 2. New York: Dover, 1951.

Stevens, Halsey. *The Life and Music of Béla Bartók*. Rev. ed. New York: Oxford University Press, 1967.

Stravinsky, Igor. *An Autobiography*. New York: W. W. Norton, 1962.

Streatfield, R. A. *Handel*. With an Introduction by J. Merrill Knapp. New York: Da Capo Press, 1964.

Strobel, Heinrich. *Paul Hindemith*. 3rd ed., rev. Mainz: Schott, 1948.

Strunk, Oliver. *Source Readings in Music History: From Classical Antiquity through the Romantic Era*. New York: W. W. Norton, 1950.

Studeny, Bruno. *Beiträge zur Geschichte der Violinsonate im 18. Jahrhundert*. Munich: Wunderhorn, 1911.

Suckling, Norman. *Fauré*. London: J. M. Dent and Sons, 1951.

Szigeti, Joseph. *A Violinist's Handbook*. London: Gerald Duckworth, 1964.

Tchaikovsky, Peter I. *The Diaries*. Translated and edited by Wladimir Lakond. New York: W. W. Norton, 1945.

Terry, Charles Sanford. *John Christian Bach*. 2nd ed. With a Foreword by H. C. Robbins-Landon. London: Oxford University Press, 1967.

Thayer, Alexander W., *Life of Beethoven*. Revised and edited by Elliott Forbes. Princeton: Princeton University Press, 1967.

Vallas, Léon. *César Franck*. Translated by Hubert Foss. London: George G. Harrap and Co., Ltd., 1951.

————, *The Theories of Claude Debussy, Musicien français*. Translated by Marie O'Brien. New York: Dover, 1967.

Vinquist, Mary, and Zaslaw, Neal, eds. *Performance Practice: A Bibliography*. New York: W. W. Norton, 1971.

Vlad, Roman. *Stravinsky*. Translated by Frederick Fuller and Ann Fuller. 2nd ed. London: Oxford University Press, 1967.

Vuillermoz, Emile. *Gabriel Fauré*. Translated by Kenneth Schapin. Philadelphia: Chilton Book Co., 1969.

Walker, Ernest. *A History of Music in England*. 3rd ed. Revised and enlarged by J. A. Westrup. London: Oxford University Press, 1952.

Warrack, John. *Carl Maria von Weber*. New York: Macmillan, 1968.

Wasielewski, Wilhelm Josef von. *Die Violine und ihre Meister*. Revised and enlarged by Waldemar von Wasielewski. Leipzig: Breitkopf & Härtel, 1927.

Webern, Anton von. *Perspectives.* Compiled by Hans Moldenhauer. Edited by Demar Irvine. Seattle: University of Washington Press, 1966.

Werner, Eric. *Mendelssohn: A New Image of the Composer and His Age.* Translated by Dika Newlin. New York: Free Press of Glencoe (Macmillan), 1963.

White, Eric Walter. *Stravinsky: The Composer and His Work.* Berkeley: University of California Press, 1966.

Wildgans, Friedrich. *Anton Webern.* Translated by Edith T. Roberts and Humphrey Searle. London: Calder and Boyars, 1966.

Williams, Peter. *Figured Bass Accompaniment.* 2 vols. Edinburgh: Edinburgh University Press, 1970.

Winternitz, Emanuel. *Musical Autographs from Monteverdi to Hindemith.* Rev. ed., 2 vols. New York: Dover Publications, 1965.

Wotquenne, Alfred. *Catalogue thématique de Charles Philippe Emmanuel Bach.* Wiesbaden: Breitkopf & Härtel, 1964.

♫ *Editions Used [for Volumes I and II]*

The following list tabulates the musical editions that are discussed in these volumes. While there are many items represented, the list (as already indicated by my Preface) does not constitute a comprehensive or exhaustive survey of the violin-keyboard sonata literature. Nor is it exclusively a compendium of preferred works. Some of these compositions are incomparable masterpieces; many are impressive works; some are the reverse, in my estimation.

It must be emphasized that, in more than one case, the edition listed is not the only one available, but is the one used by this writer, whether out of conviction or convenience. In those few instances where more than one edition of a given work or set of works is listed, it is because of special interest or because specific reference is made to each of the editions in the text.

The list is arranged as follows:

1. Alphabetically by composer (or by collection title);
2. Under composer, in numerical order by opus or subnumber, or catalog number, wherever that suits accepted practice for a given composer, or where key identification is not a part of the published title of the edition in question;
3. Otherwise, under composer, alphabetically by key;
4. Under key, major before minor.

Publisher's catalog numbers are given in brackets.

ABBREVIATIONS

HAM = *Historical Anthology of Music*
DdT = *Denkmäler deutscher Tonkunst*
DTÖ = *Denkmäler der Tonkunst in Österreich*

EDITIONS

Abaco, Evaristo Felice dall', *Sechs Sonaten aus Op. 1 für Violine und Basso continuo.* Edited by Walter Kolneder. Mainz: Schott, 1956. [4618] Sonatas 2, 4, 5, 6, 7, and 11 of opus 1.

——, *6 Solosonaten aus Op. 4, Violine, Violoncell und Klavier.* Leipzig:

Breitkopf & Härtel, n.d. [1860b] Sonatas 3, 4, 5, 6, 8, and 11 of opus 4. Note that the first volume of this edition (1860a) includes the same six sonatas of opus 1 offered in the Schott edition, catalog no. 4618, above.

Abel, Carl Friedrich. *Sonate in A dur für Violine und Klavier, Op. 13, Nr. 3.* Edited by Fritz Piersig. Leipzig: Breitkopf & Härtel, 1928. [4165] Note that the instrument listing as given by publisher contradicts prominent role of the keyboard.

————. *Sonate in B dur für Violine und Klavier.* Edited by Fritz Piersig. Leipzig: Breitkopf & Härtel, n.d. [4164]

————. *Sonata in G major for Harpsichord and Violin or Flute.* Edited by Frans Brüggen. Amsterdam: Broekmans & Van Poppel, 1960. [330]

————. *Two Sonatinas for Violin and Piano, Violoncello ad lib.* Edited by Günter Raphael. London: Hinrichsen, n.d. [H.E.16]

Albinoni, Tommaso. *Zwei Kammersonaten für Violine mit bezziffertem Bass (Klavier), Op. 6.* Edited by Walter Upmeyer. Celle: Nagel, 1928. [Nagels Musik-Archiv, Nr. 9] Sonatas 1 and 11.

————. *Sonate g-Moll für Violine und Basso continuo, Op. 6, Nr. 2.* Edited by Frederick F. Polnauer. Mainz: Schott, 1967. [5480]

————. *Tre Sonate per Violino, Violoncello e Cembalo (Pianoforte o Organo), Opera Sesta No. 4, 5, e 7.* Edited by Walther Reinhart. Zurich: Hug, 1959. [10 305]

————. *Sonate für Violine und bezifferten Bass (Violine und Klavier, Cembalo oder Orgel), Op. 6, Nr. 6.* Edited by Bernhard Paumgartner. With realization by Heinrich Nicolaus Gerber, corrected by J. S. Bach. Zurich: Hug, 1951. [9668] Note that all of the above sonatas are from the set entitled, *Trattenimenti armonici per camera divisi in dodici sonate,* 1711 ("Harmonic diversions for the chamber, devised as twelve sonatas").

Antonii, Pietro degli. *Tre Sonate per Violino e Pianoforte (Cembalo, Organo).* Edited by Bernhard Paumgartner. Zurich: Hug, 1947. [9339]

Arnold, Malcolm. *Sonata for Violin and Piano.* London: Lengnick, 1947. [3559]

————. *Sonata No. 2 for Violin and Piano (in one movement), Op. 43.* London: Patersons Publications, 1953.

Babajanian, A. *Sonata for Violin and Piano.* Moscow: Soviet Composers, 1970. [766]

Bach, Carl Philipp Emanuel. *Sonate h-Moll für Violine und konzertierendes Cembalo.* Edited by Hugo Ruf. Mainz: Schott, 1965. [5387]

————. *Sonate h-moll, für Klavier und Violine.* Edited by Hans Sitt. Leipzig: Peters, n.d. [3619a]

————. *Sonate, c-moll, für Klavier und Violine.* Edited by Hans Sitt. Leipzig: Peters, n.d. [3619b]

————. *Sonate D-dur (1731) für konzertierendes Cembalo und Violine.* Edited by Hugo Ruf and Peter Hoffmann. Baden: Ricordi, 1954. [Sy 570]

Bach, Johann Christian. *Sonatas Nos. 1-3 for Violin and Piano.* Edited by Ludwig Landshoff. From Op. X, 1773, entitled, *Six Sonatas for the Harpsi-*

chord or Piano Forte: With an Accompagnement for a Violin. London: Hinrichsen, n.d. [17a]

―――――. *Sonatas Nos. 4 and 5 for Violin and Piano*. Edited by Ludwig Landshoff. London: Hinrichsen, n.d. [17b] From opus X.

―――――. *Sonatas in D and G, Op. 16, Nos. 1 and 2, for Pianoforte, with flute or violin*. Edited by Alfred Küster. Hannover: Nagel, n.d. [Nagel Musikarchiv, 1]

―――――. *Sonate Es-dur, für Violine und Cembalo (oder Klavier)*. Edited by Heinz Zirnbauer. Mainz: Schott, 1951. [3710]

―――――. *Sonate D-dur für Violine und Klavier, Op. 16, Nr. 1*. Edited by Fritz Piersig. Leipzig: Breitkopf & Härtel, 1928. [4167]

―――――. *Sonate A-dur, Op. 16, Nr. 4, für Pianoforte, und Flöte oder Violine*. Edited by Alfred Küster. Hannover: Nagel, 1933. [Nagels Musikarchiv 103]

Bach, Johann Sebastian. *Neue Ausgabe sämtlicher Werke*. Sponsored by Johann-Sebastian-Bach-Institut of Göttingen and Bach-Archiv of Leipzig. Edition now in continuing progress, published Kassel: Bärenreiter, 1954–.

―――――. *Sechs Sonaten für Violine und Klavier (Cembalo)*. Edited by Hans Eppstein, Hans-Martin Theopold, and Karl Röhrig. Munich-Duisburg: G. Henle Verlag, 1971. [223] "According to contemporary copies and the autographs of three movements."

―――――. *Sechs Sonaten für Violino und Cembalo, BWV 1014–1019*. Edited by Rudolf Gerber. 2 vols. Kassel: Bärenreiter, 1967. [5118; 5119] "This is the original text based on: J. S. Bach, Neue Ausgabe sämtlicher Werke . . . Series VI: Chamber Music Works, Vol. I: Works for violin . . ."

―――――. *Sonate G-dur für Violine und bezifferten Bass BWV 1021*. Edited by Friedrich Blume and Adolf Busch. Wiesbaden: Breitkopf & Härtel, ca. 1929. [5936]

―――――. *Sonate e-moll für Violine mit beziffertem Bass, BWV 1023*. Edited by Walther Davisson. Wiesbaden: Breitkopf & Härtel, n.d. [6415]

Badings, Henk. *Sonate für Violine und Klavier* (1933). Mainz: Schott, 1934. [2289]

―――――. *Sonate II für Violine und Klavier*. Mainz: Schott, 1940. [3650]

―――――. *Sonata for Violin and Piano No. 3*. Amsterdam: Donemus, 1952.

Barbella, Emanuele. *Sonata I per Violino e Pianoforte*. Edited by Frederik F. Polnauer. Zurich: Hug, 1966. [10723]

Bartók, Béla. *Sonate für Violine und Klavier*, (1903). Edited by Denijs Dille and Andre Gertler. Mainz: Schott, 1968. [6032]

―――――. *Première Sonate (en 3 Mouvements), Violon et Piano*. New York: Boosey & Hawkes, 1950 (Vienna: Universal, 1923). [U.E. 7247]

―――――. *Deuxième Sonate (en 2 Mouvements), Violon et Piano*. New York: Boosey & Hawkes, 1950 (Vienna: Universal, 1923). [U.E. 7259]

Bax, Arnold. *First Sonata for Violin and Piano*. (Revised 1945). London. Chappell, 1943 (London: Murdoch, 1921). [37890]

————. *Third Sonata for Violin & Piano*. London: Chappell, 1929–1943. [40436]

Beethoven, Ludwig van. *Sonaten für Klavier und Violine*. Rev. ed. Edited by Walther Lampe and Kurt Schäffer. 2 vols. Munich-Duisburg: G. Henle, 1955. [7; 8]

Benda, Bedřich Ludwík. *Sonata in G for Violin and Piano, or Violin, Harpsichord, and Cello obbligato*. See *Violinsonaten des böhmischen Barocks*.

Benda, František [Franz]. *Quattro Sonate per Violino Solo e d'Archi con Accompagnamento*. Edited by Jan Štědroň and Bohumír Štědroň. Prague: Artia, 1962. [Musica Antiqua Bohemica, 57]

————. *Adagio un poco Andante*, from *Sonata in A*, in simply notated, and two embellished versions of the violin part, as provided by the composer: see Ferand, *Improvisation*, a volume in the Anthology of Music series. For entire sonata, in facsimile (figured-bass unrealized), see Schmitz, *Kunst der Verzierung* (see Bibliography). Finally, for the entire sonata, with realization, see the last of the *Quattro Sonate* of František Benda in the Musica Antiqua Bohemica, 57, edition, above.

————. *Sonata in F*. See Schering, *Alte Meister des Violinspiels*.

Biber, Heinrich Franz. *Acht Violinsonaten*. Edited by Guido Adler, [*DTÖ Jahrgang V/2, Band 11*. Graz: Akademische Druck- u. Verlagsanstalt, 1959. (Unrevised reprint of the DTÖ volume that appeared in Vienna, 1898.) There are two part-supplements. One contains the violin part for all eight sonatas. The other contains the part for sonatas IV and VI, which are entirely or in part written in scordatura. The first supplement gives these sonatas transcribed for normal tuning; the second, in the original notation.

————. *Sechzehn Violinsonaten*. Edited by Erwin Luntz, *DTÖ Jahrgang XII/2, Band 25*. Graz: Akademische Druck- u. Verlagsanstalt, 1959. (Unrevised reprint of the DTÖ volume that appeared in Vienna in 1905.) There are three supplementary part-books issued in this reprint: the violin part transcribed for normal tuning—including sonata XI "corrected" for the misread scordatura; the violin part of sonatas II to XV, in scordatura notation (as given also in the score volume); and the violin part of sonata XI, translated to normal tuning in the light of a proper reading of the scordatura of this piece.

————. *Surrexit Christus hodie*, from *Mysterien* sonata No. XI, in translated (nonscordatura) version, in *HAM* II, No. 238.

————. *15 Mysterien-Sonaten für Violine und Basso continuo (Klavier)*. Edited by Gustav Lenzewski. 3 vols. Frankfurt: Wilhelmiana, 1954. [F.F.12] Not in scordatura notation. These correspond to sonatas 1 through 15 of Biber, *Sechzehn Violinsonaten*, above.

————. *Fünfzehn Mysterien für Violine und Klavier nach Kupferstichen biblischen Historien*. Edited by Robert Reitz. 2 vols. Vienna: Universal, 1923. [7283; 7284] Not in scordatura notation. These correspond to sonatas 1 through 15 of Biber, *Sechzehn Violinsonaten*, above. Sole agent for *ICMI* series is Casa Editrice Leo S. Olschki, Florence.

Binder, Christlieb Siegmund. *Sonate G-dur für Violine und Klavier (Cembalo)*. Edited by Günter Hausswald. Kassel and Basel: Bärenreiter, 1950. [312]

Birkenstock, Johann Adam. *Sonate E-Dur, für Violine und Basso continuo*. Edited by Frederick F. Polnauer. Mainz: Schott, 1967. [5482] Sonata Op. 1, No. 4.

————. *Sonate Nr. 2 für Violine und Basso continuo*. Edited by Waldemar Woehl. Kassel: Nagel, 1958. [Nagels Musik-Archiv 25] Sonata Op. 2, No. 1.

Blackwood, Easley. *Sonata for Violin and Piano, Op. 7*. New York: G. Schirmer, 1961. [44815c]

Blacher, Boris. *Sonate Op. 18, für Violine und Klavier*. Berlin: Bote and Bock, 1947. [20880]

Bloch, Ernest. *Sonate Pour Violon et Piano*. New York: G. Schirmer, 1922. [43369]

Boccherini, Luigi. *Sonate per Cembalo con Violino obbligato, Op. 5*. Edited by Enrico Polo. Milan: I Classici Musicali Italiani, 1941. [*ICMI*, vol. 4] Sole agent for *ICMI* series is Casa Editrice Leo S. Olschki, Florence.

Botiarov, E. *Sonata for Violin and Piano*. Moscow: State Music Publishers, 1966. [3062]

Brahms, Johannes. *Sonaten, Klavier und Violine*. Rev. ed. Edited by Hans Otto Hiekel, Hans-Martin Theopold, and Karl Röhrig. Munich-Duisberg: G. Henle, 1967. [194]

Brahms-Dietrich-Schumann, F.A.E. *Sonata*. Edited by Erich Valentin and Otto Kobin. Wilhelmshaven: Heinrichshofen: 1935. [N234]

Britten, Benjamin. *Suite for Violin and Piano, Op. 6*. London: Boosey & Hawkes, 1935. [7720]

Busoni, Ferruccio. *Sonate für Violine und Pianoforte, Op. 29*. Leipzig: Breitkopf & Härtel, n.d. [5077]

Carpenter, John Alden. *Sonata for Violin and Piano*. New York: G. Schirmer, 1913. [23703c]

Čart, Jiří. *Sonata in C, for Violin and Piano or Violin, Harpsichord and Cello obbligato*. See *Violinsonaten des böhmischen Barocks*.

Castelnuovo-Tedesco, Mario. *Sonata—quasi una Fantasia*. Milan: Ricordi, 1930. [121626]

Cazzati, Maurizio. *Sonata Prima, Op. 55*. In Giegling, *Solo Sonata*, pp. 33-37. Also, in *HAM* II, #219.

Cima, Giovanni Paolo. *Drei Sonaten (1610)*. Edited by Karl Grebe. Hamburg: Sikorski, 1957. [472] The first of these sonatas is for violin and basso continuo, in G minor.

Copland, Aaron. *Sonata for Violin and Piano*. London: Boosey & Hawkes, 1944. [34-46]

Corelli, Arcangelo. *Zwölf Sonaten für Violine und Basso continuo, Op. 5*. Edited by Bernhard Paumgartner and Günter Kehr. 2 vols. Mainz: Schott, 1953. [4380; 4381]

————. *Sonata for Violin and Basso continuo, Op. 5, No. 9*. In Schering, *Alte*

Meister, pp. 4 ff., with all movements, fast as well as slow, showing suggested ornamental additions.

Corrette, Michel. *Sonate D-dur für Violine und obligates Cembalo.* Edited by Hugo Ruf. Mainz: Schott, 1968. [5487]

Couperin, François. *Concerts Royaux für Violine und Basso continuo, Troisième concert.* Edited by Frederick F. Polnauer. Mainz: Schott, 1970. [5782] Nos. 1, 2, and 4 are available in Schott issues 5780, 5781, 5783. (Note that some movements are scored in the edition as keyboard and violin, others in trio setting.)

Cowell, Henry. *Sonata for Violin and Piano (1945).* New York: Associated Music Publishers, 1947. [194550]

Davison, Archibald T., and Apel, Willi, eds. *Baroque, Rococo, and Pre-Classical Music.* Historical Anthology of Music, vol. 2. Cambridge: Harvard University Press, 1950.

Debussy, Claude. *Sonate pour Violon & Piano.* Paris: Durand, 1917. [9504]

Denkmäler der Tonkunst in Österreich. Vienna: Österreichisches Bundesverlag, 1894– . The series now numbers 124 volumes. Volumes 1-83 (1894–1938), in unchanged reprint from the original edition, and the later volumes of newly edited material are all issued by the present publisher, Graz: Akademischer Druck- und Verlagsanstalt.

Denkmäler deutscher Tonkunst. Leipzig: Musikgeschichtliche Kommission, 1892–1931; revised 1960. Series of 65 volumes and critical supplements issued in reprint. Wiesbaden: Breitkopf & Härtel; Graz: Akademische Druck- und Verlagsanstalt, 1958–1959.

Diamond, David. *Sonata for Violin and Piano.* New York: Schirmer, 1950. [42150]

Dittersdorf, Carl Ditters von. *Sonate für Violine und Klavier in B-dur.* Edited by Hans Mlynarczyk and Ludwig Lürman. Leipzig: Hofmeister, 1929. [1408]

———. *Sonata in G-dur für Violine und Klavier.* Edited by H. Mlynarczyk and L. Lürman. Frankfurt: Hofmeister, 1929. [10394]

Dohnanyi, Ernst von. *Sonata, Violin and Piano, Op. 21.* London and Hamburg: Simrock, 1913. [710]

Dusík, Jan Ladislav. *Sonate, Op. 69, Nos. 1, 2, Violino e Piano.* Edited by Jan Štědroň and Bohumír Štědroň. Prague: Artia, 1959. [Musica Antiqua Bohemica 41]

Dussek: see Dusík.

Duval, François. *Zwei Sonaten für Violine und Basso continuo.* Edited by Hugo Ruf. Mainz: Schott, 1953. [4168] From *Amusemens pour la Chambre, Livre VI.*

Dvarionas, B. *Sonata—Ballade for Violin and Piano.* Moscow: State Music Publishers, 1968.

Dvořák, Antonín. *Sonate, F-dur, Op. 57, für Violine und Klavier.* Rev. ed. London: Simrock, n.d. [Elite 685 (S.)]

————. *Sonatine, G-dur, Op. 100, für Violine und Klavier*. Leipzig: Breitkopf & Härtel, n.d. [4272]

Einem, Gottfried. *Sonate für Violine und Klavier, Op. 11*. Vienna: Universal, 1950. [11992]

Elgar, Edward. *Sonata Op. 82 for Violin and Piano*. London: Novello, 1919, 1947. [14540]

Emborg, Jens Laurson. *Sonate for Violin og Orgel (eller Cembalo), Op. 54*. Copenhagen: Hansen, 1932. [23037]

Enesco, Georges. *Sonate pour Piano et Violon, Op. 2*. Paris: Enoch, n.d. (Bucharest: Éditions d'État, 1956).

————. *IIème-Sonate pour Piano et Violon, Op. 6*. Paris: Enoch, n.d. (Bucharest: Éditions d'État, 1956).

————. *IIIème Sonate pour Piano et Violon, Op. 25*. Paris: Enoch, n.d. (Bucharest: Éditions d'État, 1956).

Eshpay, E. *Sonata for Violin and Piano*. Moscow: State Music Publishers, 1967. [4485]

Evlakhov, O. *Sonata for Violin and Piano*. Moscow: State Music Publishers, 1964. [319]

Fauré, Gabriel. *Sonate A-dur, Op. 13, für Violine und Klavier*. Wiesbaden: Breitkopf & Härtel, n.d. [2569]

————. *2ème Sonate pour Violon & Piano, Op. 108*. Paris: Durand, 1917. [9500]

Ferand, Ernest T. ed. *Improvisation in Nine Centuries of Western Music: An Anthology with a Historical Introduction*. Cologne: Arno Volk, 1961. In the series Anthology of Music, edited by Karl G. Fellerer.

Fesch, Willem de. *Sechs Sonaten für Violine (Flöte, Oboe, Viola) und Basso continuo*. Edited by Waldemar Woehl. 2 vols. Kassel: Bärenreiter, 1967. [Hortus musicus 127, 128] Sonatas from the set of twelve, opus 8.

Festing, Michael Christian. *Sonata in D, Op. 8, No. 5, for Violin and Continuo*. Edited by Walter Bergmann. London: Schott, 1955. [10260]

Fibich, Zdenko. *Sonata D-dur, Violino e Piano*. Edited by Jaroslav Zich. Prague: Orbis, 1950. [122]

Fine, Irving. *Sonata for Violin and Piano*. New York: Witmark, 1948. [20656-41]

Finney, Ross Lee. *Third Sonata in A for Violin and Piano*. Northampton: Valley Music Press, 1957.

Fontana, Giovanni Battista. *Sechs Sonaten für Violine und Klavier*. Edited by Friedrich Cerha. 3 vols. Vienna and Munich: Doblinger, 1962. (Diletto Musicale, nos. 13, 14, 15)

————. *Sonata [Prima]* is also reprinted in HAM II, No. 198.

————. *Tenth Sonata*. In Giegling, *Solo Sonata*, pp. 26-32.

Franck, César, *Sonate, A dur, für Violine und Klavier*. Edited by Maxim Jacobsen. New York: Peters, n.d. [3742]

Fricker, P. Racine. *Sonata for violin and piano, Op. 12*. London: Schott, 1950. [10128]

Fritz, Gaspard. *Sonate en mi mineur, Op. 2, No. 4* [for violin or flute and basso continuo]. Edited by Frank Martin. Geneva: Henn, 1931. [A. 591 592 H.]

Furtwängler, Wilhelm. *Sonate für Violine und Klavier*. Leipzig: Breitkopf & Härtel, 1938. [5668]

——. *Sonate D-Dur für Violine und Klavier*. Edited by Georg Kulenkampff. Berlin: Bote & Bock, 1940. [20584]

Gade, Niels W. *Sonate Nr. 1 in A dur für Pianoforte und Violine, Op. 6*. Leipzig: Breitkopf & Härtel, n.d. [1362] Also in editions for viola and for cello.

——. *Sonate, D-moll, für Violine und Klavier, Op. 21*. Leipzig: Breitkopf & Härtel, n.d. [1437]

Geminiani, Francesco. *Zwölf Sonaten für Violine und Basso continuo*. Edited by Walter Kolneder. 4 vols. Mainz: Schott, 1961. [5191, 5192, 5193, 5194] The twelve sonatas of Opus I(a), London, 1716. As of this printing, only Sonatas 1-3 are available in this edition [5191]. The remaining three volumes of the set [5192-4] are in preparation.

——. *Sonate a violino e basso, Op. 4*, London, 1739. There are copies of this edition in the collections of the New York Public Library and the Music Library of the University of California, Berkeley.

——. *Sonata A-Dur für Violine und Basso continuo*. Edited by Hugo Ruf. Kassel: Bärenreiter, 1962. [Hortus musicus 173] Sonata Op. 1, No. 1. Note that this is from the same opus called I(a) by Kolneder, editor of the Schott issue.

——. *Sonata D-dur für Violine und Basso continuo*. Edited by Hugo Ruf. Kassel: Bärenreiter, 1961. [Hortus musicus 174] Sonata Op. I, No. 4. Note this is from the same opus called I(a) by Kolneder, editor of the Schott issue.

——. *Sonata "Impetuosa,"* D moll. Edited by Alfred Moffat. Berlin: Simrock, 1929. [1067]. Sonata Op. I, No. 12, in a "new concert version" by Moffat.

——. *Sechs Sonaten für Violine und Basso continuo (Geminianis Bearbeitung der Sechs Sonaten für Violoncello und Basso continuo Op. V)*. Edited by Walter Kolneder. Leipzig: Peters, 1965. [9042]

——. *12 Compositioni (Violino e Pianoforte)*. Edited by Tivadar Orszagh and Laszlo Böhm. 2 vols. Budapest: Editio Musica, 1959. [*Thesaurus musicus* Nr. 7, Nr. 8] These are the twelve movements included by Geminiani as part of his *The Art of Playing the Violin*, 1751.

Gerhard, Roberto. *Gemini: Duo Concertante for Violin and Pianoforte*. London: Oxford University Press, 1970.

Giardini, Felice. *Sonate per Cembalo con Violino o Flauto, Op. 3*. Edited by Enrico Polo. Milan: I Classici Musicali Italiani, 1941. [*ICMI*, vol. 3.] Sole agent for *ICMI* series is Casa Editrice Leo S. Olschki, Florence.

Giegling, Franz, ed. *The Solo Sonata*. Cologne: Arno Volk, 1960. In the series Anthology of Music, edited by Karl G. Fellerer.

Goedike, A. *Sonata No. 1 for Violin and Piano*. Moscow: State Music Publishers, 1959. [16504]

Golubev, E. *Sonata for Violin and Piano*. Moscow: State Music Publishers, 1969. [5994]

Graun, Johann Gottlieb. *Sechs Sonaten für Violine und Continuo*. Edited by Gottfried Müller. 6 vols. Hamburg: Sikorski, 1957. [395a-f, one sonata per volume]

Graupner, Christoph. *Zwei Sonaten für Cembalo (Klavier) und Violine oder Flöte*. Edited by Adolf Hoffmann. Kassel: Bärenreiter, 1955. [Hortus musicus 121]

Grieg, Edvard. *Sonate für Klavier und Violine, F dur Op. 8*. Edited by Carl Herrmann. Leipzig: Peters, 1931. [1340]

———. *Sonate für Violine und Piano, G dur, Op. 13*. New York: Peters, 1958. [2279]

———. *Sonate für Violine und Piano, C moll, Op. 45*. New York: Peters, 1954. [2414]

Händel, Georg Friedrich. *Sieben Sonaten für Violine und Generalbass*. Edited by Stanley Sadie. Munich—Duisburg: G. Henle Verlag, 1971. In addition to the six sonatas contained in most editions, the Henle publication also includes the sonata "originally published as Opus 1 No. 6, for oboe," and marked in Handel's autograph for "Violino Solo."

———. *Sechs Sonaten für Violine und bezifferten Bass*. Edited by Johann Philipp Hinnenthal. Kassel: Bärenreiter, 1955. [4004] Hallische Händel-Ausgabe, Serie IV, Instrumentalmusik, Band 4.

Hartmann, Johann Peter Emilius. *Sonate Nr. 3, Op. 83 (G-moll) für Violine und Klavier (für Coigonoohülor)*. Copenhagen: Wilhelm Hansen, n.d. [903]

Hauptmann, Moritz. *Drei leichte Sonatinen für Pianoforte & Violine, Op. 10*. Leipzig: Peters, n.d. [2948]

Haydn, Joseph. *Sonaten für Violine und Klavier*. Rev. ed. New York: C. F. Peters, n.d. [190]

Heiden, Bernard. *Sonata for Violin and Piano (1954)*. New York: Associated Music Publishers, 1961. [95918-26]

Henriques, Fini. *Sonate pour Violon et Piano, Op. 10*. Copenhagen: Hansen, n.d. [3310]

Henze, Hans Werner. *Sonate für Violine und Klavier (1946)*. Mainz: Schott, 1948. [3859]

Hindemith, Paul. *Sonate in Es für Violine und Piano, Op. 11, No. 1*. Mainz: Schott, 1949. [1918]

———. *Sonata, Violin and Piano, Op. 11, No. 2 (in D)*. Mainz: Schott, 1920. [1919]

———. *Sonata in E, Violin and Piano (1935)*. London: Schott, 1935. [2455]

———. *Sonate für Violine und Klavier (1939)*. Mainz: Schott, 1940. [3645]

Historical Anthology of Music: see Davison and Apel.

Honegger, Arthur. *Première Sonate pour Violon et Piano*. Paris: Salabert, 1921. [E.M.S. 4398]

————. *Deuxième Sonate pour Violon et Piano*. Paris: Salabert, 1924. [6604]

Hummel, Johann Nepomuk. *Sonate B-dur für Violine und Klavier, Op. 5, Nr. 1.* Edited by Franz Samohyl. Vienna: Doblinger, 1963. [Diletto Musicale, Nr. 100]

Ibragimov, R. *Sonatina*. Moscow, State Music Publishers, 1967. [4402]

Imre, Vincze. *Sonata per Violino e Pianoforte*. Budapest: Editio Musica, 1971. [6433]

d'Indy, Vincent. *Sonate (en ut) pour Violin et Piano, Op. 59*. Paris: Durand, 1905. [6464]

Ives, Charles E. *First Sonata for Violin and Piano*. New York: Peer International, 1953. [125-35]

————. *Second Sonata for Violin and Piano*. New York: G. Schirmer, 1951. [42051c]

————. *Sonata No. 3 for Violin and Piano*. Edited by Sol Babitz and Ingolf Dahl. Bryn Mawr: Merion Music, 1951. [144-40019]

————. *Sonata No. 4 for Violin and Piano, "Children's Day at the Camp Meeting."* New York: Associated Music, 1942. [9638-21]

Janáček, Leoš. *Sonata, Violino e Piano*. Prague: Artia, 1966. [H 4347]

Kadosa, Pál. *II. Sonate für Violine und Klavier, Op. 58*. Budapest: Editio Musica, 1962. [Z. 4105]

Kammel, Antonin. *Sonata in Bb, for Violin and Piano, or Violin, Harpsichord, and Cello obbligato*. See *Violinsonaten des böhmischen Barocks*.

Khatschaturian, Karen. *Sonate für Violine und Klavier, Op. 1*. Hamburg: Sikorski, 1957. [2120]

Kirchhoff, Gottfried. *Zwölf Sonaten für Violine und Cembalo* [basso continuo]. Edited by Walter Serauky and Ludwig Bus. 2 vols. Mainz: Schott, 1960. [5060; 5061]

Kirchner, Leon. *Sonata Concertante, for Violin and Piano*. New York: Mercury Music, 1955.

Klebe, Giselher. *Sonate für Violine und Klavier, Op. 14*. Mainz: Schott, 1953. [4478]

Kleven, Arvid. *Sonate No. I, Op. 10, for Violin og Piano*. Copenhagen: Wilhelm Hansen, 1925. [2472]

Kliuzner, Boris. *Sonata for Violin and Piano*. Moscow: Music State Publishers, 1966. [1960]

Kuss, M. *Sonata for Violin and Piano*. Moscow: Soviet Composers, 1969. [765]

Laurušas, V. *Sonata for Violin and Piano*. Moscow: Music State Publishers, 1967. [724]

Leclair, Jean-Marie. *Zwölf Sonaten für Violine und Generalbass nebst einem Trio für Violine, Violoncell und Generalbass [Op. 2], 2. Buch der Sonaten, Paris circa 1732*. Edited by Robert Eitner. Publikation aelterer praktischer unde theoretischer Musikwerke, vol. XXVII. Leipzig: Breitkopf & Härtel, 1903 (reprinted New York: Broude, 1966). Despite the title, there are twelve pieces in all; the trio is number 8 of the dozen.

————. *Sonatas for Violin and Basso Continuo, Op. 5, Op. 9, and Op. 15.* Edited by Robert E. Preston. New Haven or Madison (Wisconsin): A-R Editions—Recent Researches in the Music of the Baroque Era, Vol IV: Opus 5, Sonatas I-V 1968; Vol V: Opus 5, Sonatas VI-XII 1969; Vol X: Opus 9, Sonatas I-VI 1970; Vol XI: Opus 9, Sonatas VII-XII, Opus 15, Posthumous Sonata, 1971

————. *Six Sonates pour Violon et Clavecin ou Piano.* Edited by Marc Pincherle and Laurence Boulay. 6 vols. L'Oiseau-Lyre, 1952. [Book I, No. 8 (Op. 1/8), 181; Book II, No. 1 (Op. 2/1), 180; Book II, No. 12 (Op. 2/12), 184; Book III, No. 1 (Op. 5/1), 182; Book III, No. 4 (Op. 5/4), 185; Book IV, No. 4 (Op. 9/4), 183.]

————. *Sonate H-Moll für Violine und Basso continuo, Op. V, Nr. 5.* Edited by Hugo Ruf. Kassel: Bärenreiter, 1958. [3414]

————. *Sonate a-Moll für Violine und Basso continuo, Op. IX, Nr. 5.* Edited by Frederick F. Polnauer. Mainz: Schott, 1969. [5778]

Le Duc, Simon. *Vier Sonaten für Violine und Basso continuo.* Edited by Elma Doflein. 2 vols. Mainz: Schott, 1964. [Op. IV/1, IV/6, 4708; Op. I/1, IV/4, 4709]

Legrenzi, Giovanni. *Sonate für Violine und Violoncello mit Basso continuo, Op. 10, 1, Nr. 4.* Edited by Karl Gustav Fellerer. Kassel: Bärenreiter, 1951. [Hortus musicus 84]

Liatoshinsky, B. *Sonata for Violin and Piano.* Moscow: Soviet Composers, 1962. [2746]

Locatelli, Pietro. *Sei Sonate da Camera per Violino e Basso dall' Op. 6.* Edited by Giacomo Benvenuti, Enrico Polo, and Michelangelo Abbado. Milan: I Classici Musicali Italiani, 1956. [*ICMI*, vol. 14] Includes sonatas 1 through 6 of the twelve sonatas in this opus. Sole agent for *ICMI* series is Casa Editrice Leo S. Olschki, Florence.

————. *Sonata in Re Minore, Op. VI, N. 12 per Violino e Basso.* Edited by Michelangelo Abbado. Milan: Ricordi, 1970. [131693]

————. *Sonata in Re maggiore per Violine e Pianoforte.* Edited by Cesare Barison. Milan: Carisch, 1965. [21704]

————. *Sonata in Sol maggiore.* Edited by A. Poltronieri. Milan: Carisch, 1946. [20333]

————. *Sonata da Camera g-Moll, für Violine und bezifferten Bass.* Edited by J. Bachmair. Leipzig: Breitkopf & Härtel, 1959. [3358]

Lonati, Carlo Ambrogio. *Sonata Quinta.* In Giegling, *Solo Sonata.*

Loránd, István. *Sonata per violino e pianoforte.* Budapest: Editio Musica, 1969. [Z.6049]

Marini, Biagio. *Sonata, "La Giardana."* In Schering, *Geschichte der Musik in Beispielen*, No. 182. From Marini's opus 1, 1617.

―――. *Sonata per il violino per sonar con due corde.* In Schering, *Geschichte der Musik in Beispielen*, No. 183. From Marini's opus 8, 1628.

―――. *Sonate, D-moll, für Violine, Streich-bass (Gambe oder Violoncello) und Basso continuo.* Edited by Werner Danckert. Kassel: Bärenreiter, 1955. [Hortus musicus 129]

Martin, Frank. *Sonate (1931–32) pour Violon et Piano.* Zurich: Universal, 1959. [12874 Z]

Martinon, Jean. *Duo: Musique en forme de Sonate pour Violon et Piano, Op. 47.* Mainz: Schott, 1959. [4791]

―――. *2e Sonatine pour Violon et Piano, Op. 19, No 2.* Paris: Braun, 1944. [2864]

Martinu, Bohuslav. *Sonate [No. 1] pour Violon et Piano.* Paris: Leduc, 1930. [17,688]

―――. *Sonate pour Violon et Piano.* Paris: Salabert, 1932. [R.D.7479]

―――. *Sonatina per Violino e Piano.* Edited by Victor Napp. Prague: Artia, 1970. [H.2172]

Mascitti, Michele. *Sechs Kammersonaten für Violine und Klavier, Op. 2.* Edited by Walter Kolneder. 2 vols. Heidelberg: Willy Müller, 1963. [2181; 2182]

Medtner, Nikolay. *Sonata Epica, Op. 57, for Violin and Piano.* London: Novello, n.d. [16790]

―――. *Sonate No. 2 für Violine und Klavier, G-dur, Op. 44.* Leipzig: Zimmermann, n.d. [11213]

Mendelssohn, Felix. *Sonata in F major for Violin and Piano.* Edited by Yehudi Menuhin. New York: Peters, 1953. [6075]

―――. *Sonate (F moll) für Klavier und Violine, Op. 4.* Edited by Friedrich Hermann. Leipzig: Peters, n.d. [1732]

Mihalovici, Marcel. *2ème Sonate Op. 45, pour Violon et Piano.* Paris: Heugel, 1954. [31654]

Milhaud, Darius. *Sonate pour Violon et Piano (1911).* Paris: Durand, 1914. [9180]

―――. *2e Sonate pour Violon et Piano,* Paris: Durand, 1919. [9746]

Milman, M. *Sonata for Violin and Piano.* Moscow: Soviet Composers, 1969.

Monasipov, A. *Sonata for Violin and Piano.* Moscow, Soviet Composers, 1967. [4456]

Mondonville, Jean-Joseph. *Sonate D-Dur, für Violine und Basso continuo.* Edited by Frederick F. Polnauer. Mainz: Schott, 1967. [5484] Sonata Op. 1, No. 3.

―――. *Sonate C-dur, für Violine und Basso continuo.* Edited by Frederick F. Polnauer. Mainz: Schott, 1967. [5485] Sonata Op. 1, No. 4.

―――. *Pièces de Clavecin en Sonates [Op. 3]* Edited by Marc Pincherle. Paris: Heugel, 1969. Publications de la Société française de Musicologie, Première Série, Tome IX.

―――. *Sonate F-dur für Violine und Cembalo.* Edited by Walter Höckner. Locarno: Heinrichshofen, 1963. [Pegasus PE 6057] Sonata II, from op. 3.

————. *Sonata C-dur, Op. 4, Nr. 2, für Violine und Basso continuo.* Edited by Frederick F. Polnauer. Wilhelmshaven: Heinrichshofen, 1970. [Pegasus, N 1256]

Montalbano, Bartolomeo. *Sinfonia No. 4, "Geloso."* In Giegling, *Solo Sonata,* pp. 23-25.

Mozart, Wolfgang Amadeus. *Jugendsonaten I: Vier Sonaten für Klavier (Cembalo) und Violine, KV 6-9.* Edited by Eduard Reeser. Kassel: Bärenreiter, 1967. [4755]. "Revised separate edition, based on W. A. Mozart, *Neue Ausgabe sämtlicher Werke Series VIII, Chamber Music, Category 23, Sonatas and Variations for Pianoforte and Violin, Vol. 1.*"

————. *Jugendsonaten II: Sechs Sonaten für Klavier (Cembalo), Violine (oder Flöte) und Violoncello, KV 10-15.* Edited by Wolfgang Plath and Wolfgang Rehm. Kassel: Bärenreiter, 1969. [4756]. "Revised separate edition, based on: W. A. Mozart, *Neue Ausgabe sämtlicher Werke . . . Series VIII, Chamber Music, Category 22, Section 2: Pianoforte Trios . . .*"

————. *Jugendsonaten III: Sechs Sonaten für Klavier (Cembalo) und Violine, KV 26-31.* Edited by Eduard Reeser. Kassel: Bärenreiter, 1964. [4757]. "Revised separate edition, based on: W. A. Mozart, *Neue Ausgabe sämtlicher Werke . . . Series VIII, Chamber Music, Category 23, Sonatas and Variations for Pianoforte and Violin, Vol. 1.*"

————. *Sonaten für Klavier und Violine [K. 296-570].* Edited by Ernst Fritz Schmid, Walter Lampe, and Karl Röhrig. 2 vols. Munich-Duisburg: G. Henle, 1956. [78; 79]

Muffat, Georg. *Sonate, D-dur, für Violine und Basso continuo.* Edited by Walter Kolneder. Mainz: Schott, 1969. [Schott 5797]

Nardini, Pietro. *Sonata in Si Bemolle Maggiore per Violino e Basso.* Edited by Michelangelo Abbado. Milan: Ricordi, 1970. [131694] ". . . the last of the seven [sonatas of Nardini] published by Cartier in his Anthology [*L'art du Violon,* Paris, 1801]."

————. *Sonate D dur, Violine und Klavier.* Edited by Carl Flesch. New York: C. F. Peters, 1931. [4167]

————. *Six Sonatas for Violin and Piano.* Edited by Paul Doktor and Mildred J. Johnson. New York: G. Schirmer, 1967. [1852]

Niaga, G. *Sonata for Violin and Piano.* Moscow: Soviet Composers, 1961. [2577]

Nielsen, Carl. *Sonata No. 1 for Violin and Piano, Op. 9.* Copenhagen: Wilhelm Hansen, n.d. [11759]

————. *Sonate Op. 35, Nr. 2, für Violine und Klavier.* Copenhagen: Hansen, 1919. [1982]

Nozeman, Jacobus. *Tre Sonate a Violino e Basso continuo, Opera Prima (ca. 1724).* Edited by Willem Noske and Hans Schouwman. Amsterdam: Broekmans & Van Poppel, 1954. [Society for old Netherlands music, Chamber music Series No. 1] Sonatas Op. 1, Nos. 1, 3, and 4.

Paganini, Niccolo. *Six Sonatas for Violin and Piano, Op. 2.* New York: Paragon, 1957. [20]

————. *Six Sonatas for Violin and Piano, Op. 3.* New York: Paragon, 1957. [21]

Pepusch, Johann Christoph. *Sechs Sonaten für Violine und Klavier (Cembalo), Violoncello (Gambe) ad lib.* Edited by Dietz Degen and Gustav Lenzewski. Mainz: Schott, 1940. [36088]

Pijper, Willem. *Sonata for Violin and Piano, No. 2.* Amsterdam: Donemus, 1952.

Pisendel, Johann Georg. *Sonate für Violine und Cembalo (Klavier).* Edited by Günter Hausswald. Mainz: Schott, 1954. [4162]

Piston, Walter. *Sonata for Violin and Piano, (1939).* New York: Associated Music Publishers, 1940. [96232-30]

————. *Sonatina for Violin & Harpsichord (Piano).* New York: Boosey and Hawkes, 1948. [16239]

Pizzetti, Ildebrando. *Sonata in A major for Violin and Piano (1919).* London: Chester, 1920. [327]

Pleyel, Ignatz Joseph. *Duets: Piano and Violin, Op. 8.* Edited by Friedrich Hermann. London, Galliard, n.d. [6042a]

————. *Duets: Piano and Violin, Op. 44.* Edited by Friedrich Hermann. London: Augener, n.d. [9642]

Porpora, Niccolo. *Sonate in G-moll für Violine mit beziffertem Bass.* Edited by A. Moffat. Hamburg: Simrock, 1932.

Porter, Quincy. *Second Sonata for Violin and Piano.* New York: Peters, 1964 (Original copyright, 1933). [SPAM 32]

Poulenc, Francis. *Sonate pour Violon et Piano.* Corrected edition (violin part edited by Ginette Neveu). Paris: Eschig, 1949. [6411]

Prokofieff, Sergei. *Sonate für Violine und Klavier, Op. 80.* Edited by David Oistrakh. [Sonata number 1 in F minor] Leipzig: Peters, n.d. [4718]

————. *Sonata Op. 94 [and Op. 94 bis], for Flute or Violin and Piano.* Edited by Joseph Szigeti. [Sonata number 1 in D] New York: MCA Music, 1948–1965. [05143-024]

Pugnani, Gaetano. *Sonata III, Oeuvre 6.* Edited by Claude Arrieu. Paris: Ricordi, 1957. [1554] This numbering is from the so-identified Paris edition. The sonata is identical with number 3 of Opus 7, the original London publication.

————. *Sei Sonate a Violino e Basso, Opera 7.* Amsterdam: A. J. Heuwekemeyer; Mechelen/Leuven: De Monte, 1970. [Reprint edition 1970/021]. Note that this is a facsimile of the original edition, without realized basso continuo.

————. *Sonata in mi maggiore n. 1 per Violino e Basso.* Edited by Michelangelo Abbado. Milan: Ricordi, 1972. [131798] This is sonata Opus 8, No. 1.

Ravel, Maurice. *Sonate pour Violin et Piano.* Paris: Durand, 1927. [11273]

Reger, Max. *4. Sonate C-dur, Violine und Klavier, Op. 72.* Rev. ed. Edited by Theodor Prusse. Berlin: Bote and Bock, 1967. [16921 (958)]

————. *5. Sonate fis-moll, Violine und Klavier, Op. 84*. Rev. ed. Edited by Theodor Prusse. Berlin: Bote and Bock, 1965. [17057 (945)]

————. *Kleine Sonate d-moll, Hausmusik, Op. 103b, Nr. 1, Violine und Klavier*. Berlin: Bote and Bock, 1937. [17265 (251)]

————. *Kleine Sonate A-dur, Hausmusik, Op. 103b, Nr. 2, Violine und Klavier*. Berlin: Bote and Bock, 1965. [17266 (252)]

————. *Sonate e-moll, Violine und Klavier, Op. 122*. Berlin: Bote and Bock, 1971. [17688 (1135)]

————. *Sonate c moll, für Violine und Klavier, Op. 139*. Leipzig: Peters, 1915. [3985]

Respighi, Ottorino. *Sonata in Si minore, per Violino e Pianoforte*. Milan: Ricordi, 1919, reprinted 1967. [117619]

Richter, Franz Xaver. *Sechs Kammersonaten für obligates Cembalo (Klavier), Querflöte (Violine) und Violoncello, Op. 2*. Edited by Walter Upmeyer. Kassel: Bärenreiter, 1965. [Hortus musicus 86] Only this volume, with sonatas 1-3, has appeared.

Riegger, Wallingford. *Sonatina for Violin and Piano*. New York: Marks, 1948. [12512-20]

Ries, Ferdinand. *Drei Sonatinen für Violine und Klavier, Op. 30*. Berlin: Ries & Erler, 1969. [11.255]

————. *Grande Sonate für Violine und Klavier, Op. 83*. Berlin: Ries & Erler, 1969. [11.256]

Riisager, Knudage. *Sonate, Violon et Piano (1923)*. Copenhagen: Wilhelm Hansen, n.d. [2456]

Roussel, Albert. *1ère Sonate en re mineur, pour piano et violon*. Revised by Roussel in 1931. Paris: Salabert, 1931 (originally by Rouart-Lerolle, 1909). [4770]

————. *2e Sonate pour Violon et Piano, Op. 28*. Paris: Durand, 1925. [10, 757]

Rubbra, Edmund. *Sonata No. 2 for Violin and Piano*. London: Oxford University Press, 1937.

————. *Sonata No. 3 for Violin and Piano, Op. 133*. London: Lengnick, 1968. [4231]

Saint-Saëns, Camille. *1ère Sonate, Op. 75, pour Piano et Violon*. Paris: Durand, n.d. [3541]

————. *2ème Sonate pour Violon et Piano, Op. 102*. Paris: Durand, 1896. [5099]

Salmanov, V. *Sonata No. 2 for Violin and Piano*. Leningrad: State Music Publishers, 1967. [630]

Satie, Erik. *Choses vues à Droite et à Gauche (Sans Lunettes), Piano et Violon*. Paris: Rouart-Lerolle (Salabert), 1916. [R.L. 10.074]

Schering, Arnold, ed. *Alte Meister des Violinspiels*. Leipzig: Peters, 1909. [3226]

————, comp. and ed. *Geschichte der Musik in Beispielen*: Leipzig, Breitkopf & Härtel, 1931 (reprinted New York: Broude Bros., 1950).

Schmelzer, Johann Heinrich. *Sonatae Unarum Fidium*. Edited by Friedrich Cerha. 2 vols. Vienna: Universal, 1960. [13301; 13302]

———. *Sonatae Unarum Fidium, 1644—Violinsonaten handschriftlicher Überlieferung*. Edited by Erich Schenck. [DTÖ, Band 93].

Schobert, Johann. *Ausgewählte Werke*. Edited by Hugo Riemann. Revised by Hans Jochim Moser [DdT, series 1, Vol. 39].

———. *Sonate A-dur, für Cembalo und Violine*. Edited by Walter Kramolisch. Kassel: Nagel, 1962. [Nagels Musik-Archiv, 199]

Schoeck, Othmar. *Sonate für Violine und Klavier, Op. 46*. Zurich: Hug, 1934. [7719]

Schoenberg, Arnold. *Phantasy for Violin with Piano Accompaniment, Op. 47*. New York: C. F. Peters, 1952. [6060]

Schubert, Franz. *Sonatinen für Klavier und Violine, Op. 137*. Rev. ed. Edited by Günter Henle and Karl Röhrig. Munich-Duisburg: G. Henle, 1955. [6]

———. *Duos für Klavier und Violine*. Edited by Carl Hermann. New York: Peters, 1934. [156b] Includes Rondeau brillant, Op. 70; Fantaisie in C, Op. 159; Introduction and Variations, Op. 160; and Duo (Sonata) in A, Op. 162.

Schulz, Johann Abraham Peter. *Sonata D-dur, für Violine und Cembalo (Klavier)*. Edited by Willi Hillemann. Wilhelmshaven: Heinrich Noetzel, 1961. [Pegasus, N 3258]

Schumann, Robert. *Sonaten für Klavier und Violine, Opp. 105, 121*. Edited by Friedrich Hermann. Frankfurt: Peters, 1928–1956. [2367]

———. *Sonata No. 3 in A minor, Violin and Piano*. Edited by O. W. Neighbour. Mainz: Schott, 1956. [10505]

Seiber, Matyas. *Sonata (1960) for Violin and Piano*. London: Schott, 1963. [10747]

Senallié, Jean Baptiste. *Sonata in D minor, for Violin and Keyboard*. Edited by John A. Parkinson. London: Oxford University Press, 1963.

Shnaper, B. *Sonata in D minor for Violin and Piano*. Moscow: State Music Publishers, 1966. [2902]

Shostakovich, Dmitri. *Sonata for Violin and Pianoforte, Op. 134*. Violin part edited by David Oistrakh. Moscow: State Music Publishers, 1970. [6709]

Sibelius, Jean. *Sonatine for Violin and Piano, Op. 80*. Edited and revised by Julia A. Burt. Copenhagen: Hansen, 1921–1949. [17734]

Sidon, Samuel Peter. *Sonate mit Suite für Violine und Generalbass*. Edited by Max Seiffert. Leipzig: Kistner & Siegel, n.d. [28340]

Sinding, Christian. *Sonate (C-dur) für Violine und Pianoforte, Op. 12*. Copenhagen: Hansen, n.d. [11062]

Sjnitke, A. *Sonate No. 1 for Violin and Piano*. Moscow: State Music Publishers, 1969. [6090]

Sjögren, Emil. *Sonate Nr. 2 e-moll, Op. 24, für Violine und Pianoforte*. Copenhagen: Hansen, n.d. [20677]

Smith, David Stanley. *Sonata for Violin and Piano, Op. 51*. New York: G. Schirmer, 1924.

Somis, Giovanni Battista. *Sonate (Sol majeur) arrangée pour Violon avec accompagnement de Piano.* Edited by J. Salmon. Paris: Ricordi, 1918. [378]

——. *Sonate, g-moll, Op. IV, Nr. 5, für Violine und Basso continuo.* Edited by Hugo Ruf. Heidelberg: Willy Müller, 1966. [1828]

Stamic, Jan Václav [Johann Stamitz]. *Sonata Sol maggiore, Op. 6a.* Edited by František Brož. Prague: Artia, 1956. [Musica Antiqua Bohemica 28]

Strauss, Richard. *Sonate für Violine und Klavier, Op. 18, in Es-dur.* Vienna: Universal, n.d. [1047]

Stravinsky, Igor. *Duo Concertant pour violon et piano.* Violin part with collaboration of Samuel Dushkin. London: Boosey & Hawkes, 1947 (Paris: Edition Russe, 1933). [16373]

Tailleferre, Germaine. *Sonate pour piano et violon.* Paris: Durand, 1923. [10256]

Tardos, Béla. *Sonate pour Violon et Piano.* Budapest: Editio Musica, 1969. [Z. 6157]

Tartini, Giuseppe. *Sei Sonate per Violino e Pianoforte, Op. 5.* Edited by Ettore Bonelli. Padua: Zanibon, 1951. [3829]

——. *6 Sonate per Violino e Pianoforte.* Edited by Enrico Polo. Milan: Ricordi, 1921. [177]

——. *Sonata in G minor for Violin and Piano.* Edited by Leopold Auer. New York: Carl Fischer, 1919. [B 2665]

——. *3 Sonaten, F dur, G dur, E moll, Violine und Klavier.* Edited by Friedrich Hermann. Leipzig: Peters, n.d. [1099a]

——. *Teufelstriller-Sonate, G-moll-Sonate.* Edited by Friedrich Hermann. Leipzig: Peters, n.d. [1099b]

——. *Sonaten, C dur, D dur.* Edited by Friedrich Hermann. Leipzig: Peters, n.d. [1099c]

Telemann, Georg Philipp. *Sonate, F-dur, für Violine und Basso continuo.* Edited by Hugo Ruf. Mainz: Schott, 1965. [5477] This sonata is Solo No. 1 from the *Essercizii Musici.*

——. *Sonate A-dur, für Violine und Basso continuo.* Edited by Hugo Ruf. Mainz: Schott, 1965. [5478] This sonata is Solo No. 7 from the *Essercizii Musici.*

——. *Sechs Sonaten für Violine und Basso continuo.* Edited by Wilhelm Friedrich. Mainz: Schott, 1954. [4221] This is the set of sonatas published by Telemann in Frankfurt in 1715.

——. *Zwölf Methodische Sonaten, 1-6 für Violine oder Querflöte und Basso continuo, 7-12 für Querflöte oder Violine und Basso continuo, Hamburg 1728 und 1732.* Edited by Max Seiffert. Kassel: Bärenreiter, 1955. [2951]

——. *Sechs Sonatinen für Violine und Cembalo (Klavier).* Edited by Willi Maertens and Walter Heinz Bernstein. Leipzig: Peters, 1967. [9096]

——. *Tafelmusik II: Solo A-dur für Violine und Basso continuo.* Edited by Johann Philipp Hinnenthal. Kassel: Bärenreiter, 1966. [3542] "Separate edition for practical use from Volume XIII of 'Georg Philipp Telemann, Musi-kalische Werke,' published by the Gesellschaft für Musikforschung."

———. *Sonata IV, C-dur, für Violine und Cembalo (Klavier)*. Edited by Gott-hold Frotscher. Leipzig: Peters/Litolff, 1951. [5644] Source not given. This sonata, short and slight, does not duplicate any other listed here.

———. *Sonata, C moll, für Violine und Cembalo*. Leipzig: Breitkopf & Härtel, 1938. [4176]

Toch, Ernst. *Sonate [No. 2], Op. 44, für Violine und Piano*. Mainz: Schott, 1928. [1240]

Tremais (no first name). *Sonate F moll*. In Schering, *Alte Meister*, pp. 57-68.

Ustvolskaya, G. *Sonata for Violin and Piano*. Moscow: State Music Publishers, 1966. [463]

Valentini, Giuseppe. *Sonata d-Moll, für Violine und Basso continuo*. Edited by Hugo Ruf. Mainz: Schott, 1968. [5784]

———. *Sonata in Sol, per Violino e Pianoforte*. Edited by Ottorino Respighi. Milan: Ricordi, 1921. [270]

Vaughan-Williams, Ralph. *Sonata in A minor for Violin and Pianoforte*. Lon-don: Oxford University Press, 1956.

Antonio Veracini, *Sonata da Camera Op. 3, No. 2*. Edited by Frederick F. Pol-nauer. London: Chester, 1970. [453]

Veracini, Francesco Maria. *Sonaten für Violine (Flöte) und Bass*. Edited by Franz Bär. 3 vols. Kassel: Bärenreiter, 1950. [F major, 347; G major, 348; D minor, 349]

———. *Zwölf Sonaten für Violine und Klavier (Cembalo), Op. I*. Edited by Walter Kolneder. 4 vols. Leipzig: Peters, 1958. [4937a-d]

———. *Sonate accademiche für Violine und Klavier (Cembalo), op. 2*. Edited by Walter Kolneder. 12 vols. Leipzig: Peters, 1961–1971. [9011 a-m] Each *Sonata accademica*, from no. 1 through no. 12, appears in its own volume of this edition, from catalog suffix *a* through *m* (there is no *j*).

———. *Zwölf Sonaten nach Arcangelo Corelli Op. 5, für Violine und Basso continuo*. Edited by Walter Kolneder. 4 vols. Mainz: Schott, 1961. [5157; 5158; 5170; 5171]

Villa-Lobos, Heitor. *Première Sonate-Fantaisie, Désespérance, pour Piano et Violon*. Paris: Eschig, 1929. [2465]

———. *Deuxième Sonate-Fantaisie pour Violon et Piano*. Paris: Eschig, 1953. [6673]

———. *Troisième Sonate pour Violon et Piano*. Paris: Eschig, 1953. [6690]

Violinsonaten des böhmischen Barocks. Edited by Richard Tillinger. Prague: Artia, 1967. [Musica Viva Historica 18] Sonatas of Jiří Cart, Antonin Kam-mel, and Bedřich Ludwík Benda.

Viotti, Giovanni Battista. *Six Sonatas à violon seul et basse, 2e Livre*. Paris: Nadermann, ca. 1800. This edition is contained in the collection of the Music Division of the New York Public Library. That same collection also contains the composer's *Six Sonates pour violon et basse* . . . *Oeuvre 4, 1ᵉʳ Livre de sonates,* Paris: Boyer, 17_?.

Vitali, Giovanni Battista. *Artifici Musicali, Op. XIII.* Edited by Louise Rood and Gertrude P. Smith. Northampton: Smith College, 1959. [Smith College Music Archives, XIV]

Vitali, Tommaso Antonio. *Concerto Di Sonate, Op. 4, for Violin, Violoncello, and Continuo.* Edited by Doris Silbert, Gertrude Parker Smith, and Louise Rood. Northampton: Smith College, n.d. [Smith College Music Archives, XII]

―――. *Sonate für Violine/Violoncello und Cembalo, Op. 4, No. XI.* Edited by J. P. Hinnenthal. Kassel: Bärenreiter, 1959. [Hortus musicus 38]

Vivaldi, Antonio. *Zwölf Sonaten für Violine und Basso Continuo, Op. 2.* Edited by Willi Hillemann. 2 vols. Mainz: Schott, 1953. [4212; 4213]

―――. *XII Sonate per Violino e Basso, [Op. 2].* Edited by S. A. Luciani. Milan: Instituto di Alta Cultura, n.d. Based on the same first edition of opus 2 as the Schott edition, above, the Luciani edition is a miniature score, showing the violin part and the figured-bass line, unrealized.

―――. *Vier Sonaten für Violine und Basso continuo, Op. V/1-4.* Edited by Walter Upmeyer. Kassel: Nagel, 1954. [Nagels Musik-Archiv 162]

―――. *Vier Sonaten für Violine und Basso continuo, "fatto per il Maestro Pisendel."* Edited by Hans Grüss and Walter H. Bernstein. Leipzig: Deutscher Verlag für Musik, 1965. [8101]

―――. *Sonata in Re per Violino e basso (F. XIII n. 6).* Edited by Ottorino Respighi. Milan: Ricordi, 1921–1970. [128437]

―――. *Sonata, G-moll, a Violino solo con Basso continuo.* Edited by Walter Upmeyer. Kassel: Bärenreiter, 1953. [Hortus musicus 102] This sonata is not duplicated in any other edition shown here.

Vodička, Václav. *Sei Sonate, Violino e Cembalo.* Edited by Camillo Schoenbaum. Prague: Artia, 1962. [Musica Antiqua Bohemica 54]

Vorisek, Jan Hugo. *Sonata, Op. 5, Violino e Piano.* Edited by Jan Štědroň and Bohumír Štědroň. Prague: Artia, 1956. [Musica Antiqua Bohemica 30]

Walter, Bruno. *Sonate A-dur für Violine und Klavier.* Vienna: Universal, 1910. [2598]

Walther, Johann Jakob. *Scherzi da Violino solo con il Basso continuo, 1676.* Edited by Gustav Beckmann. Kassel: Nagel, 1953. [EdM, Band 17, Kammermusik 3] "Unaltered reprint of vol. 17, 1941, of *Das Erbe deutscher Musik.*"

―――. *Sonate mit Suite für Violine und Generalbass (Hortulus Chelicus 1688, Nr. 2).* Edited by Max Seiffert. Leipzig: Kistner & Siegel, 1930. [Organum, Dritte Reihe, Nr. 28]

―――. *Sonate für Violine und Basso continuo.* Edited by Erna Bethan. Kassel: Nagel, ca. 1931. [Nagels Musik-Archiv 89] This is sonata number 4 of the *Scherzi* set.

Walton, William. *Sonata for Violin and Piano.* London: Oxford University Press, 1950.

Weber, Ben. *Sonata da Camera for Violin and Piano, Op. 30*. New York: Boosey & Hawkes, 1954. [Fromm Music Foundation 9]

Weber, Carl Maria von. *Sechs Sonaten für Klavier und Violine, Op. 10(b)*. Edited by Ewald Zimmermann, Hans-Martin Theopold, and Karl Röhrig. Munich-Duisburg: G. Henle, 1965. [182]

Webern, Anton. *Vier Stücke für Geige und Klavier, Op. 7*. Vienna: Universal, 1922. [6642]

Wolf-Ferrari, Ermanno. *Sonate a-moll, Op. 10, Violino & Piano*. Hamburg: Rahter, 1902. [Elite Edition 202]

Zbinden, Julien-François. *Sonata per Violino e Pianoforte, Op. 15*. Milan: Zerboni, 1956. [5278]

✿ Acknowledgments

Music examples in this volume are reproduced by the following permissions, gratefully acknowledged. (Publishers' catalog numbers are shown in brackets. For full bibliographic listings, see Editions Used.)

Béla Bartók, *Sonate für Violine und Klavier* (1903) (Dille and Gertler [6032]. © 1968 by Schott & Co. Reprint permission granted by Belwin-Mills Publishing Corp., exclusive agents for the copyright holder.

———, *Première Sonate (en 3 Mouvements), Violon et Piano* [UE7247]. © 1923 by Universal Edition; © 1950 by Boosey and Hawkes. Reprint permission granted by Universal Editions (London) Ltd., and by Boosey and Hawkes, Inc., for U.S.

———, *Deuxième Sonate (en 2 mouvements), Violon et Piano* [UE7259]. © 1923 by Universal edition; © 1950 by Boosey and Hawkes. Reprint permission granted by Universal Edition (London) Ltd., and by Boosey and Hawkes, Inc., for the U.S.

Ludwig van Beethoven, *Sonaten für Klavier und Violine* (Lampe and Schäffer) [7,8]. © 1955 by G. Henle Verlag. Reprint permission granted by the publisher.

Johannes Brahms, *Sonaten, Klavier und Violine* (Hiekel) [194]. Revised edition. © 1967 by G. Henle Verlag. Reprint permission granted by the publisher.

Benjamin Britten, *Suite for Violin and Piano, Op. 6* [7720]. © 1935 by Boosey and Hawkes, Inc. Reprint permission granted by the publisher.

Aaron Copland, *Sonata for Violin and Piano* [34-46]. © 1944 by Boosey and Hawkes, Inc. Reprint permission granted by the publisher.

Claude Debussy, *Sonate pour Violon et Piano* [9504]. © 1917 by Durand et Cie. Reprint permission granted by the publisher and by Elkan-Vogel, Inc., sole representatives, U.S.A.

Robert Donington, *The Interpretation of Early Music*, 2nd ed. © 1965 by St. Martin's Press, New York. Reprint permission granted by the publisher.

Antonin Dvořák, *Sonate, F-dur, Op. 57, für Violine und Klavier*, rev. ed. [Elite

685 (S.)]. Reprint permission granted by the publisher, Richard Schauer (for Simrock), and by Associated Music Publishers, New York, sole agents for the U.S.A.

————, *Sonatine, G-dur, Op. 100, für Violine und Klavier* [4272]. Reprint permission granted by the publisher, Breitkopf and Härtel, and by Associated Music Publishers, New York, sole agents for the U.S.A.

Gabriel Fauré, *Sonate, A-dur, Op. 13, für Violine und Klavier* [2569]. Reprint permission granted by the publisher, Breitkopf and Härtel, and by Associated Music Publishers, New York, sole agents for the U.S.A.

César Franck, *Sonate, A-dur für Violine und Klavier* (Jacobsen) [3742]. By permission of C. F. Peters Corp., New York.

Roberto Gerhard, *Gemini, Duo Concertante for Violin and Pianoforte*. © 1970 by Oxford University Press. Reprint permission granted by the publisher.

Edvard Grieg, *Sonate für Klavier und Violine, F-dur*, Opus 8 (Hermann) [P1340]. © 1931 by C. F. Peters. Reprint permission granted by the publisher.

————, *Sonate für Violine und Piano, G-dur*, Opus 13 [P2279]. © 1958 by C. F. Peters. Reprint permission granted by the publisher.

————, *Sonate für Violine und Piano, C-moll*, Opus 45 [P2414]. By permission of C. F. Peters Corp., New York.

Paul Hindemith, *Sonate in Es für Violine und Piano*, Opus 11, Nr. 1 [1918]. © 1949 by Schott & Co. Reprint permission granted by Belwin-Mills Publishing Corp., exclusive agents for the copyright owner.

————, *Sonate in D, für Violine und Piano, Opus* 11, Nr. 2 [1919]. © 1920 by Schott & Co. Reprint permission granted by Belwin-Mills Publishing Corp., exclusive agents of the copyright owner.

————, *Sonata in E, Violin and Piano* (1935) [2455]. © 1935 by Schott & Co. Reprint permission granted by Belwin-Mills Publishing Corp., exclusive agents for the copyright owner.

————, *Sonate für Violine und Klavier* (1939) [3645]. © 1940 by Schott & Co. Reprint permission granted by Belwin-Mills Publishing Corp., exclusive agents for the copyright owner.

Leon Kirchner, *Sonata Concertante, for Violin and Piano*. © 1955 by Mercury Music Corp. Used by permission.

Felix Mendelssohn, *Sonata in F major for Violin and Piano* (Menuhin) [P6075]. © 1953 by C. F. Peters Corp. Reprint permission granted by the publisher.

————, *Sonate für Klavier und Violine, F-moll* (Hermann) [P1732]. By permission of C. F. Peters Corp., New York.

Wolfgang Amadeus Mozart, *Sonaten für Klavier und Violine* (Schmid) [78, 79: Sonatas K. 296-570, in two volumes]. © 1956 by G. Henle Verlag. Reprint permission granted by the publisher.

Carl Nielsen, *Sonata No. 1 for Violin and Piano, Op. 9* [11759]. © by Wilhelm Hansen, Musik-Forlag, Copenhagen. Reprint permission granted by the publisher and by G. Schirmer, Inc., New York, agents for the U.S.A.

————, *Sonate Op. 35, Nr. 2, für Violine und Klavier* [1982]. © 1919 by Wilhelm Hansen, Musik-Forlag, Copenhagen. Reprint permission granted by the publisher and by G. Schirmer, Inc., New York, agents for the U.S.A.

Sergei Prokofieff, *Sonate für Violine und Klavier, Opus 80* (Oistrakh) [4718].
By permission of C. F. Peters Corp., New York.
———, *Sonata Opus 94 for Flute or Violin and Piano* (Szigeti) [05143-024].
© 1948, 1965 by MCA Music, a Division of MCA, Inc., 445 Park Avenue,
New York, New York 10022. Used by permission. All rights reserved.

Maurice Ravel, *Sonate pour Violon et Piano* [11,273]. © 1927 by Durand et
Cie. Reprint permission granted by the publisher and by Elkan-Vogel, Inc.,
sole representatives, U.S.A.

Erik Satie, *Choses vues à Droite et à Gauche (Sans Lunettes), Piano et Violon*
[R.L.10.074]. © 1916 by Rouart-Lerolle et Cie (Salabert). Reprint permission granted by Editions Salabert and by Belwin-Mills Publishing Corp., sole
agents for the U.S.A.

Arnold Schoenberg, *Phantasy for Violin with Piano Accompaniment, Opus 47*
[P6060]. © 1952 by Henmar Press Inc. Reprint permission granted by the
publisher.

Franz Schubert, *Sonatinen für Klavier und Violine, Opus 137* (Henle and
Rohrig) [6]. Revised edition. © 1955 by G. Henle Verlag. Reprint permis-
sion granted by the publisher.
———, *Duos für Klavier und Violine* (Hermann) [P156b]. © 1934 by C. F.
Peters Corp. Reprint permission granted by the publisher.

Robert Schumann, *Sonaten für Klavier und Violine, Opus 105, 121* (Hermann)
[P2367]. © 1928 by C. F. Peters Corp. © renewed 1956 by C. F. Peters Corp.
Reprint permission granted by the publisher.

Matyas Seiber, *Sonata (1960) for Violin and Piano* [10747]. © 1963 by Schott
& Co., London. Reprint permission granted by the publisher and by Belwin-
Mills Publishing Corp., exclusive agents for the copyright owner.

Dmitri Shostakovich, *Sonata for Violin and Pianoforte, Op. 134* (Oistrakh)
[6709]. Used by permission of MCA Music, a Division of MCA, Inc., 445
Park Avenue, New York, New York 10022. All rights reserved.

Richard Strauss, *Sonate für Violine und Klavier, Op. 18, in Es-dur* [1047]. Reprint permission granted by the publisher, Universal Edition A.G., Vienna,
and by Theodore Presser Co., sole representative, U.S.A., Canada and Mexico.

Igor Stravinsky, *Duo Concertant pour violon et piano* [16373]. © 1947 by
Boosey and Hawkes, Inc. Reprint permission granted by the publisher.

William Walton, *Sonata for Violin and Piano.* © 1950 by Oxford University
Press. Reprint permission granted by the publisher.

Ben Weber, *Sonata da Camera for Violin and Piano, Op. 30* [Fromm Music
Foundation 9]. © 1954 by Boosey and Hawkes. Reprinted by permission.

Anton Webern, *Vier Stücke für Geige und Klavier, Op. 7* [6642]. © 1922 by
Universal Edition. Reprint permission granted by Universal Edition A.G.,
Vienna, and by Theodore Presser Company, sole representative, U.S.A.,
Canada and Mexico.

Index

Composers whose duo sonatas are considered in this volume are shown below in bold-face type. All references to duo sonatas are presented at the *end* of the listing for the given composer. The sonatas (whether so titled, or as "sonatina," "duo," or "suite") listed are for violin and piano—or piano and violin!—unless otherwise indicated. They are listed numerically according to opus or title number, where such has been provided; in numerical order within a set of works; otherwise, in alphabetical order according to key (with major preceding minor); and, where it was felt necessary for identification, with the year of composition or publication given in parentheses.

Names of patrons, employers, and dedicatees are unlisted, with a few rare exceptions. So also for publishers.

Page references are given in italics.

The text of this book was set on the linotype in Electra
by Maryland Linotype Composition Company, Baltimore, Maryland.
The display type is Bell.
Musical autography and preparation of excerpts from
editions by Wilmia Polnauer. Designed by Jacqueline Schuman.